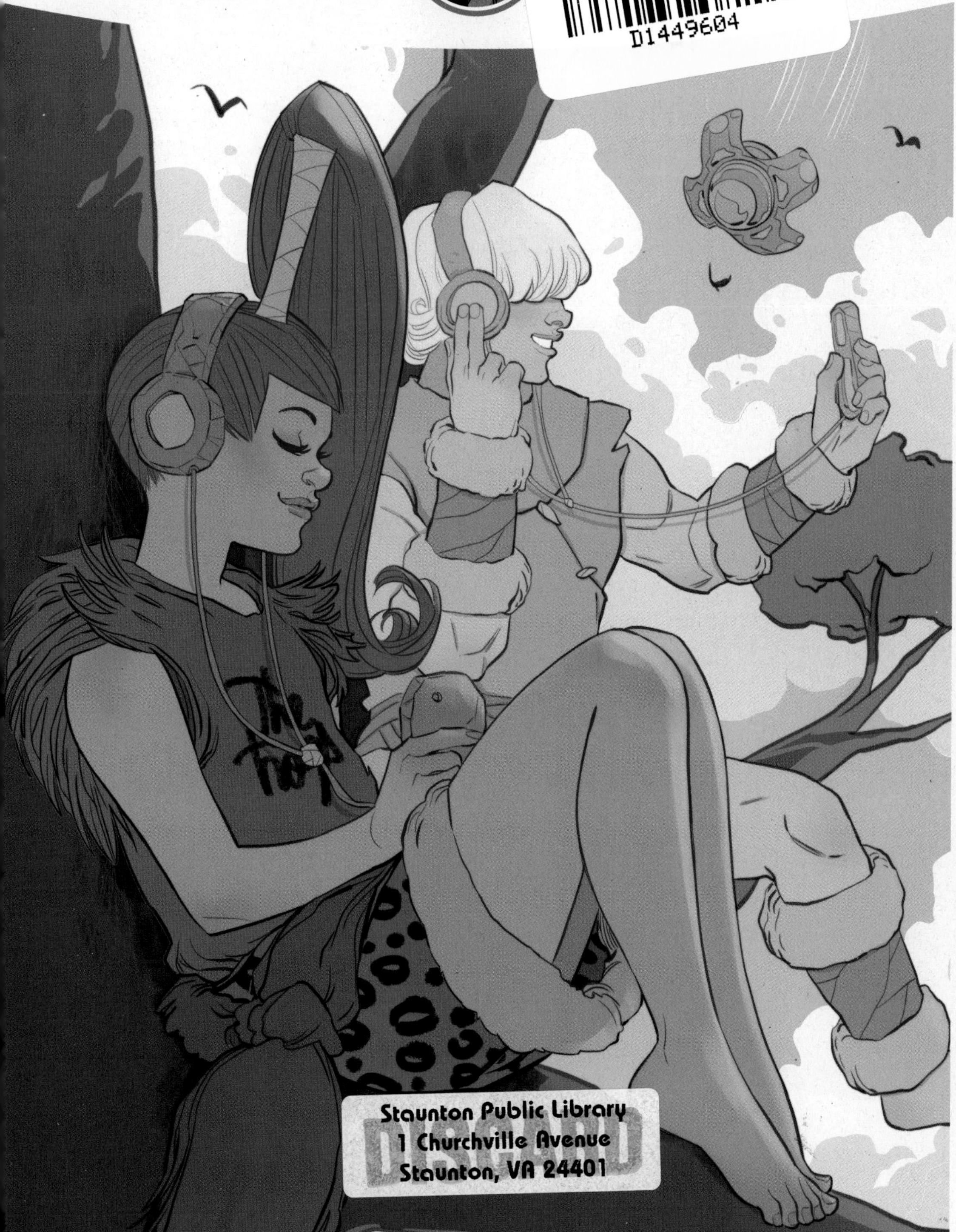

THE FLINTSTONES
VOL. 2

THE FLINTSTONES

VOL.2

MARK RUSSELL writer
STEVE PUGH RICK LEONARDI
SCOTT HANNA artists
CHRIS CHUCKRY colorist
DAVE SHARPE letterer
STEVE PUGH collection cover artist

MARIE JAVINS Editor - Original Series BRITTANY HOLZHERR Associate Editor - Original Series
JEB WOODARD Group Editor - Collected Editions ERIKA ROTHBERG Editor - Collected Edition
STEVE COOK Design Director - Books CURTIS KING JR. Publication Design

BOB HARRAS Senior VP - Editor-in-Chief, DC Comics
PAT McCALLUM Executive Editor, DC Comics

DIANE NELSON President DAN DiDIO Publisher JIM LEE Publisher GEOFF JOHNS President & Chief Creative Officer
AMIT DESAI Executive VP - Business & Marketing Strategy, Direct to Consumer & Global Franchise Management
SAM ADES Senior VP & General Manager, Digital Services BOBBIE CHASE VP & Executive Editor, Young Reader & Talent Development
MARK CHIARELLO Senior VP - Art, Design & Collected Editions JOHN CUNNINGHAM Senior VP - Sales & Trade Marketing
ANNE DePIES Senior VP - Business Strategy, Finance & Administration DON FALLETTI VP - Manufacturing Operations
LAWRENCE GANEM VP - Editorial Administration & Talent Relations ALISON GILL Senior VP - Manufacturing & Operations
HANK KANALZ Senior VP - Editorial Strategy & Administration JAY KOGAN VP - Legal Affairs JACK MAHAN VP - Business Affairs
NICK J. NAPOLITANO VP - Manufacturing Administration EDDIE SCANNELL VP - Consumer Marketing
COURTNEY SIMMONS Senior VP - Publicity & Communications JIM (SKI) SOKOLOWSKI VP - Comic Book Specialty Sales & Trade Marketing
NANCY SPEARS VP - Mass, Book, Digital Sales & Trade Marketing MICHELE R. WELLS VP - Content Strategy

THE FLINTSTONES VOL. 2

Published by DC Comics. Compilation and all new material Copyright © 2017 Hanna-Barbera. All Rights Reserved. Originally published in single magazine form in THE FLINTSTONES 7-12. Copyright © 2017 Hanna-Barbera. All Rights Reserved. All characters, their distinctive likenesses and related elements featured in this publication are trademarks of Hanna-Barbera. DC Logo: ™ and © DC Comics. The stories, characters and incidents featured in this publication are entirely fictional. DC Comics does not read or accept unsolicited submissions of ideas, stories or artwork.

DC Comics, 2900 West Alameda Ave., Burbank, CA 91505
Printed by Solisco Printers, Scott, QC, Canada. 9/1/17. First Printing.
ISBN: 978-1-4012-7398-9

Library of Congress Cataloging-in-Publication Data is available.

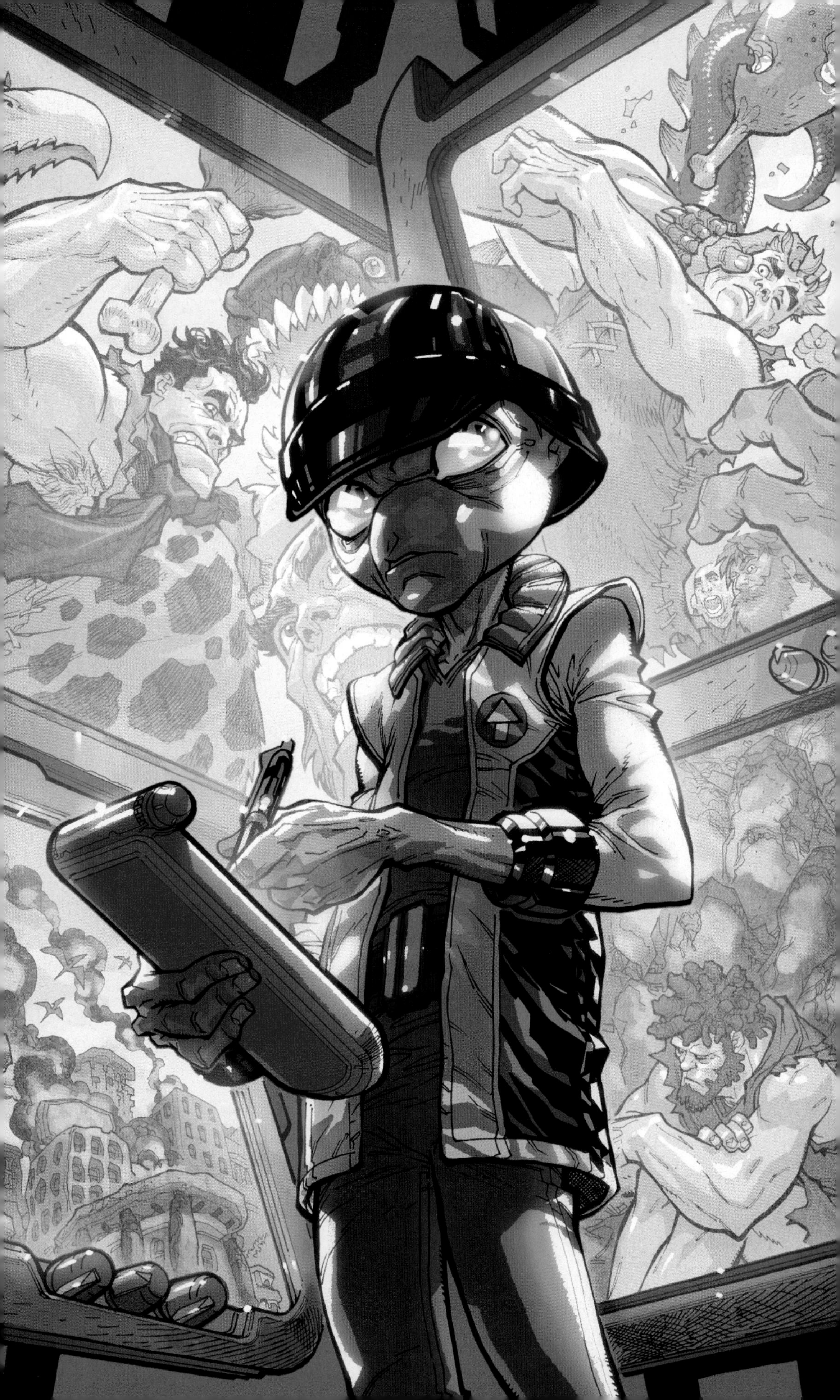

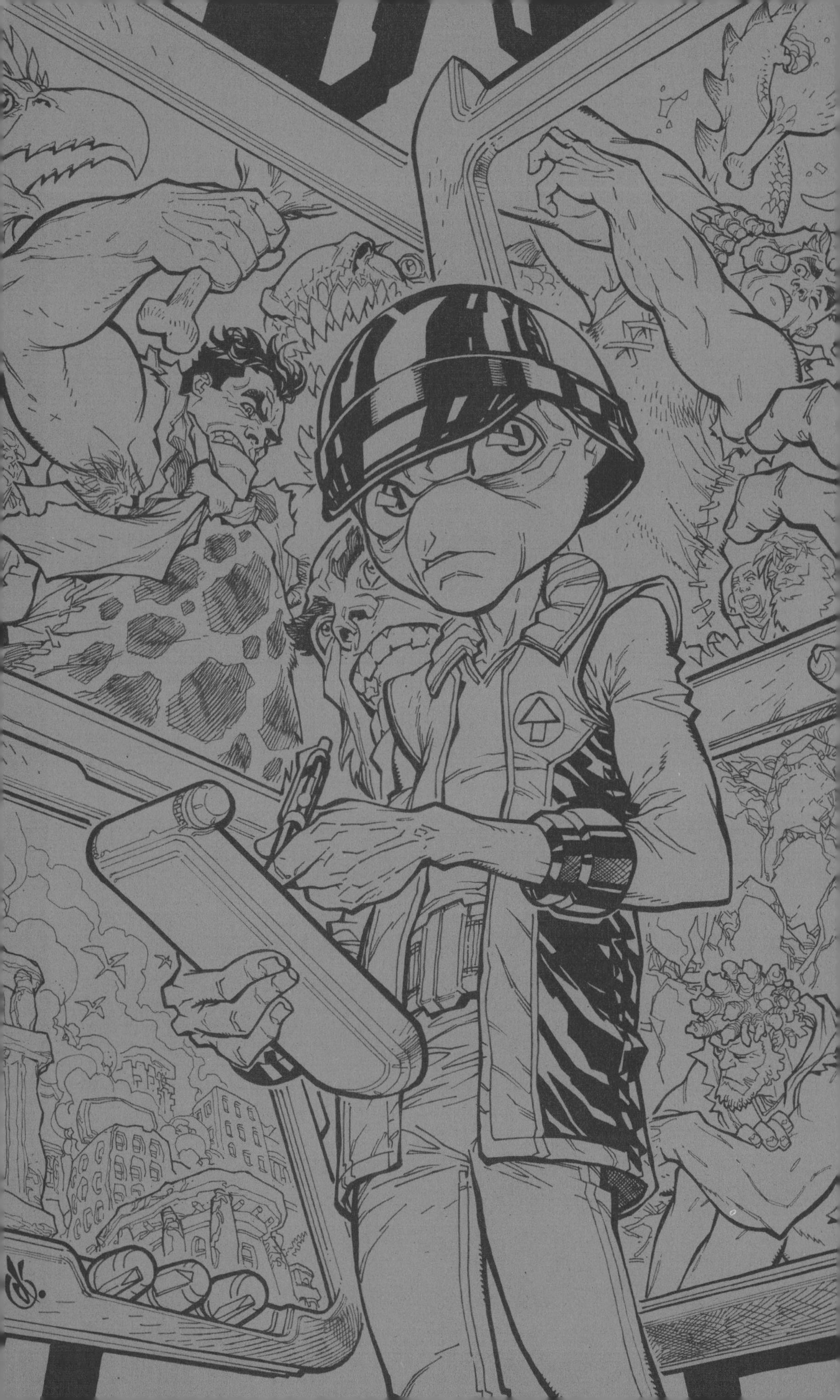

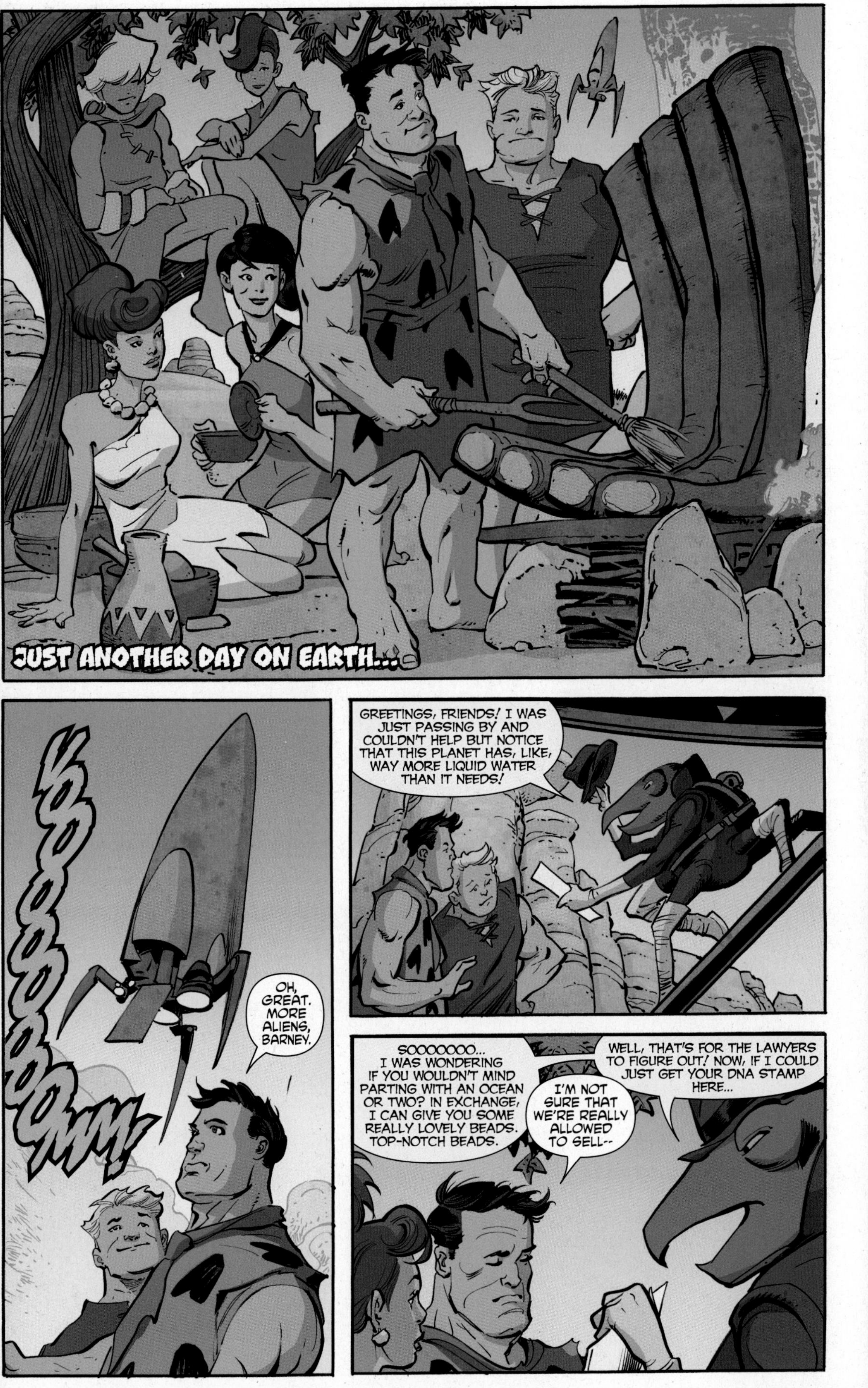
JUST ANOTHER DAY ON EARTH...
VOOOOOOOOOOOMM!
OH, GREAT. MORE ALIENS, BARNEY.
GREETINGS, FRIENDS! I WAS JUST PASSING BY AND COULDN'T HELP BUT NOTICE THAT THIS PLANET HAS, LIKE, WAY MORE LIQUID WATER THAN IT NEEDS!
SOOOOOOO... I WAS WONDERING IF YOU WOULDN'T MIND PARTING WITH AN OCEAN OR TWO? IN EXCHANGE, I CAN GIVE YOU SOME REALLY LOVELY BEADS. TOP-NOTCH BEADS.
I'M NOT SURE THAT WE'RE REALLY ALLOWED TO SELL--
WELL, THAT'S FOR THE LAWYERS TO FIGURE OUT! NOW, IF I COULD JUST GET YOUR DNA STAMP HERE...

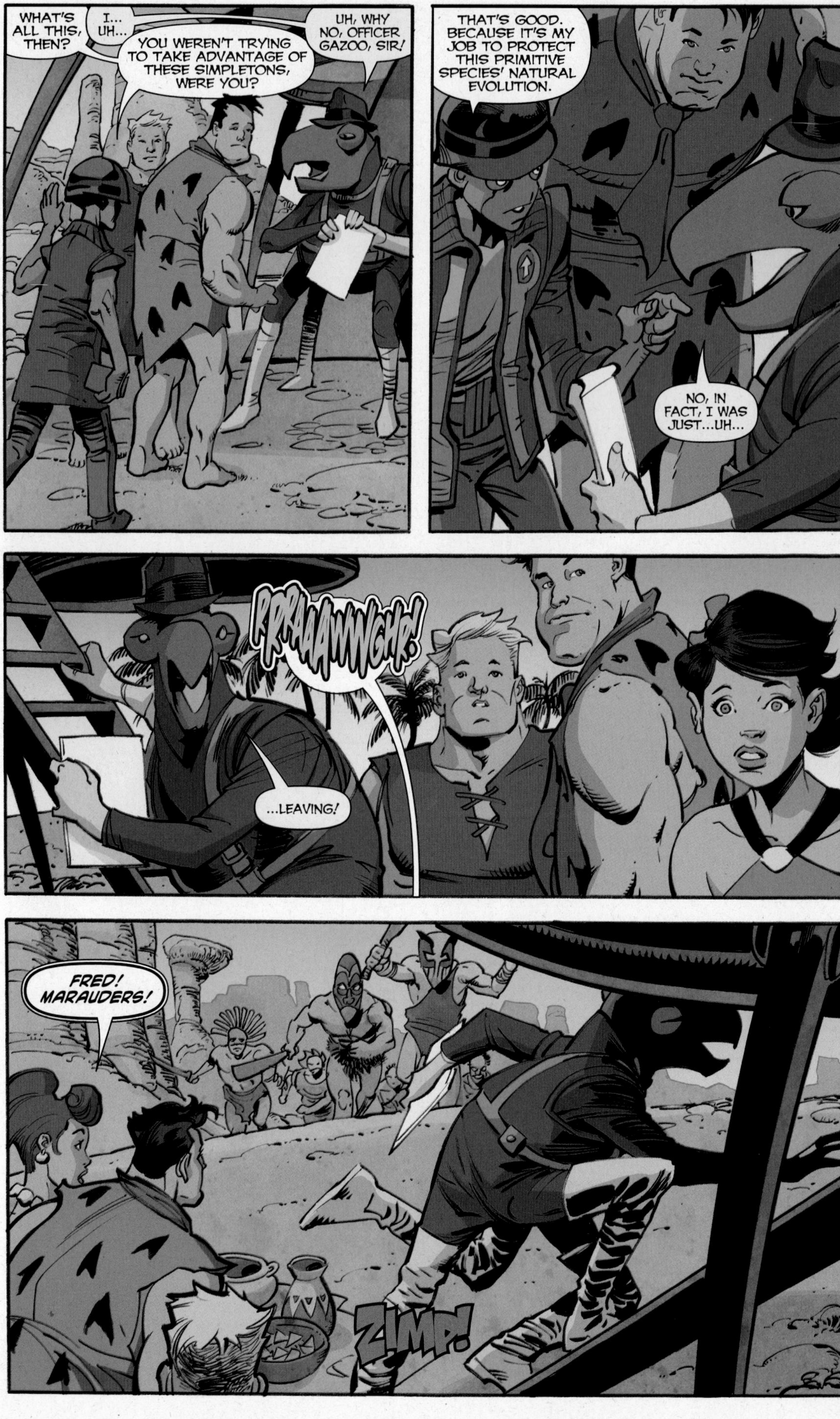
WHAT'S ALL THIS, THEN?
I... UH...
YOU WEREN'T TRYING TO TAKE ADVANTAGE OF THESE SIMPLETONS, WERE YOU?
UH, WHY NO, OFFICER GAZOO, SIR!
THAT'S GOOD. BECAUSE IT'S MY JOB TO PROTECT THIS PRIMITIVE SPECIES' NATURAL EVOLUTION.
NO, IN FACT, I WAS JUST...UH...
RRRAAAWWNGHR!
...LEAVING!
FRED! MARAUDERS!
ZIMP!

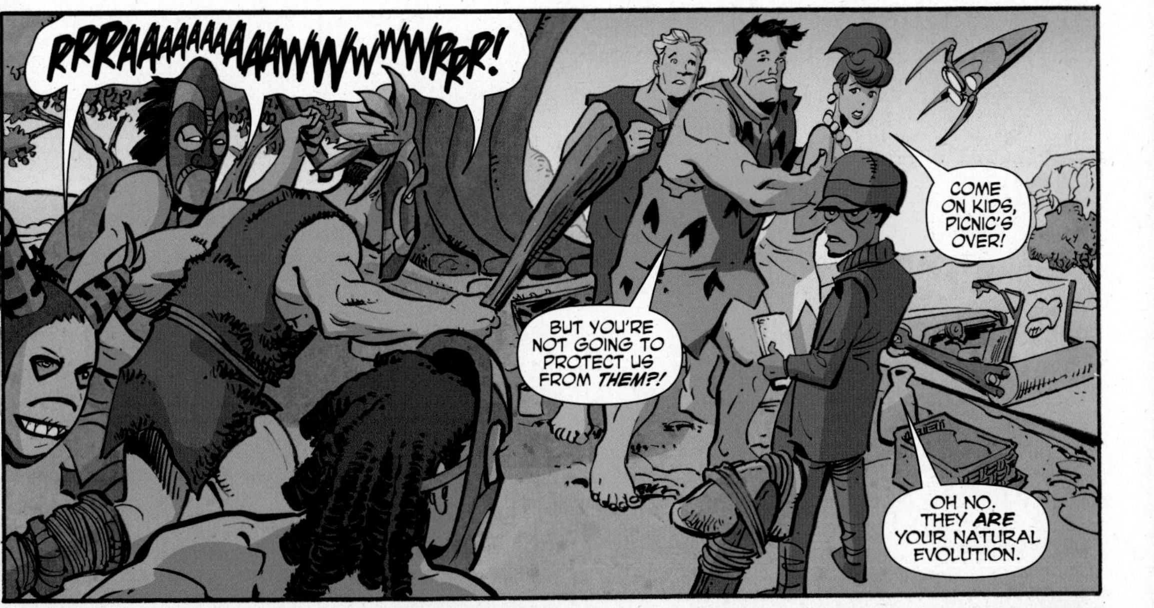
RRRAAAAAAAAWWWWWRRR!
COME ON KIDS, PICNIC'S OVER!
BUT YOU'RE NOT GOING TO PROTECT US FROM *THEM?!*
OH NO. THEY *ARE* YOUR NATURAL EVOLUTION.

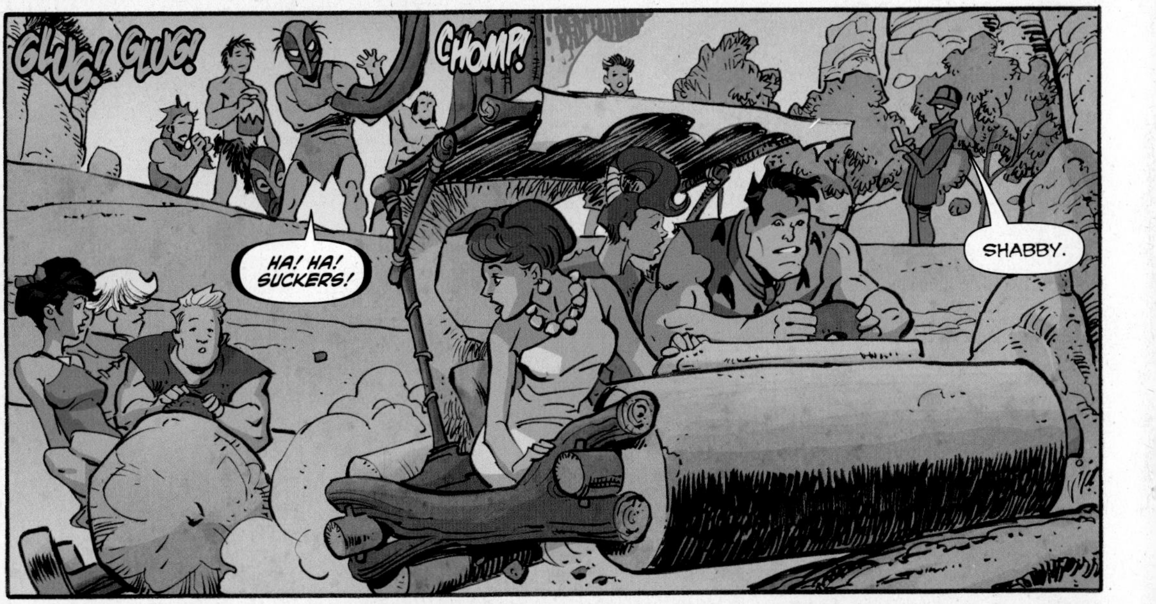
GLUG! GLUG!
CHOMP!
HA! HA! SUCKERS!
SHABBY.

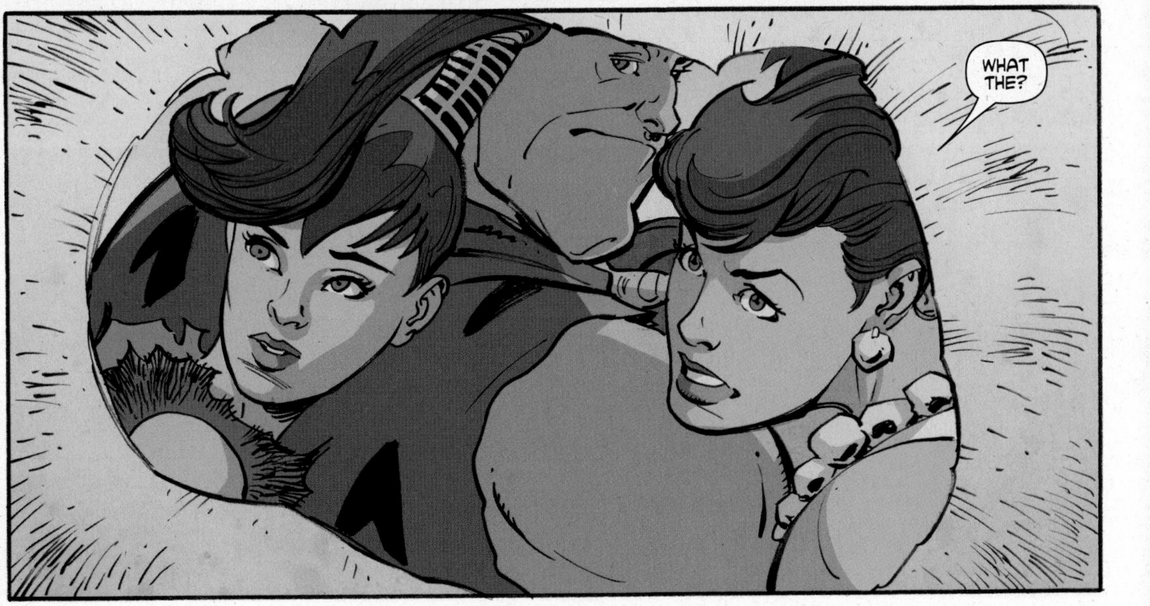
WHAT THE?

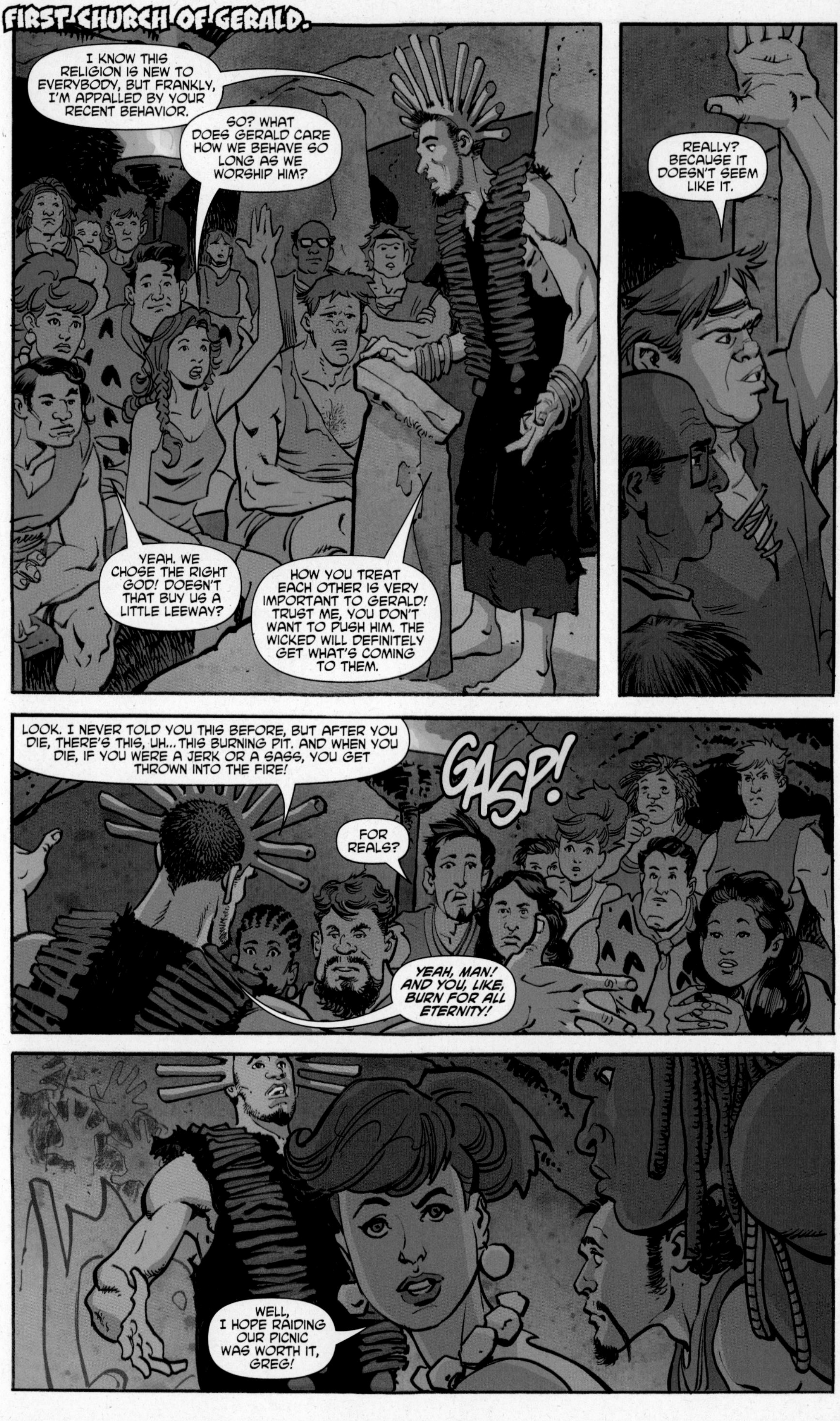
FIRST CHURCH OF GERALD.
I KNOW THIS RELIGION IS NEW TO EVERYBODY, BUT FRANKLY, I'M APPALLED BY YOUR RECENT BEHAVIOR.
SO? WHAT DOES GERALD CARE HOW WE BEHAVE SO LONG AS WE WORSHIP HIM?
YEAH. WE CHOSE THE RIGHT GOD! DOESN'T THAT BUY US A LITTLE LEEWAY?
HOW YOU TREAT EACH OTHER IS VERY IMPORTANT TO GERALD! TRUST ME, YOU DON'T WANT TO PUSH HIM. THE WICKED WILL DEFINITELY GET WHAT'S COMING TO THEM.
REALLY? BECAUSE IT DOESN'T SEEM LIKE IT.
LOOK. I NEVER TOLD YOU THIS BEFORE, BUT AFTER YOU DIE, THERE'S THIS, UH... THIS BURNING PIT. AND WHEN YOU DIE, IF YOU WERE A JERK OR A SASS, YOU GET THROWN INTO THE FIRE!
GASP!
FOR REALS?
YEAH, MAN! AND YOU, LIKE, BURN FOR ALL ETERNITY!
WELL, I HOPE RAIDING OUR PICNIC WAS WORTH IT, GREG!

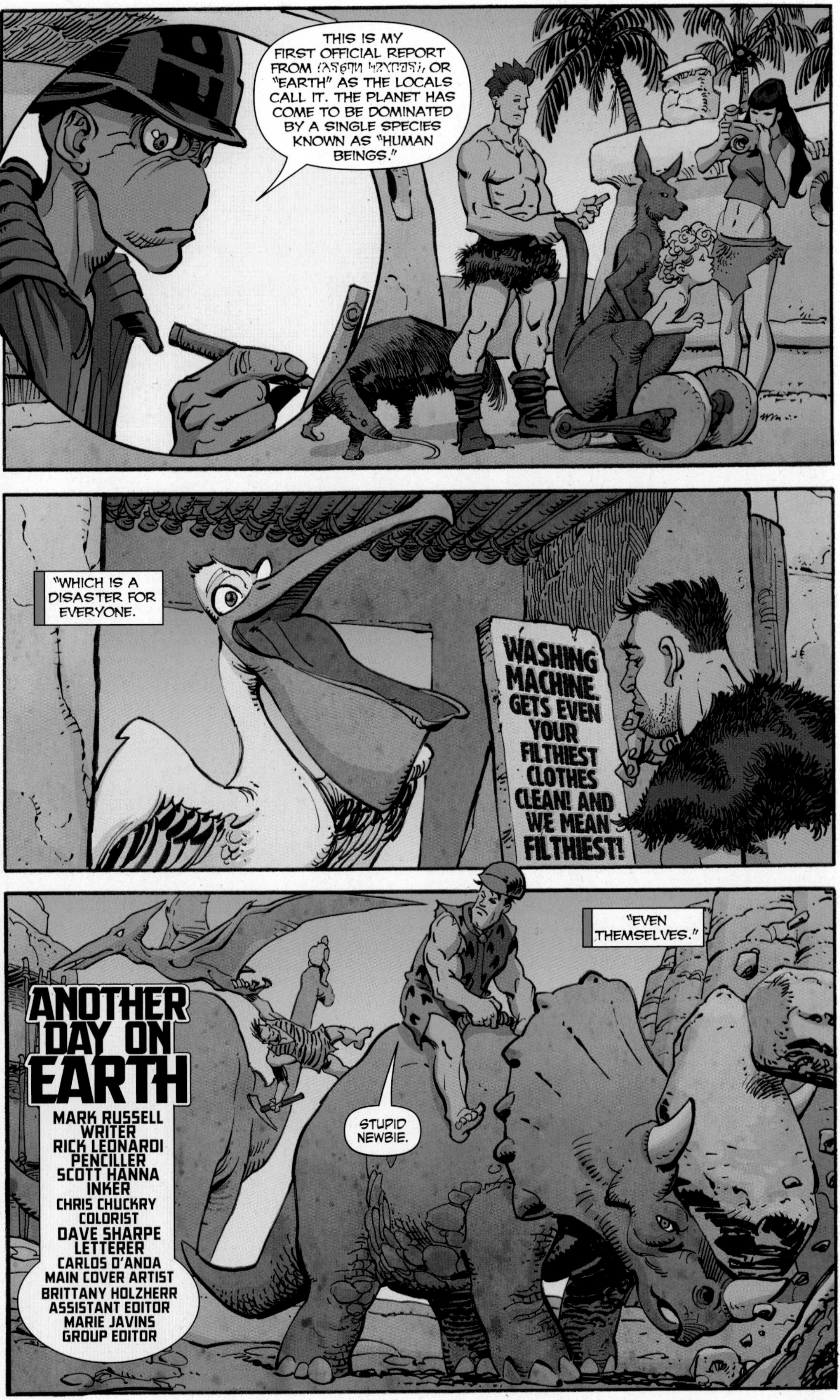
THIS IS MY FIRST OFFICIAL REPORT FROM , OR "EARTH" AS THE LOCALS CALL IT. THE PLANET HAS COME TO BE DOMINATED BY A SINGLE SPECIES KNOWN AS "HUMAN BEINGS."
"WHICH IS A DISASTER FOR EVERYONE.
WASHING MACHINE. GETS EVEN YOUR FILTHIEST CLOTHES CLEAN! AND WE MEAN FILTHIEST!
"EVEN THEMSELVES."
ANOTHER DAY ON EARTH
MARK RUSSELL WRITER
RICK LEONARDI PENCILLER
SCOTT HANNA INKER
CHRIS CHUCKRY COLORIST
DAVE SHARPE LETTERER
CARLOS D'ANDA MAIN COVER ARTIST
BRITTANY HOLZHERR ASSISTANT EDITOR
MARIE JAVINS GROUP EDITOR
STUPID NEWBIE.

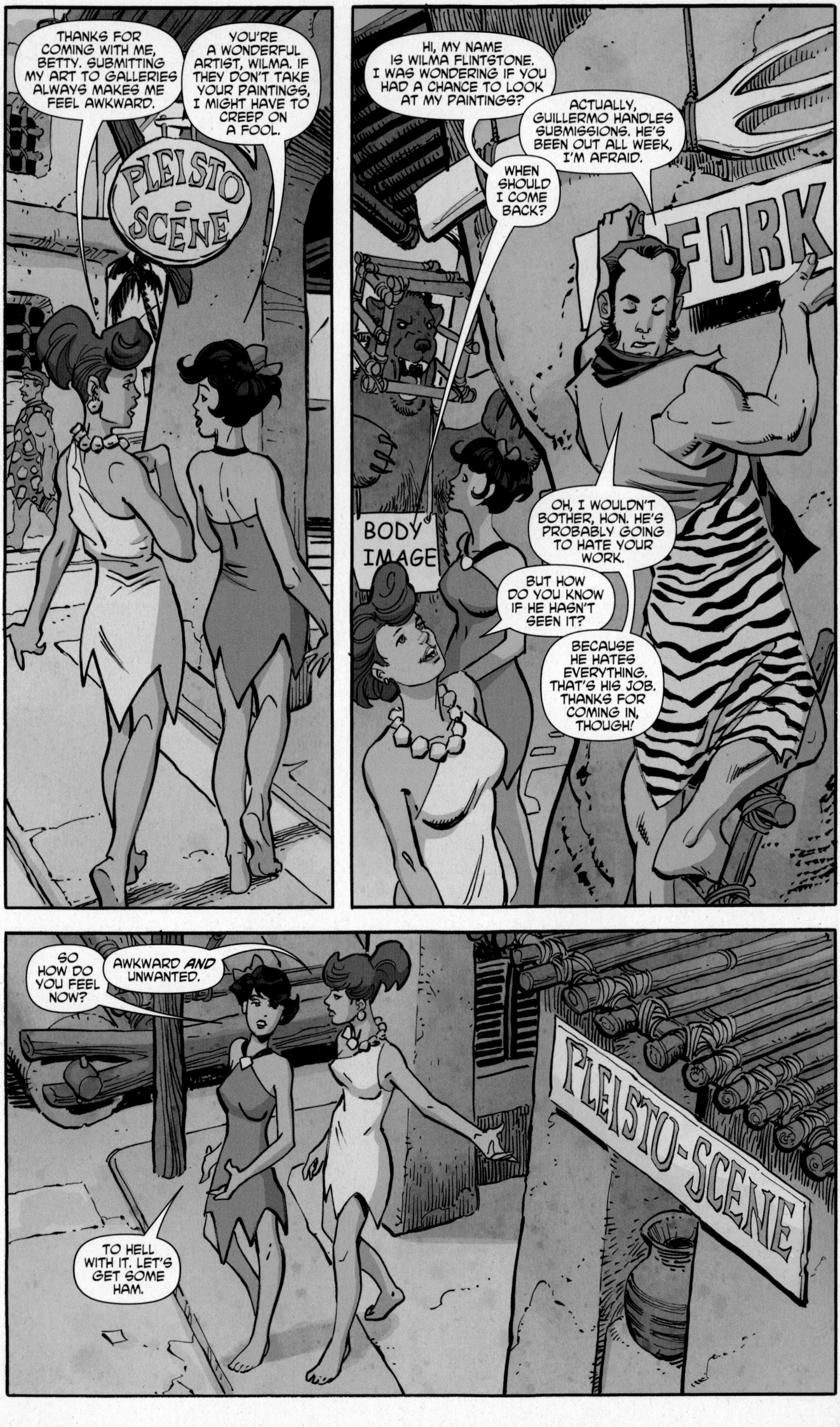

THANKS FOR COMING WITH ME, BETTY. SUBMITTING MY ART TO GALLERIES ALWAYS MAKES ME FEEL AWKWARD.
YOU'RE A WONDERFUL ARTIST, WILMA. IF THEY DON'T TAKE YOUR PAINTINGS, I MIGHT HAVE TO CREEP ON A FOOL.
PLEISTO - SCENE
HI, MY NAME IS WILMA FLINTSTONE. I WAS WONDERING IF YOU HAD A CHANCE TO LOOK AT MY PAINTINGS?
ACTUALLY, GUILLERMO HANDLES SUBMISSIONS. HE'S BEEN OUT ALL WEEK, I'M AFRAID.
WHEN SHOULD I COME BACK?
FORK
OH, I WOULDN'T BOTHER, HON. HE'S PROBABLY GOING TO HATE YOUR WORK.
BODY IMAGE
BUT HOW DO YOU KNOW IF HE HASN'T SEEN IT?
BECAUSE HE HATES EVERYTHING. THAT'S HIS JOB. THANKS FOR COMING IN, THOUGH!
SO HOW DO YOU FEEL NOW?
AWKWARD ***AND*** UNWANTED.
PLEISTO-SCENE
TO HELL WITH IT. LET'S GET SOME HAM.

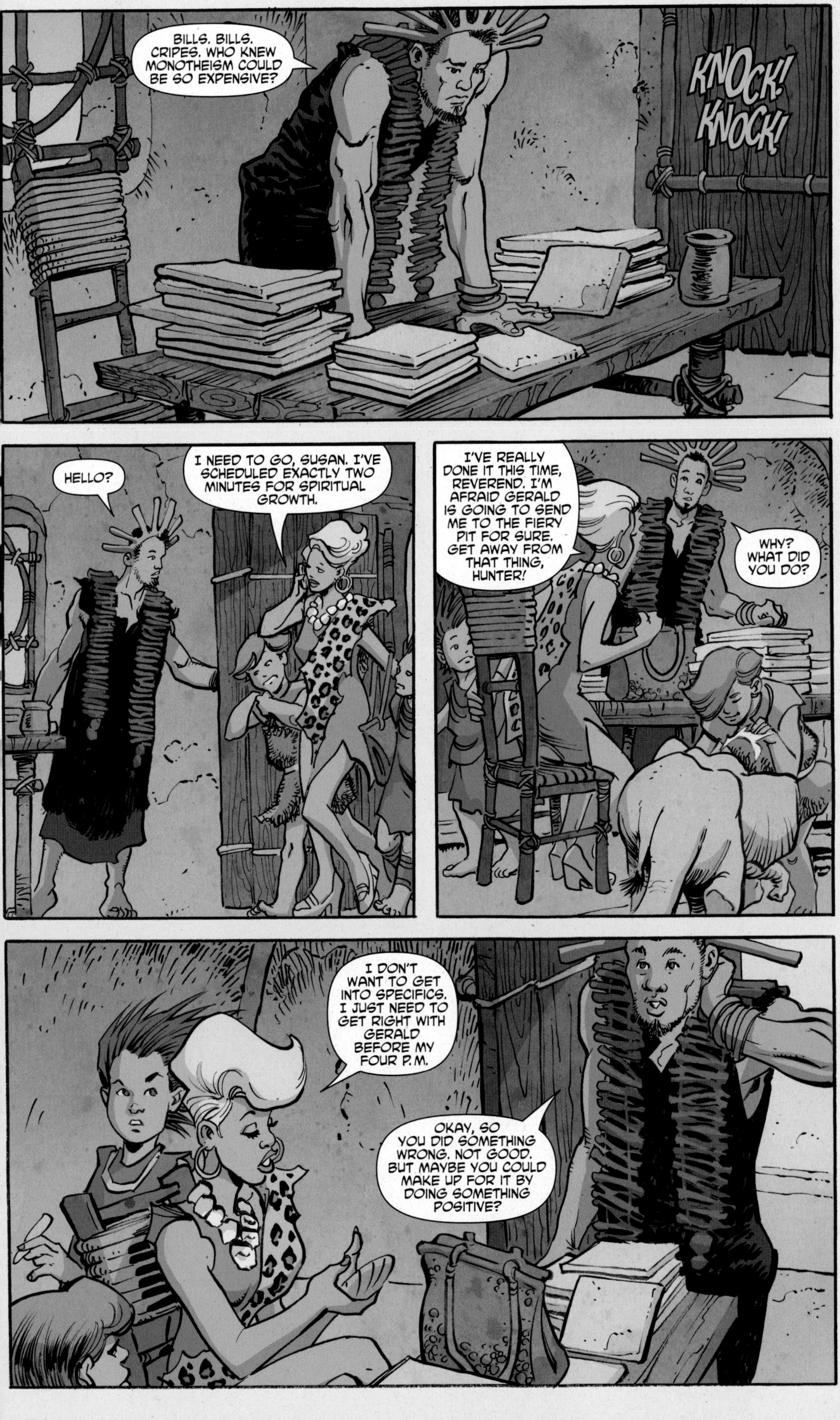
BILLS. BILLS. CRIPES. WHO KNEW MONOTHEISM COULD BE SO EXPENSIVE?
KNOCK! KNOCK!
HELLO?
I NEED TO GO, SUSAN. I'VE SCHEDULED EXACTLY TWO MINUTES FOR SPIRITUAL GROWTH.
I'VE REALLY DONE IT THIS TIME, REVEREND. I'M AFRAID GERALD IS GOING TO SEND ME TO THE FIERY PIT FOR SURE. GET AWAY FROM THAT THING, HUNTER!
WHY? WHAT DID YOU DO?
I DON'T WANT TO GET INTO SPECIFICS. I JUST NEED TO GET RIGHT WITH GERALD BEFORE MY FOUR P.M.
OKAY, SO YOU DID SOMETHING WRONG. NOT GOOD. BUT MAYBE YOU COULD MAKE UP FOR IT BY DOING SOMETHING POSITIVE?

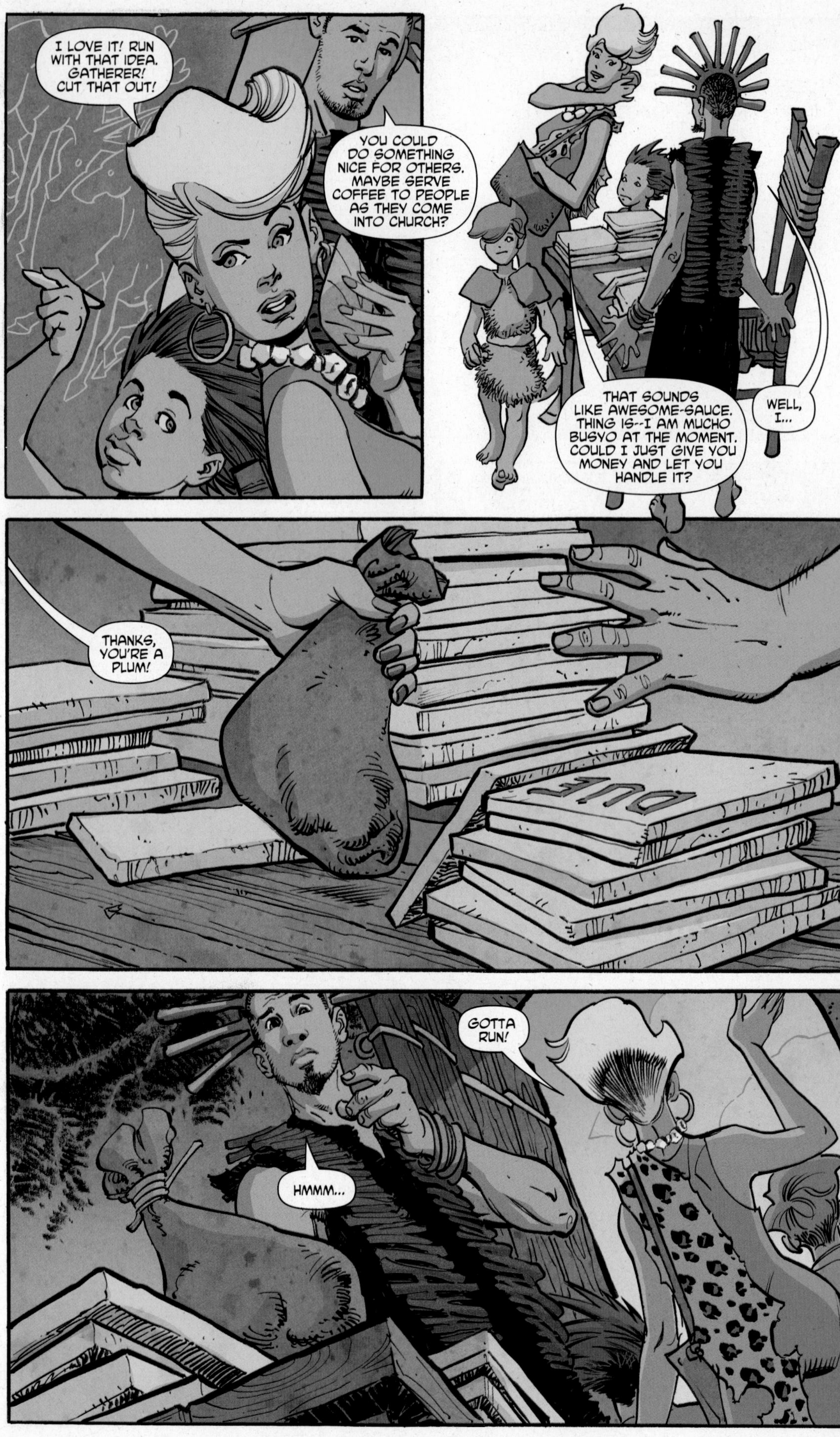
I LOVE IT! RUN WITH THAT IDEA. GATHERER! CUT THAT OUT!
YOU COULD DO SOMETHING NICE FOR OTHERS. MAYBE SERVE COFFEE TO PEOPLE AS THEY COME INTO CHURCH?
WELL, I...
THAT SOUNDS LIKE AWESOME-SAUCE. THING IS--I AM MUCHO BUSYO AT THE MOMENT. COULD I JUST GIVE YOU MONEY AND LET YOU HANDLE IT?
THANKS, YOU'RE A PLUM!
DUE
GOTTA RUN!
HMMM...

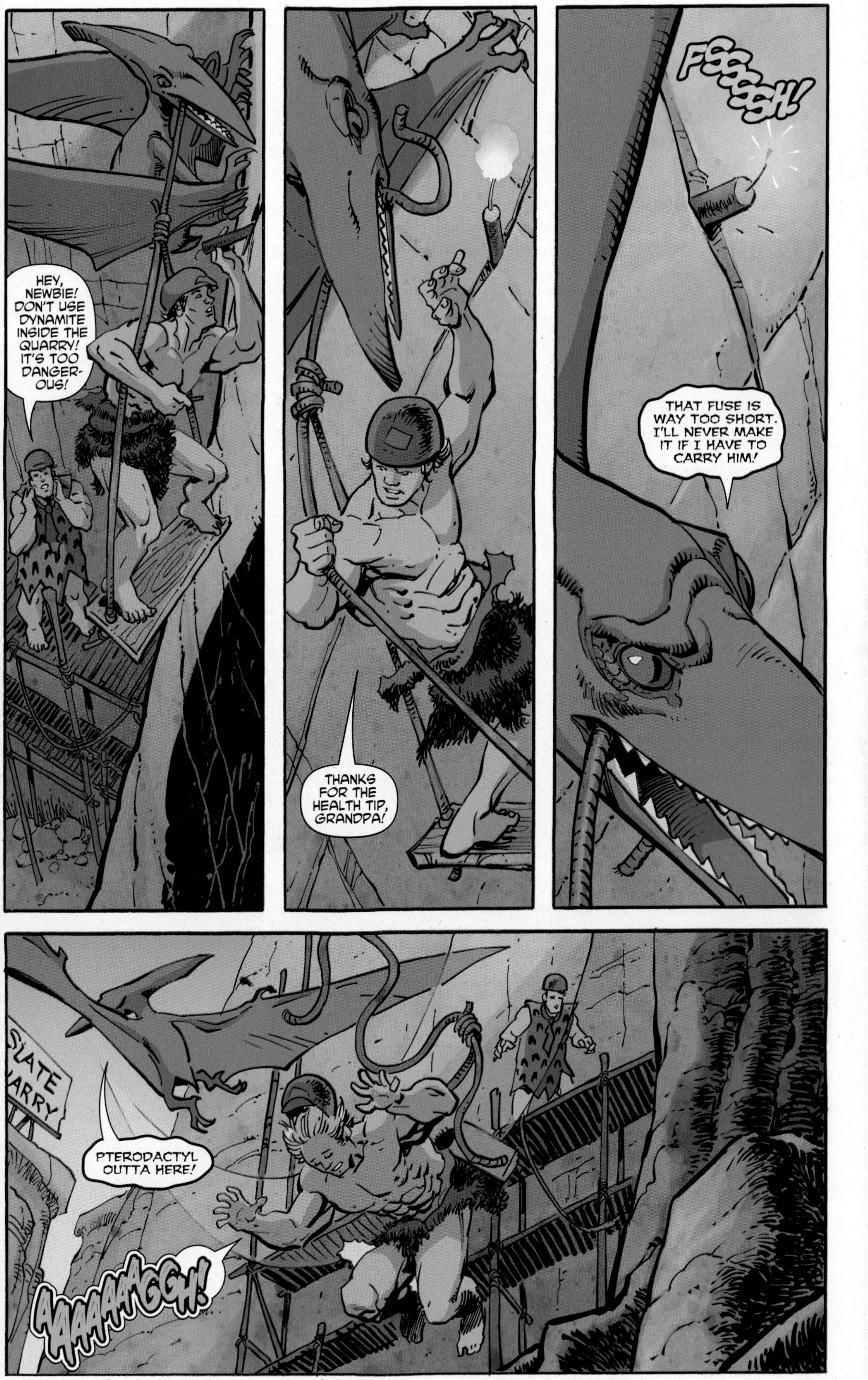

HEY, NEWBIE! DON'T USE DYNAMITE INSIDE THE QUARRY! IT'S TOO DANGER-OUS!
THANKS FOR THE HEALTH TIP, GRANDPA!
FSSSSH!
THAT FUSE IS WAY TOO SHORT. I'LL NEVER MAKE IT IF I HAVE TO CARRY HIM!
SLATE
ARRY
PTERODACTYL OUTTA HERE!
AAAAAAAGGH!

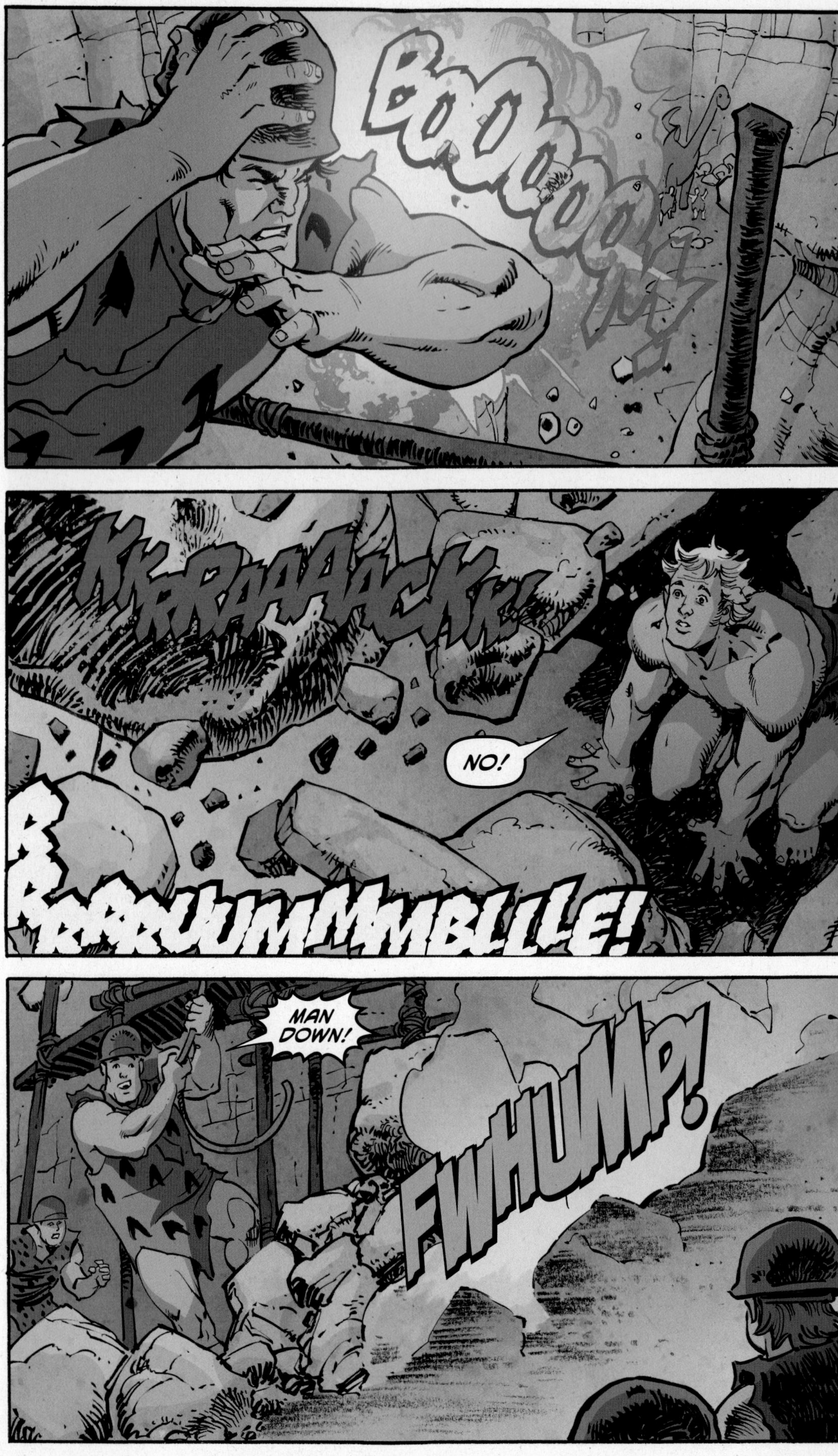

BOOOOOM!
KKRAAAACKK!
NO!
RRRUUMMMBLLLE!
MAN DOWN!
FWHUMP!

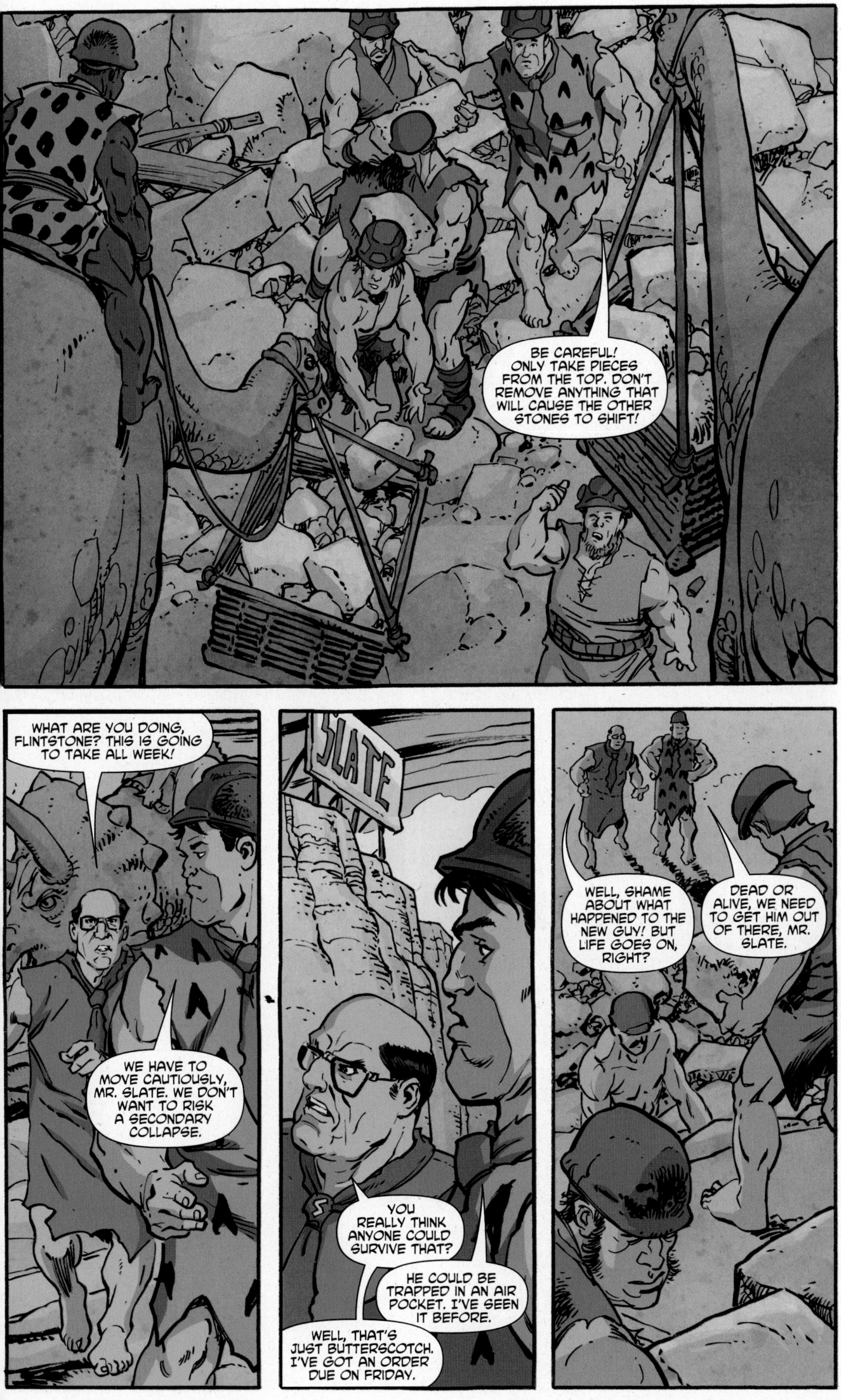
BE CAREFUL! ONLY TAKE PIECES FROM THE TOP. DON'T REMOVE ANYTHING THAT WILL CAUSE THE OTHER STONES TO SHIFT!
WHAT ARE YOU DOING, FLINTSTONE? THIS IS GOING TO TAKE ALL WEEK!
WE HAVE TO MOVE CAUTIOUSLY, MR. SLATE. WE DON'T WANT TO RISK A SECONDARY COLLAPSE.
SLATE
YOU REALLY THINK ANYONE COULD SURVIVE THAT?
HE COULD BE TRAPPED IN AN AIR POCKET. I'VE SEEN IT BEFORE.
WELL, THAT'S JUST BUTTERSCOTCH. I'VE GOT AN ORDER DUE ON FRIDAY.
WELL, SHAME ABOUT WHAT HAPPENED TO THE NEW GUY! BUT LIFE GOES ON, RIGHT?
DEAD OR ALIVE, WE NEED TO GET HIM OUT OF THERE, MR. SLATE.

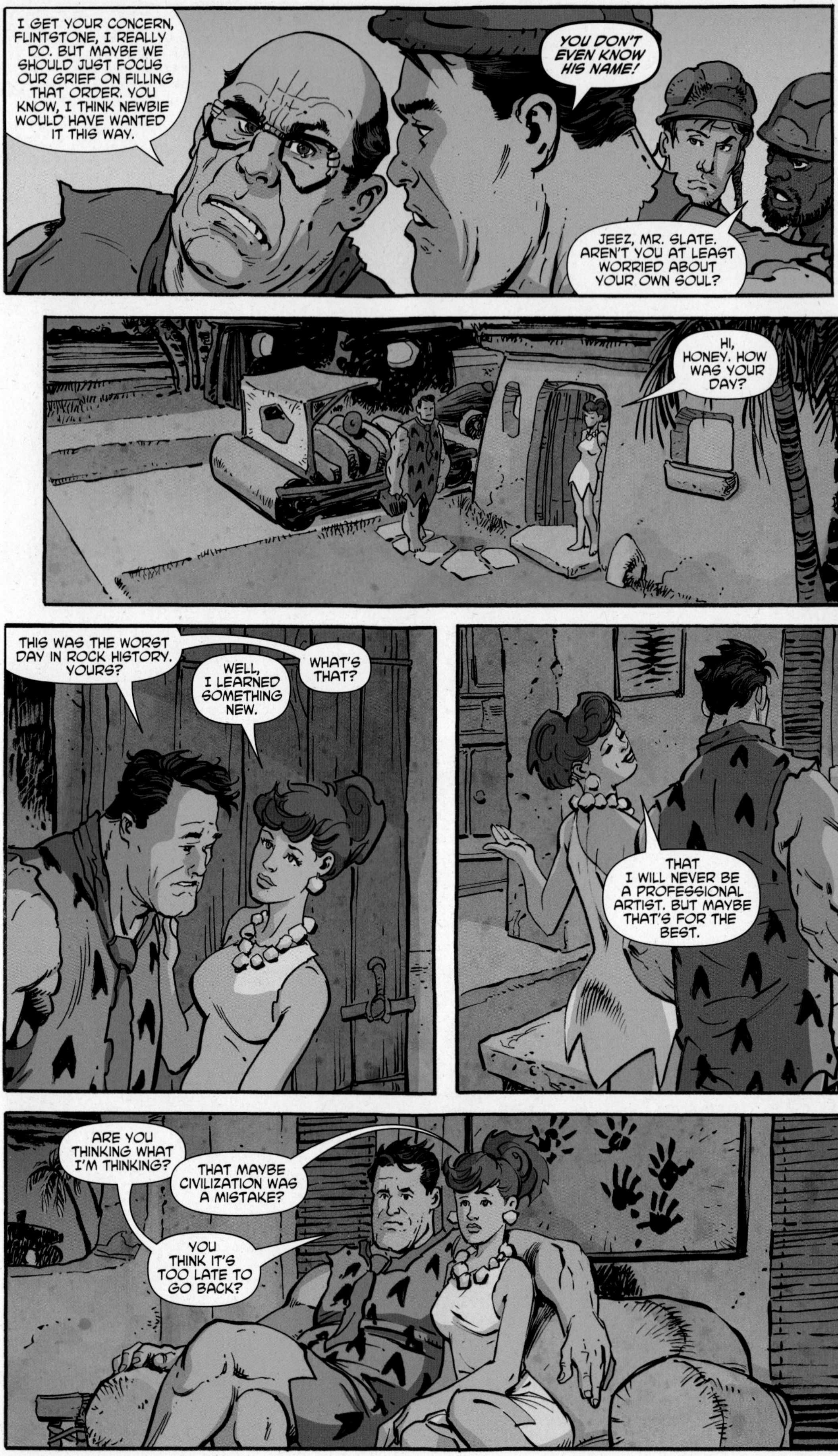

I GET YOUR CONCERN, FLINTSTONE, I REALLY DO. BUT MAYBE WE SHOULD JUST FOCUS OUR GRIEF ON FILLING THAT ORDER. YOU KNOW, I THINK NEWBIE WOULD HAVE WANTED IT THIS WAY.
YOU DON'T EVEN KNOW HIS NAME!
JEEZ, MR. SLATE. AREN'T YOU AT LEAST WORRIED ABOUT YOUR OWN SOUL?
HI, HONEY. HOW WAS YOUR DAY?
THIS WAS THE WORST DAY IN ROCK HISTORY. YOURS?
WELL, I LEARNED SOMETHING NEW.
WHAT'S THAT?
THAT I WILL NEVER BE A PROFESSIONAL ARTIST. BUT MAYBE THAT'S FOR THE BEST.
ARE YOU THINKING WHAT I'M THINKING?
THAT MAYBE CIVILIZATION WAS A MISTAKE?
YOU THINK IT'S TOO LATE TO GO BACK?

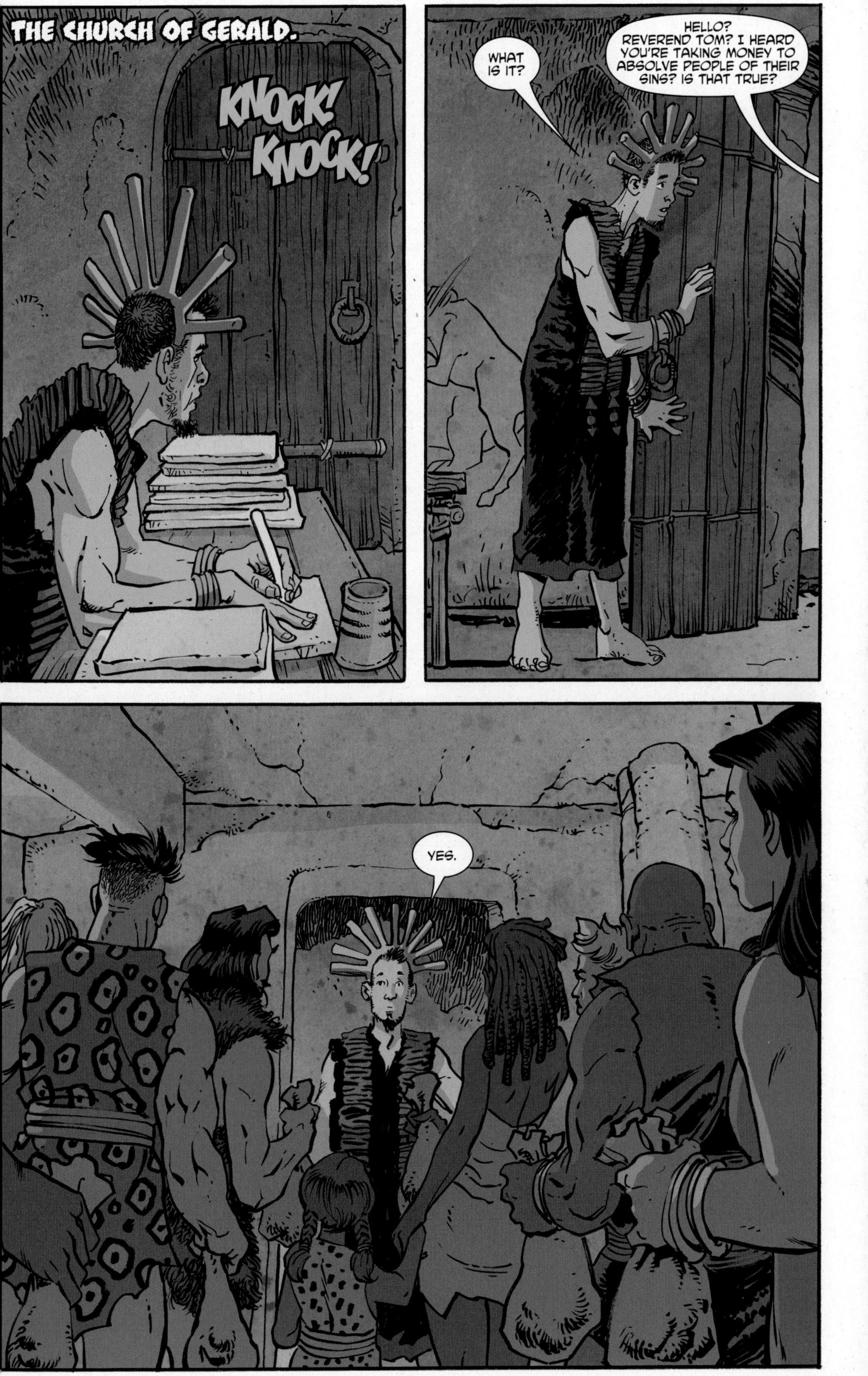
THE CHURCH OF GERALD.
KNOCK! KNOCK!
WHAT IS IT?
HELLO? REVEREND TOM? I HEARD YOU'RE TAKING MONEY TO ABSOLVE PEOPLE OF THEIR SINS? IS THAT TRUE?
YES.

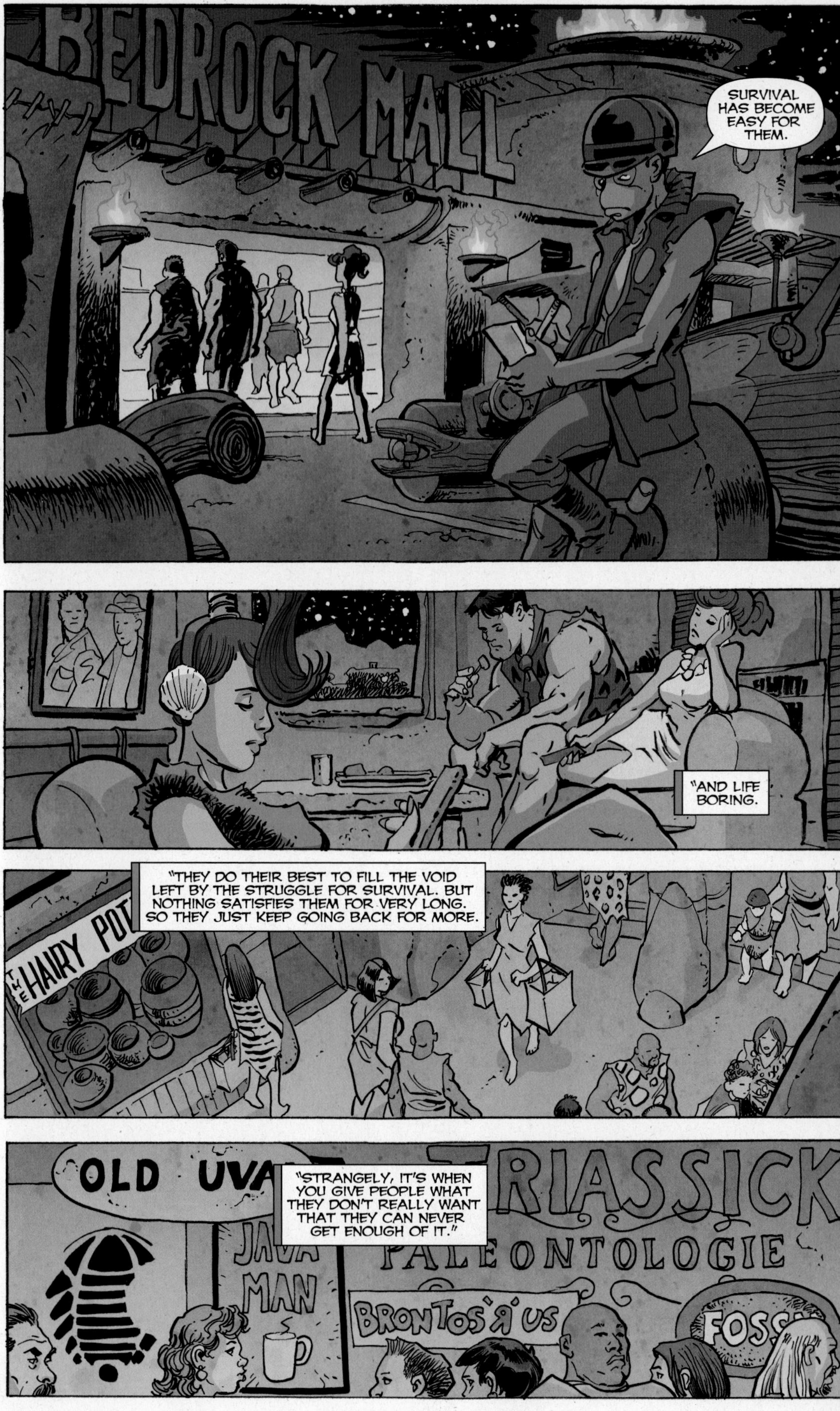
BEDROCK MALL
SURVIVAL HAS BECOME EASY FOR THEM.
"AND LIFE BORING.
"THEY DO THEIR BEST TO FILL THE VOID LEFT BY THE STRUGGLE FOR SURVIVAL. BUT NOTHING SATISFIES THEM FOR VERY LONG. SO THEY JUST KEEP GOING BACK FOR MORE.
THE HAIRY POT
OLD UVA
"STRANGELY, IT'S WHEN YOU GIVE PEOPLE WHAT THEY DON'T REALLY WANT THAT THEY CAN NEVER GET ENOUGH OF IT."
JAVA MAN
RIASSICK
PALEONTOLOGIE
BRONTOS 'Я' US
FOSS

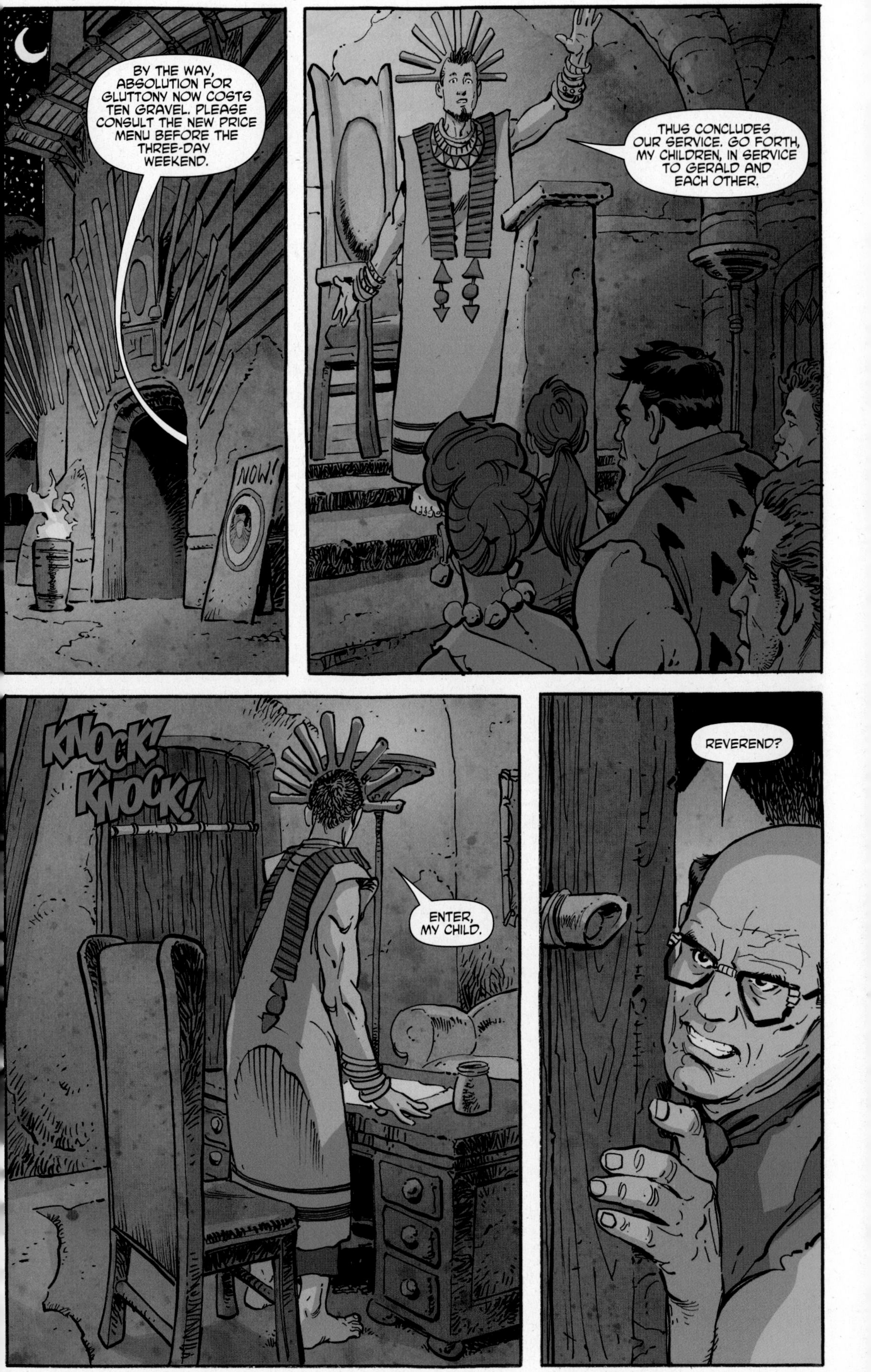
BY THE WAY, ABSOLUTION FOR GLUTTONY NOW COSTS TEN GRAVEL. PLEASE CONSULT THE NEW PRICE MENU BEFORE THE THREE-DAY WEEKEND.
NOW!
THUS CONCLUDES OUR SERVICE. GO FORTH, MY CHILDREN, IN SERVICE TO GERALD AND EACH OTHER.
KNOCK! KNOCK!
ENTER, MY CHILD.
REVEREND?

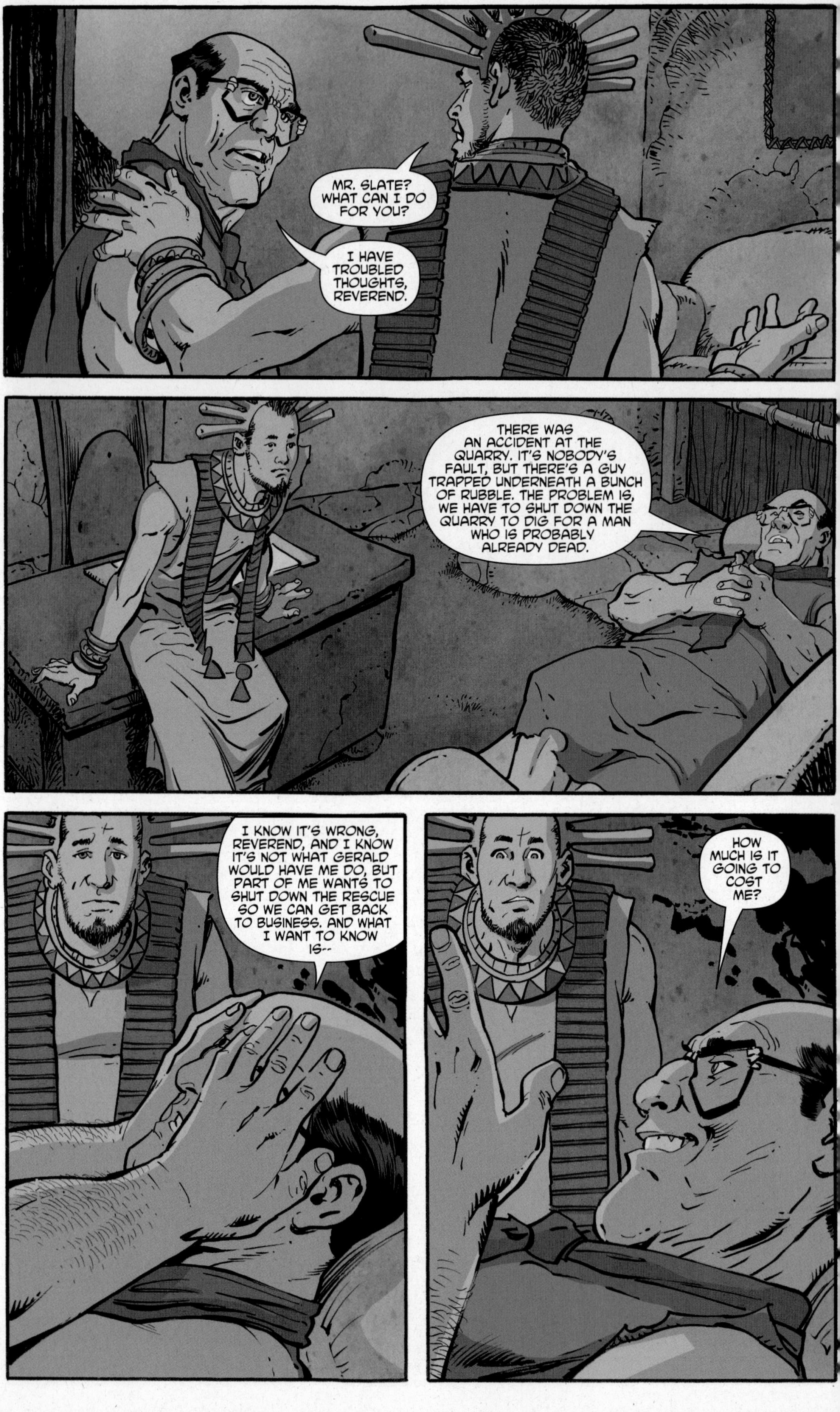
MR. SLATE? WHAT CAN I DO FOR YOU?
I HAVE TROUBLED THOUGHTS, REVEREND.
THERE WAS AN ACCIDENT AT THE QUARRY. IT'S NOBODY'S FAULT, BUT THERE'S A GUY TRAPPED UNDERNEATH A BUNCH OF RUBBLE. THE PROBLEM IS, WE HAVE TO SHUT DOWN THE QUARRY TO DIG FOR A MAN WHO IS PROBABLY ALREADY DEAD.
I KNOW IT'S WRONG, REVEREND, AND I KNOW IT'S NOT WHAT GERALD WOULD HAVE ME DO, BUT PART OF ME WANTS TO SHUT DOWN THE RESCUE SO WE CAN GET BACK TO BUSINESS. AND WHAT I WANT TO KNOW IS--
HOW MUCH IS IT GOING TO COST ME?

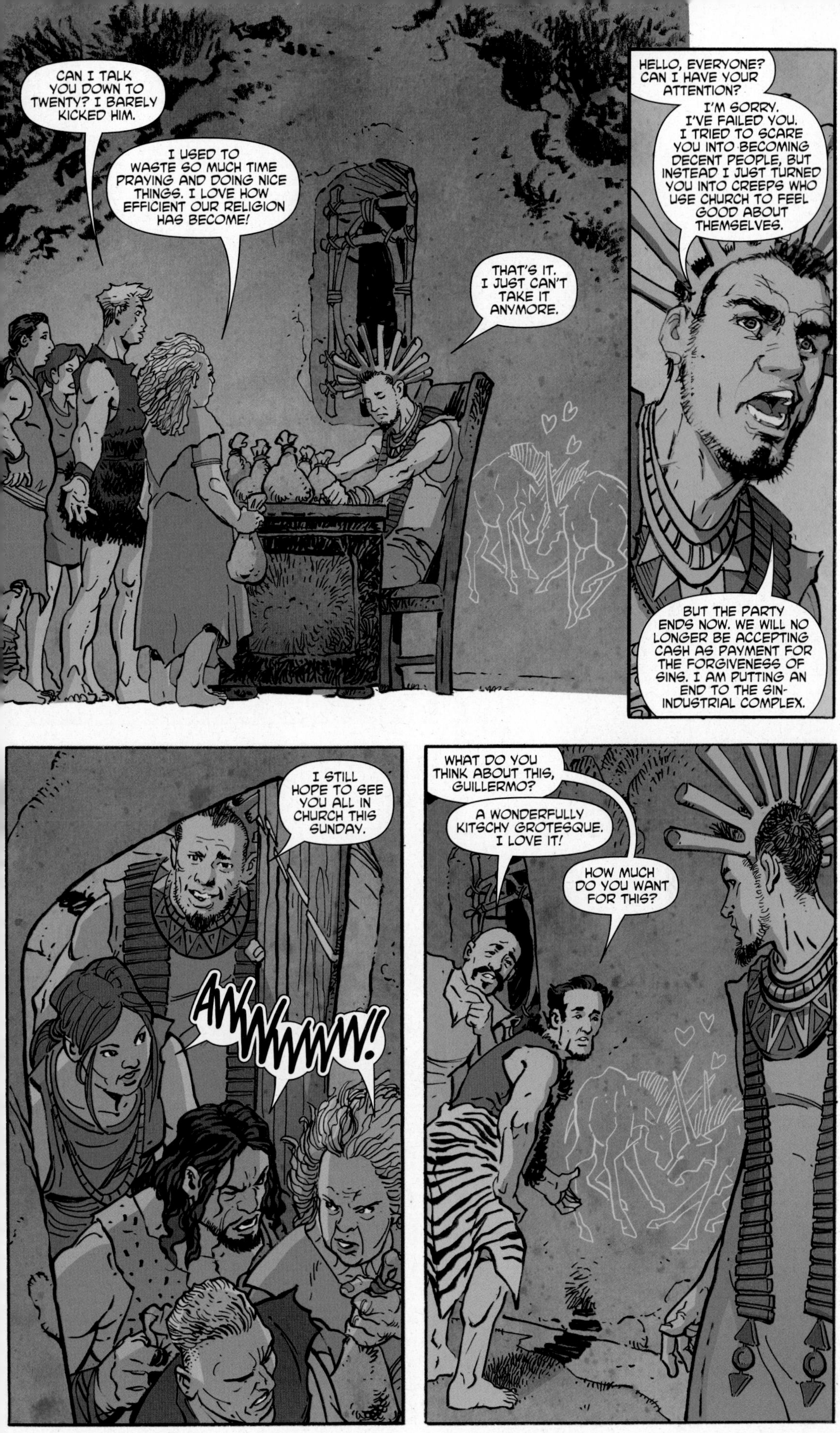
CAN I TALK YOU DOWN TO TWENTY? I BARELY KICKED HIM.
I USED TO WASTE SO MUCH TIME PRAYING AND DOING NICE THINGS. I LOVE HOW EFFICIENT OUR RELIGION HAS BECOME!
THAT'S IT. I JUST CAN'T TAKE IT ANYMORE.
HELLO, EVERYONE? CAN I HAVE YOUR ATTENTION?
I'M SORRY. I'VE FAILED YOU. I TRIED TO SCARE YOU INTO BECOMING DECENT PEOPLE, BUT INSTEAD I JUST TURNED YOU INTO CREEPS WHO USE CHURCH TO FEEL GOOD ABOUT THEMSELVES.
BUT THE PARTY ENDS NOW. WE WILL NO LONGER BE ACCEPTING CASH AS PAYMENT FOR THE FORGIVENESS OF SINS. I AM PUTTING AN END TO THE SIN-INDUSTRIAL COMPLEX.
I STILL HOPE TO SEE YOU ALL IN CHURCH THIS SUNDAY.
AWWWWW!
WHAT DO YOU THINK ABOUT THIS, GUILLERMO?
A WONDERFULLY KITSCHY GROTESQUE. I LOVE IT!
HOW MUCH DO YOU WANT FOR THIS?

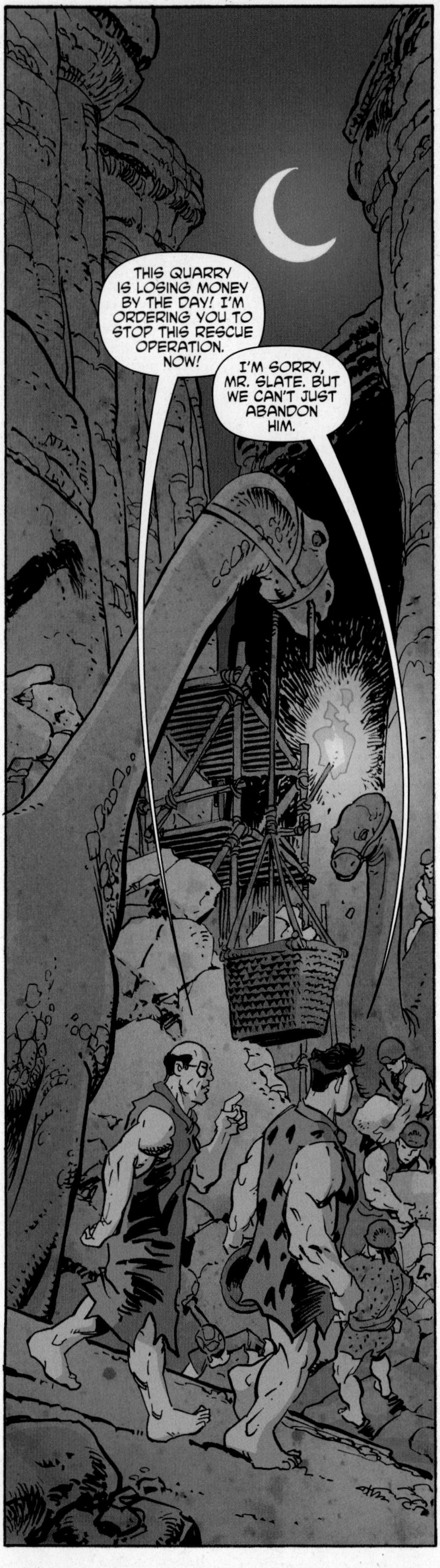
THIS QUARRY IS LOSING MONEY BY THE DAY! I'M ORDERING YOU TO STOP THIS RESCUE OPERATION. NOW!
I'M SORRY, MR. SLATE. BUT WE CAN'T JUST ABANDON HIM.

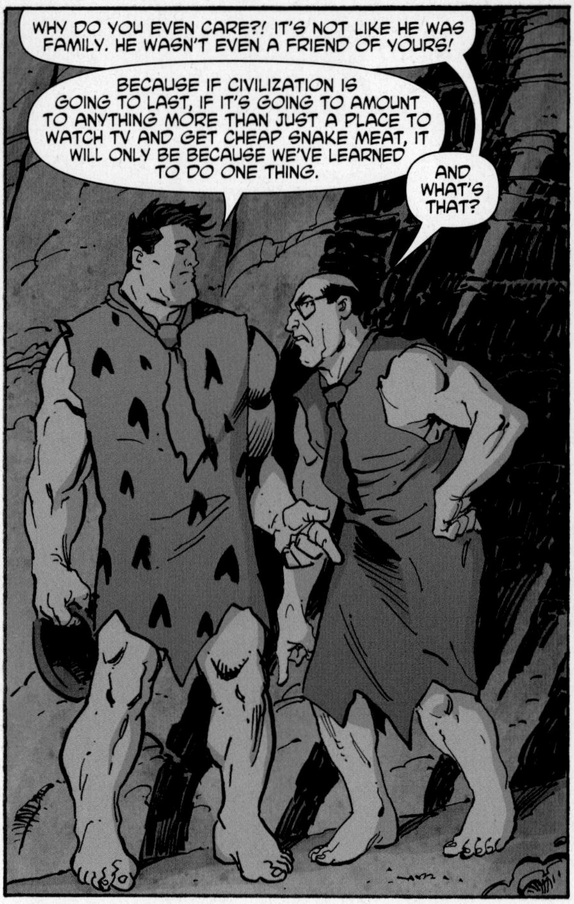
WHY DO YOU EVEN CARE?! IT'S NOT LIKE HE WAS FAMILY. HE WASN'T EVEN A FRIEND OF YOURS!
BECAUSE IF CIVILIZATION IS GOING TO LAST, IF IT'S GOING TO AMOUNT TO ANYTHING MORE THAN JUST A PLACE TO WATCH TV AND GET CHEAP SNAKE MEAT, IT WILL ONLY BE BECAUSE WE'VE LEARNED TO DO ONE THING.
AND WHAT'S THAT?

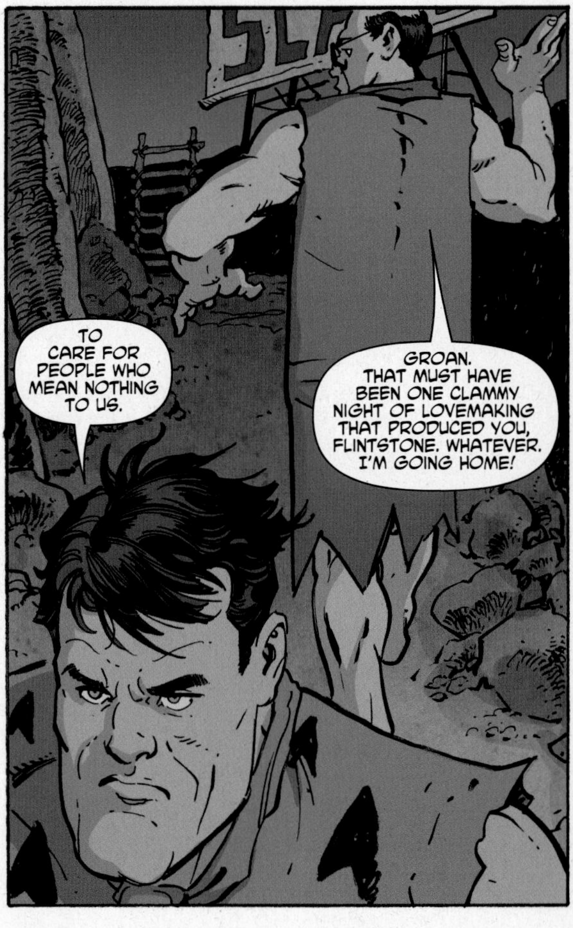
TO CARE FOR PEOPLE WHO MEAN NOTHING TO US.
GROAN. THAT MUST HAVE BEEN ONE CLAMMY NIGHT OF LOVEMAKING THAT PRODUCED YOU, FLINTSTONE. WHATEVER. I'M GOING HOME!

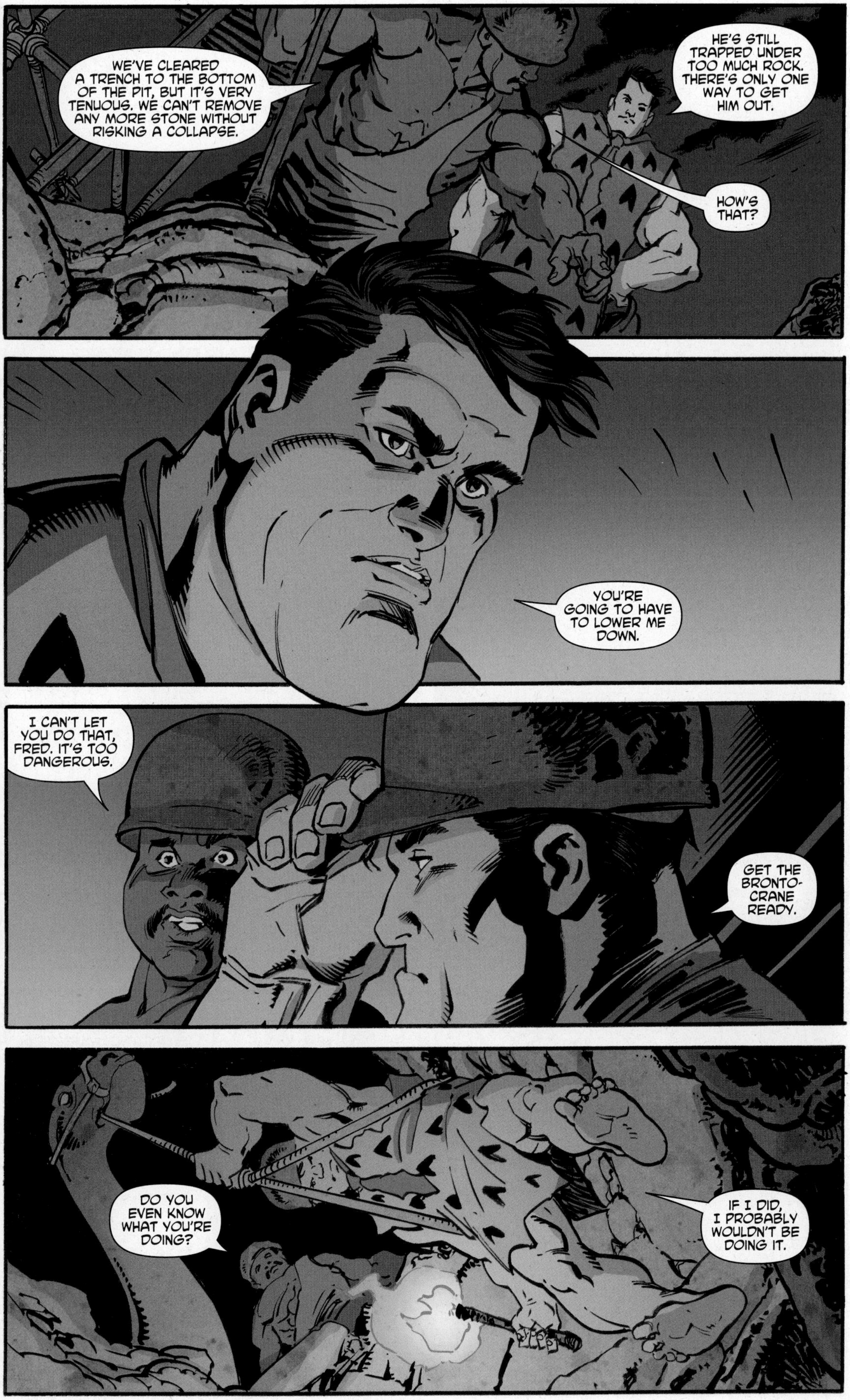
WE'VE CLEARED A TRENCH TO THE BOTTOM OF THE PIT, BUT IT'S VERY TENUOUS. WE CAN'T REMOVE ANY MORE STONE WITHOUT RISKING A COLLAPSE.
HE'S STILL TRAPPED UNDER TOO MUCH ROCK. THERE'S ONLY ONE WAY TO GET HIM OUT.
HOW'S THAT?
YOU'RE GOING TO HAVE TO LOWER ME DOWN.
I CAN'T LET YOU DO THAT, FRED. IT'S TOO DANGEROUS.
GET THE BRONTO-CRANE READY.
DO YOU EVEN KNOW WHAT YOU'RE DOING?
IF I DID, I PROBABLY WOULDN'T BE DOING IT.

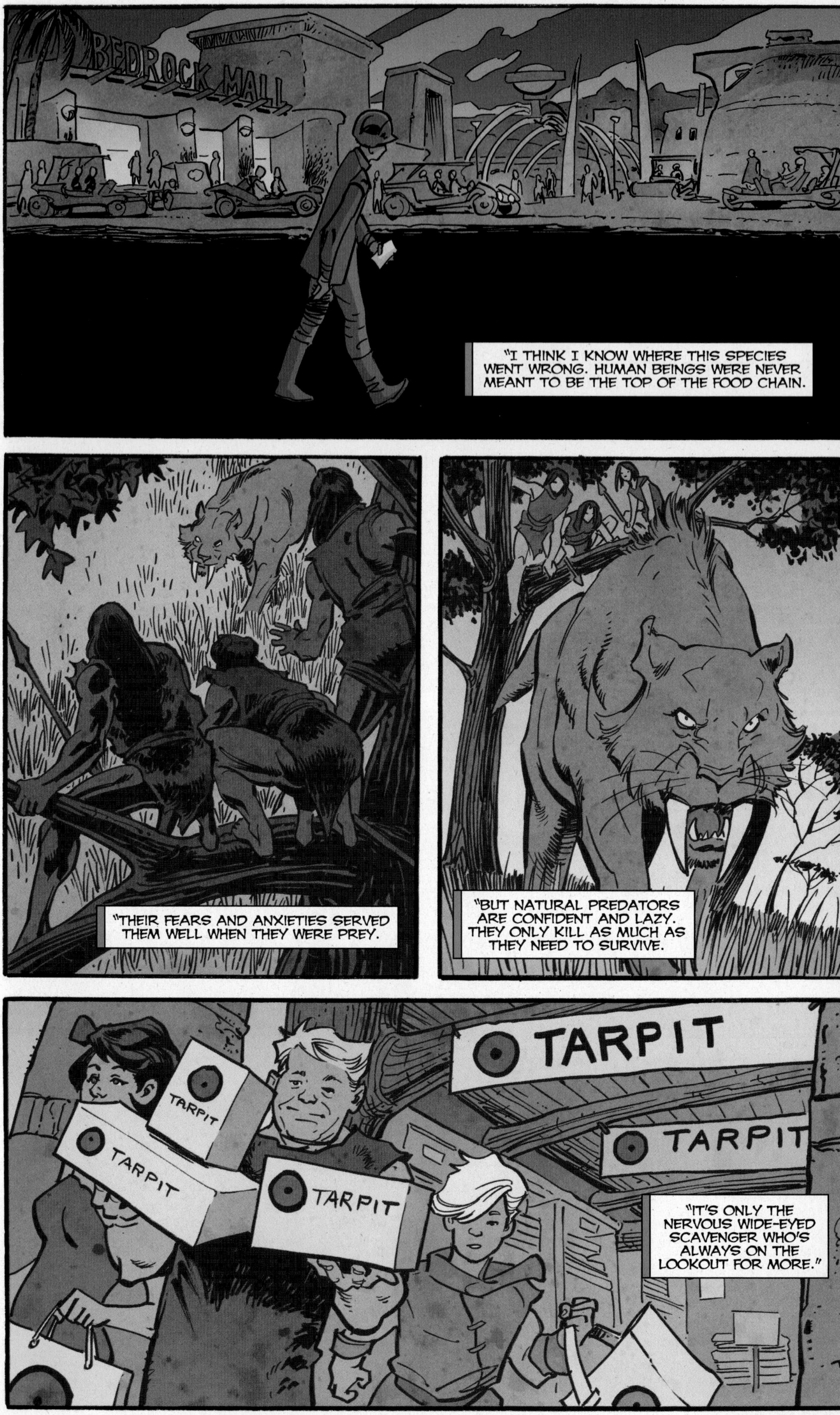
BEDROCK MALL
"I THINK I KNOW WHERE THIS SPECIES WENT WRONG. HUMAN BEINGS WERE NEVER MEANT TO BE THE TOP OF THE FOOD CHAIN.
"THEIR FEARS AND ANXIETIES SERVED THEM WELL WHEN THEY WERE PREY.
"BUT NATURAL PREDATORS ARE CONFIDENT AND LAZY. THEY ONLY KILL AS MUCH AS THEY NEED TO SURVIVE.
TARPIT
TARPIT
TARPIT
TARPIT
TARPIT
"IT'S ONLY THE NERVOUS WIDE-EYED SCAVENGER WHO'S ALWAYS ON THE LOOKOUT FOR MORE."

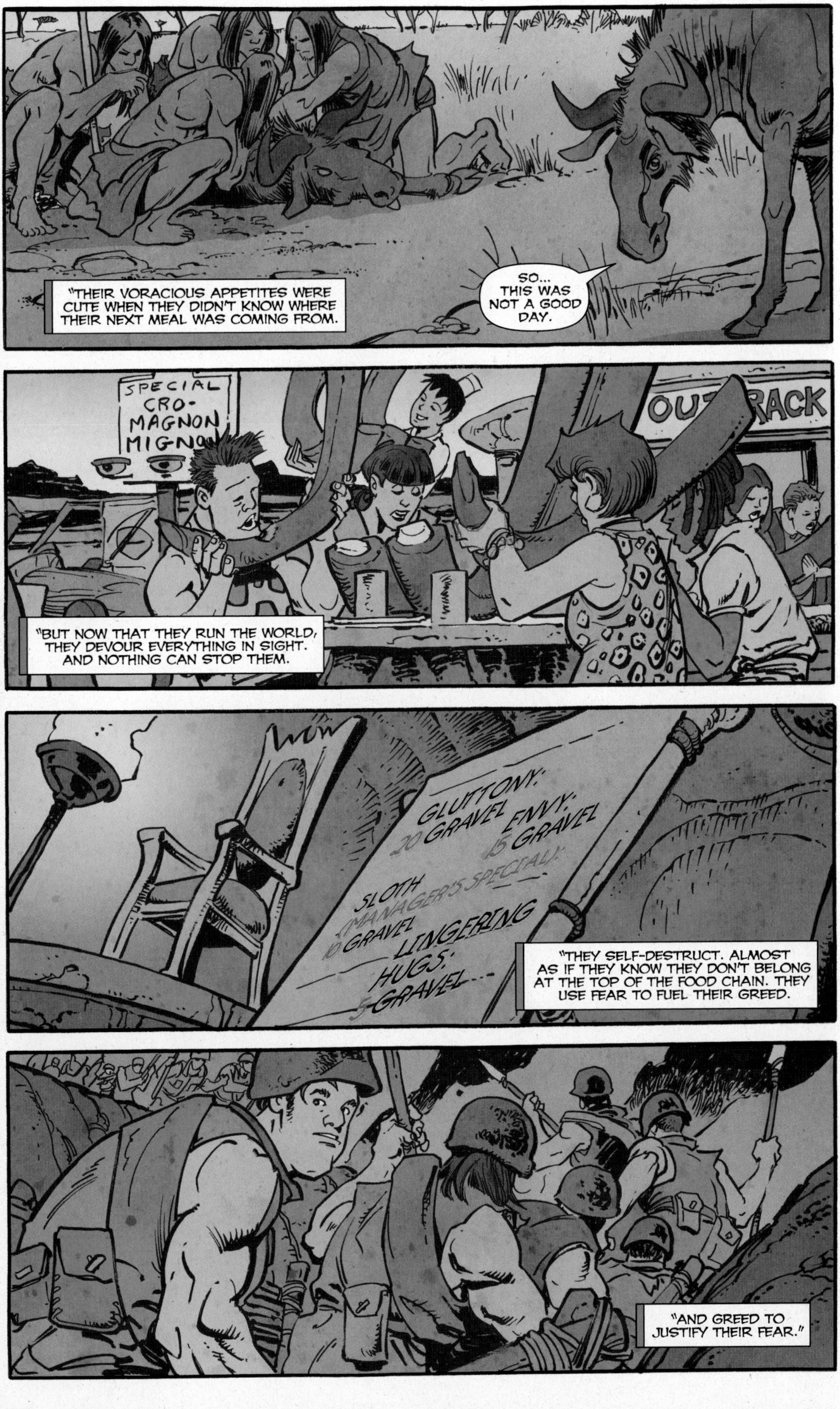

"THEIR VORACIOUS APPETITES WERE CUTE WHEN THEY DIDN'T KNOW WHERE THEIR NEXT MEAL WAS COMING FROM.
SO... THIS WAS NOT A GOOD DAY.
SPECIAL CRO-MAGNON MIGNO
"BUT NOW THAT THEY RUN THE WORLD, THEY DEVOUR EVERYTHING IN SIGHT. AND NOTHING CAN STOP THEM.
GLUTTONY: 20 GRAVEL
ENVY: 15 GRAVEL
SLOTH (MANAGER'S SPECIAL) 10 GRAVEL
LINGERING HUGS: 5 GRAVEL...
"THEY SELF-DESTRUCT. ALMOST AS IF THEY KNOW THEY DON'T BELONG AT THE TOP OF THE FOOD CHAIN. THEY USE FEAR TO FUEL THEIR GREED.
"AND GREED TO JUSTIFY THEIR FEAR."

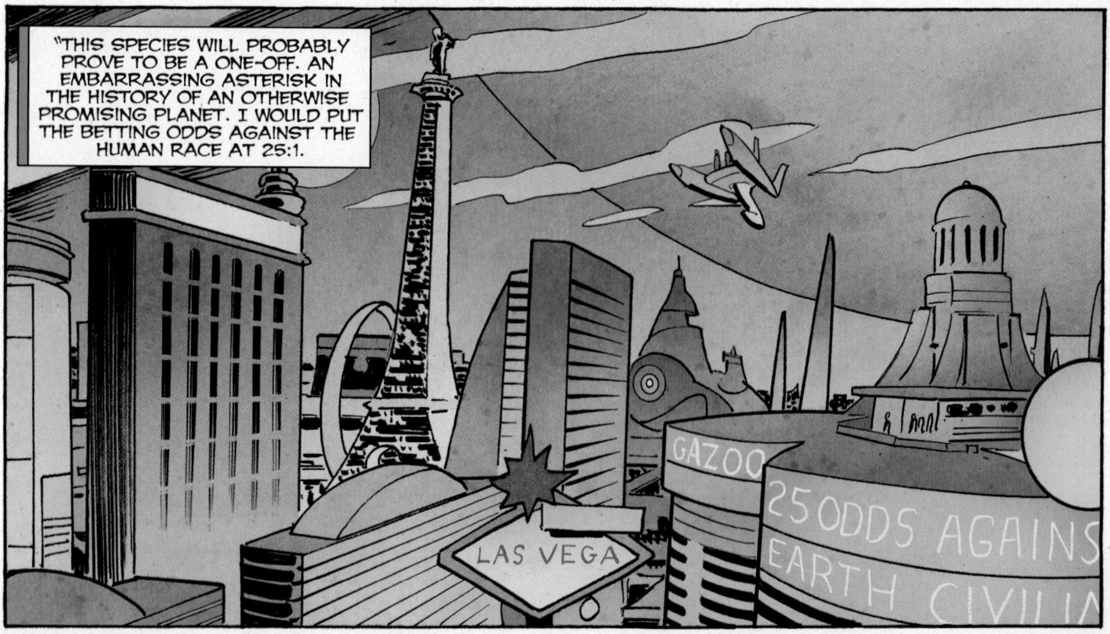
"THIS SPECIES WILL PROBABLY PROVE TO BE A ONE-OFF. AN EMBARRASSING ASTERISK IN THE HISTORY OF AN OTHERWISE PROMISING PLANET. I WOULD PUT THE BETTING ODDS AGAINST THE HUMAN RACE AT 25:1.
LAS VEGA
GAZOO
25 ODDS AGAINS
EARTH CIVILI

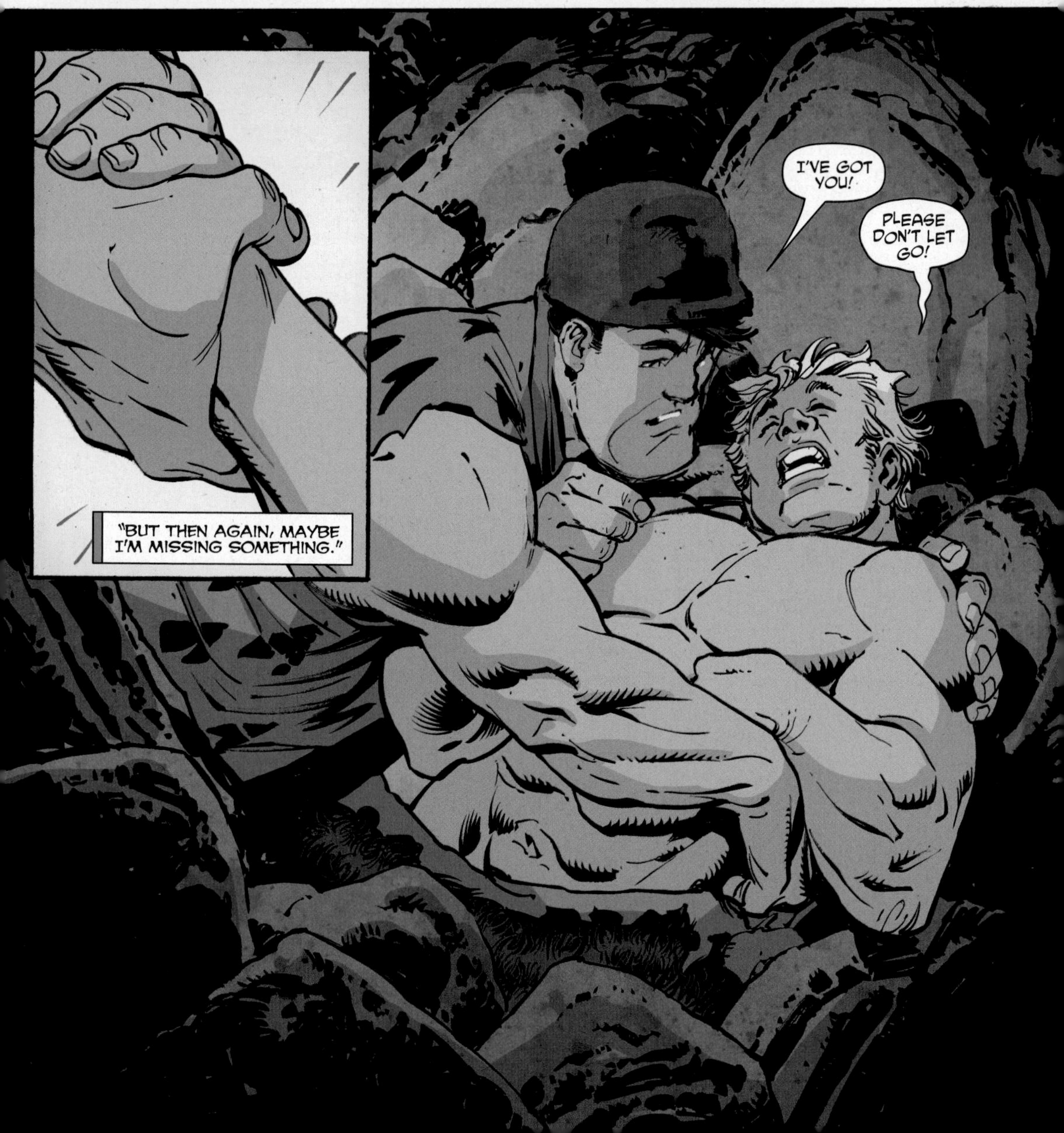
"BUT THEN AGAIN, MAYBE I'M MISSING SOMETHING."
I'VE GOT YOU!
PLEASE DON'T LET GO!

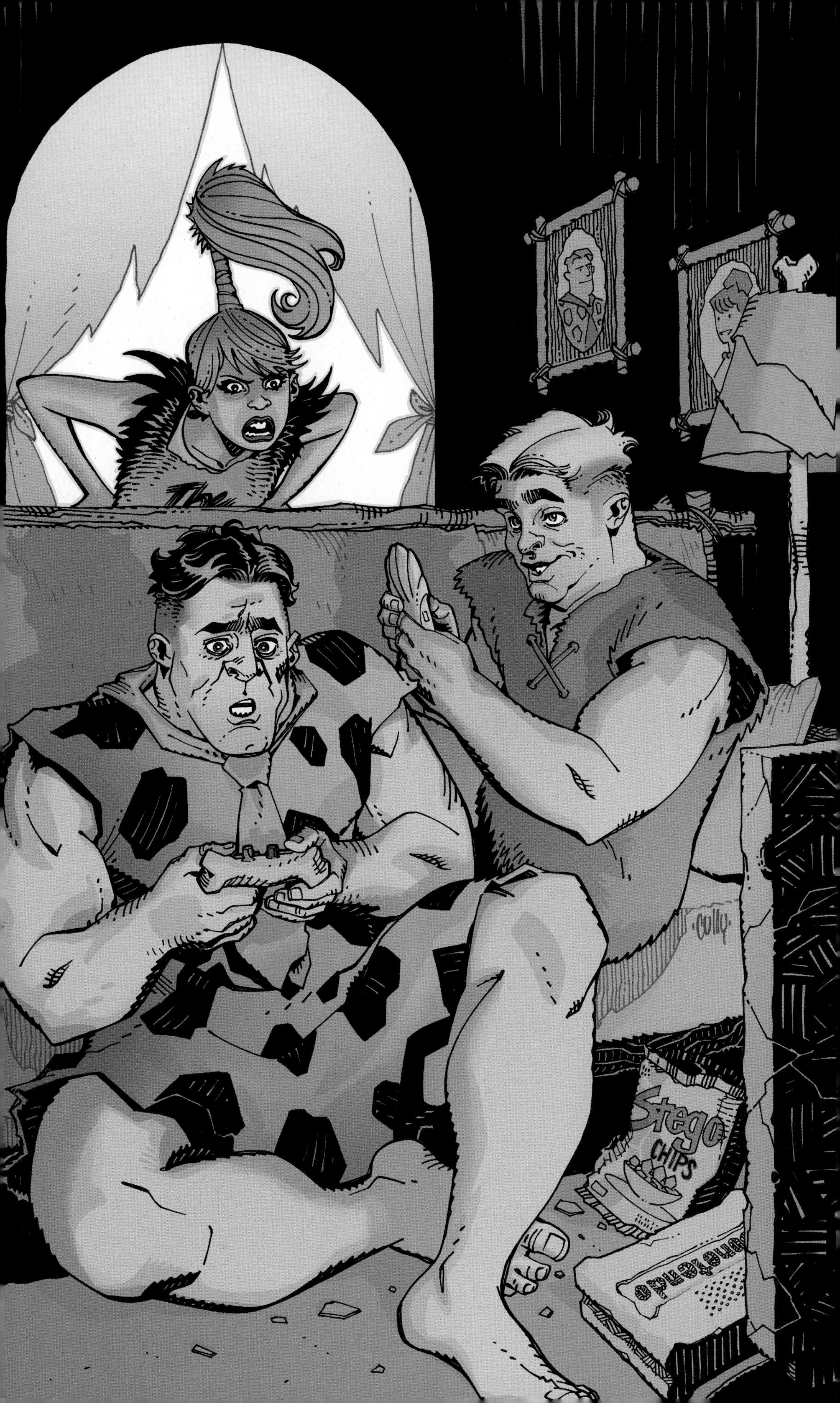
Stego
CHIPS

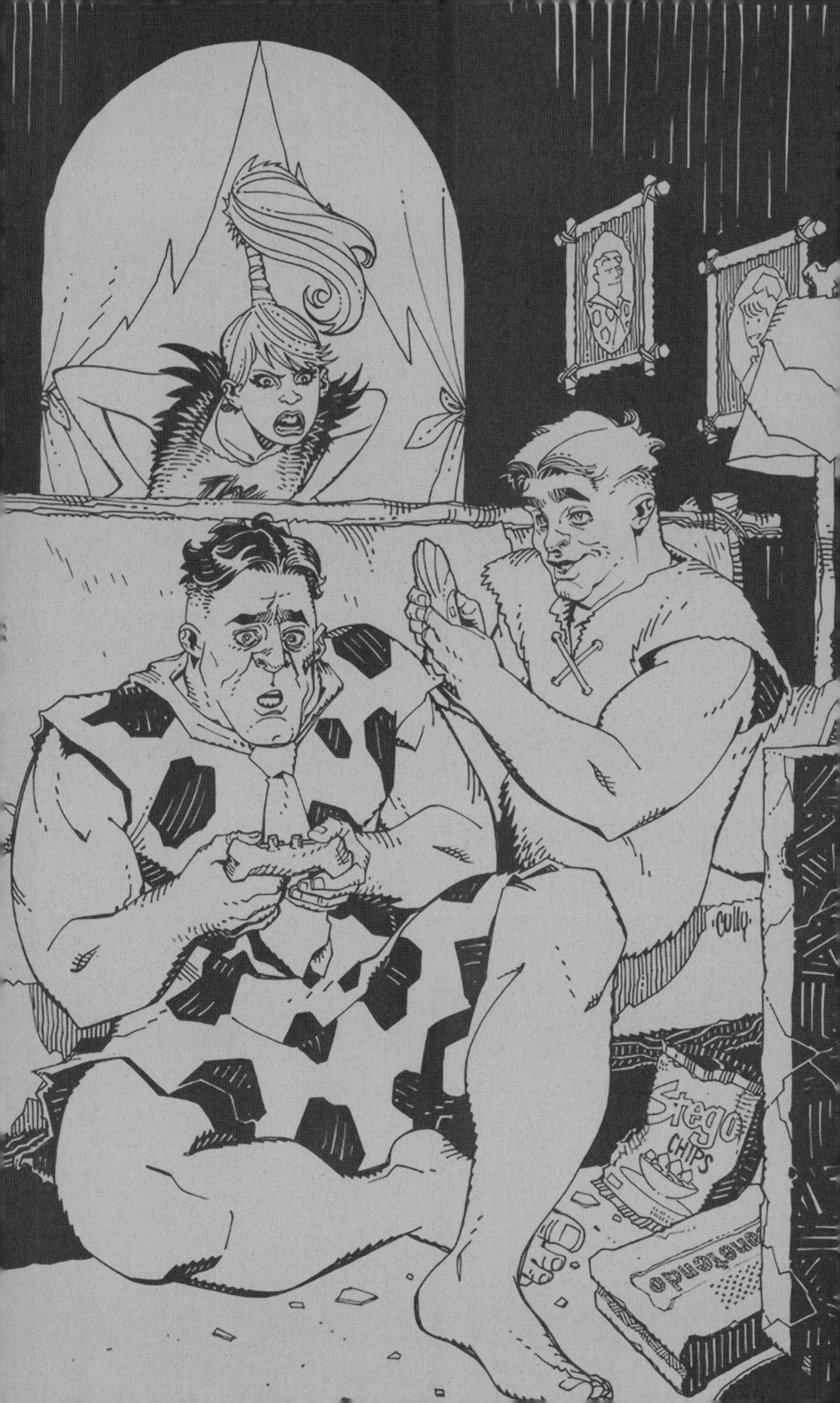
Stego
CHIPS

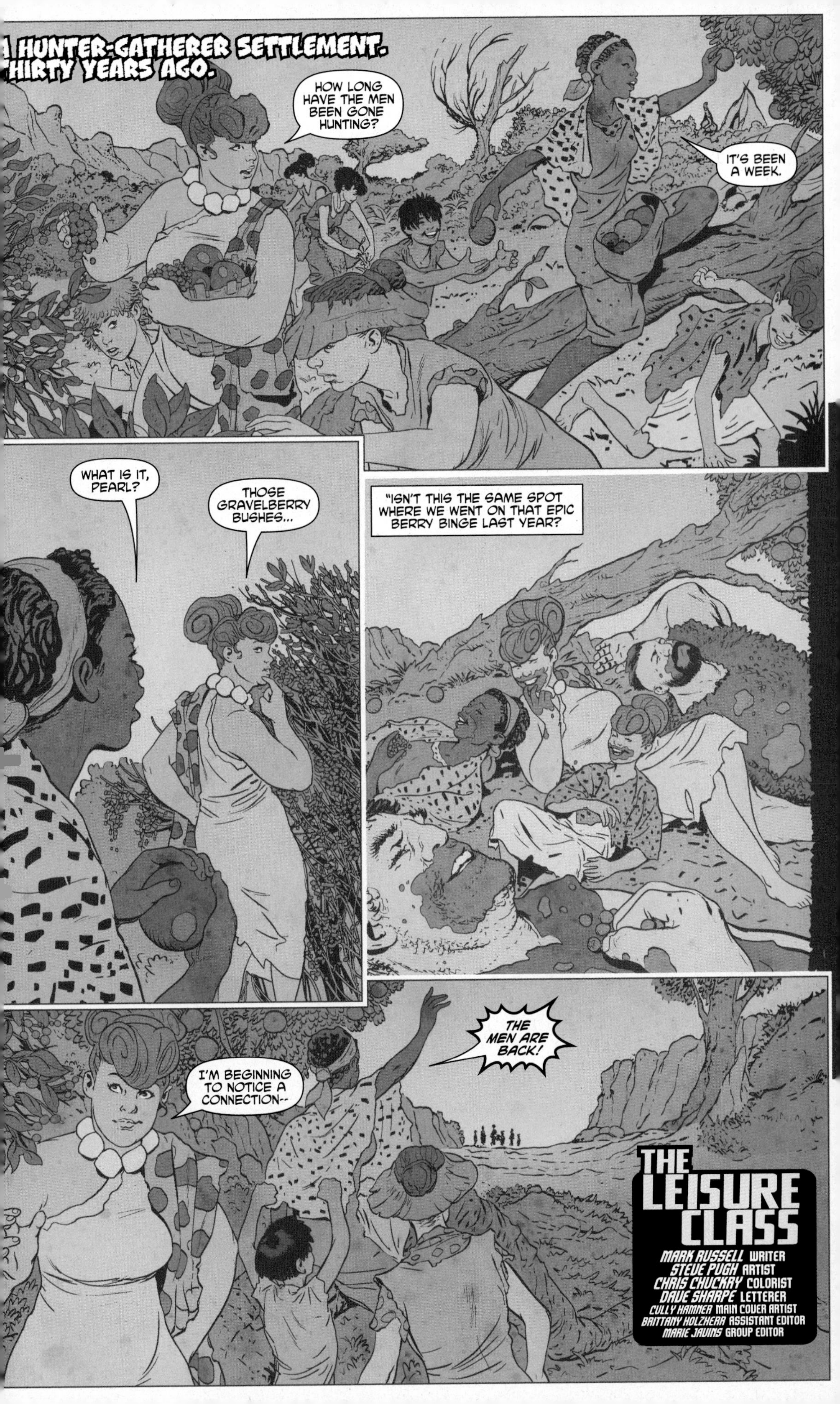
A HUNTER-GATHERER SETTLEMENT. THIRTY YEARS AGO.
HOW LONG HAVE THE MEN BEEN GONE HUNTING?
IT'S BEEN A WEEK.
WHAT IS IT, PEARL?
THOSE GRAVELBERRY BUSHES...
"ISN'T THIS THE SAME SPOT WHERE WE WENT ON THAT EPIC BERRY BINGE LAST YEAR?
I'M BEGINNING TO NOTICE A CONNECTION--
THE MEN ARE BACK!
THE LEISURE CLASS
MARK RUSSELL WRITER
STEVE PUGH ARTIST
CHRIS CHUCKRY COLORIST
DAVE SHARPE LETTERER
CULLY HAMNER MAIN COVER ARTIST
BRITTANY HOLZHERR ASSISTANT EDITOR
MARIE JAVINS GROUP EDITOR

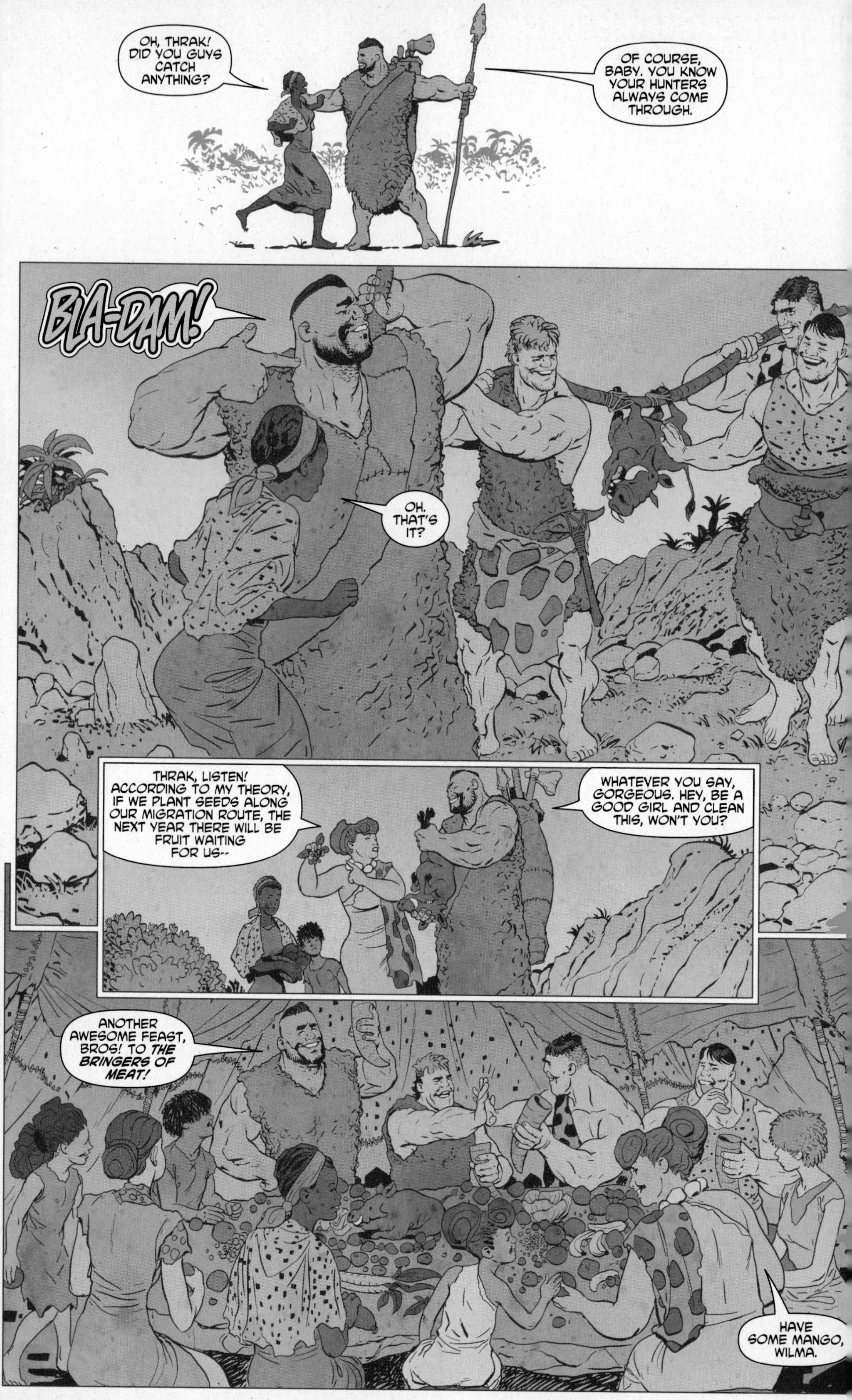
OH, THRAK! DID YOU GUYS CATCH ANYTHING?
OF COURSE, BABY. YOU KNOW YOUR HUNTERS ALWAYS COME THROUGH.
BLA-DAM!
OH. THAT'S IT?
THRAK, LISTEN! ACCORDING TO MY THEORY, IF WE PLANT SEEDS ALONG OUR MIGRATION ROUTE, THE NEXT YEAR THERE WILL BE FRUIT WAITING FOR US--
WHATEVER YOU SAY, GORGEOUS. HEY, BE A GOOD GIRL AND CLEAN THIS, WON'T YOU?
ANOTHER AWESOME FEAST, BROS! TO *THE BRINGERS OF MEAT!*
HAVE SOME MANGO, WILMA.

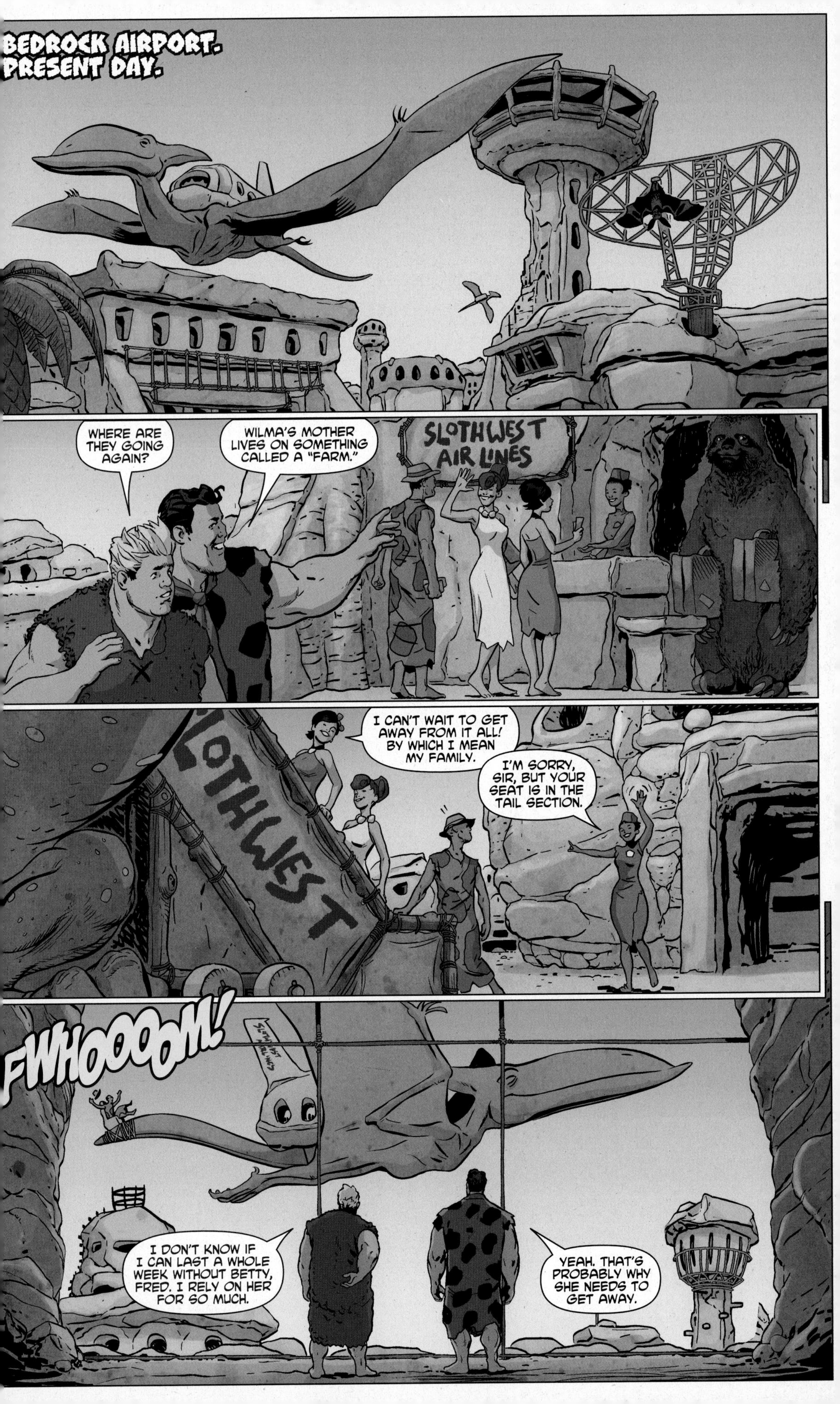
BEDROCK AIRPORT. PRESENT DAY.
WHERE ARE THEY GOING AGAIN?
WILMA'S MOTHER LIVES ON SOMETHING CALLED A "FARM."
SLOTHWEST AIR LINES
I CAN'T WAIT TO GET AWAY FROM IT ALL! BY WHICH I MEAN MY FAMILY.
I'M SORRY, SIR, BUT YOUR SEAT IS IN THE TAIL SECTION.
SLOTHWEST
FWHOOOOM!
I DON'T KNOW IF I CAN LAST A WHOLE WEEK WITHOUT BETTY, FRED. I RELY ON HER FOR SO MUCH.
YEAH. THAT'S PROBABLY WHY SHE NEEDS TO GET AWAY.

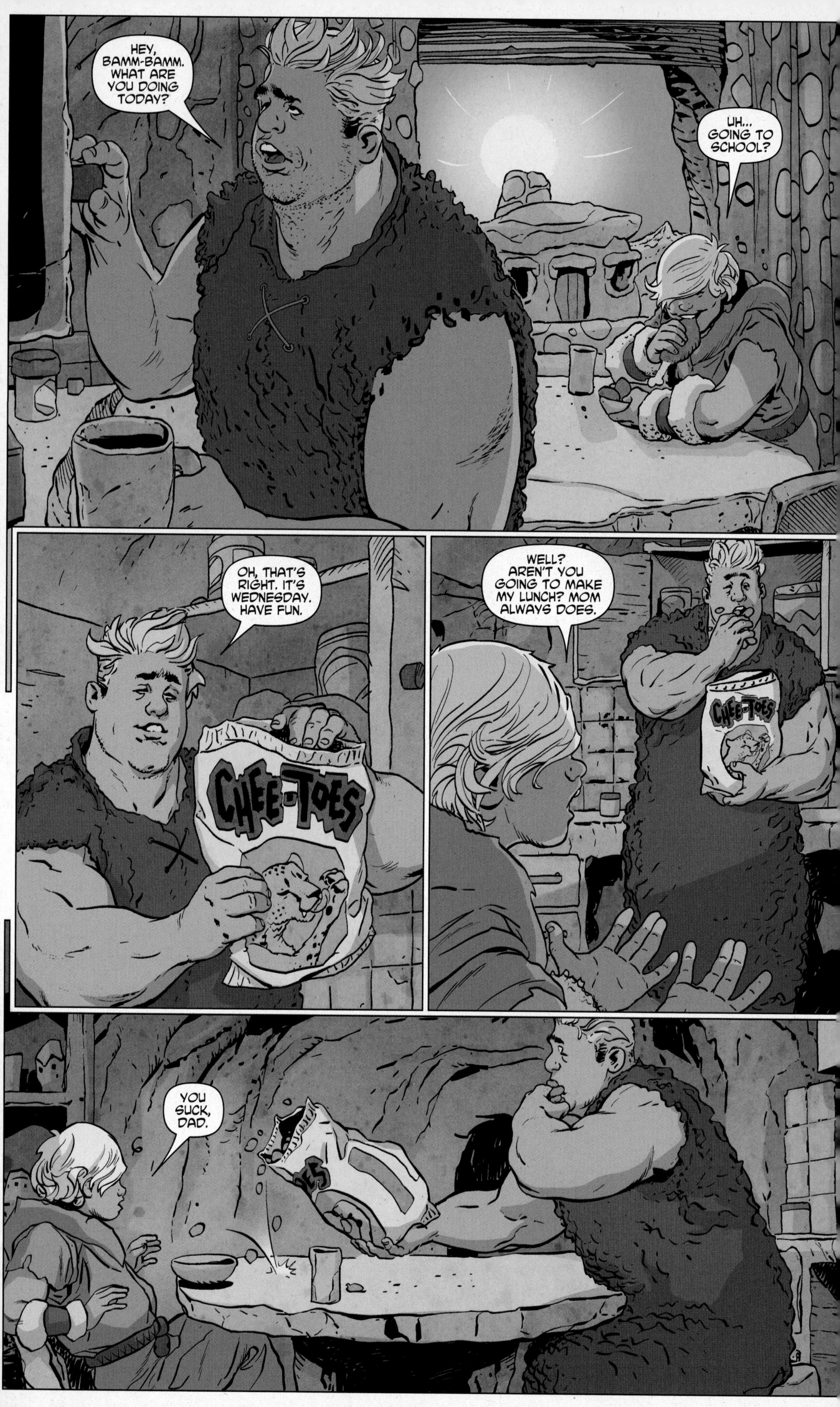
HEY, BAMM-BAMM. WHAT ARE YOU DOING TODAY?
UH... GOING TO SCHOOL?
OH, THAT'S RIGHT. IT'S WEDNESDAY. HAVE FUN.
CHEE-TOES
WELL? AREN'T YOU GOING TO MAKE MY LUNCH? MOM ALWAYS DOES.
CHEE-TOES
YOU SUCK, DAD.

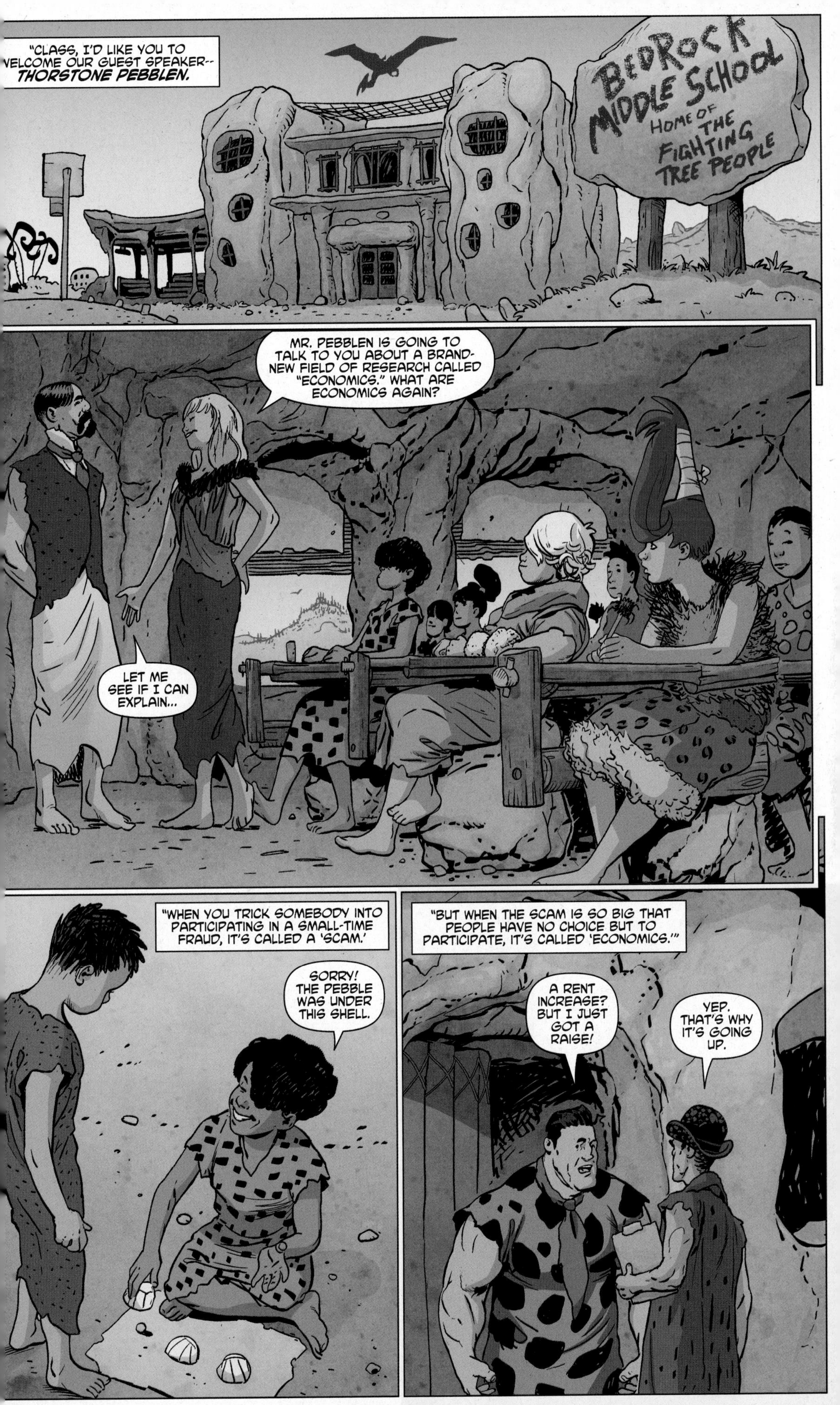
"CLASS, I'D LIKE YOU TO WELCOME OUR GUEST SPEAKER-- THORSTONE PEBBLEN.
BEDROCK MIDDLE SCHOOL HOME OF THE FIGHTING TREE PEOPLE
MR. PEBBLEN IS GOING TO TALK TO YOU ABOUT A BRAND-NEW FIELD OF RESEARCH CALLED "ECONOMICS." WHAT ARE ECONOMICS AGAIN?
LET ME SEE IF I CAN EXPLAIN...
"WHEN YOU TRICK SOMEBODY INTO PARTICIPATING IN A SMALL-TIME FRAUD, IT'S CALLED A 'SCAM.'
SORRY! THE PEBBLE WAS UNDER THIS SHELL.
"BUT WHEN THE SCAM IS SO BIG THAT PEOPLE HAVE NO CHOICE BUT TO PARTICIPATE, IT'S CALLED 'ECONOMICS.'"
A RENT INCREASE? BUT I JUST GOT A RAISE!
YEP. THAT'S WHY IT'S GOING UP.

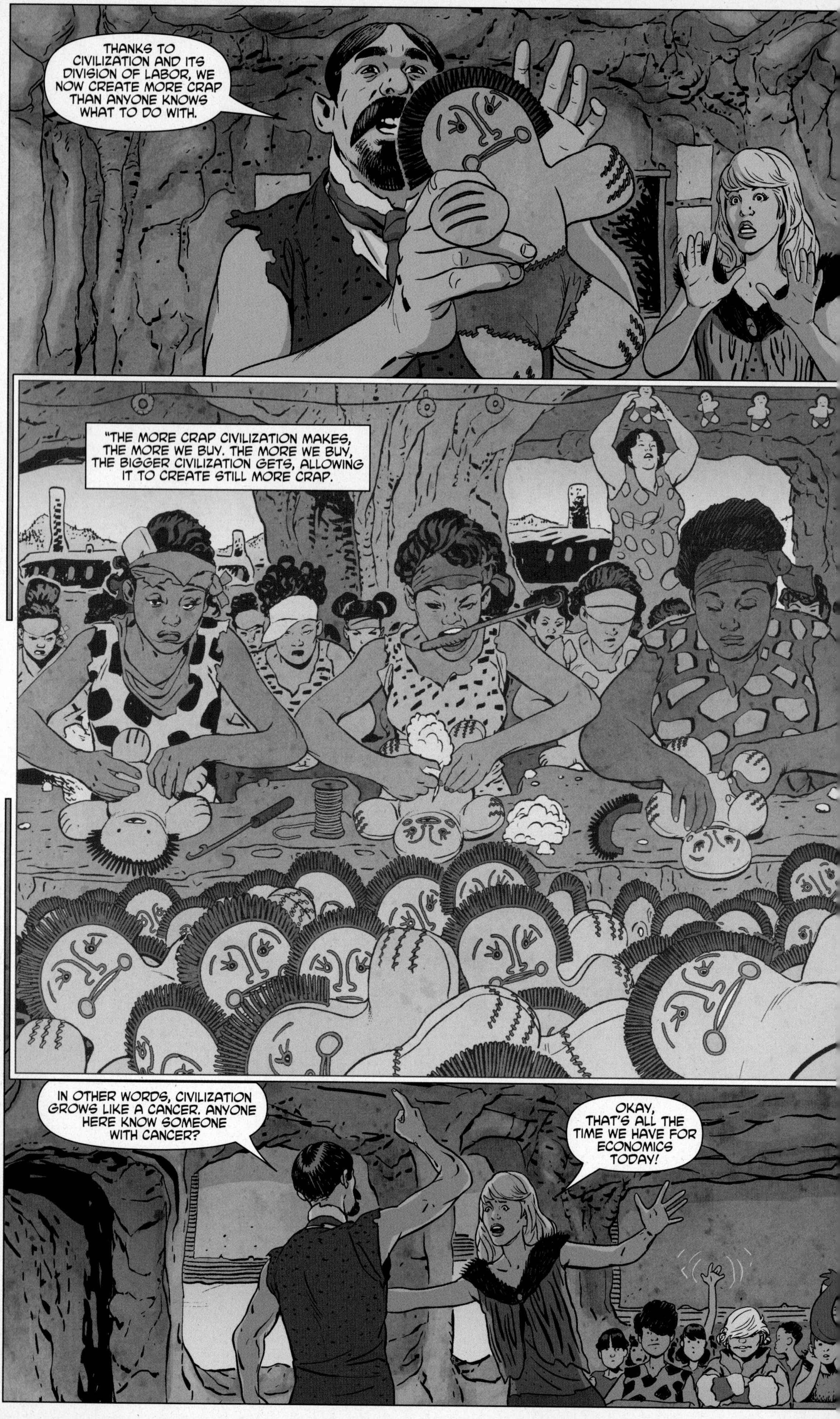
THANKS TO CIVILIZATION AND ITS DIVISION OF LABOR, WE NOW CREATE MORE CRAP THAN ANYONE KNOWS WHAT TO DO WITH.
"THE MORE CRAP CIVILIZATION MAKES, THE MORE WE BUY. THE MORE WE BUY, THE BIGGER CIVILIZATION GETS, ALLOWING IT TO CREATE STILL MORE CRAP.
IN OTHER WORDS, CIVILIZATION GROWS LIKE A CANCER. ANYONE HERE KNOW SOMEONE WITH CANCER?
OKAY, THAT'S ALL THE TIME WE HAVE FOR ECONOMICS TODAY!

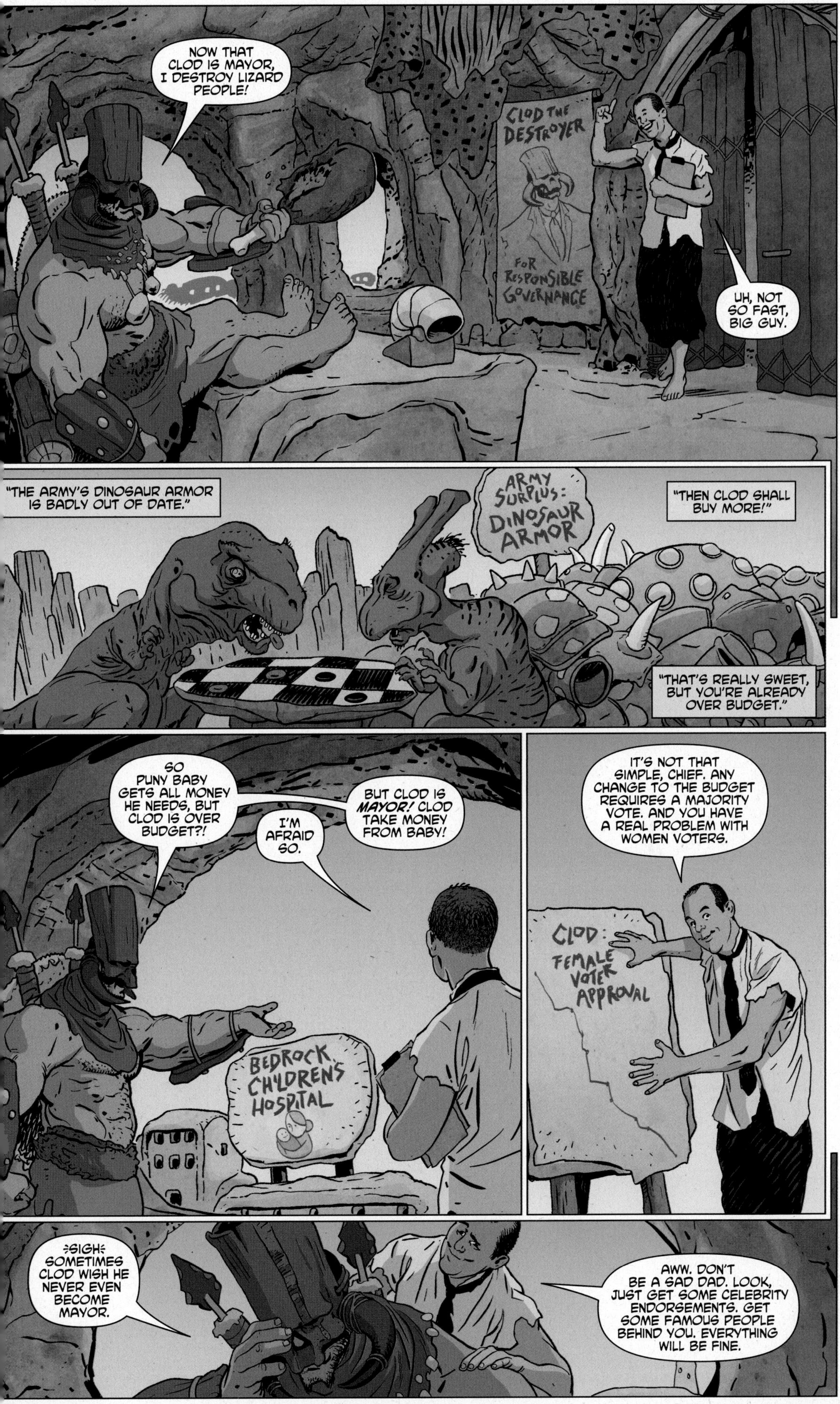
NOW THAT CLOD IS MAYOR, I DESTROY LIZARD PEOPLE!
CLOD THE DESTROYER
FOR RESPONSIBLE GOVERNANCE
UH, NOT SO FAST, BIG GUY.
"THE ARMY'S DINOSAUR ARMOR IS BADLY OUT OF DATE."
ARMY SURPLUS: DINOSAUR ARMOR
"THEN CLOD SHALL BUY MORE!"
"THAT'S REALLY SWEET, BUT YOU'RE ALREADY OVER BUDGET."
SO PUNY BABY GETS ALL MONEY HE NEEDS, BUT CLOD IS OVER BUDGET?!
I'M AFRAID SO.
BUT CLOD IS *MAYOR!* CLOD TAKE MONEY FROM BABY!
BEDROCK CHILDREN'S HOSPITAL
IT'S NOT THAT SIMPLE, CHIEF. ANY CHANGE TO THE BUDGET REQUIRES A MAJORITY VOTE. AND YOU HAVE A REAL PROBLEM WITH WOMEN VOTERS.
CLOD: FEMALE VOTER APPROVAL
SIGH SOMETIMES CLOD WISH HE NEVER EVEN BECOME MAYOR.
AWW. DON'T BE A SAD DAD. LOOK, JUST GET SOME CELEBRITY ENDORSEMENTS. GET SOME FAMOUS PEOPLE BEHIND YOU. EVERYTHING WILL BE FINE.

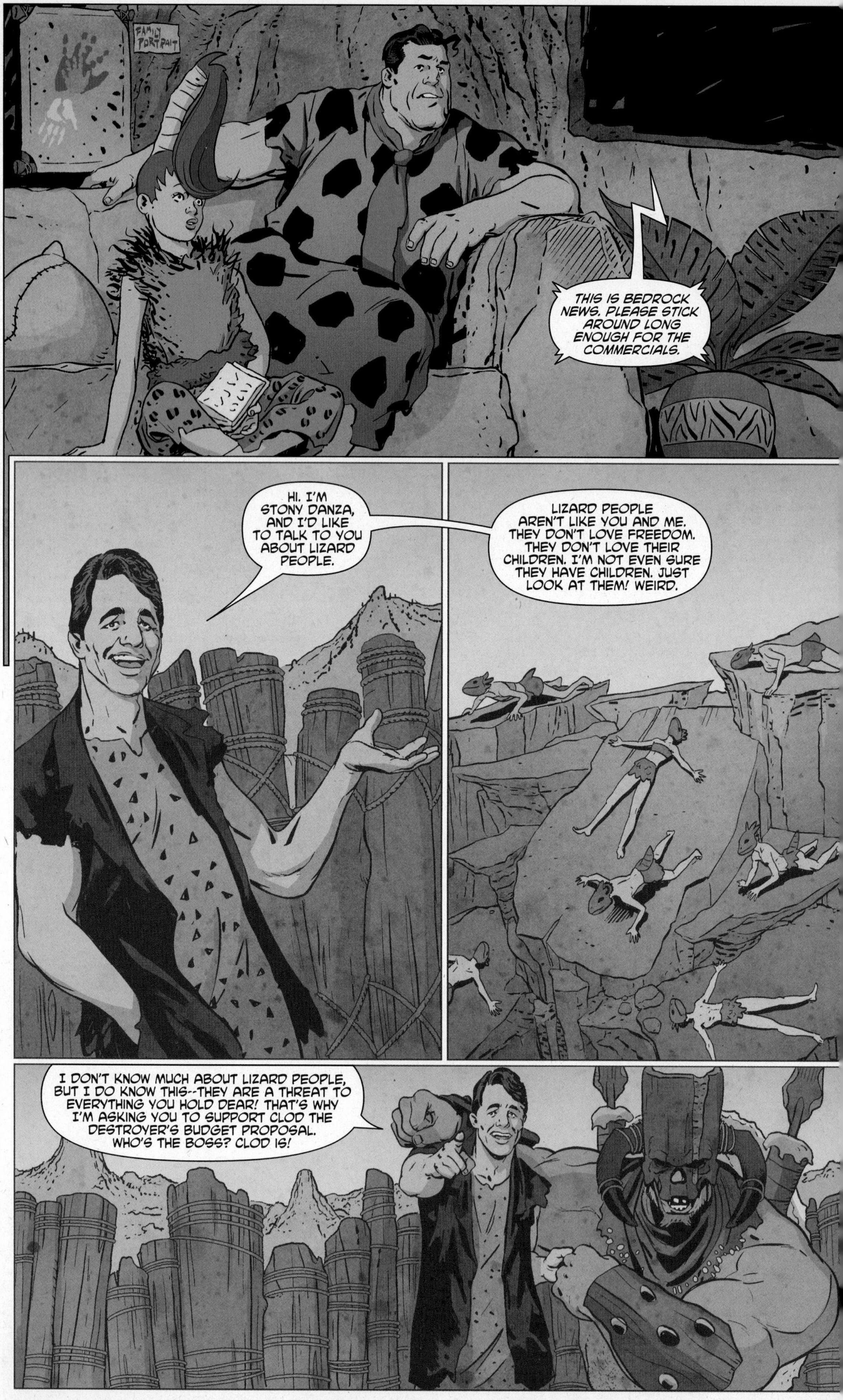
FAMILY PORTRAIT
THIS IS BEDROCK NEWS. PLEASE STICK AROUND LONG ENOUGH FOR THE COMMERCIALS.
HI. I'M STONY DANZA, AND I'D LIKE TO TALK TO YOU ABOUT LIZARD PEOPLE.
LIZARD PEOPLE AREN'T LIKE YOU AND ME. THEY DON'T LOVE FREEDOM. THEY DON'T LOVE THEIR CHILDREN. I'M NOT EVEN SURE THEY HAVE CHILDREN. JUST LOOK AT THEM! WEIRD.
I DON'T KNOW MUCH ABOUT LIZARD PEOPLE, BUT I DO KNOW THIS--THEY ARE A THREAT TO EVERYTHING YOU HOLD DEAR! THAT'S WHY I'M ASKING YOU TO SUPPORT CLOD THE DESTROYER'S BUDGET PROPOSAL. WHO'S THE BOSS? CLOD IS!

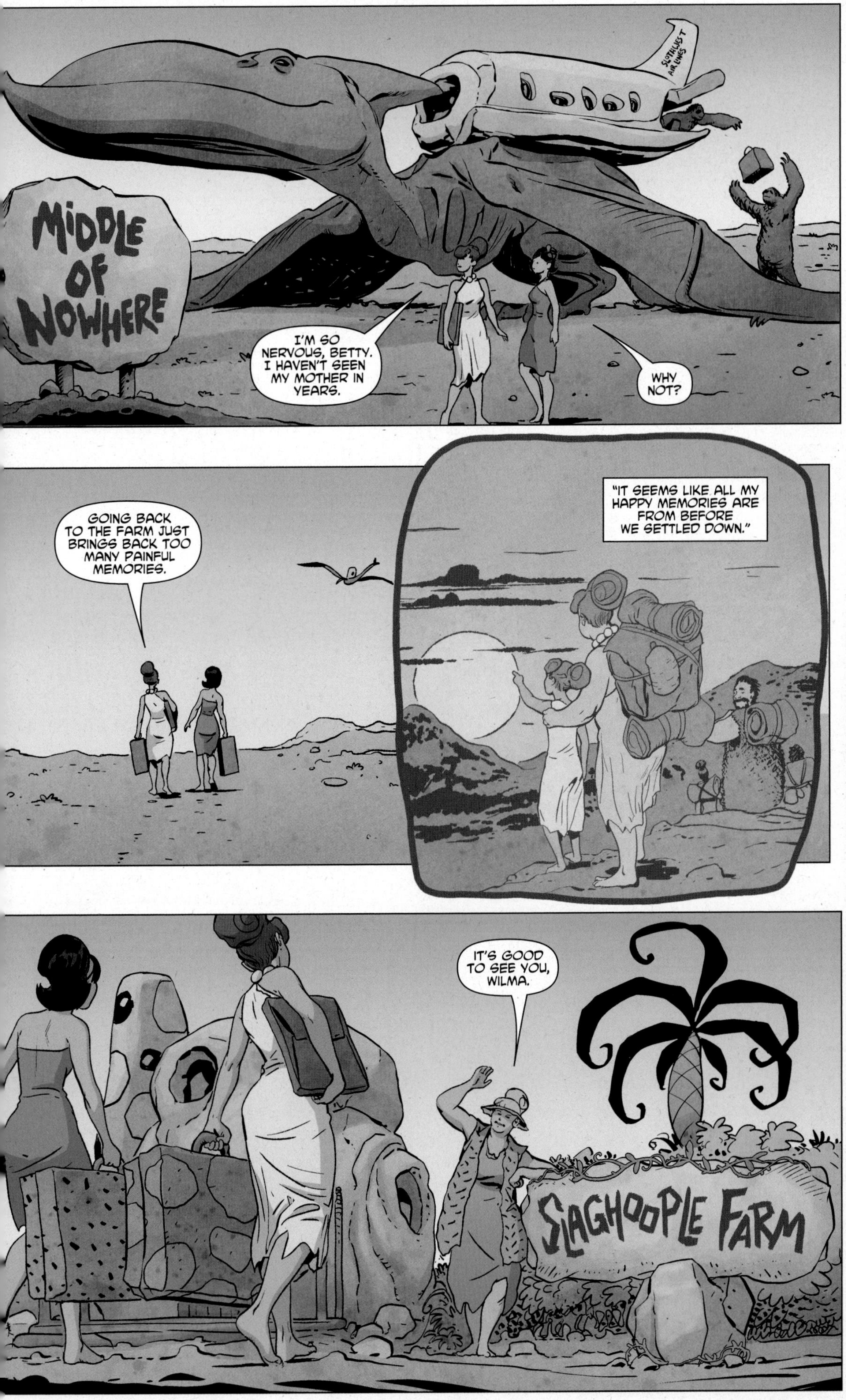
SLOTHLIEST AIR LINES
MIDDLE OF NOWHERE
I'M SO NERVOUS, BETTY. I HAVEN'T SEEN MY MOTHER IN YEARS.
WHY NOT?
GOING BACK TO THE FARM JUST BRINGS BACK TOO MANY PAINFUL MEMORIES.
"IT SEEMS LIKE ALL MY HAPPY MEMORIES ARE FROM BEFORE WE SETTLED DOWN."
IT'S GOOD TO SEE YOU, WILMA.
SLAGHOOPLE FARM

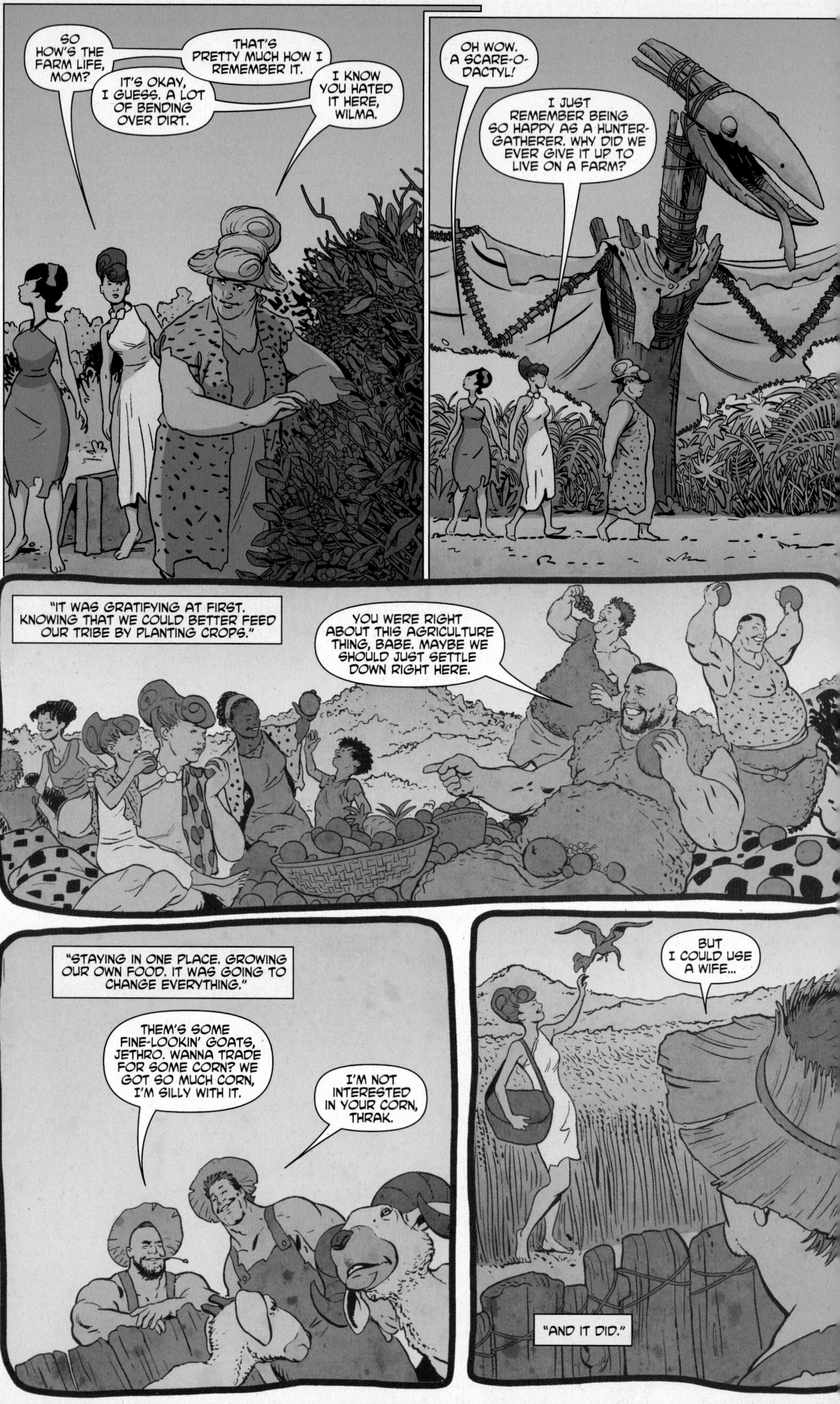
SO HOW'S THE FARM LIFE, MOM?
IT'S OKAY, I GUESS. A LOT OF BENDING OVER DIRT.
THAT'S PRETTY MUCH HOW I REMEMBER IT.
I KNOW YOU HATED IT HERE, WILMA.
OH WOW. A SCARE-O-DACTYL!
I JUST REMEMBER BEING SO HAPPY AS A HUNTER-GATHERER. WHY DID WE EVER GIVE IT UP TO LIVE ON A FARM?
"IT WAS GRATIFYING AT FIRST. KNOWING THAT WE COULD BETTER FEED OUR TRIBE BY PLANTING CROPS."
YOU WERE RIGHT ABOUT THIS AGRICULTURE THING, BABE. MAYBE WE SHOULD JUST SETTLE DOWN RIGHT HERE.
"STAYING IN ONE PLACE. GROWING OUR OWN FOOD. IT WAS GOING TO CHANGE EVERYTHING."
THEM'S SOME FINE-LOOKIN' GOATS, JETHRO. WANNA TRADE FOR SOME CORN? WE GOT SO MUCH CORN, I'M SILLY WITH IT.
I'M NOT INTERESTED IN YOUR CORN, THRAK.
BUT I COULD USE A WIFE...
"AND IT DID."

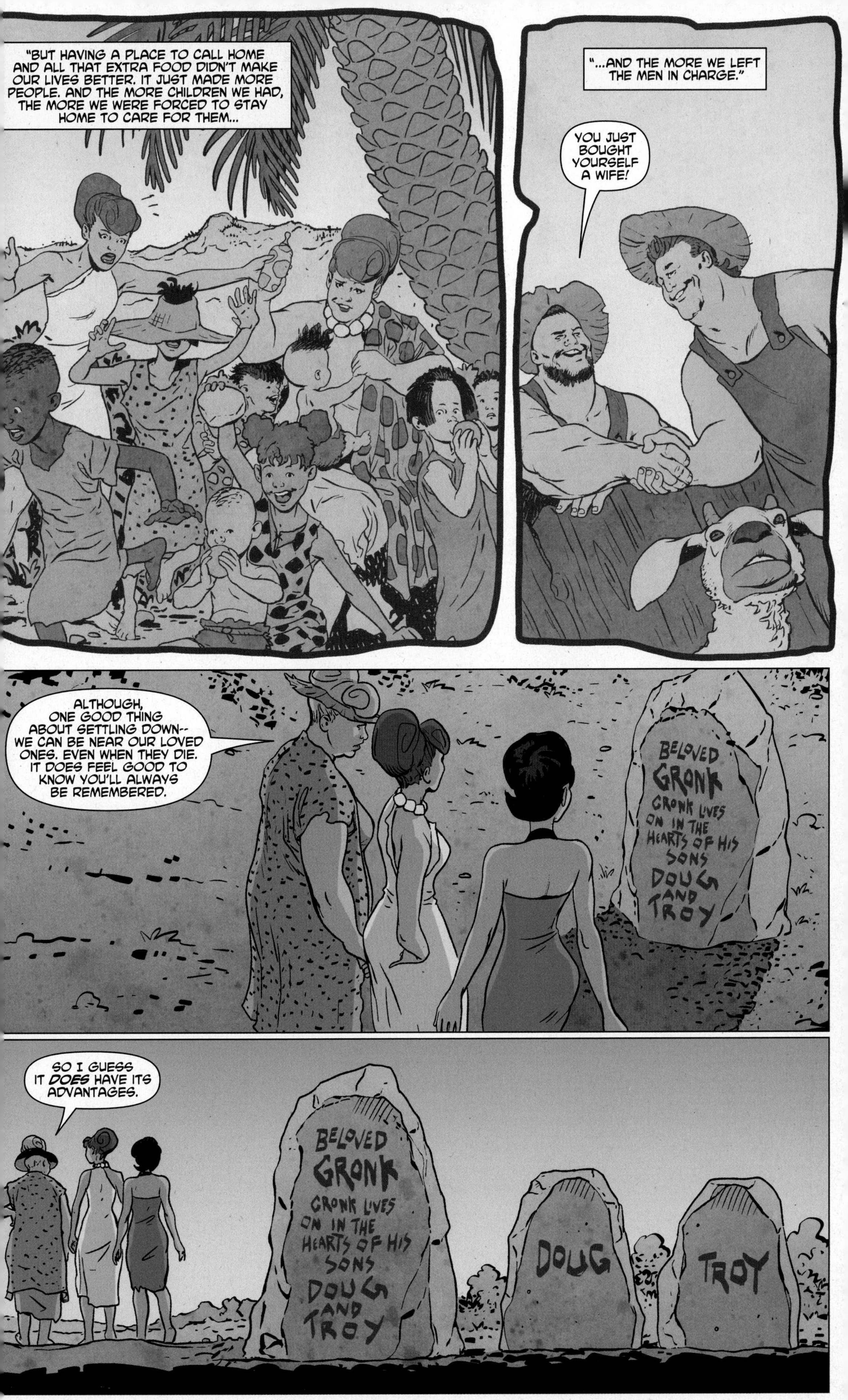
"BUT HAVING A PLACE TO CALL HOME AND ALL THAT EXTRA FOOD DIDN'T MAKE OUR LIVES BETTER. IT JUST MADE MORE PEOPLE. AND THE MORE CHILDREN WE HAD, THE MORE WE WERE FORCED TO STAY HOME TO CARE FOR THEM...
"...AND THE MORE WE LEFT THE MEN IN CHARGE."
YOU JUST BOUGHT YOURSELF A WIFE!
ALTHOUGH, ONE GOOD THING ABOUT SETTLING DOWN-- WE CAN BE NEAR OUR LOVED ONES. EVEN WHEN THEY DIE. IT DOES FEEL GOOD TO KNOW YOU'LL ALWAYS BE REMEMBERED.
BELOVED GRONK GRONK LIVES ON IN THE HEARTS OF HIS SONS DOUG AND TROY
SO I GUESS IT *DOES* HAVE ITS ADVANTAGES.
BELOVED GRONK GRONK LIVES ON IN THE HEARTS OF HIS SONS DOUG AND TROY
DOUG
TROY

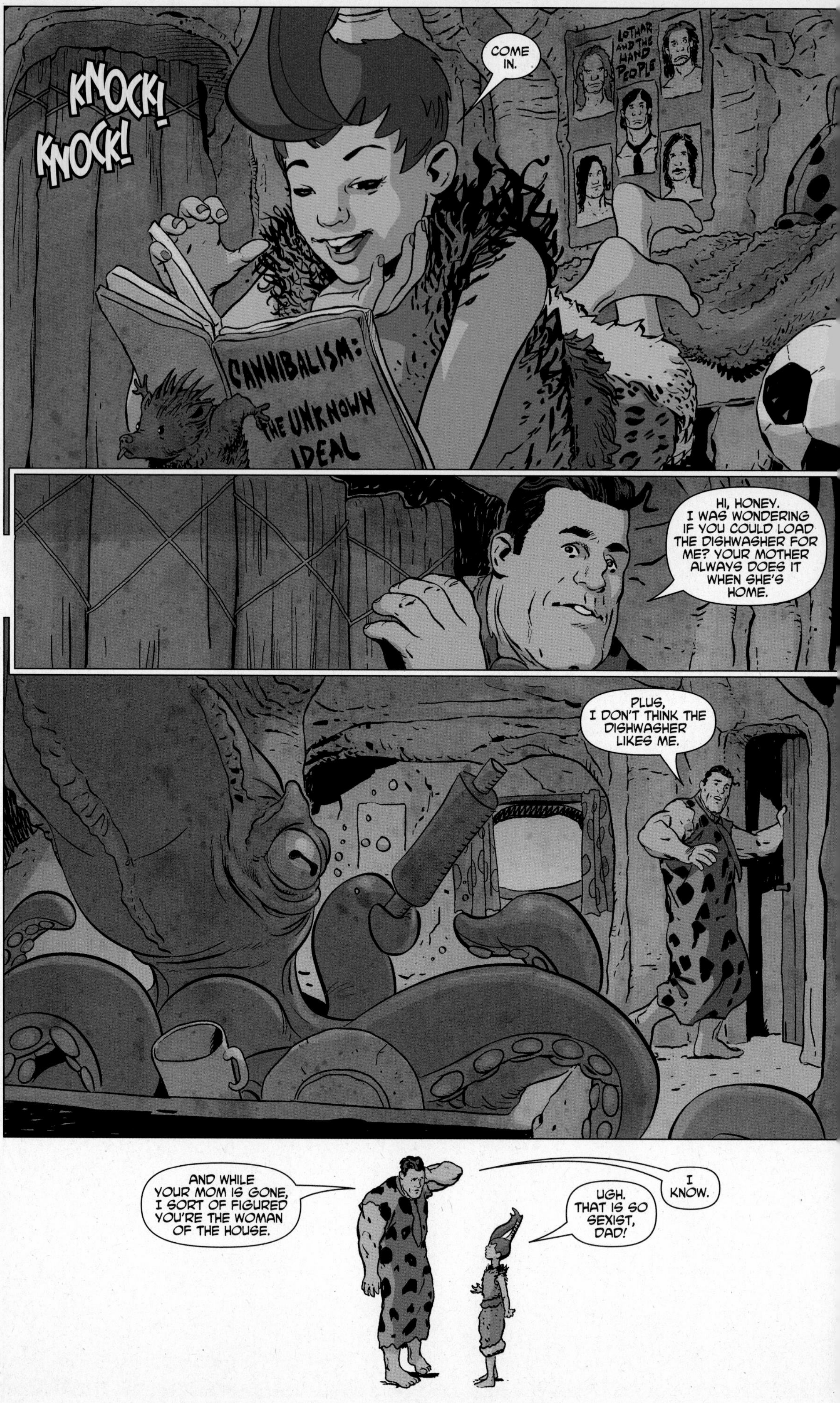
KNOCK! KNOCK!
COME IN.
LOTHAR AND THE HAND PEOPLE
CANNIBALISM: THE UNKNOWN IDEAL
HI, HONEY. I WAS WONDERING IF YOU COULD LOAD THE DISHWASHER FOR ME? YOUR MOTHER ALWAYS DOES IT WHEN SHE'S HOME.
PLUS, I DON'T THINK THE DISHWASHER LIKES ME.
AND WHILE YOUR MOM IS GONE, I SORT OF FIGURED YOU'RE THE WOMAN OF THE HOUSE.
UGH. THAT IS SO SEXIST, DAD!
I KNOW.

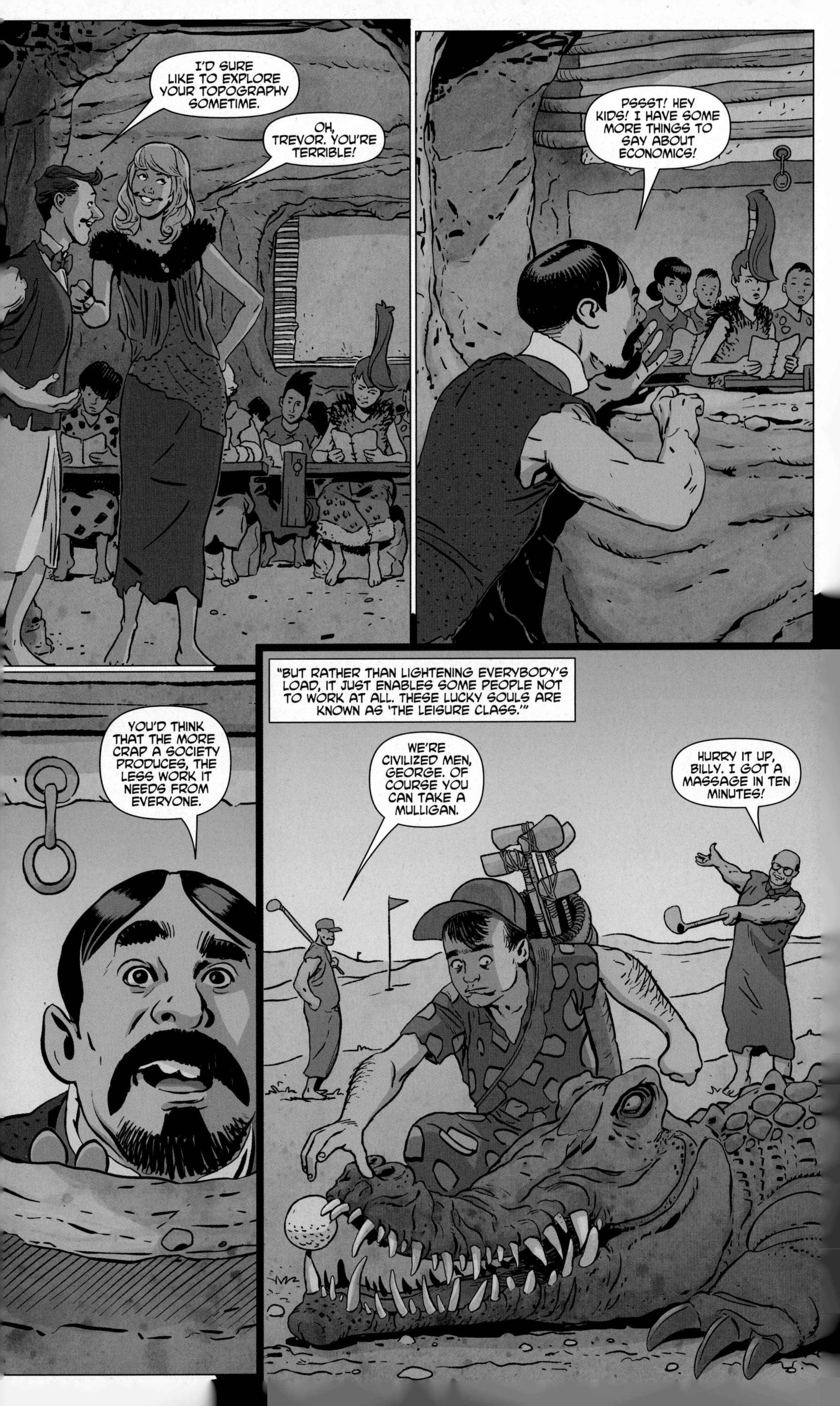
I'D SURE LIKE TO EXPLORE YOUR TOPOGRAPHY SOMETIME.
OH, TREVOR. YOU'RE TERRIBLE!
PSSST! HEY KIDS! I HAVE SOME MORE THINGS TO SAY ABOUT ECONOMICS!
YOU'D THINK THAT THE MORE CRAP A SOCIETY PRODUCES, THE LESS WORK IT NEEDS FROM EVERYONE.
"BUT RATHER THAN LIGHTENING EVERYBODY'S LOAD, IT JUST ENABLES SOME PEOPLE NOT TO WORK AT ALL. THESE LUCKY SOULS ARE KNOWN AS 'THE LEISURE CLASS.'"
WE'RE CIVILIZED MEN, GEORGE. OF COURSE YOU CAN TAKE A MULLIGAN.
HURRY IT UP, BILLY. I GOT A MASSAGE IN TEN MINUTES!

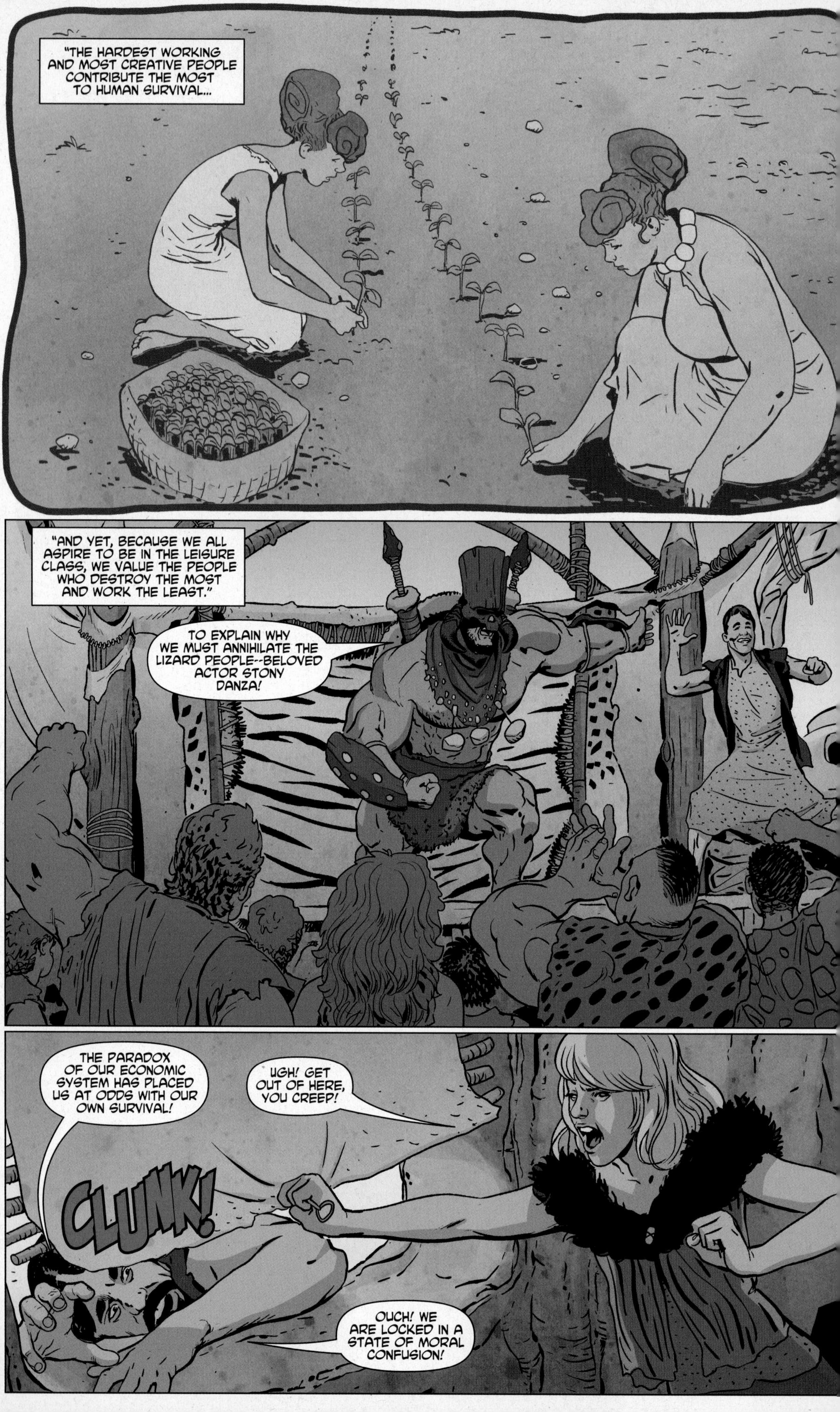
"THE HARDEST WORKING AND MOST CREATIVE PEOPLE CONTRIBUTE THE MOST TO HUMAN SURVIVAL...
"AND YET, BECAUSE WE ALL ASPIRE TO BE IN THE LEISURE CLASS, WE VALUE THE PEOPLE WHO DESTROY THE MOST AND WORK THE LEAST."
TO EXPLAIN WHY WE MUST ANNIHILATE THE LIZARD PEOPLE--BELOVED ACTOR STONY DANZA!
THE PARADOX OF OUR ECONOMIC SYSTEM HAS PLACED US AT ODDS WITH OUR OWN SURVIVAL!
UGH! GET OUT OF HERE, YOU CREEP!
CLUNK!
OUCH! WE ARE LOCKED IN A STATE OF MORAL CONFUSION!

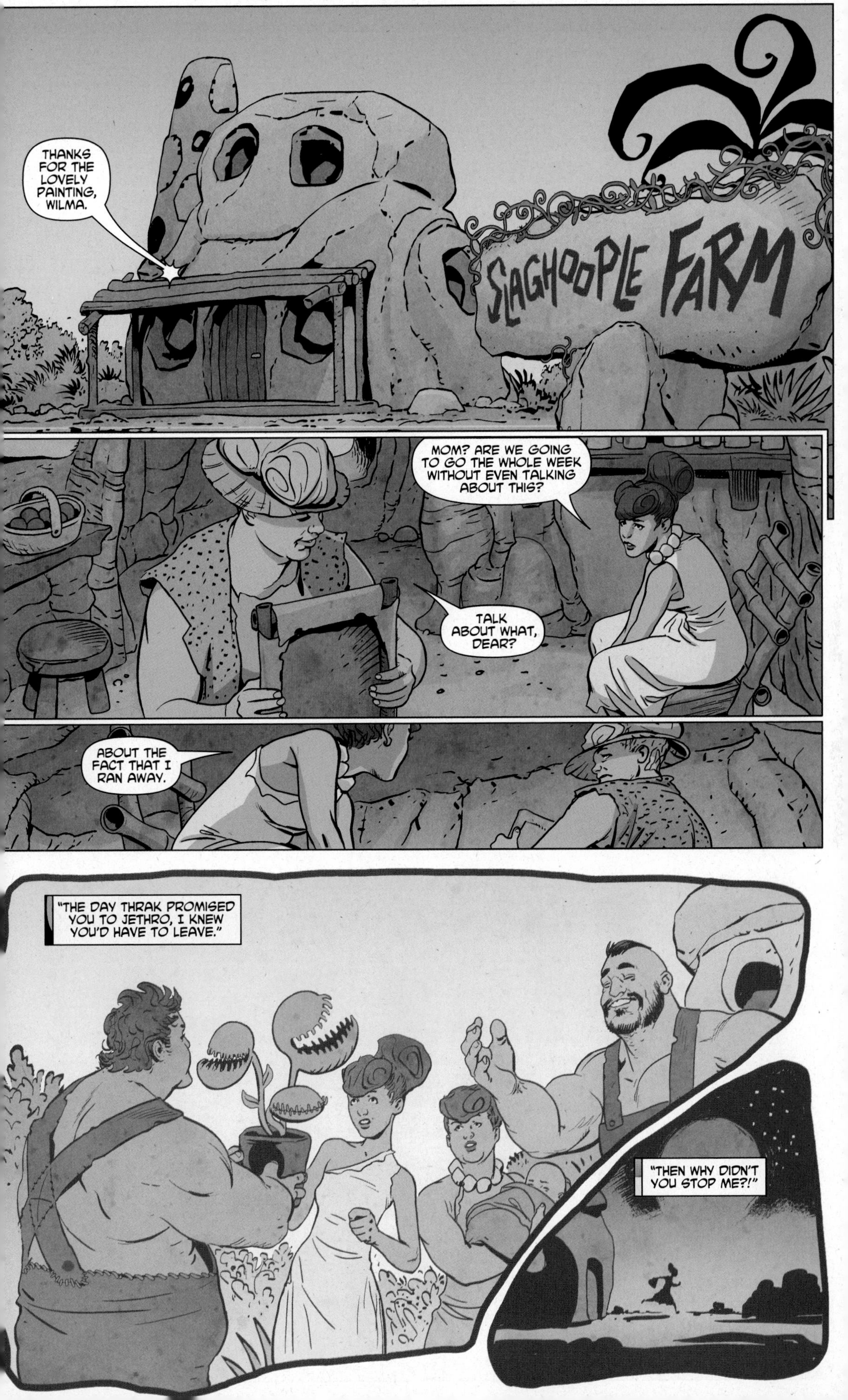
THANKS FOR THE LOVELY PAINTING, WILMA.
SLAGHOOPLE FARM
MOM? ARE WE GOING TO GO THE WHOLE WEEK WITHOUT EVEN TALKING ABOUT THIS?
TALK ABOUT WHAT, DEAR?
ABOUT THE FACT THAT I RAN AWAY.
"THE DAY THRAK PROMISED YOU TO JETHRO, I KNEW YOU'D HAVE TO LEAVE."
"THEN WHY DIDN'T YOU STOP ME?!"

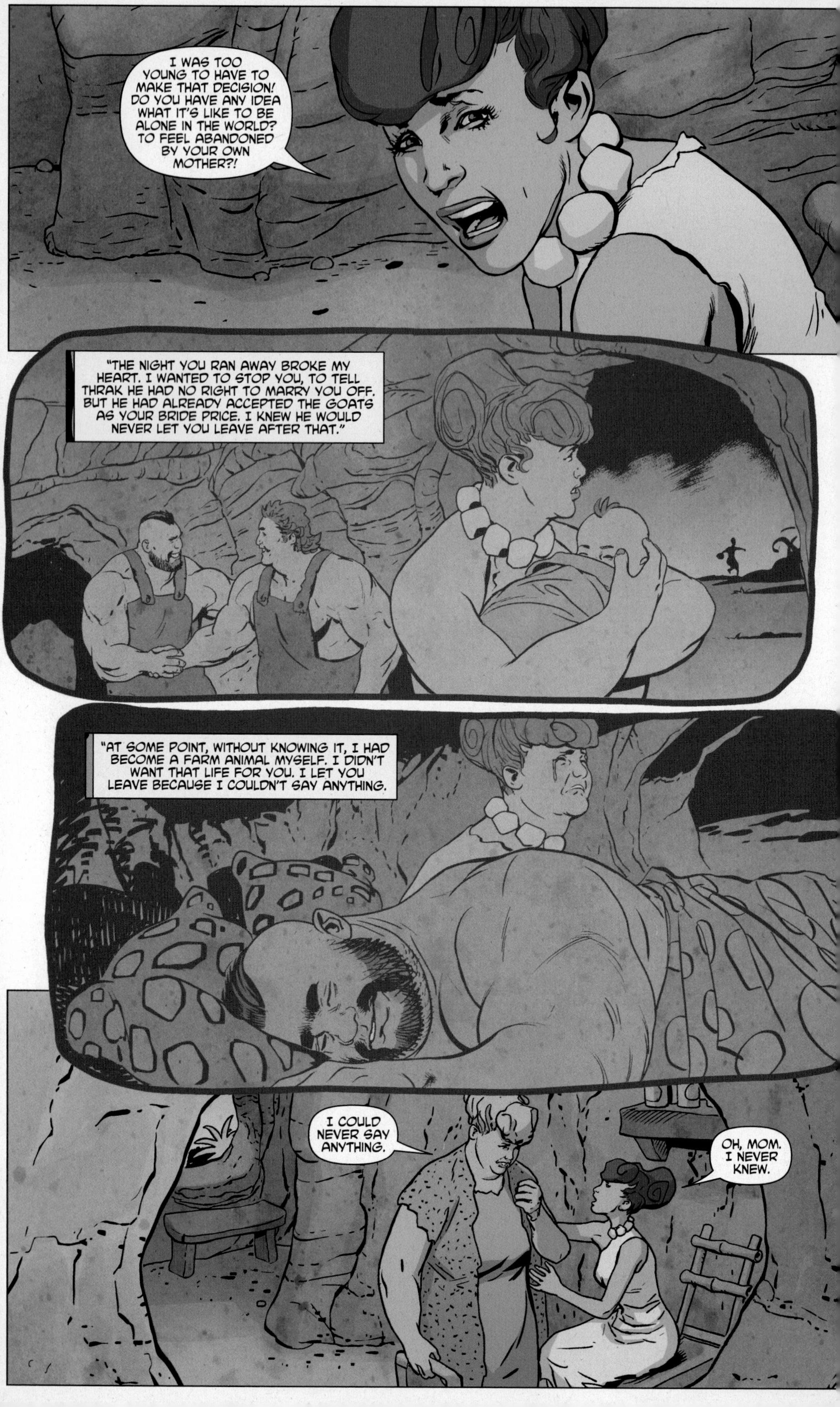

I WAS TOO YOUNG TO HAVE TO MAKE THAT DECISION! DO YOU HAVE ANY IDEA WHAT IT'S LIKE TO BE ALONE IN THE WORLD? TO FEEL ABANDONED BY YOUR OWN MOTHER?!
"THE NIGHT YOU RAN AWAY BROKE MY HEART. I WANTED TO STOP YOU, TO TELL THRAK HE HAD NO RIGHT TO MARRY YOU OFF. BUT HE HAD ALREADY ACCEPTED THE GOATS AS YOUR BRIDE PRICE. I KNEW HE WOULD NEVER LET YOU LEAVE AFTER THAT."
"AT SOME POINT, WITHOUT KNOWING IT, I HAD BECOME A FARM ANIMAL MYSELF. I DIDN'T WANT THAT LIFE FOR YOU. I LET YOU LEAVE BECAUSE I COULDN'T SAY ANYTHING.
I COULD NEVER SAY ANYTHING.
OH, MOM. I NEVER KNEW.

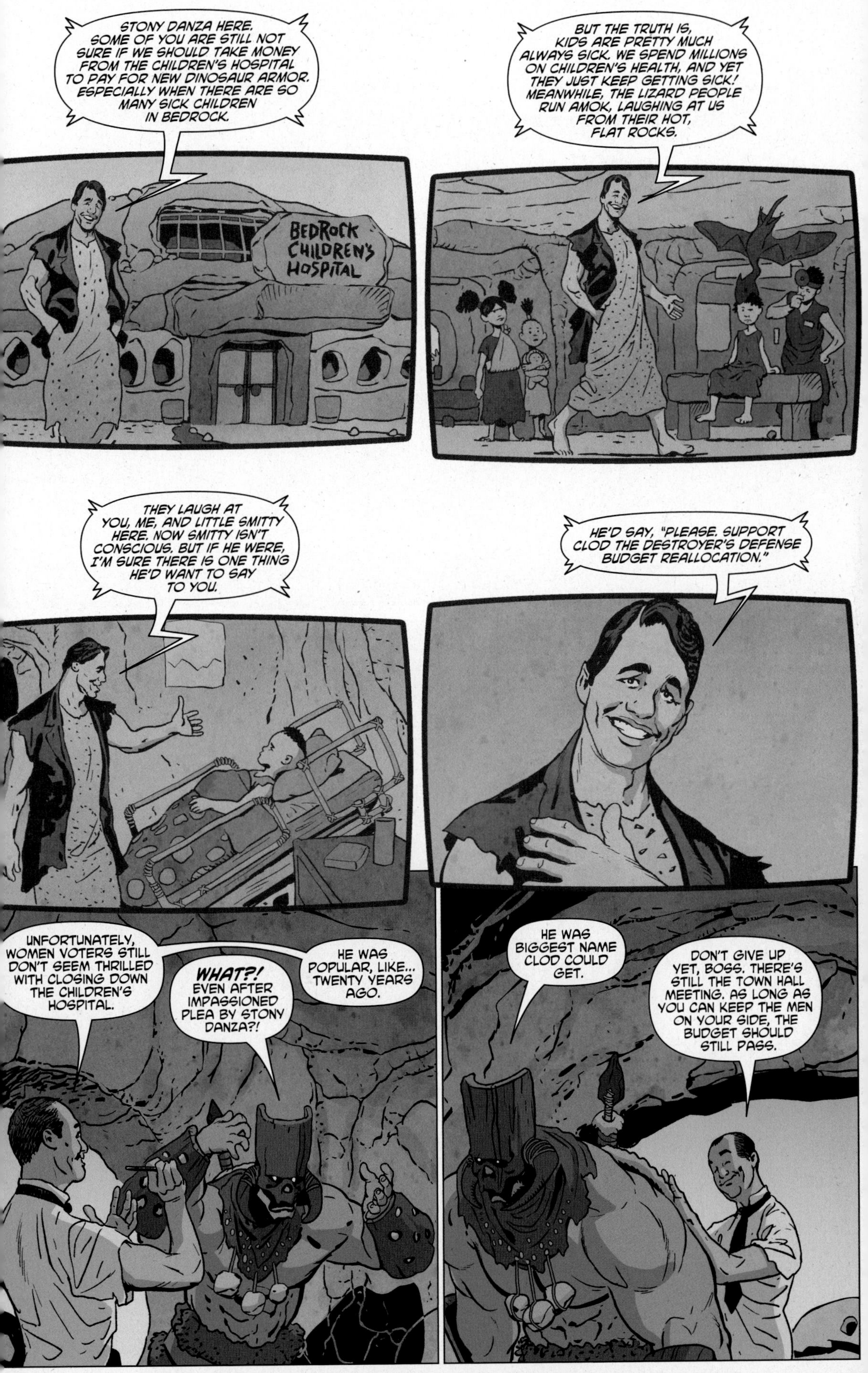
STONY DANZA HERE. SOME OF YOU ARE STILL NOT SURE IF WE SHOULD TAKE MONEY FROM THE CHILDREN'S HOSPITAL TO PAY FOR NEW DINOSAUR ARMOR. ESPECIALLY WHEN THERE ARE SO MANY SICK CHILDREN IN BEDROCK.
BEDROCK CHILDREN'S HOSPITAL
BUT THE TRUTH IS, KIDS ARE PRETTY MUCH ALWAYS SICK. WE SPEND MILLIONS ON CHILDREN'S HEALTH, AND YET THEY JUST KEEP GETTING SICK! MEANWHILE, THE LIZARD PEOPLE RUN AMOK, LAUGHING AT US FROM THEIR HOT, FLAT ROCKS.
THEY LAUGH AT YOU, ME, AND LITTLE SMITTY HERE. NOW SMITTY ISN'T CONSCIOUS. BUT IF HE WERE, I'M SURE THERE IS ONE THING HE'D WANT TO SAY TO YOU.
HE'D SAY, "PLEASE. SUPPORT CLOD THE DESTROYER'S DEFENSE BUDGET REALLOCATION."
UNFORTUNATELY, WOMEN VOTERS STILL DON'T SEEM THRILLED WITH CLOSING DOWN THE CHILDREN'S HOSPITAL.
WHAT?! EVEN AFTER IMPASSIONED PLEA BY STONY DANZA?!
HE WAS POPULAR, LIKE... TWENTY YEARS AGO.
HE WAS BIGGEST NAME CLOD COULD GET.
DON'T GIVE UP YET, BOSS. THERE'S STILL THE TOWN HALL MEETING. AS LONG AS YOU CAN KEEP THE MEN ON YOUR SIDE, THE BUDGET SHOULD STILL PASS.

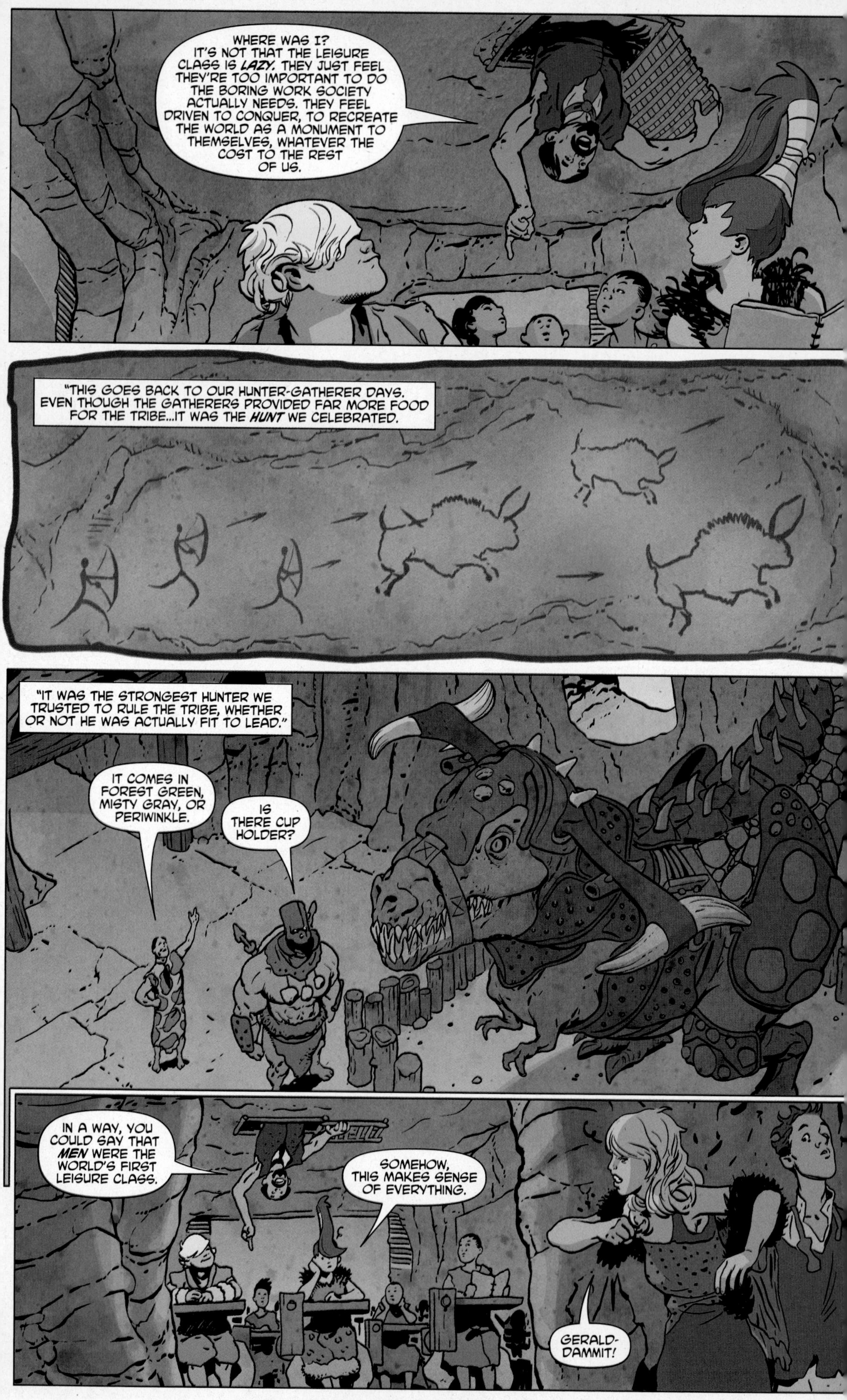

WHERE WAS I? IT'S NOT THAT THE LEISURE CLASS IS *LAZY.* THEY JUST FEEL THEY'RE TOO IMPORTANT TO DO THE BORING WORK SOCIETY ACTUALLY NEEDS. THEY FEEL DRIVEN TO CONQUER, TO RECREATE THE WORLD AS A MONUMENT TO THEMSELVES, WHATEVER THE COST TO THE REST OF US.
"THIS GOES BACK TO OUR HUNTER-GATHERER DAYS. EVEN THOUGH THE GATHERERS PROVIDED FAR MORE FOOD FOR THE TRIBE...IT WAS THE *HUNT* WE CELEBRATED.
"IT WAS THE STRONGEST HUNTER WE TRUSTED TO RULE THE TRIBE, WHETHER OR NOT HE WAS ACTUALLY FIT TO LEAD."
IT COMES IN FOREST GREEN, MISTY GRAY, OR PERIWINKLE.
IS THERE CUP HOLDER?
IN A WAY, YOU COULD SAY THAT *MEN* WERE THE WORLD'S FIRST LEISURE CLASS.
SOMEHOW, THIS MAKES SENSE OF EVERYTHING.
GERALD-DAMMIT!

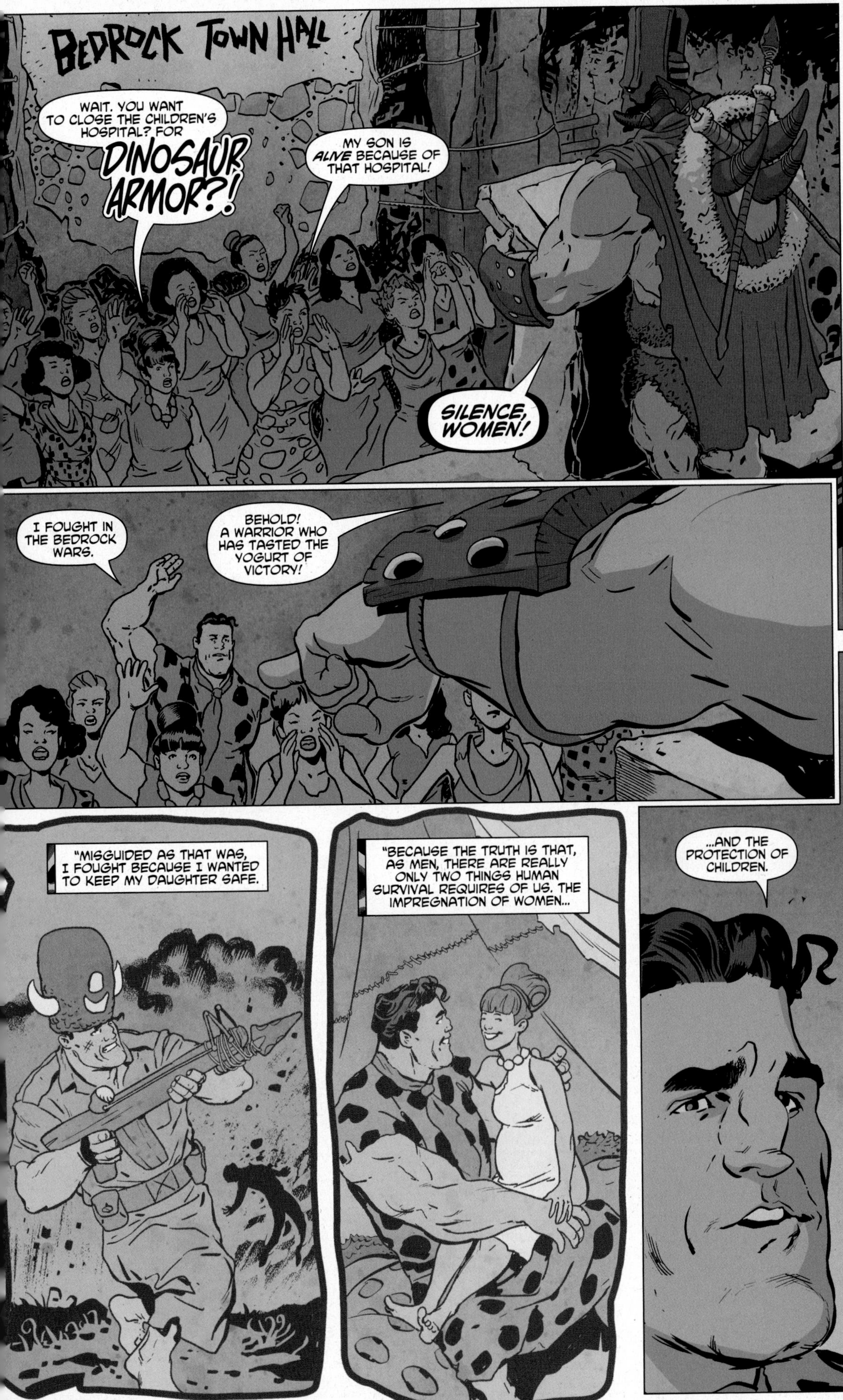
BEDROCK TOWN HALL
WAIT. YOU WANT TO CLOSE THE CHILDREN'S HOSPITAL? FOR DINOSAUR ARMOR?!
MY SON IS ALIVE BECAUSE OF THAT HOSPITAL!
SILENCE, WOMEN!
I FOUGHT IN THE BEDROCK WARS.
BEHOLD! A WARRIOR WHO HAS TASTED THE YOGURT OF VICTORY!
"MISGUIDED AS THAT WAS, I FOUGHT BECAUSE I WANTED TO KEEP MY DAUGHTER SAFE.
"BECAUSE THE TRUTH IS THAT, AS MEN, THERE ARE REALLY ONLY TWO THINGS HUMAN SURVIVAL REQUIRES OF US. THE IMPREGNATION OF WOMEN...
...AND THE PROTECTION OF CHILDREN.

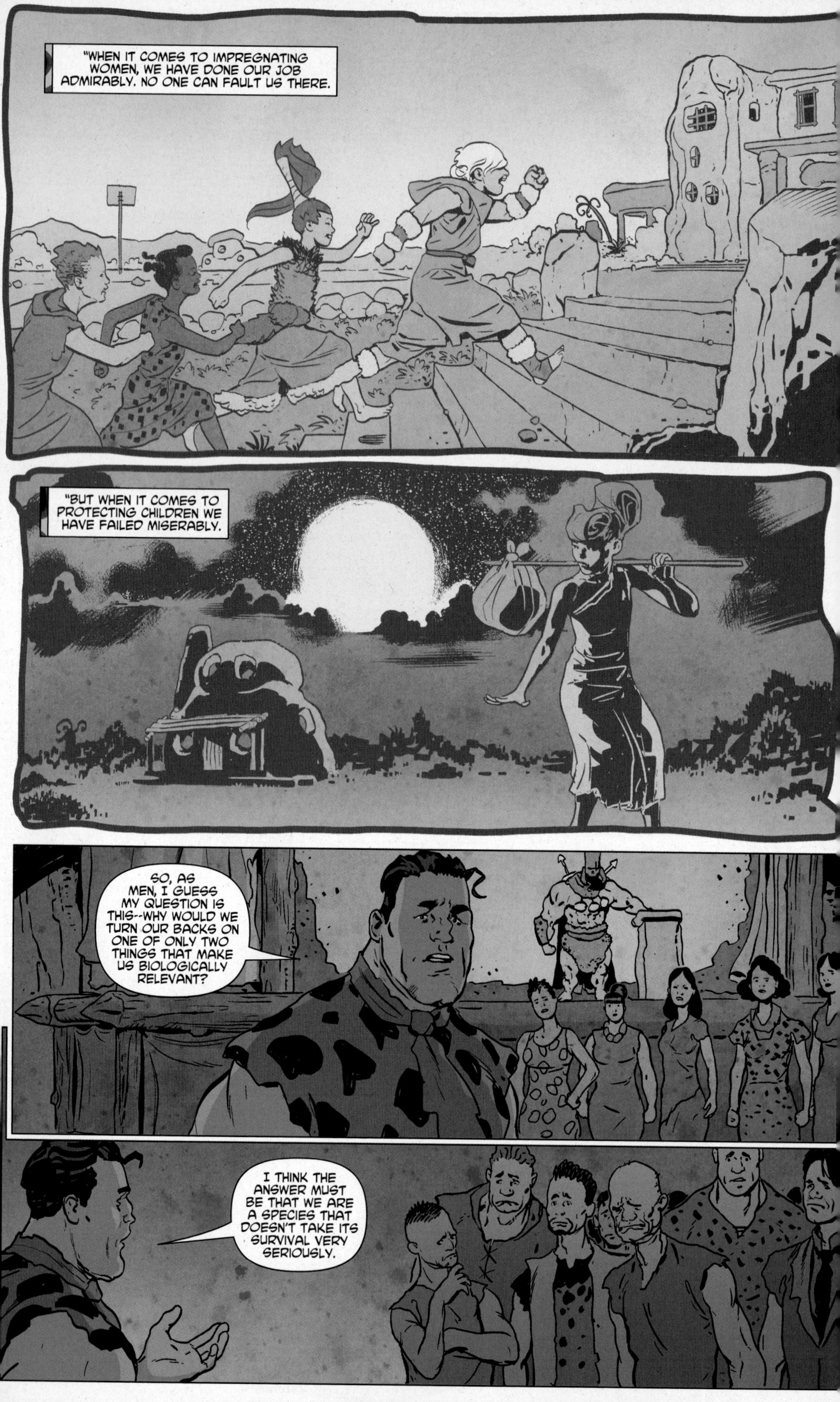
"WHEN IT COMES TO IMPREGNATING WOMEN, WE HAVE DONE OUR JOB ADMIRABLY. NO ONE CAN FAULT US THERE.
"BUT WHEN IT COMES TO PROTECTING CHILDREN WE HAVE FAILED MISERABLY.
SO, AS MEN, I GUESS MY QUESTION IS THIS--WHY WOULD WE TURN OUR BACKS ON ONE OF ONLY TWO THINGS THAT MAKE US BIOLOGICALLY RELEVANT?
I THINK THE ANSWER MUST BE THAT WE ARE A SPECIES THAT DOESN'T TAKE ITS SURVIVAL VERY SERIOUSLY.

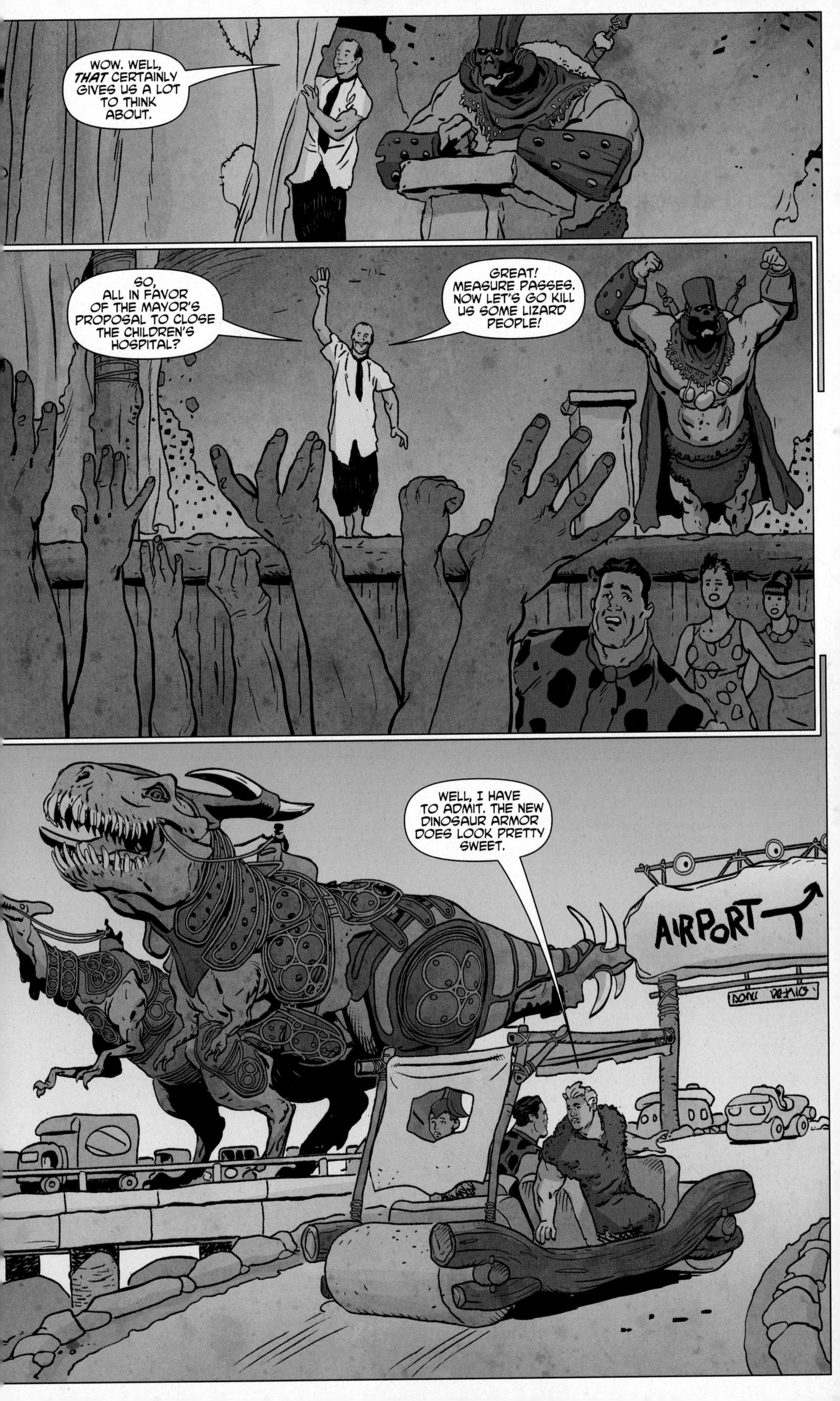

WOW. WELL, *THAT* CERTAINLY GIVES US A LOT TO THINK ABOUT.
SO, ALL IN FAVOR OF THE MAYOR'S PROPOSAL TO CLOSE THE CHILDREN'S HOSPITAL?
GREAT! MEASURE PASSES. NOW LET'S GO KILL US SOME LIZARD PEOPLE!
WELL, I HAVE TO ADMIT. THE NEW DINOSAUR ARMOR DOES LOOK PRETTY SWEET.
AIRPORT

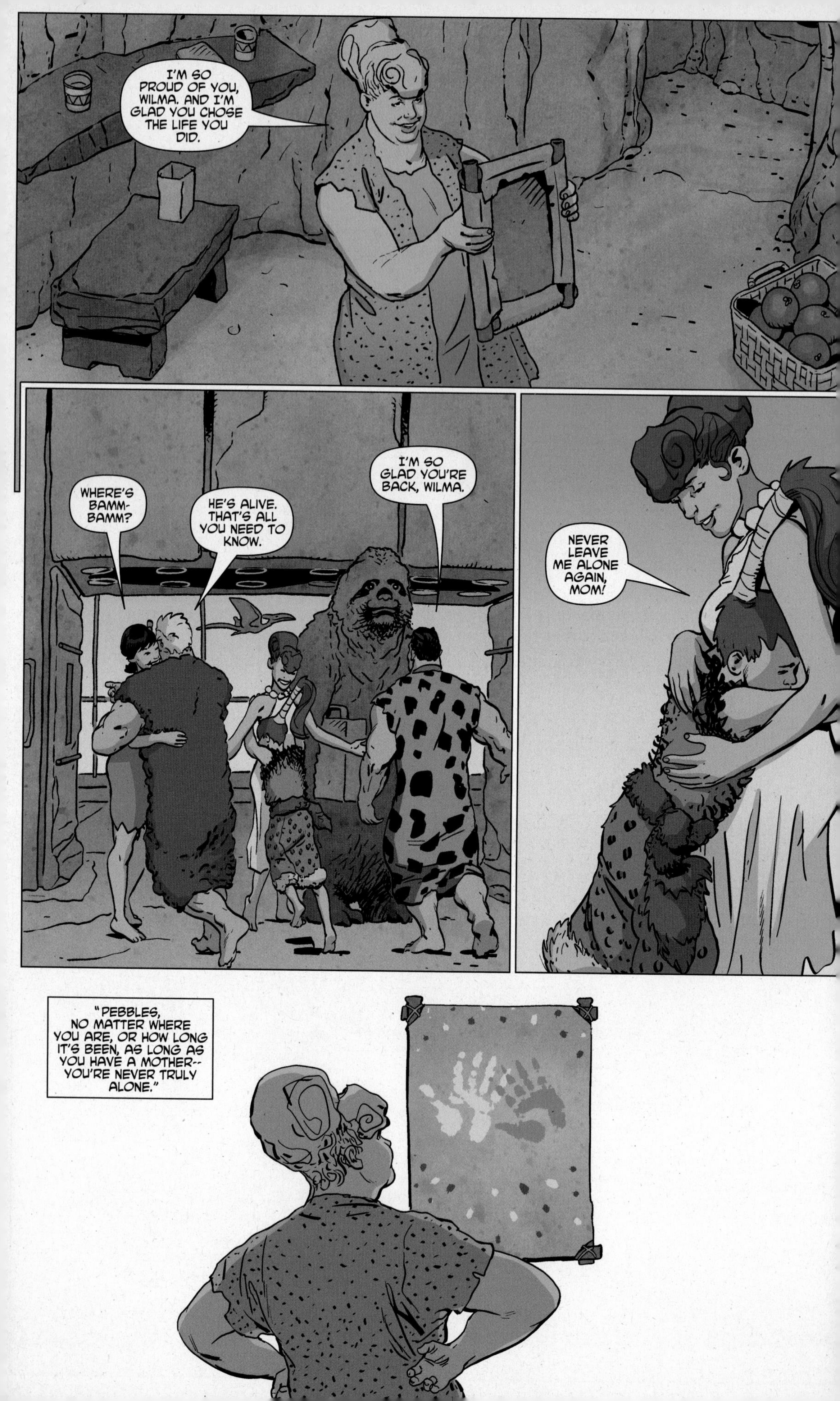
I'M SO PROUD OF YOU, WILMA. AND I'M GLAD YOU CHOSE THE LIFE YOU DID.
WHERE'S BAMM-BAMM?
HE'S ALIVE. THAT'S ALL YOU NEED TO KNOW.
I'M SO GLAD YOU'RE BACK, WILMA.
NEVER LEAVE ME ALONE AGAIN, MOM!
"PEBBLES, NO MATTER WHERE YOU ARE, OR HOW LONG IT'S BEEN, AS LONG AS YOU HAVE A MOTHER-- YOU'RE NEVER TRULY ALONE."

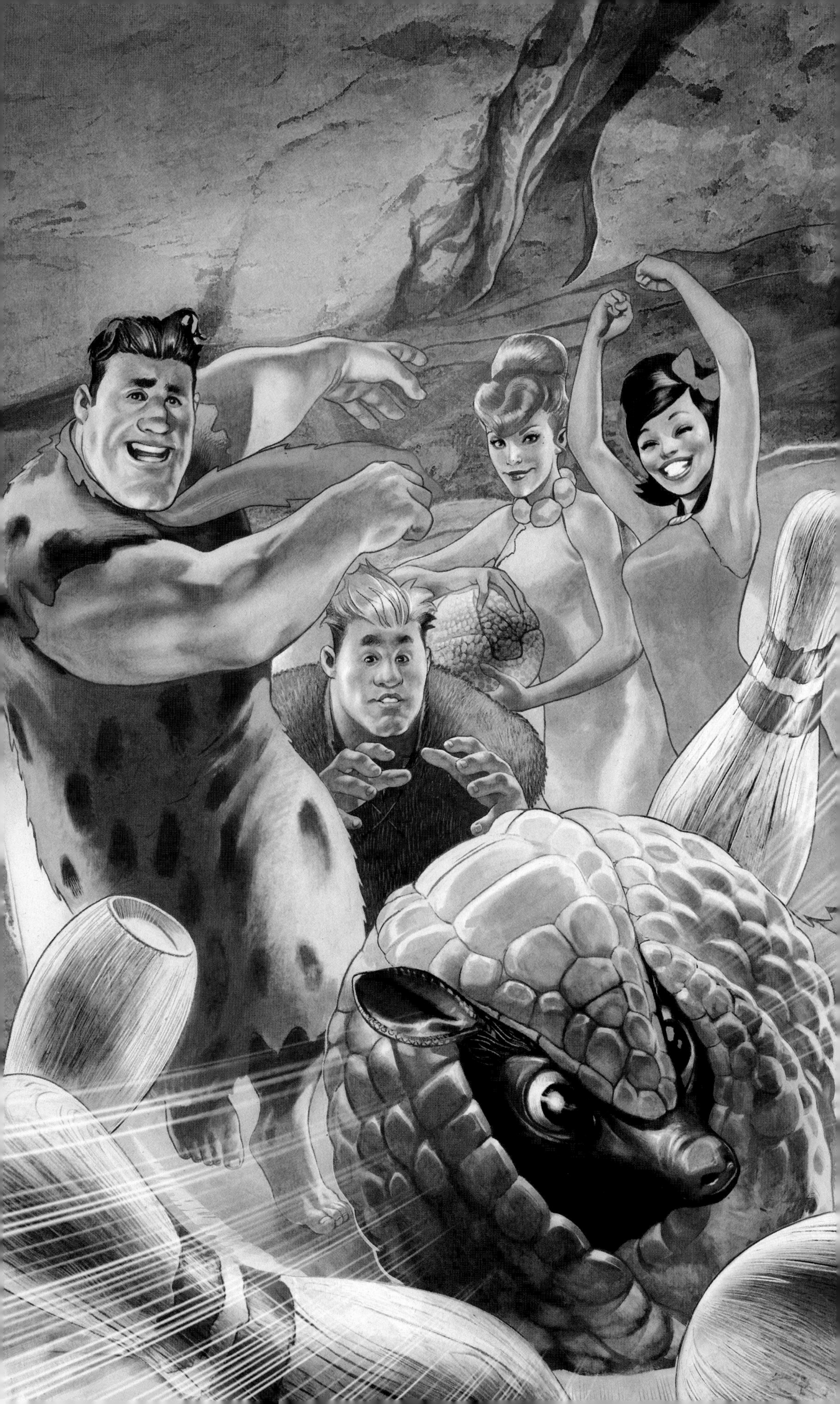

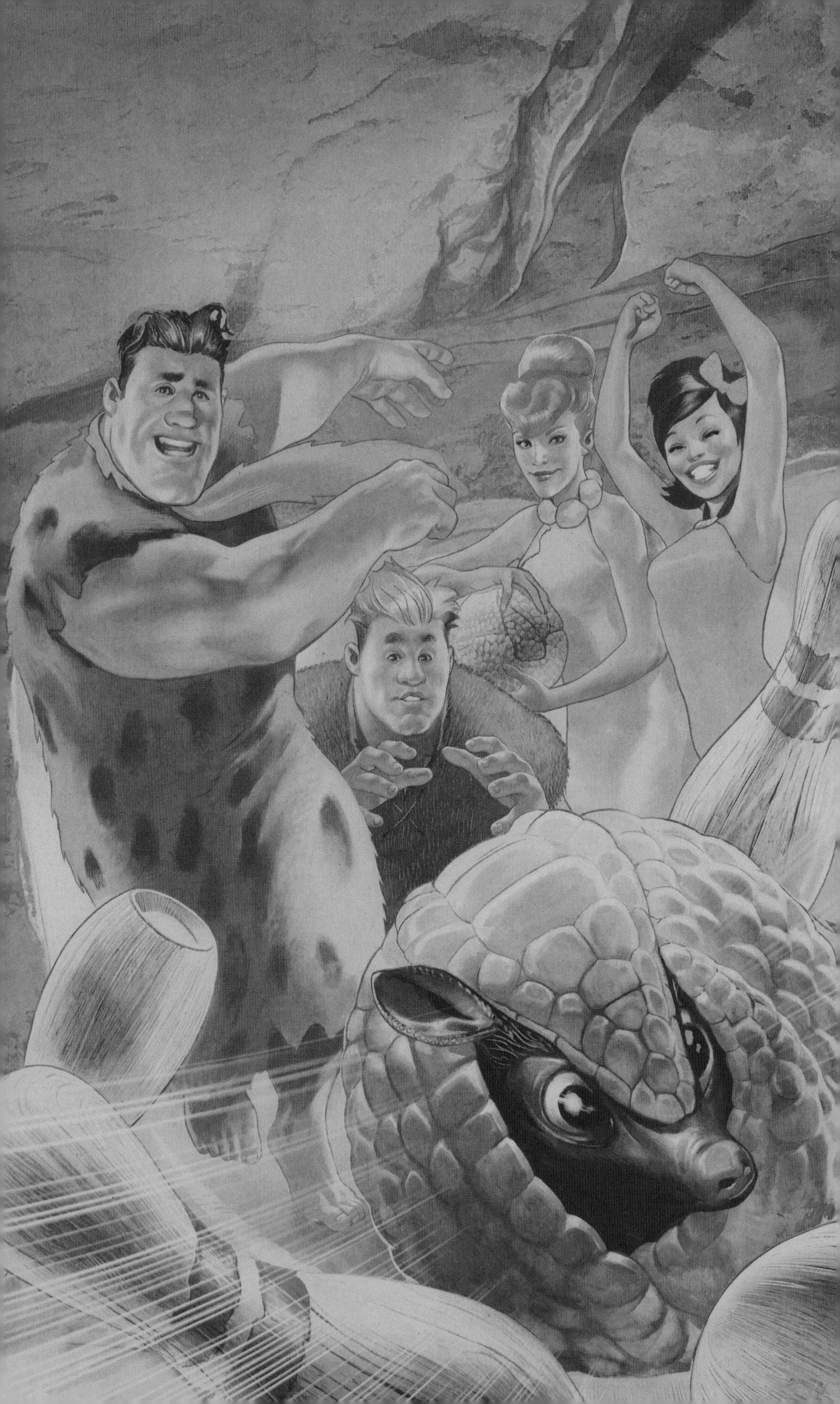

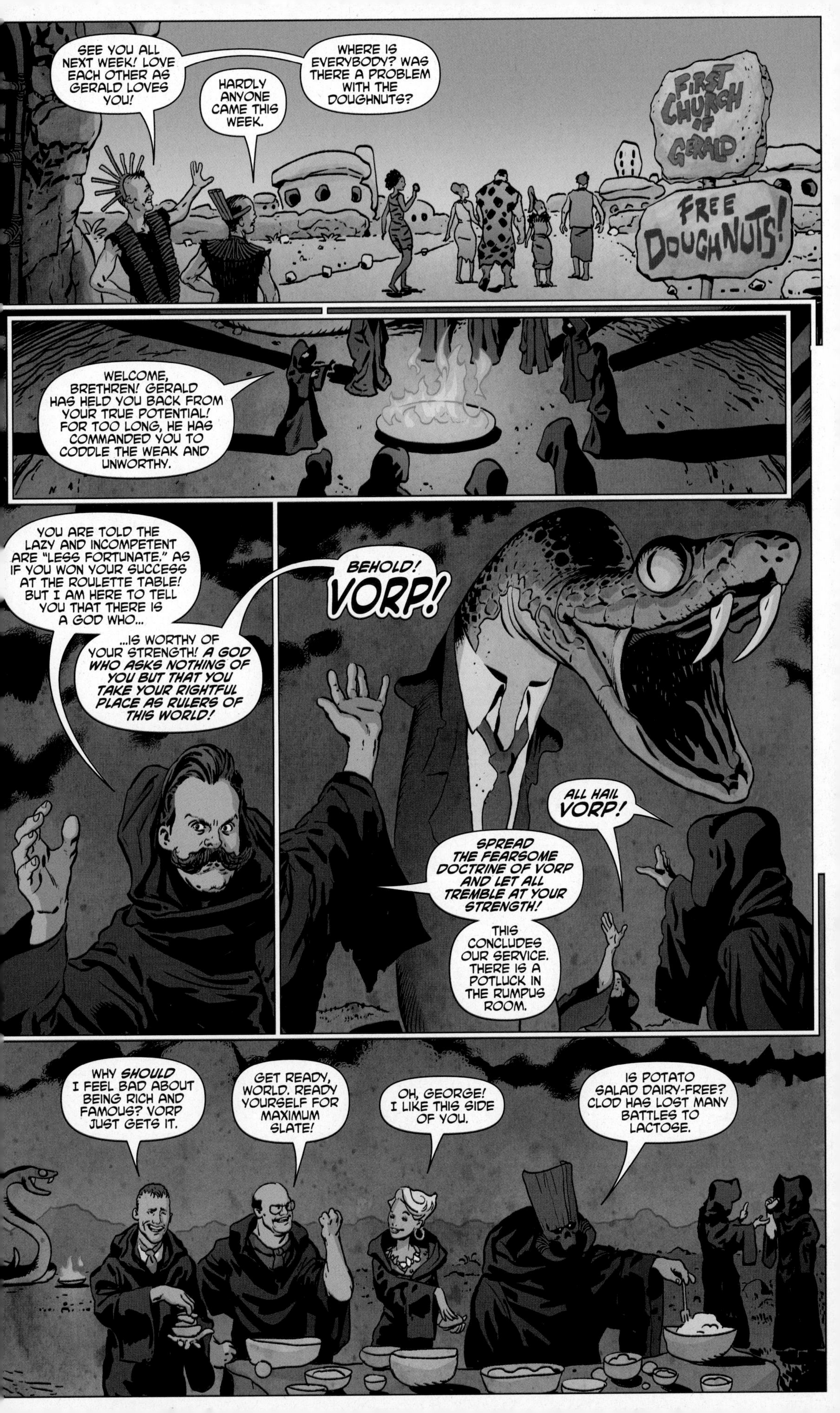
SEE YOU ALL NEXT WEEK! LOVE EACH OTHER AS GERALD LOVES YOU!
HARDLY ANYONE CAME THIS WEEK.
WHERE IS EVERYBODY? WAS THERE A PROBLEM WITH THE DOUGHNUTS?
FIRST CHURCH OF GERALD
FREE DOUGHNUTS!
WELCOME, BRETHREN! GERALD HAS HELD YOU BACK FROM YOUR TRUE POTENTIAL! FOR TOO LONG, HE HAS COMMANDED YOU TO CODDLE THE WEAK AND UNWORTHY.
YOU ARE TOLD THE LAZY AND INCOMPETENT ARE "LESS FORTUNATE." AS IF YOU WON YOUR SUCCESS AT THE ROULETTE TABLE! BUT I AM HERE TO TELL YOU THAT THERE IS A GOD WHO...
...IS WORTHY OF YOUR STRENGTH! A GOD WHO ASKS NOTHING OF YOU BUT THAT YOU TAKE YOUR RIGHTFUL PLACE AS RULERS OF THIS WORLD!
BEHOLD! VORP!
ALL HAIL VORP!
SPREAD THE FEARSOME DOCTRINE OF VORP AND LET ALL TREMBLE AT YOUR STRENGTH!
THIS CONCLUDES OUR SERVICE. THERE IS A POTLUCK IN THE RUMPUS ROOM.
WHY SHOULD I FEEL BAD ABOUT BEING RICH AND FAMOUS? VORP JUST GETS IT.
GET READY, WORLD. READY YOURSELF FOR MAXIMUM SLATE!
OH, GEORGE! I LIKE THIS SIDE OF YOU.
IS POTATO SALAD DAIRY-FREE? CLOD HAS LOST MANY BATTLES TO LACTOSE.

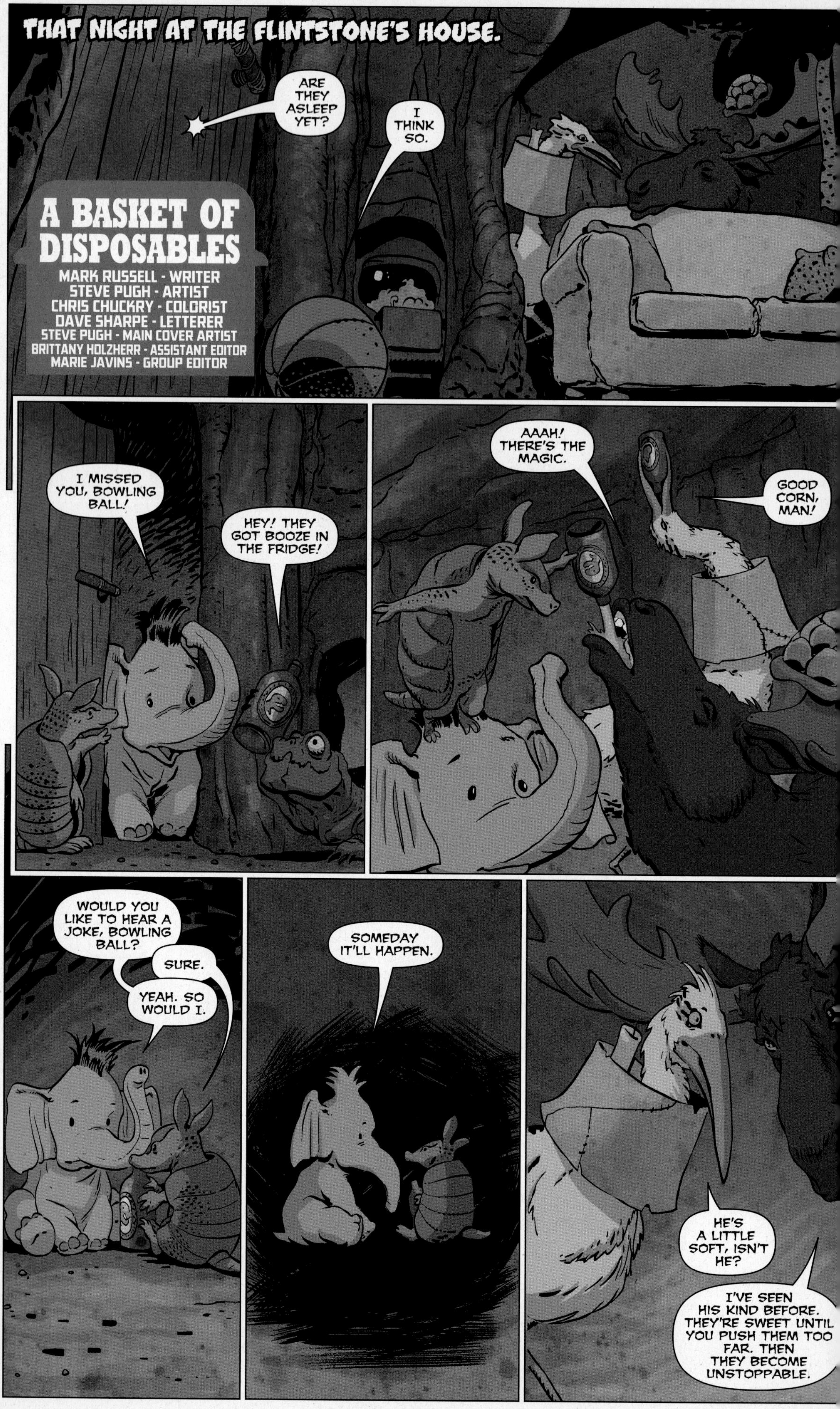
THAT NIGHT AT THE FLINTSTONE'S HOUSE.
ARE THEY ASLEEP YET?
I THINK SO.
A BASKET OF DISPOSABLES
MARK RUSSELL - WRITER
STEVE PUGH - ARTIST
CHRIS CHUCKRY - COLORIST
DAVE SHARPE - LETTERER
STEVE PUGH - MAIN COVER ARTIST
BRITTANY HOLZHERR - ASSISTANT EDITOR
MARIE JAVINS - GROUP EDITOR
I MISSED YOU, BOWLING BALL!
HEY! THEY GOT BOOZE IN THE FRIDGE!
AAAH! THERE'S THE MAGIC.
GOOD CORN, MAN!
WOULD YOU LIKE TO HEAR A JOKE, BOWLING BALL?
SURE.
YEAH. SO WOULD I.
SOMEDAY IT'LL HAPPEN.
HE'S A LITTLE SOFT, ISN'T HE?
I'VE SEEN HIS KIND BEFORE. THEY'RE SWEET UNTIL YOU PUSH THEM TOO FAR. THEN THEY BECOME UNSTOPPABLE.

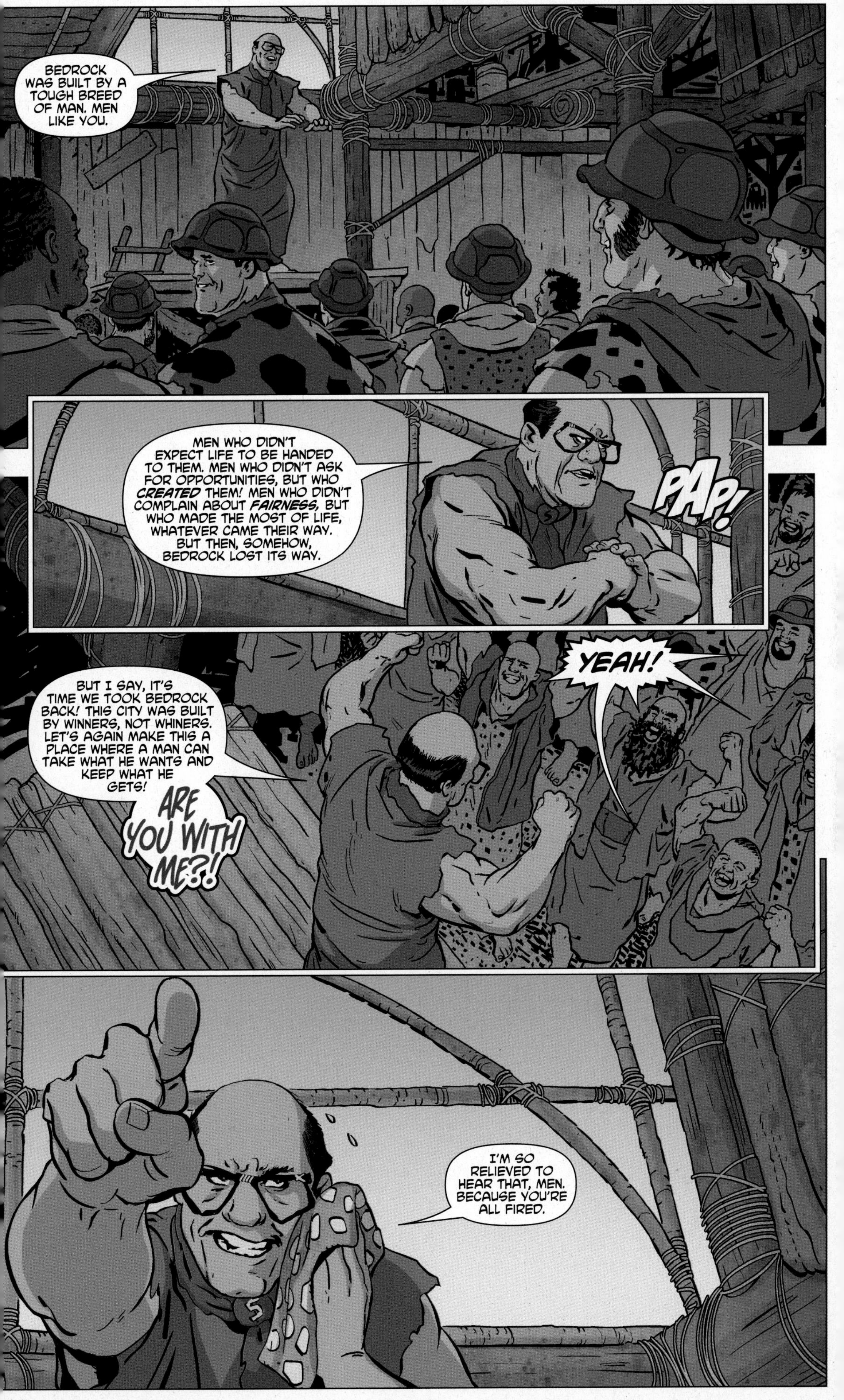
BEDROCK WAS BUILT BY A TOUGH BREED OF MAN. MEN LIKE YOU.
MEN WHO DIDN'T EXPECT LIFE TO BE HANDED TO THEM. MEN WHO DIDN'T ASK FOR OPPORTUNITIES, BUT WHO CREATED THEM! MEN WHO DIDN'T COMPLAIN ABOUT FAIRNESS, BUT WHO MADE THE MOST OF LIFE, WHATEVER CAME THEIR WAY. BUT THEN, SOMEHOW, BEDROCK LOST ITS WAY.
PAP!
BUT I SAY, IT'S TIME WE TOOK BEDROCK BACK! THIS CITY WAS BUILT BY WINNERS, NOT WHINERS. LET'S AGAIN MAKE THIS A PLACE WHERE A MAN CAN TAKE WHAT HE WANTS AND KEEP WHAT HE GETS!
ARE YOU WITH ME?!
YEAH!
I'M SO RELIEVED TO HEAR THAT, MEN. BECAUSE YOU'RE ALL FIRED.

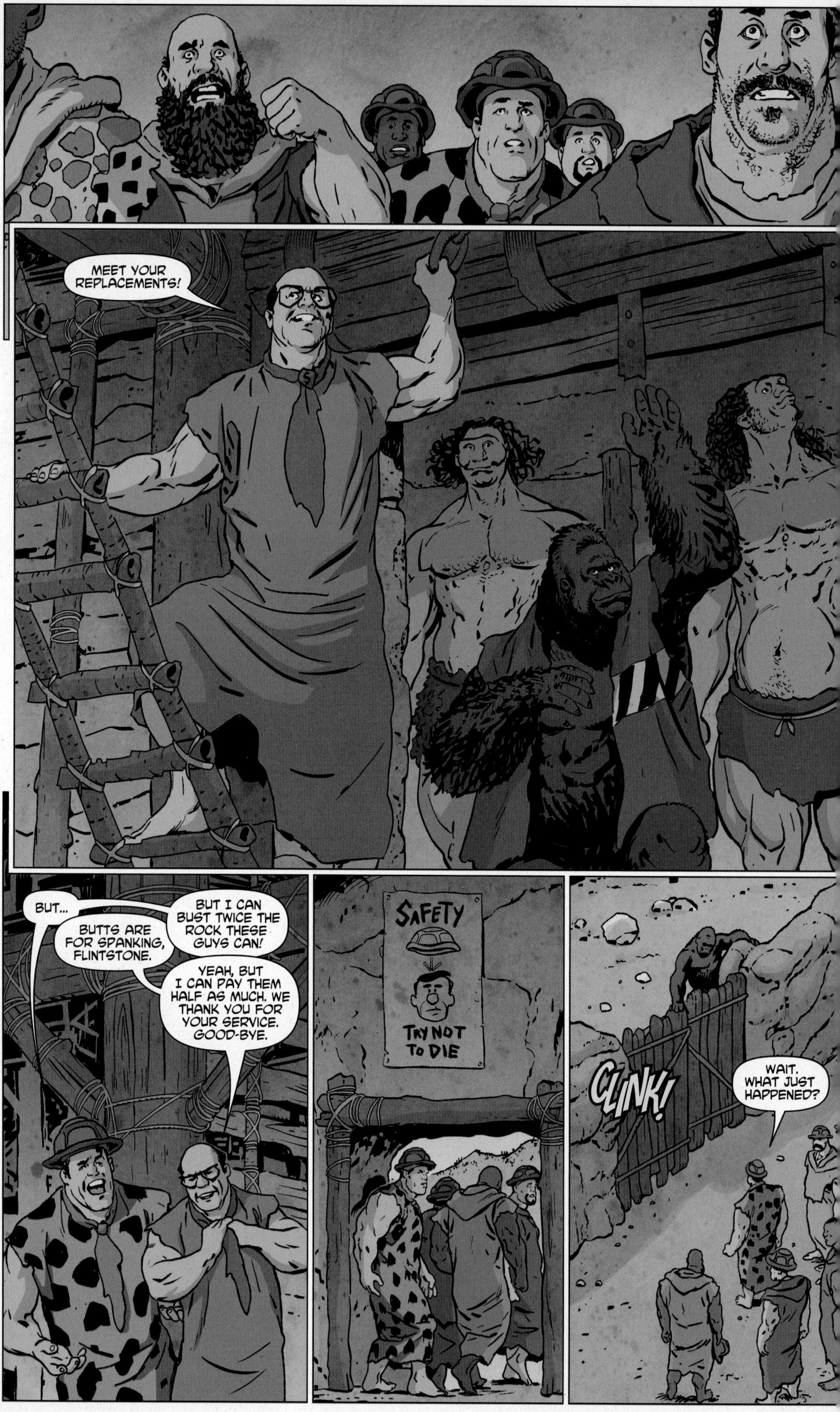

MEET YOUR REPLACEMENTS!
BUT...
BUT I CAN BUST TWICE THE ROCK THESE GUYS CAN!
BUTTS ARE FOR SPANKING, FLINTSTONE.
YEAH, BUT I CAN PAY THEM HALF AS MUCH. WE THANK YOU FOR YOUR SERVICE. GOOD-BYE.
SAFETY
TRY NOT TO DIE
CLINK!
WAIT. WHAT JUST HAPPENED?

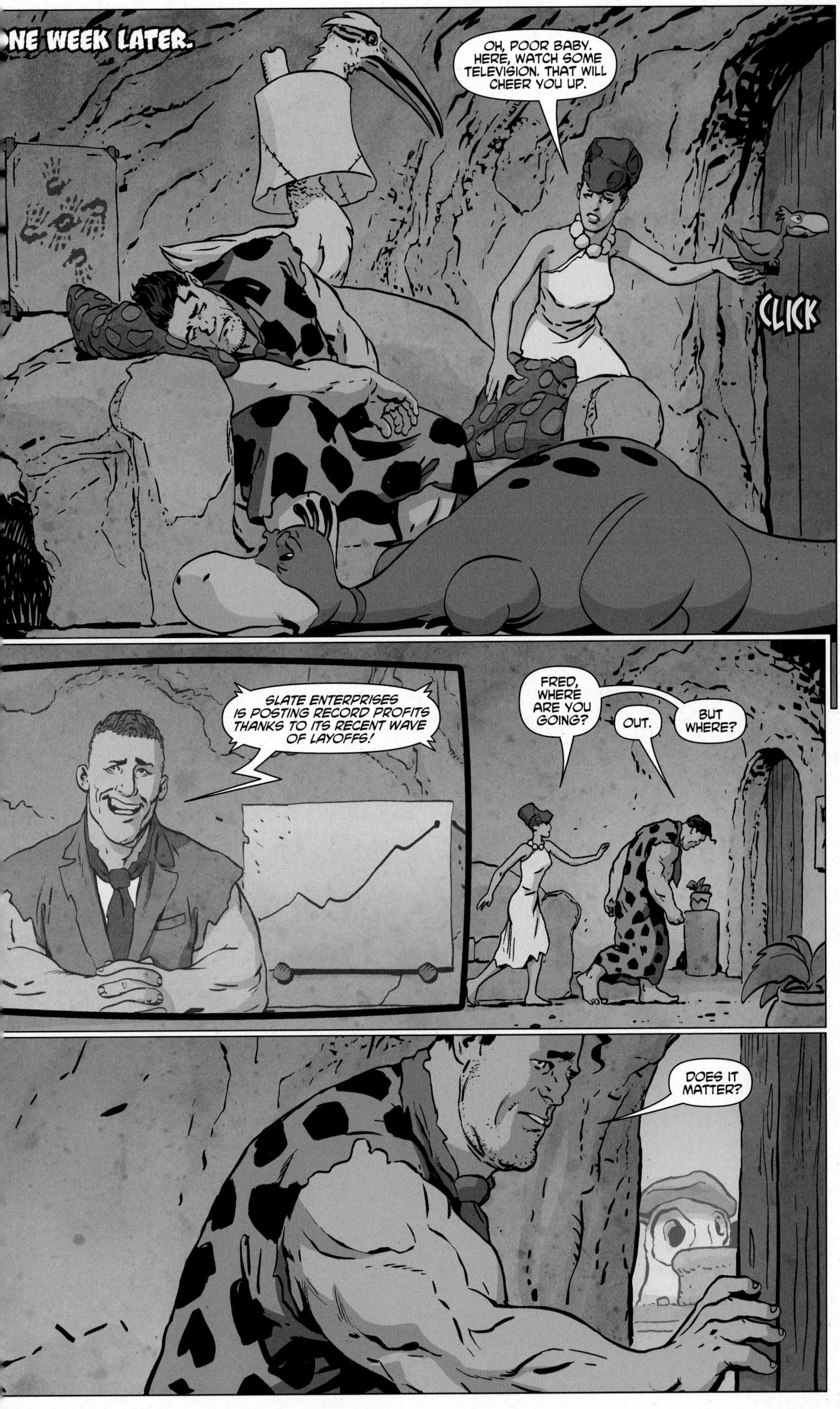
NE WEEK LATER.
OH, POOR BABY. HERE, WATCH SOME TELEVISION. THAT WILL CHEER YOU UP.
CLICK
SLATE ENTERPRISES IS POSTING RECORD PROFITS THANKS TO ITS RECENT WAVE OF LAYOFFS!
FRED, WHERE ARE YOU GOING?
OUT.
BUT WHERE?
DOES IT MATTER?

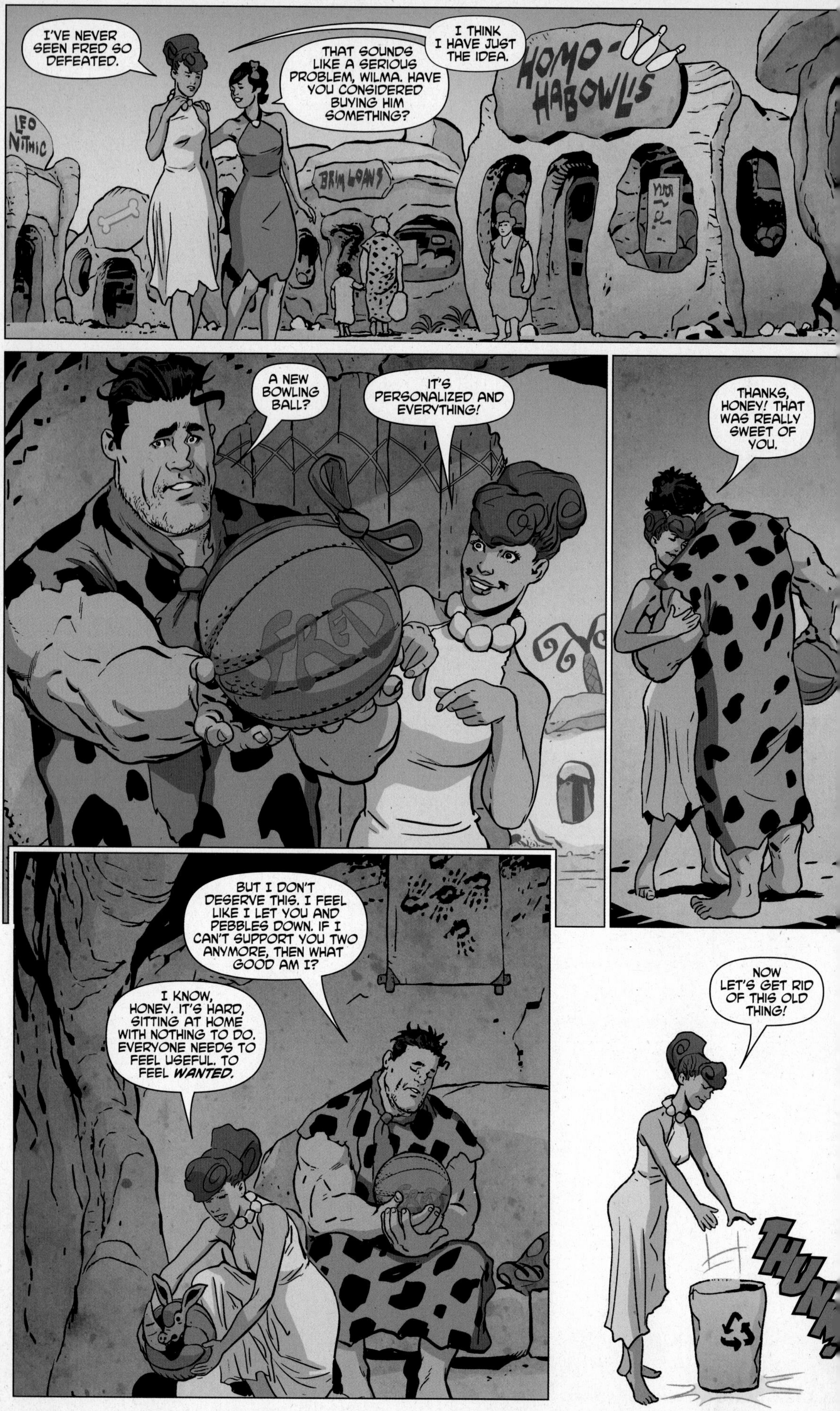
I'VE NEVER SEEN FRED SO DEFEATED.
THAT SOUNDS LIKE A SERIOUS PROBLEM, WILMA. HAVE YOU CONSIDERED BUYING HIM SOMETHING?
I THINK I HAVE JUST THE IDEA.
HOMO-HABOWLIS
LEO NITHIC
BRIM LOANS
A NEW BOWLING BALL?
IT'S PERSONALIZED AND EVERYTHING!
FRED
THANKS, HONEY! THAT WAS REALLY SWEET OF YOU.
BUT I DON'T DESERVE THIS. I FEEL LIKE I LET YOU AND PEBBLES DOWN. IF I CAN'T SUPPORT YOU TWO ANYMORE, THEN WHAT GOOD AM I?
I KNOW, HONEY. IT'S HARD, SITTING AT HOME WITH NOTHING TO DO. EVERYONE NEEDS TO FEEL USEFUL. TO FEEL *WANTED.*
NOW LET'S GET RID OF THIS OLD THING!
THUNK

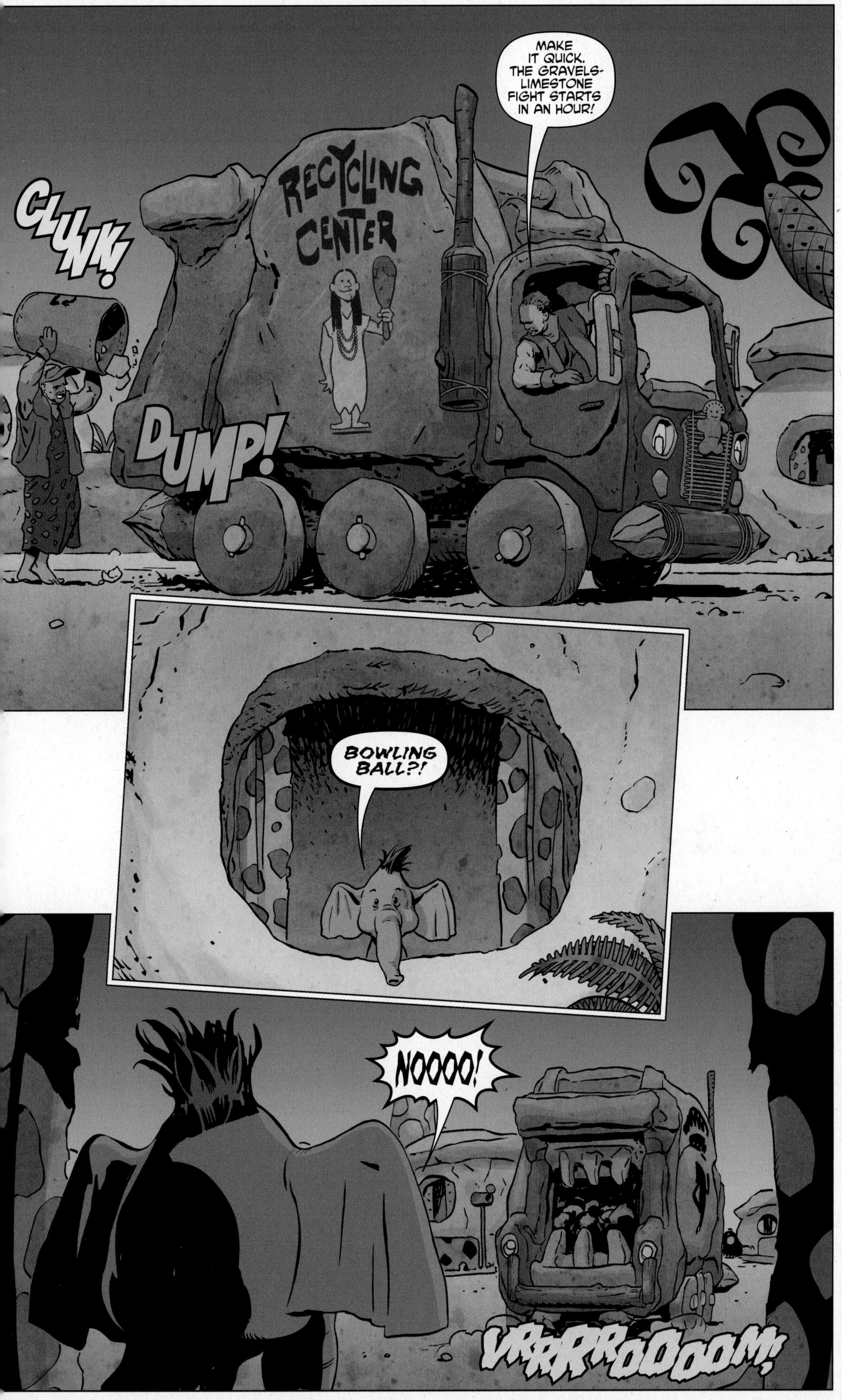
MAKE IT QUICK. THE GRAVELS-LIMESTONE FIGHT STARTS IN AN HOUR!
CLUNK!
RECYCLING CENTER
DUMP!
BOWLING BALL?!
NOOOO!
VRRRROOOOOM!

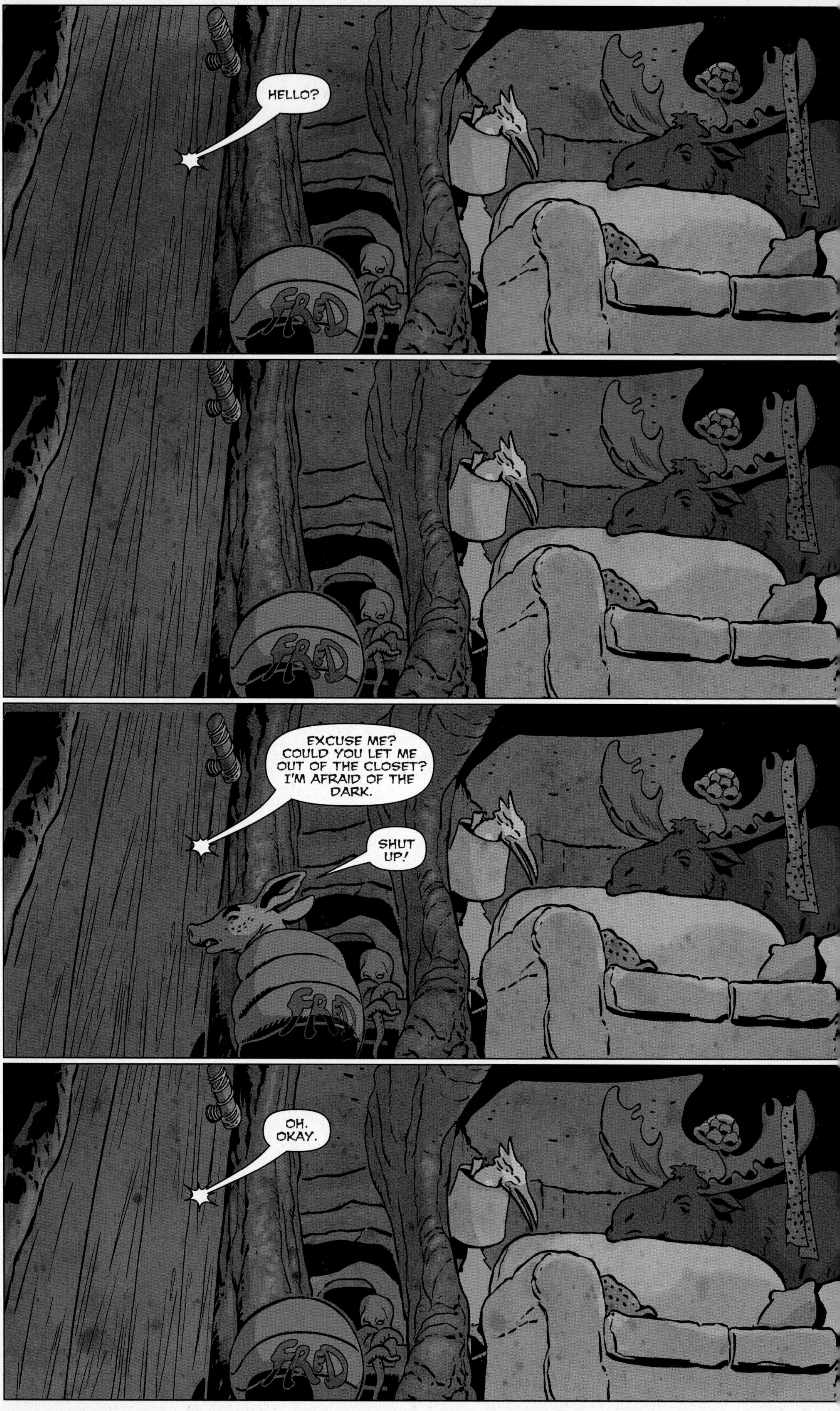
HELLO?
EXCUSE ME? COULD YOU LET ME OUT OF THE CLOSET? I'M AFRAID OF THE DARK.
SHUT UP!
OH. OKAY.
FRED

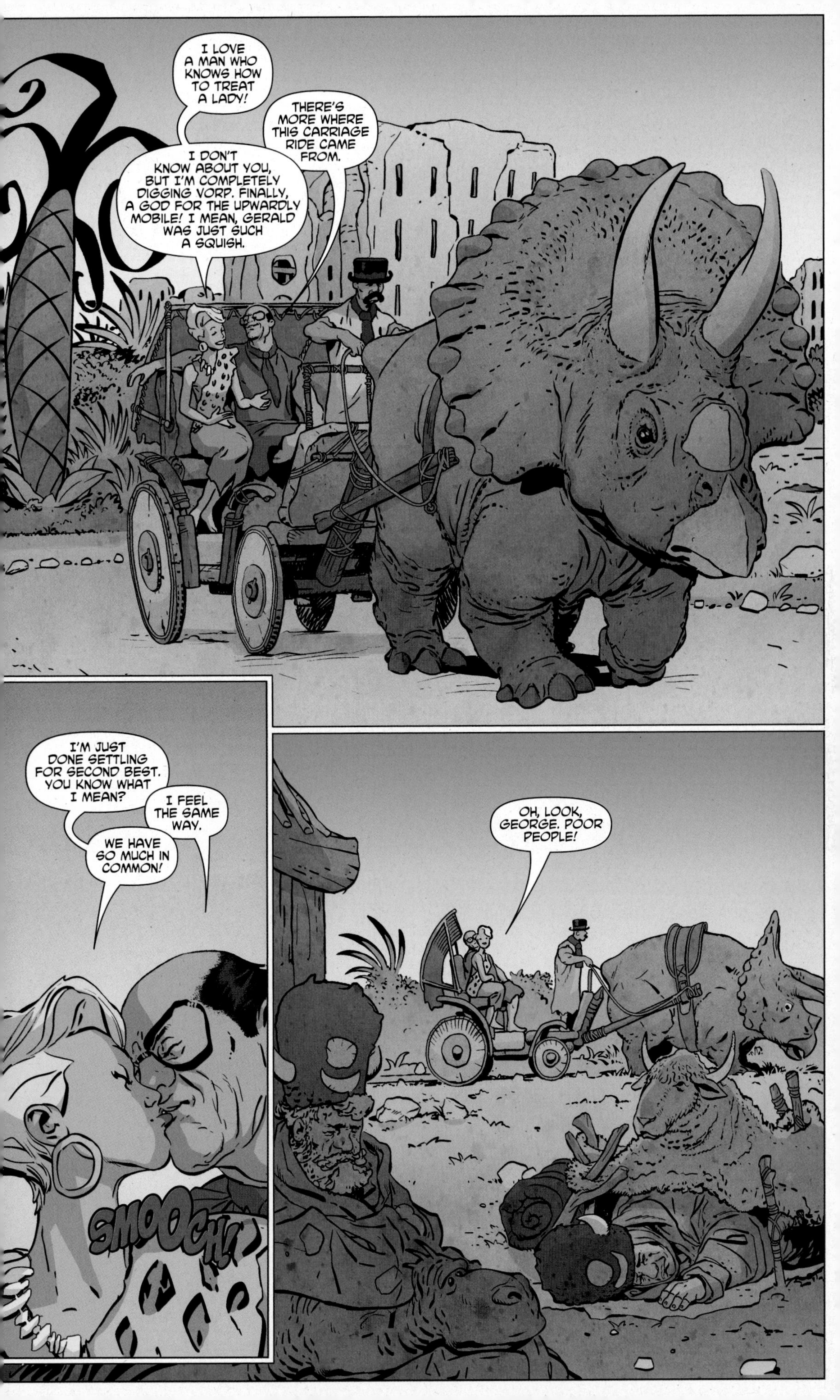
I LOVE A MAN WHO KNOWS HOW TO TREAT A LADY!
THERE'S MORE WHERE THIS CARRIAGE RIDE CAME FROM.
I DON'T KNOW ABOUT YOU, BUT I'M COMPLETELY DIGGING VORP. FINALLY, A GOD FOR THE UPWARDLY MOBILE! I MEAN, GERALD WAS JUST SUCH A SQUISH.
I'M JUST DONE SETTLING FOR SECOND BEST. YOU KNOW WHAT I MEAN?
I FEEL THE SAME WAY.
WE HAVE SO MUCH IN COMMON!
SMOOCH!
OH, LOOK, GEORGE. POOR PEOPLE!

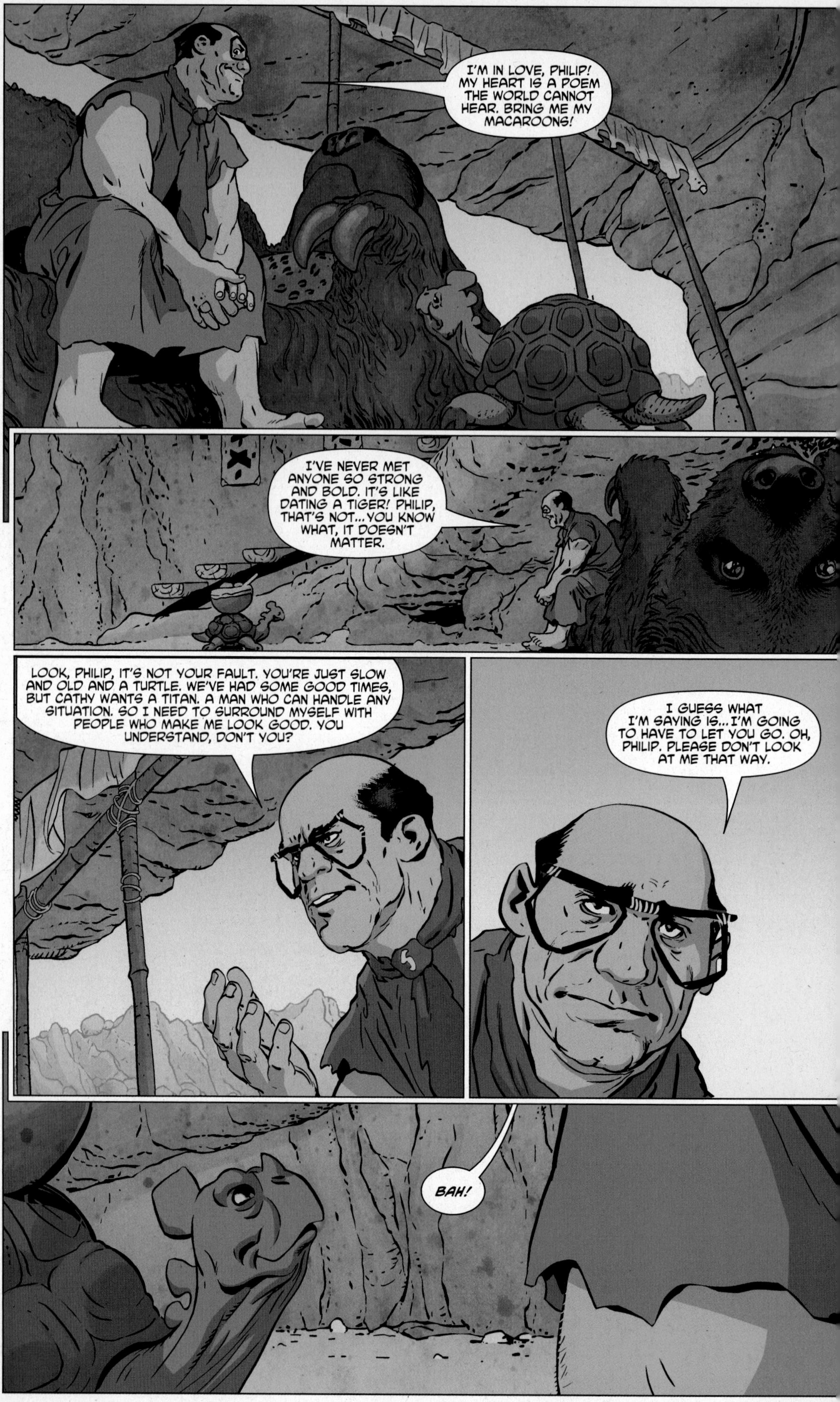
I'M IN LOVE, PHILIP! MY HEART IS A POEM THE WORLD CANNOT HEAR. BRING ME MY MACAROONS!
I'VE NEVER MET ANYONE SO STRONG AND BOLD. IT'S LIKE DATING A TIGER! PHILIP, THAT'S NOT...YOU KNOW WHAT, IT DOESN'T MATTER.
LOOK, PHILIP, IT'S NOT YOUR FAULT. YOU'RE JUST SLOW AND OLD AND A TURTLE. WE'VE HAD SOME GOOD TIMES, BUT CATHY WANTS A TITAN. A MAN WHO CAN HANDLE ANY SITUATION. SO I NEED TO SURROUND MYSELF WITH PEOPLE WHO MAKE ME LOOK GOOD. YOU UNDERSTAND, DON'T YOU?
I GUESS WHAT I'M SAYING IS...I'M GOING TO HAVE TO LET YOU GO. OH, PHILIP. PLEASE DON'T LOOK AT ME THAT WAY.
BAH!

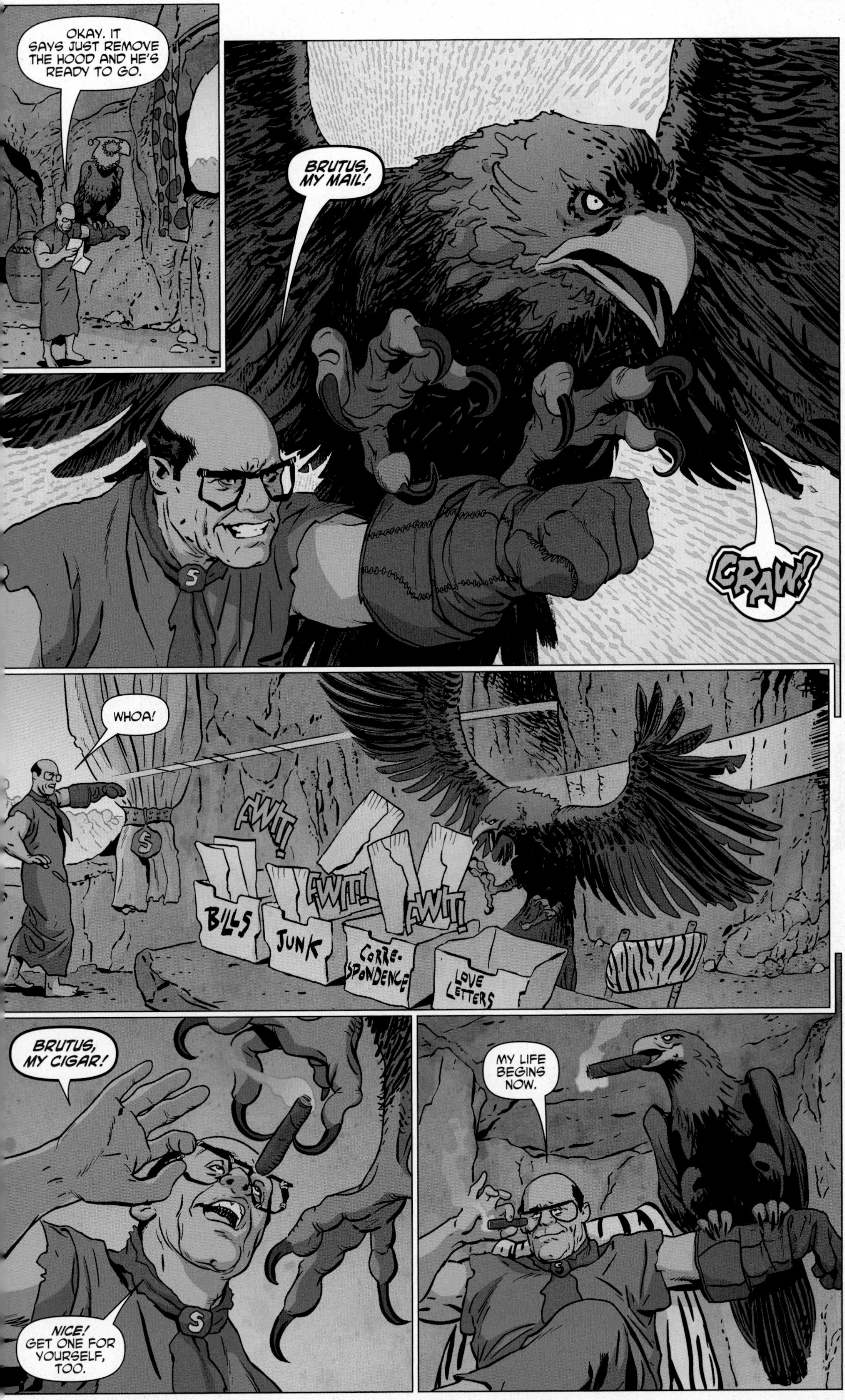
OKAY. IT SAYS JUST REMOVE THE HOOD AND HE'S READY TO GO.
BRUTUS, MY MAIL!
CRAW!
WHOA!
FWIT!
FWIT!
FWIT!
BILLS
JUNK
CORRE-SPONDENCE
LOVE LETTERS
BRUTUS, MY CIGAR!
NICE! GET ONE FOR YOURSELF, TOO.
MY LIFE BEGINS NOW.

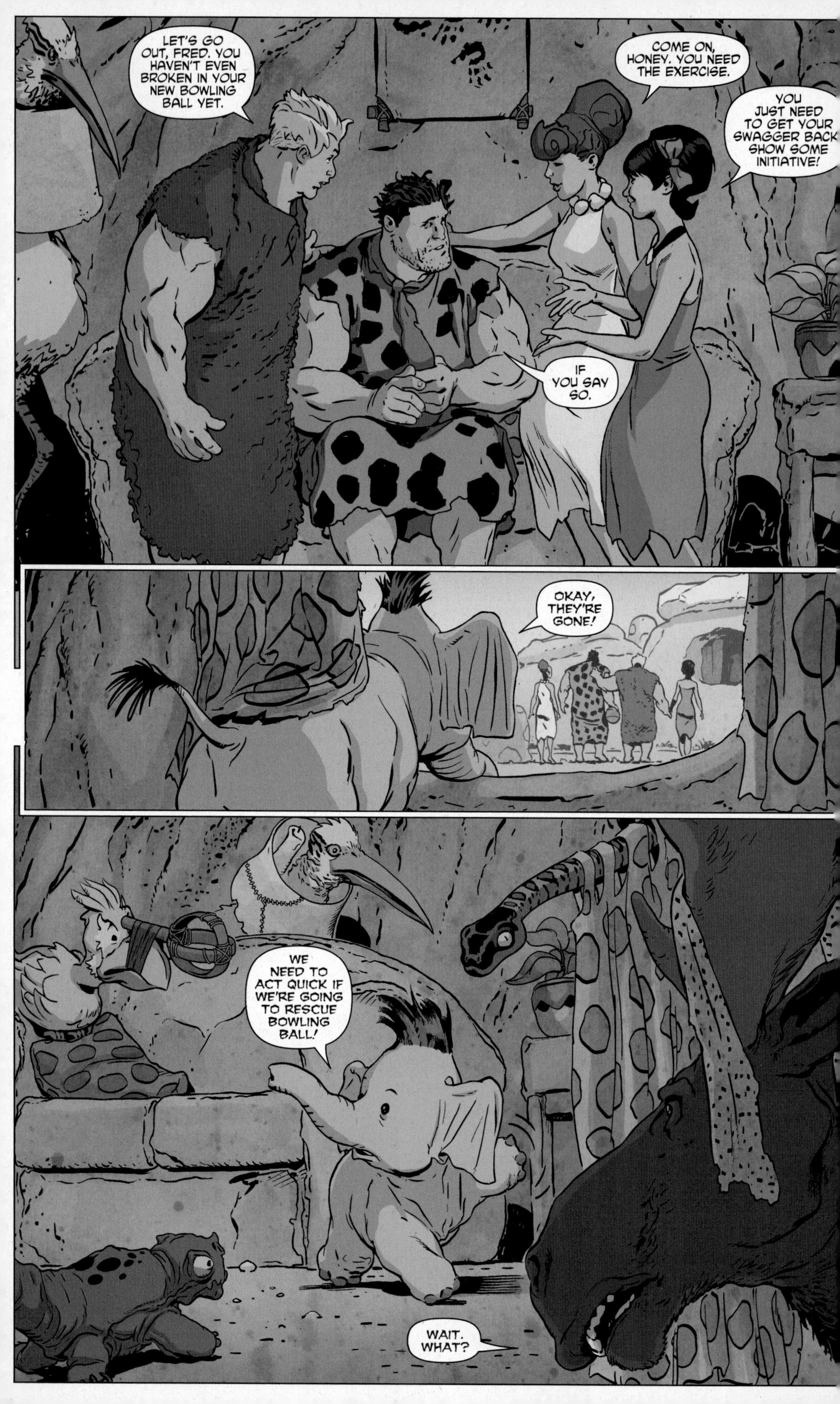
LET'S GO OUT, FRED. YOU HAVEN'T EVEN BROKEN IN YOUR NEW BOWLING BALL YET.
COME ON, HONEY. YOU NEED THE EXERCISE.
YOU JUST NEED TO GET YOUR SWAGGER BACK SHOW SOME INITIATIVE!
IF YOU SAY SO.
OKAY, THEY'RE GONE!
WE NEED TO ACT QUICK IF WE'RE GOING TO RESCUE BOWLING BALL!
WAIT. WHAT?

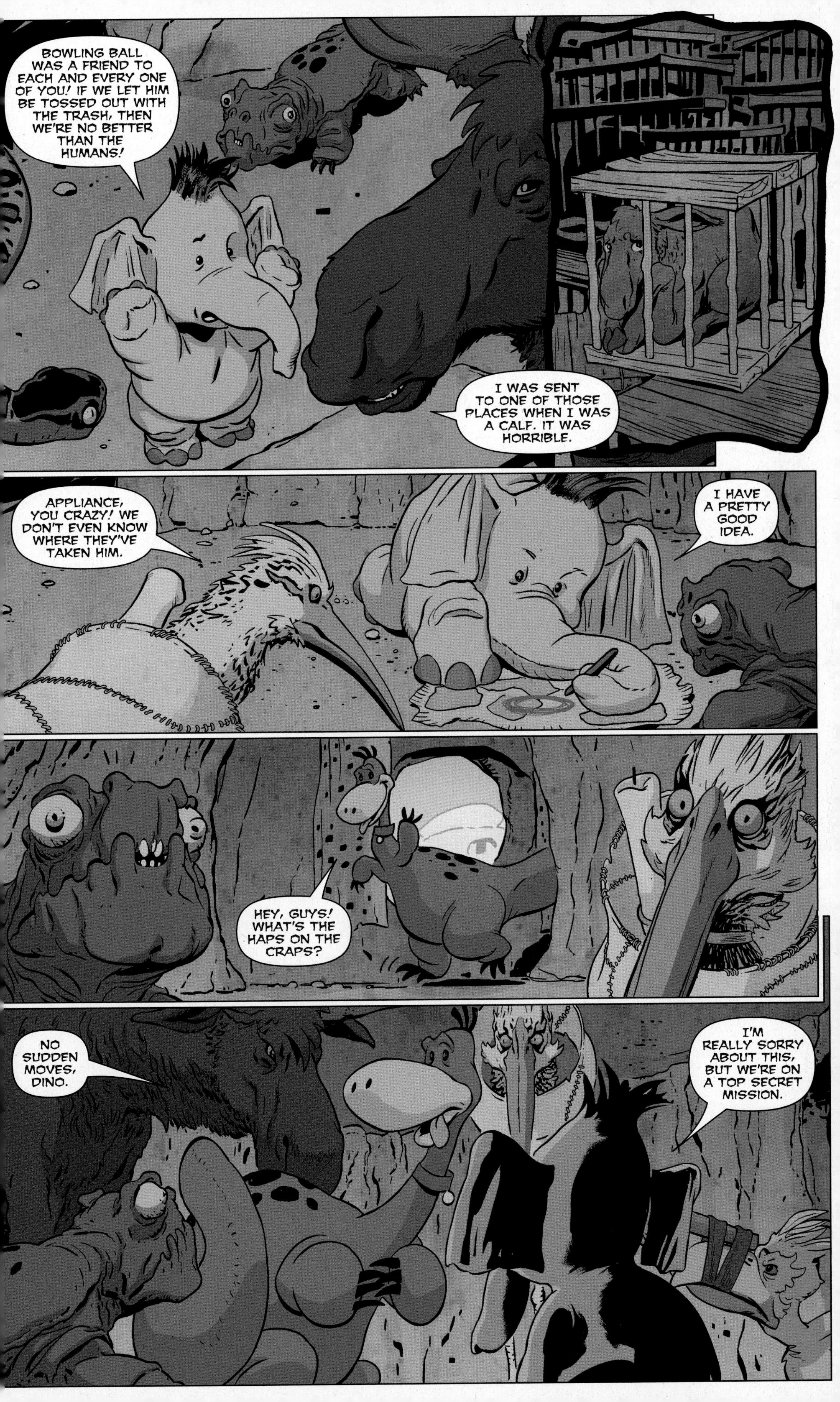
BOWLING BALL WAS A FRIEND TO EACH AND EVERY ONE OF YOU! IF WE LET HIM BE TOSSED OUT WITH THE TRASH, THEN WE'RE NO BETTER THAN THE HUMANS!
I WAS SENT TO ONE OF THOSE PLACES WHEN I WAS A CALF. IT WAS HORRIBLE.
APPLIANCE, YOU CRAZY! WE DON'T EVEN KNOW WHERE THEY'VE TAKEN HIM.
I HAVE A PRETTY GOOD IDEA.
HEY, GUYS! WHAT'S THE HAPS ON THE CRAPS?
NO SUDDEN MOVES, DINO.
I'M REALLY SORRY ABOUT THIS, BUT WE'RE ON A TOP SECRET MISSION.

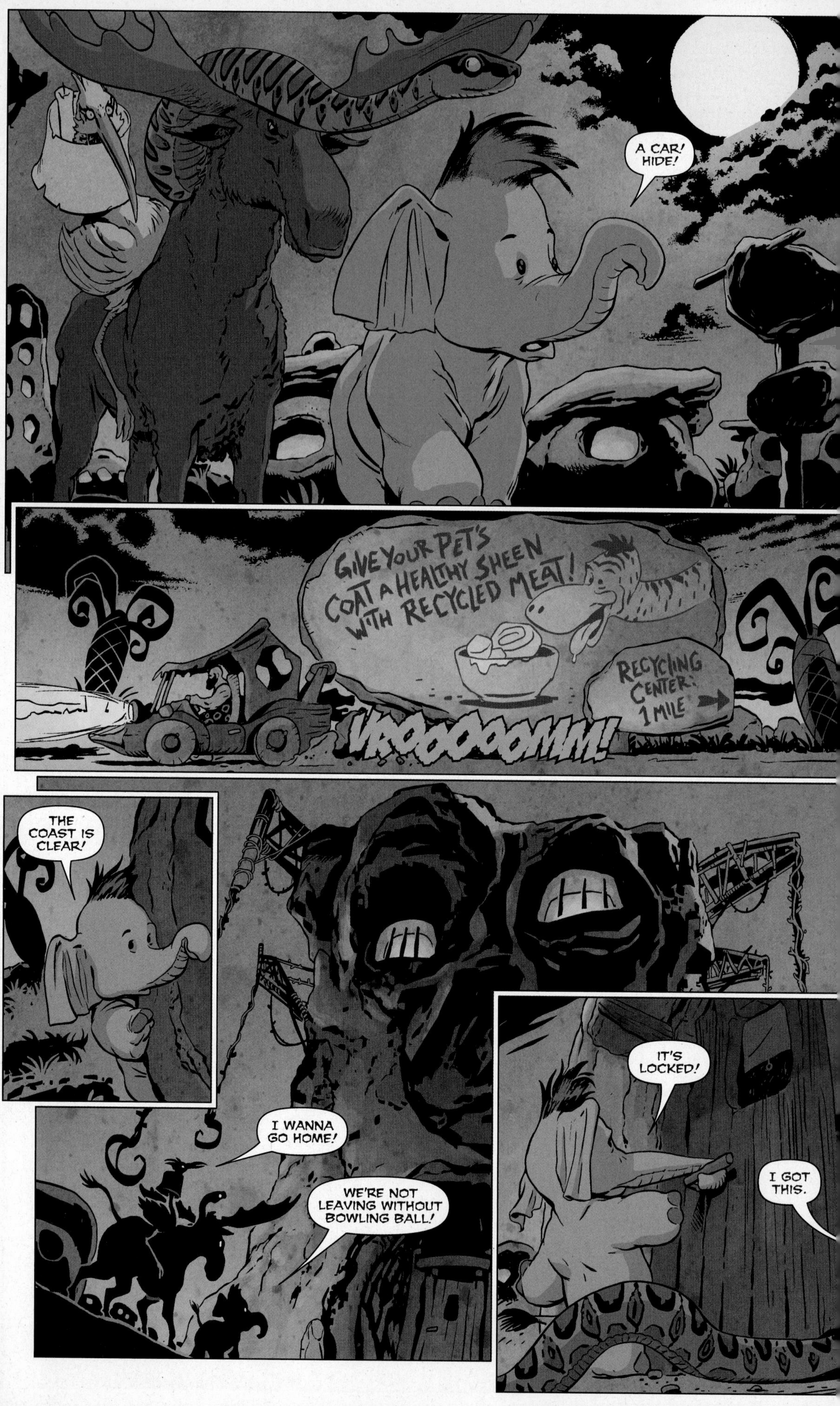

A CAR! HIDE!
GIVE YOUR PET'S COAT A HEALTHY SHEEN WITH RECYCLED MEAT!
RECYCLING CENTER: 1 MILE
VROOOOOOMM!
THE COAST IS CLEAR!
I WANNA GO HOME!
WE'RE NOT LEAVING WITHOUT BOWLING BALL!
IT'S LOCKED!
I GOT THIS.

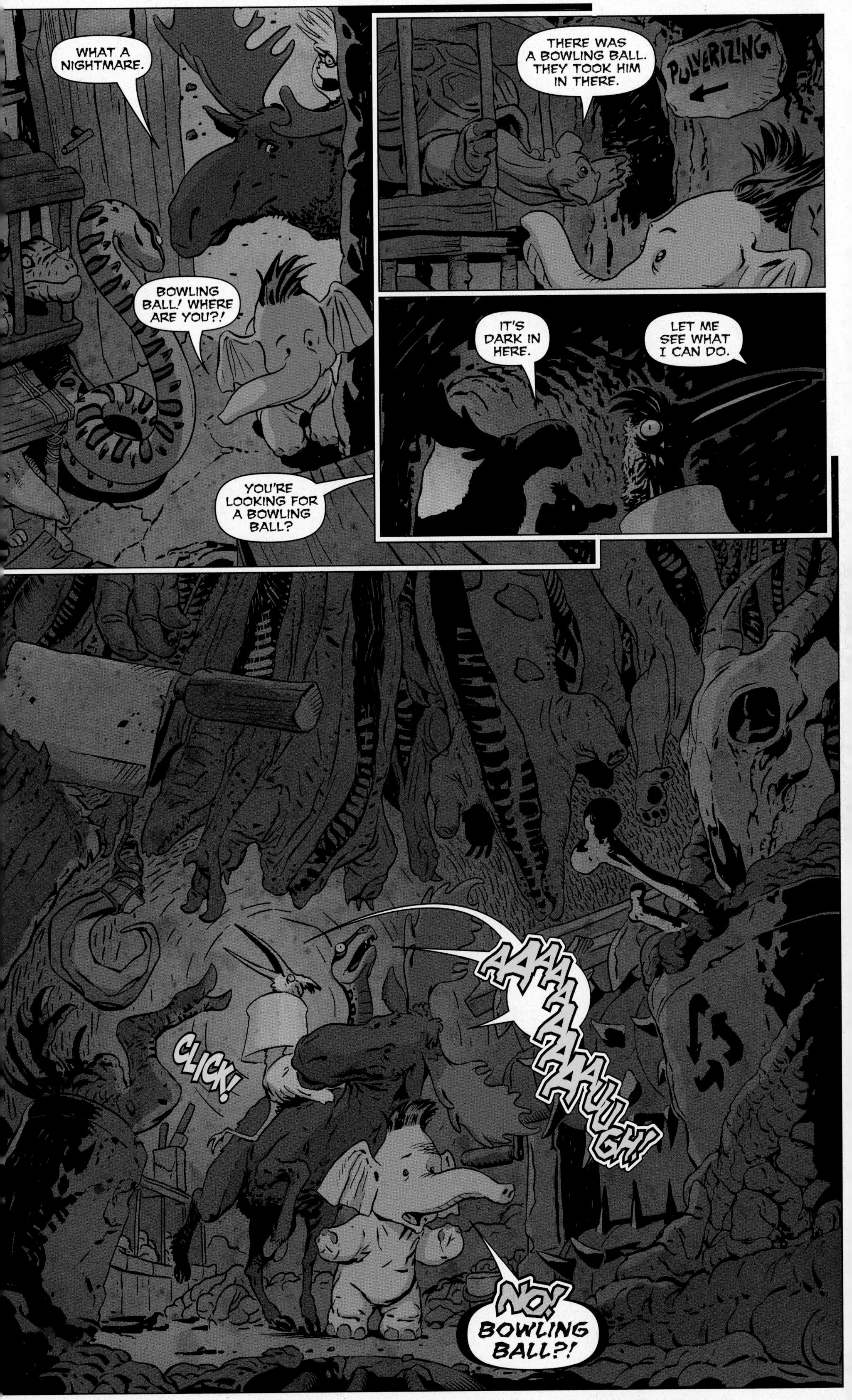
WHAT A NIGHTMARE.
BOWLING BALL! WHERE ARE YOU?!
YOU'RE LOOKING FOR A BOWLING BALL?
THERE WAS A BOWLING BALL. THEY TOOK HIM IN THERE.
PULVERIZING
IT'S DARK IN HERE.
LET ME SEE WHAT I CAN DO.
CLICK!
AAAAAAAAAUUGH!
NO! BOWLING BALL?!

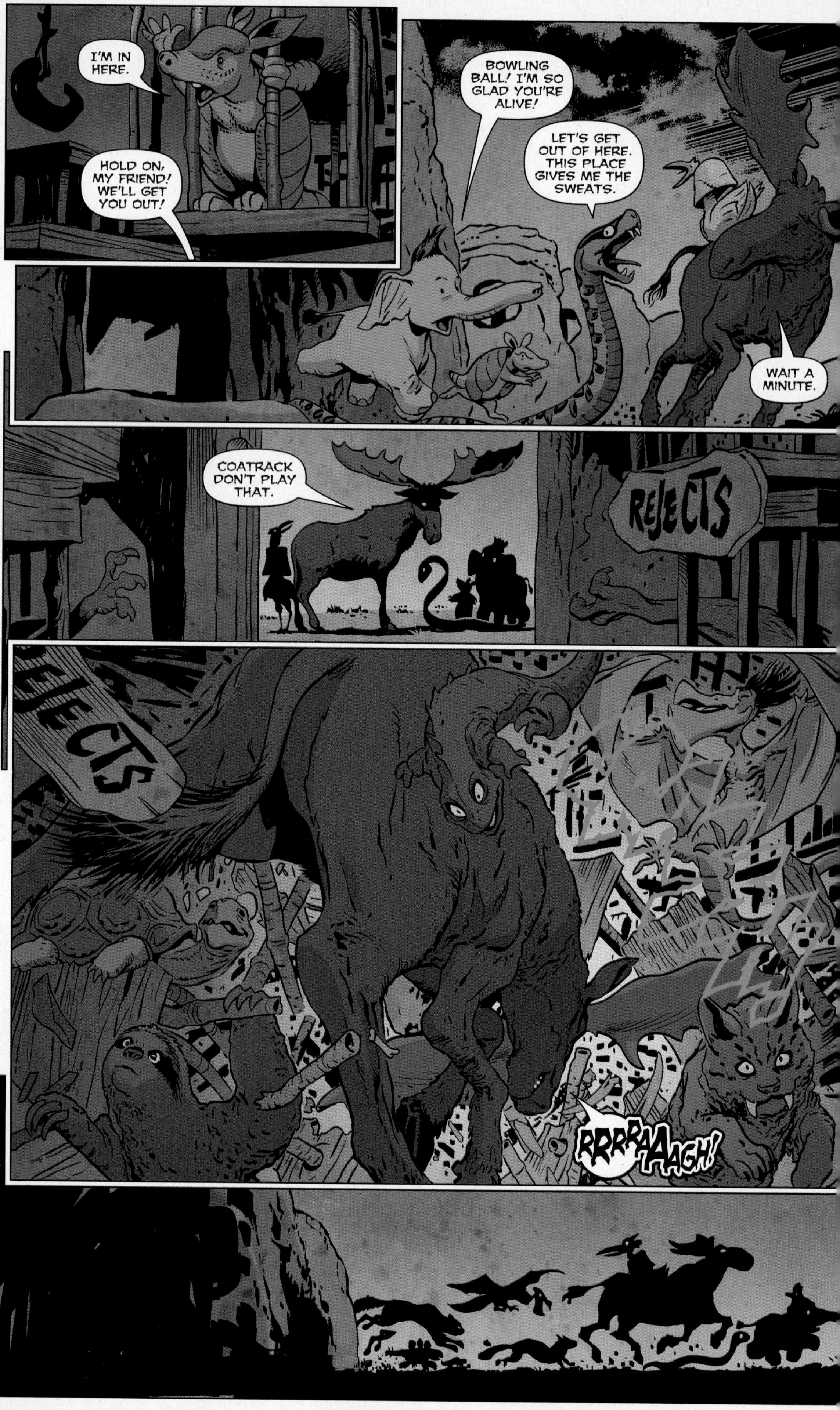
I'M IN HERE.
HOLD ON, MY FRIEND! WE'LL GET YOU OUT!
BOWLING BALL! I'M SO GLAD YOU'RE ALIVE!
LET'S GET OUT OF HERE. THIS PLACE GIVES ME THE SWEATS.
WAIT A MINUTE.
COATRACK DON'T PLAY THAT.
REJECTS
REJECTS
RRRRAAAGH!

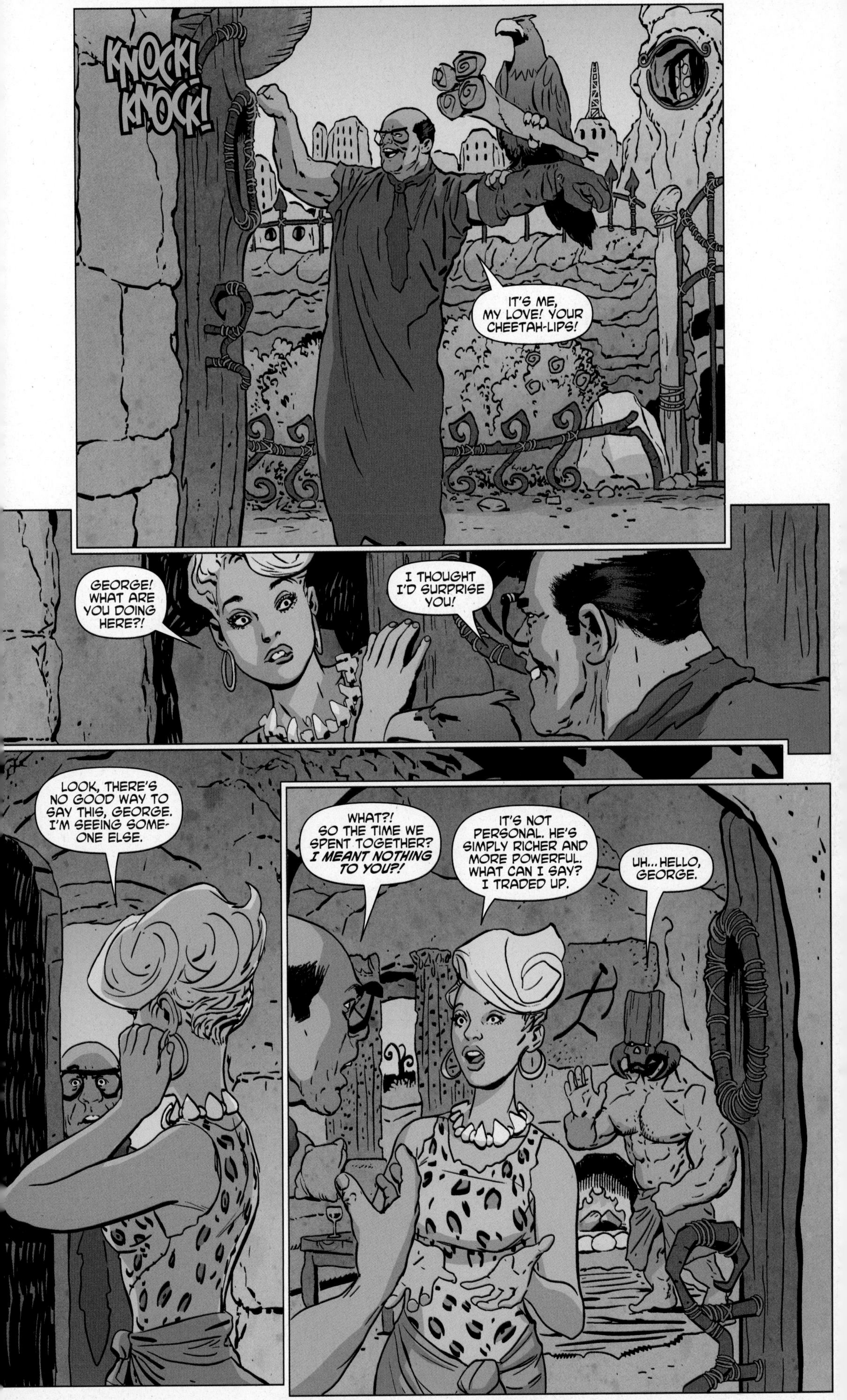
KNOCK! KNOCK!
IT'S ME, MY LOVE! YOUR CHEETAH-LIPS!
GEORGE! WHAT ARE YOU DOING HERE?!
I THOUGHT I'D SURPRISE YOU!
LOOK, THERE'S NO GOOD WAY TO SAY THIS, GEORGE. I'M SEEING SOME-ONE ELSE.
WHAT?! SO THE TIME WE SPENT TOGETHER? *I MEANT NOTHING TO YOU?!*
IT'S NOT PERSONAL. HE'S SIMPLY RICHER AND MORE POWERFUL. WHAT CAN I SAY? I TRADED UP.
UH... HELLO, GEORGE.

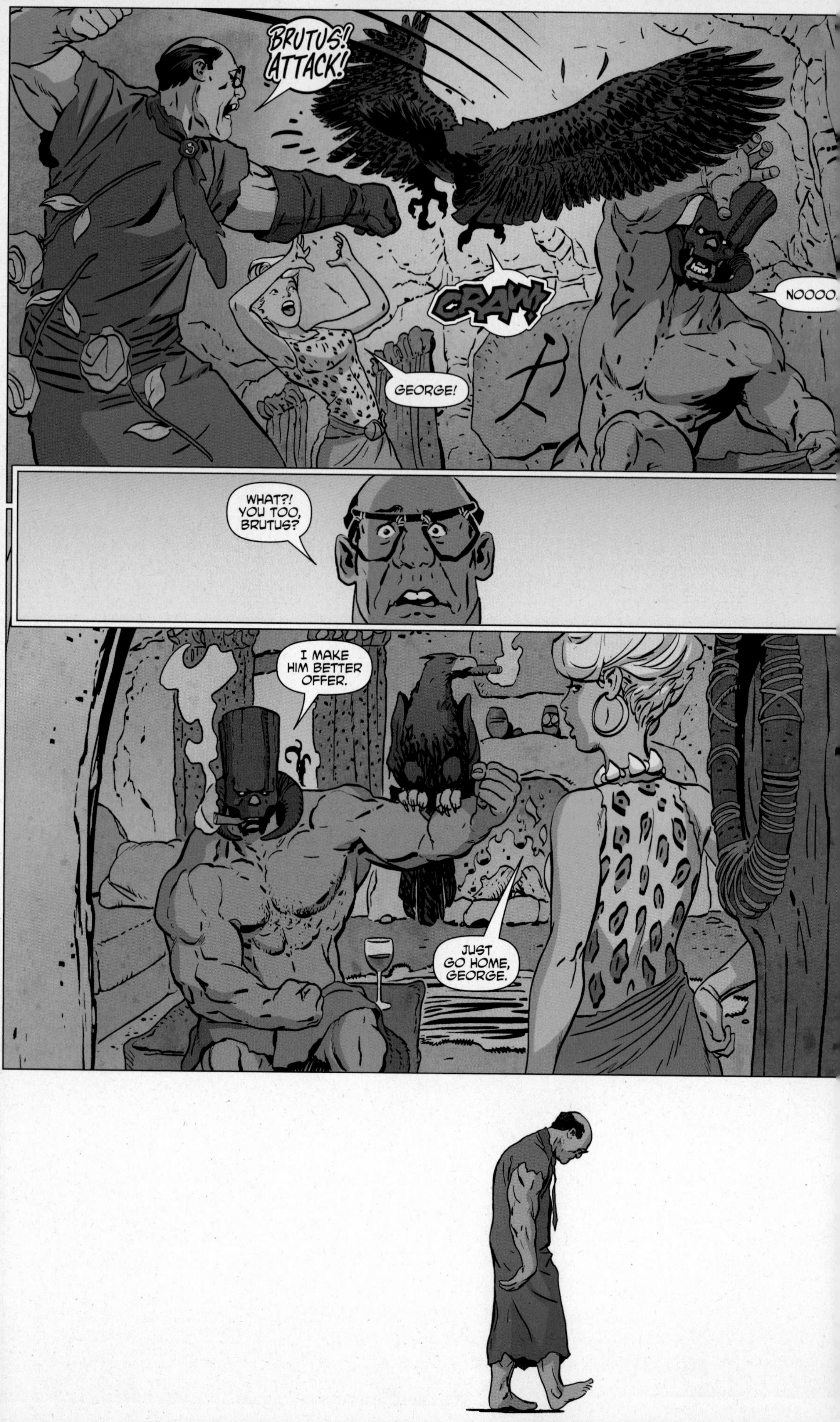

BRUTUS! ATTACK!
CRAW!
NOOOO..
GEORGE!
WHAT?! YOU TOO, BRUTUS?
I MAKE HIM BETTER OFFER.
JUST GO HOME, GEORGE.

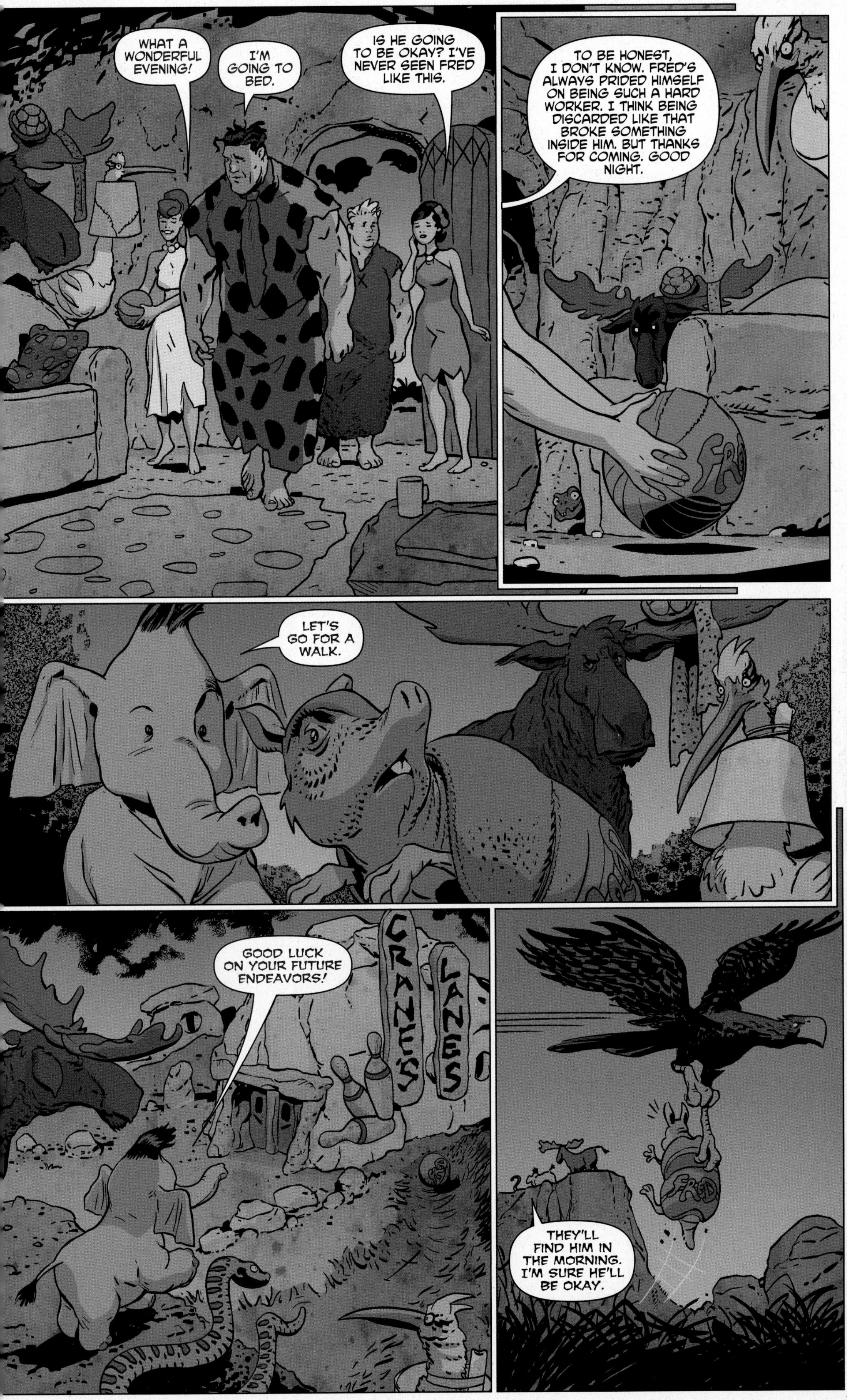
WHAT A WONDERFUL EVENING!
I'M GOING TO BED.
IS HE GOING TO BE OKAY? I'VE NEVER SEEN FRED LIKE THIS.
TO BE HONEST, I DON'T KNOW. FRED'S ALWAYS PRIDED HIMSELF ON BEING SUCH A HARD WORKER. I THINK BEING DISCARDED LIKE THAT BROKE SOMETHING INSIDE HIM. BUT THANKS FOR COMING. GOOD NIGHT.
FRED
LET'S GO FOR A WALK.
GOOD LUCK ON YOUR FUTURE ENDEAVORS!
CRANE'S
LANES
FRED
THEY'LL FIND HIM IN THE MORNING. I'M SURE HE'LL BE OKAY.

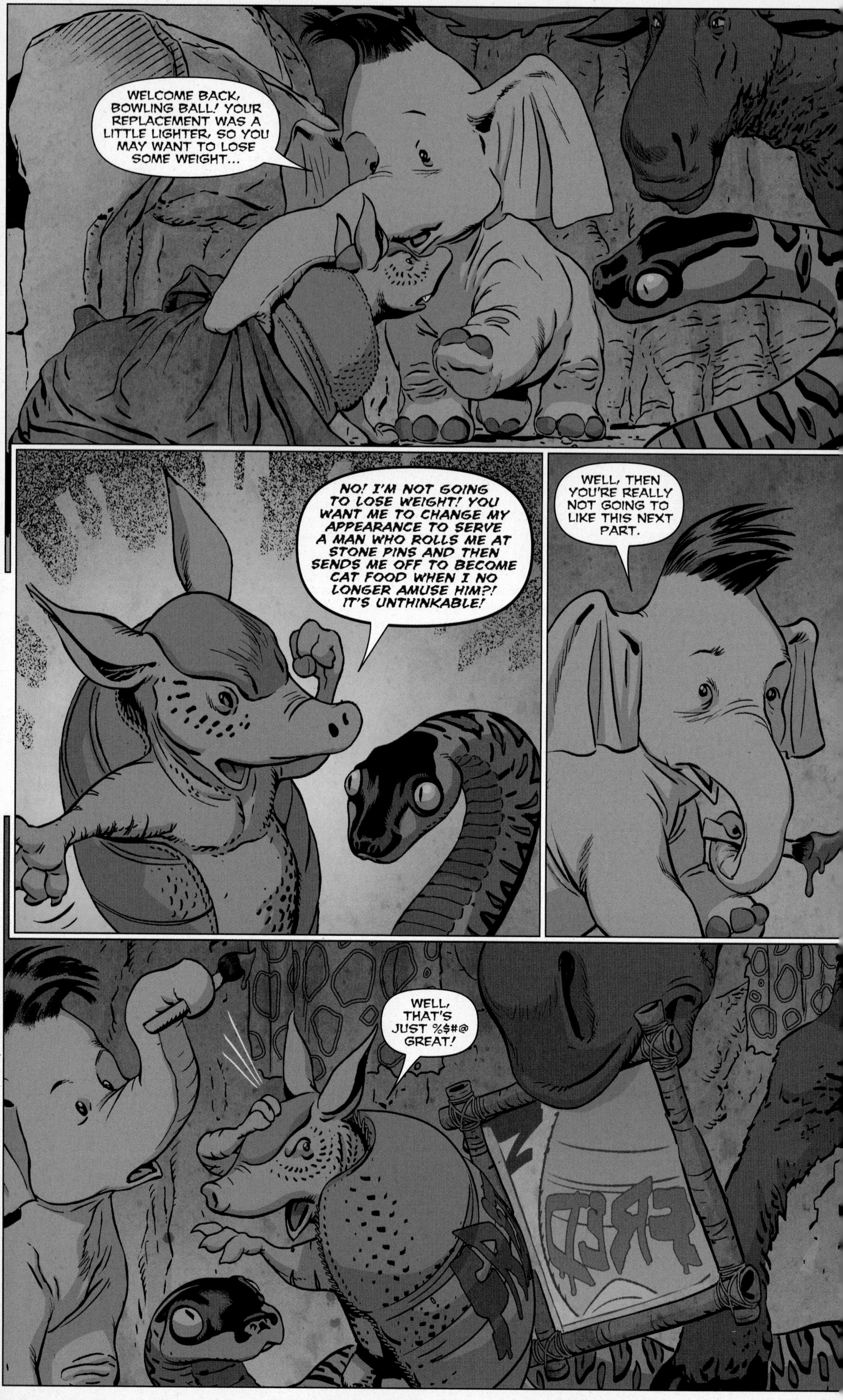
WELCOME BACK, BOWLING BALL! YOUR REPLACEMENT WAS A LITTLE LIGHTER, SO YOU MAY WANT TO LOSE SOME WEIGHT...
NO! I'M NOT GOING TO LOSE WEIGHT! YOU WANT ME TO CHANGE MY APPEARANCE TO SERVE A MAN WHO ROLLS ME AT STONE PINS AND THEN SENDS ME OFF TO BECOME CAT FOOD WHEN I NO LONGER AMUSE HIM?! IT'S UNTHINKABLE!
WELL, THEN YOU'RE REALLY NOT GOING TO LIKE THIS NEXT PART.
WELL, THAT'S JUST %$#@ GREAT!

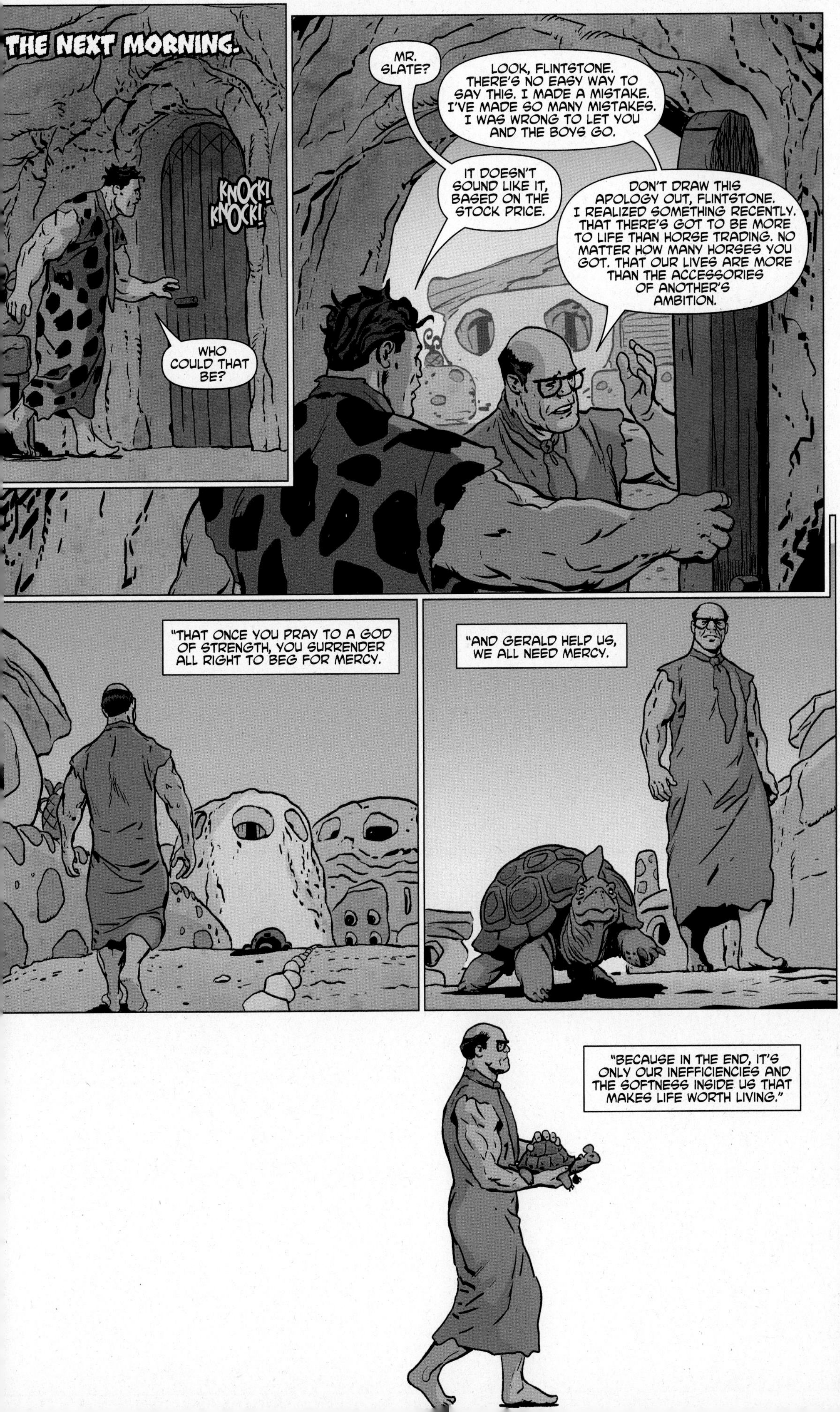

THE NEXT MORNING.
KNOCK! KNOCK!
WHO COULD THAT BE?
MR. SLATE?
LOOK, FLINTSTONE. THERE'S NO EASY WAY TO SAY THIS. I MADE A MISTAKE. I'VE MADE SO MANY MISTAKES. I WAS WRONG TO LET YOU AND THE BOYS GO.
IT DOESN'T SOUND LIKE IT, BASED ON THE STOCK PRICE.
DON'T DRAW THIS APOLOGY OUT, FLINTSTONE. I REALIZED SOMETHING RECENTLY. THAT THERE'S GOT TO BE MORE TO LIFE THAN HORSE TRADING. NO MATTER HOW MANY HORSES YOU GOT. THAT OUR LIVES ARE MORE THAN THE ACCESSORIES OF ANOTHER'S AMBITION.
"THAT ONCE YOU PRAY TO A GOD OF STRENGTH, YOU SURRENDER ALL RIGHT TO BEG FOR MERCY.
"AND GERALD HELP US, WE ALL NEED MERCY.
"BECAUSE IN THE END, IT'S ONLY OUR INEFFICIENCIES AND THE SOFTNESS INSIDE US THAT MAKES LIFE WORTH LIVING."

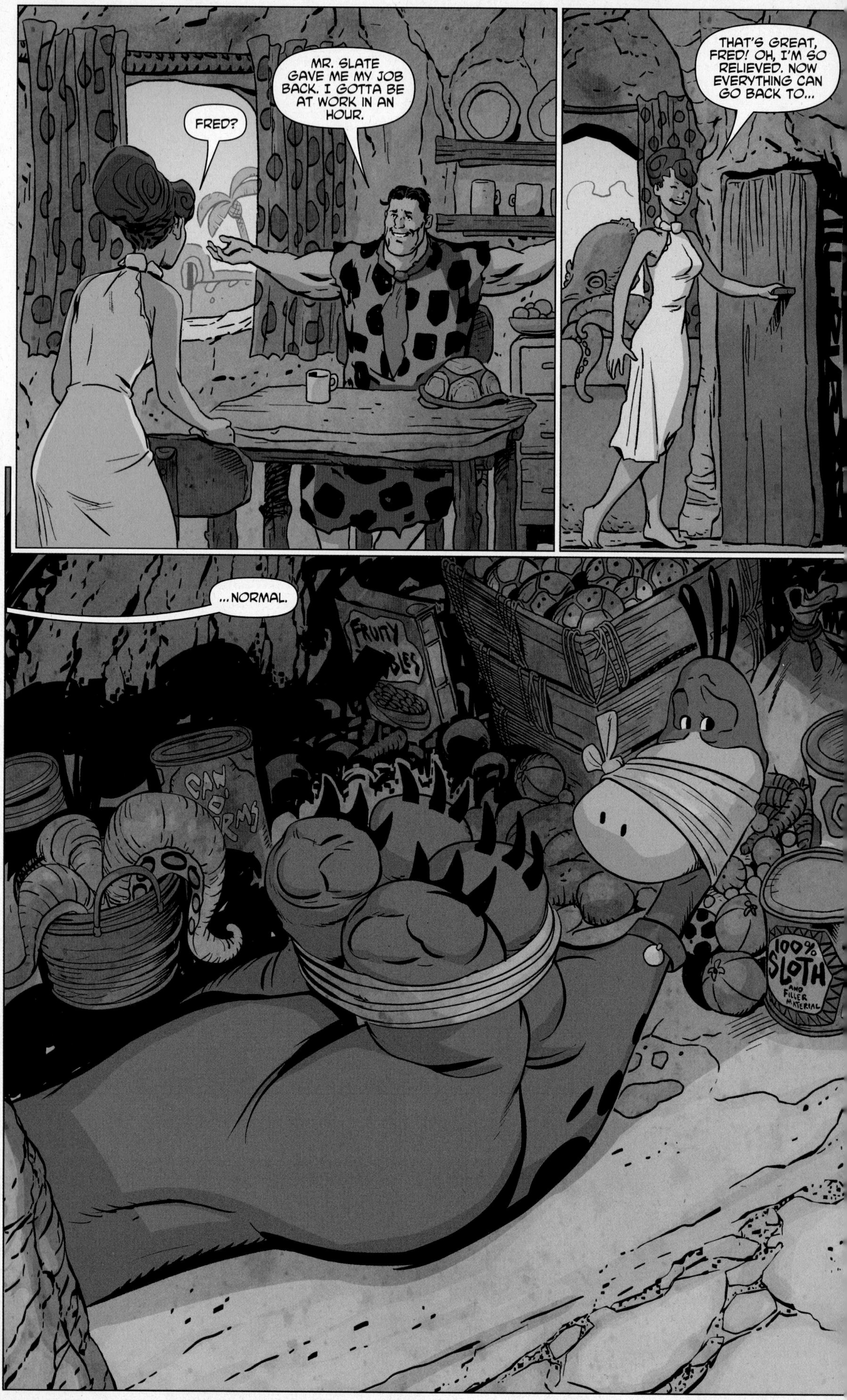

FRED?
MR. SLATE GAVE ME MY JOB BACK. I GOTTA BE AT WORK IN AN HOUR.
THAT'S GREAT, FRED! OH, I'M SO RELIEVED. NOW EVERYTHING CAN GO BACK TO...
...NORMAL.
FRUITY
CAN O' WORMS
100% SLOTH
AND FILLER MATERIAL

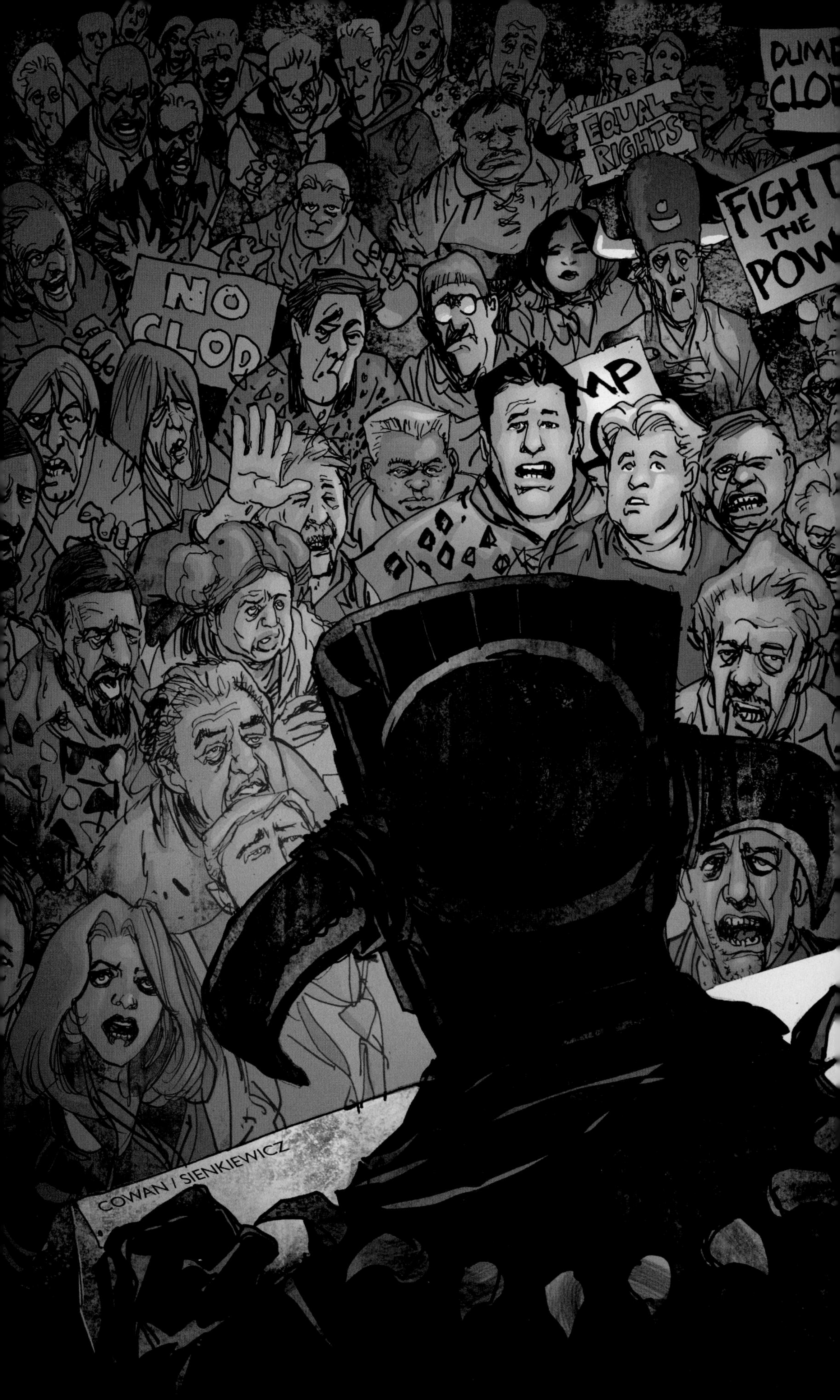
DUMP CLOD
EQUAL RIGHTS
FIGHT THE POW
NO CLOD
MP
COWAN / SIENKIEWICZ

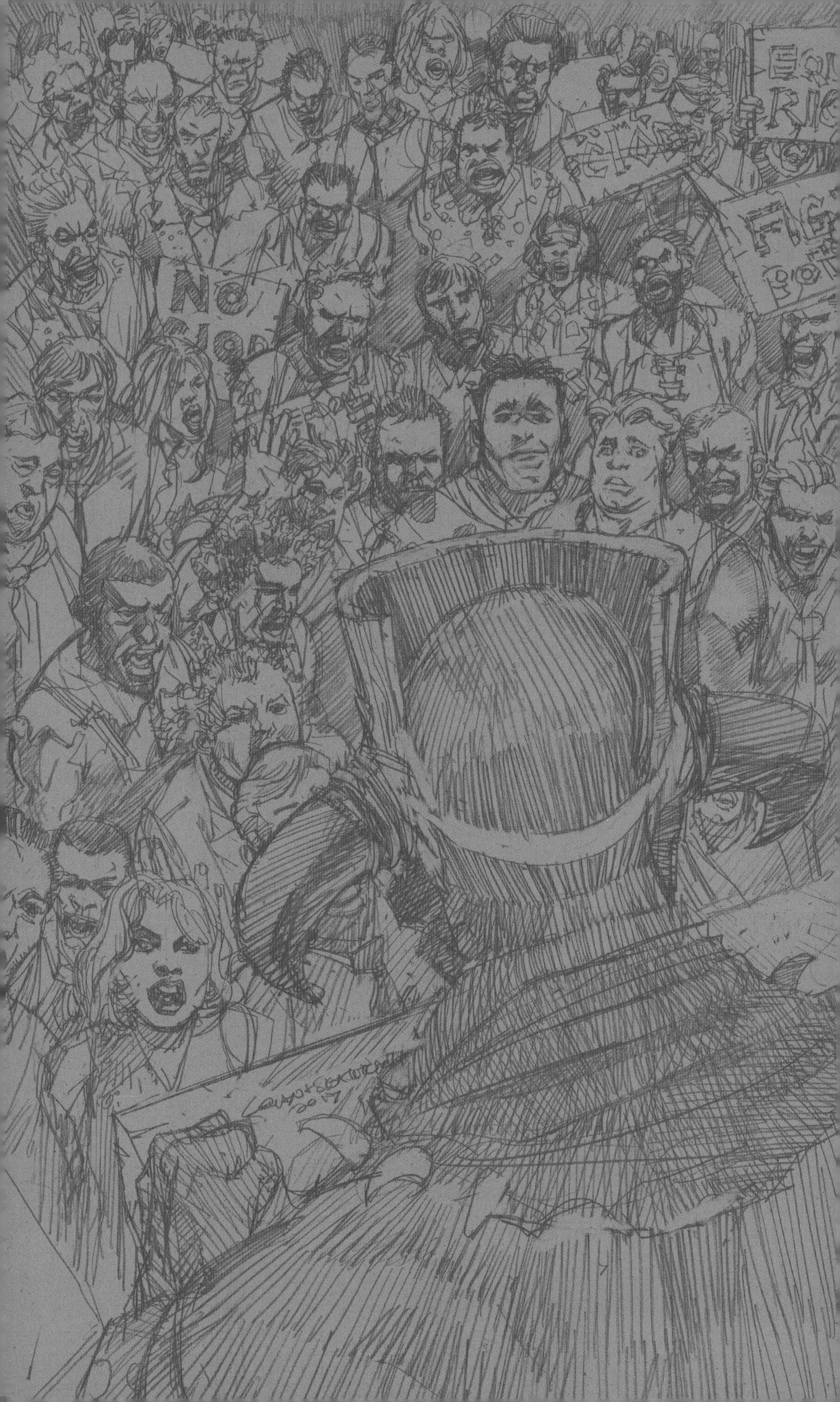
NO

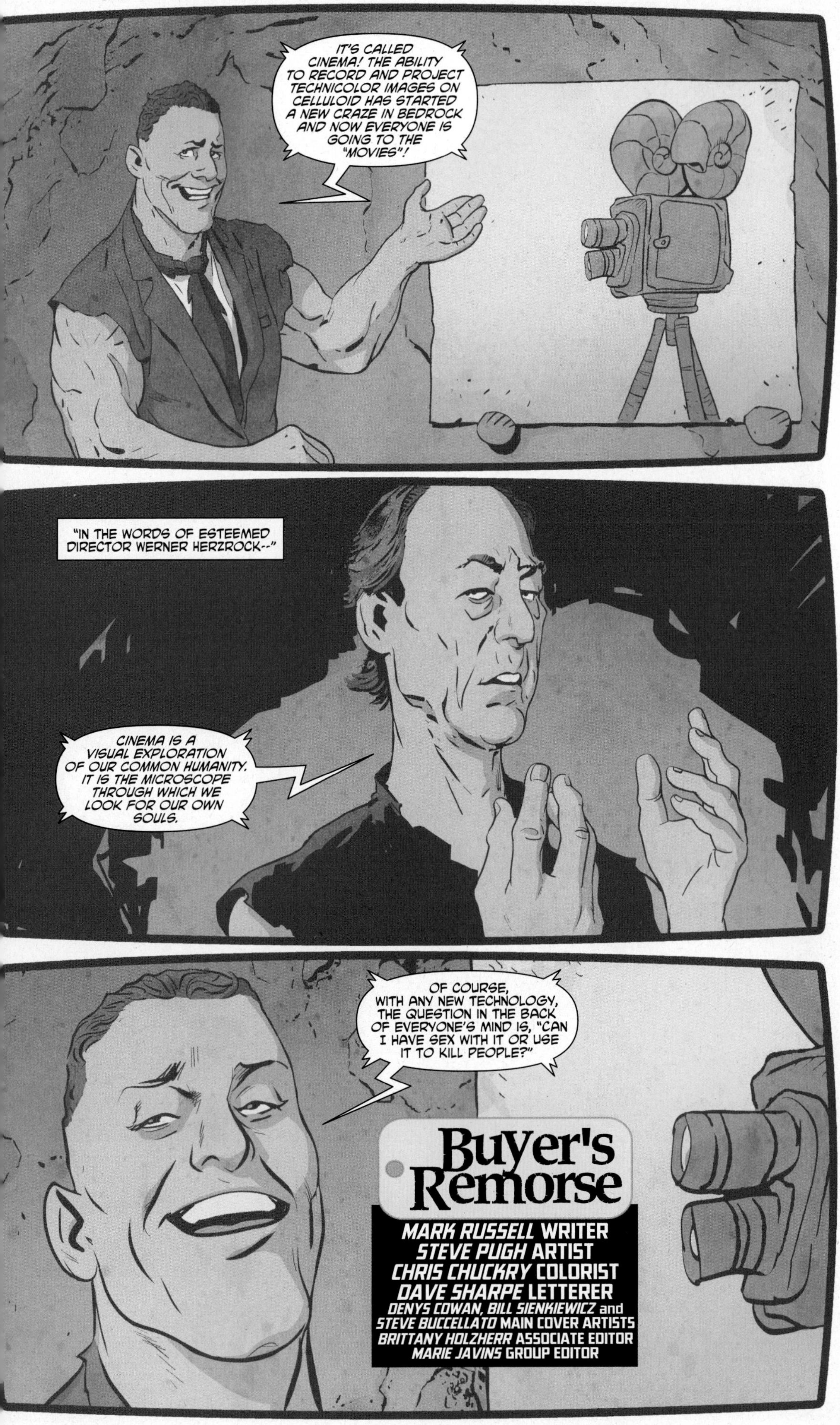
IT'S CALLED CINEMA! THE ABILITY TO RECORD AND PROJECT TECHNICOLOR IMAGES ON CELLULOID HAS STARTED A NEW CRAZE IN BEDROCK AND NOW EVERYONE IS GOING TO THE "MOVIES"!
"IN THE WORDS OF ESTEEMED DIRECTOR WERNER HERZROCK--"
CINEMA IS A VISUAL EXPLORATION OF OUR COMMON HUMANITY. IT IS THE MICROSCOPE THROUGH WHICH WE LOOK FOR OUR OWN SOULS.
OF COURSE, WITH ANY NEW TECHNOLOGY, THE QUESTION IN THE BACK OF EVERYONE'S MIND IS, "CAN I HAVE SEX WITH IT OR USE IT TO KILL PEOPLE?"
Buyer's Remorse
MARK RUSSELL WRITER
STEVE PUGH ARTIST
CHRIS CHUCKRY COLORIST
DAVE SHARPE LETTERER
DENYS COWAN, BILL SIENKIEWICZ and STEVE BUCCELLATO MAIN COVER ARTISTS
BRITTANY HOLZHERR ASSOCIATE EDITOR
MARIE JAVINS GROUP EDITOR

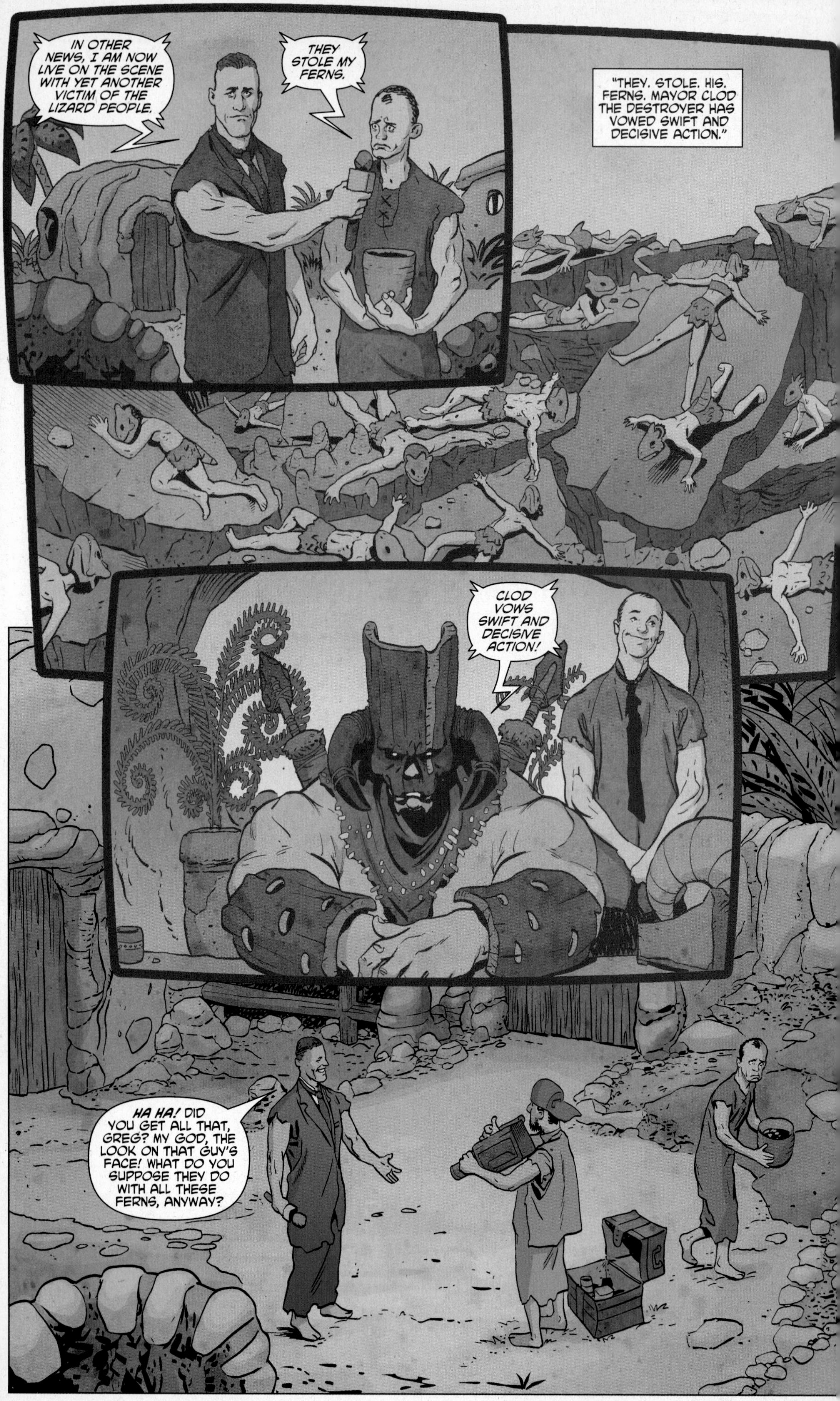
IN OTHER NEWS, I AM NOW LIVE ON THE SCENE WITH YET ANOTHER VICTIM OF THE LIZARD PEOPLE.
THEY STOLE MY FERNS.
"THEY. STOLE. HIS. FERNS. MAYOR CLOD THE DESTROYER HAS VOWED SWIFT AND DECISIVE ACTION."
CLOD VOWS SWIFT AND DECISIVE ACTION!
HA HA! DID YOU GET ALL THAT, GREG? MY GOD, THE LOOK ON THAT GUY'S FACE! WHAT DO YOU SUPPOSE THEY DO WITH ALL THESE FERNS, ANYWAY?

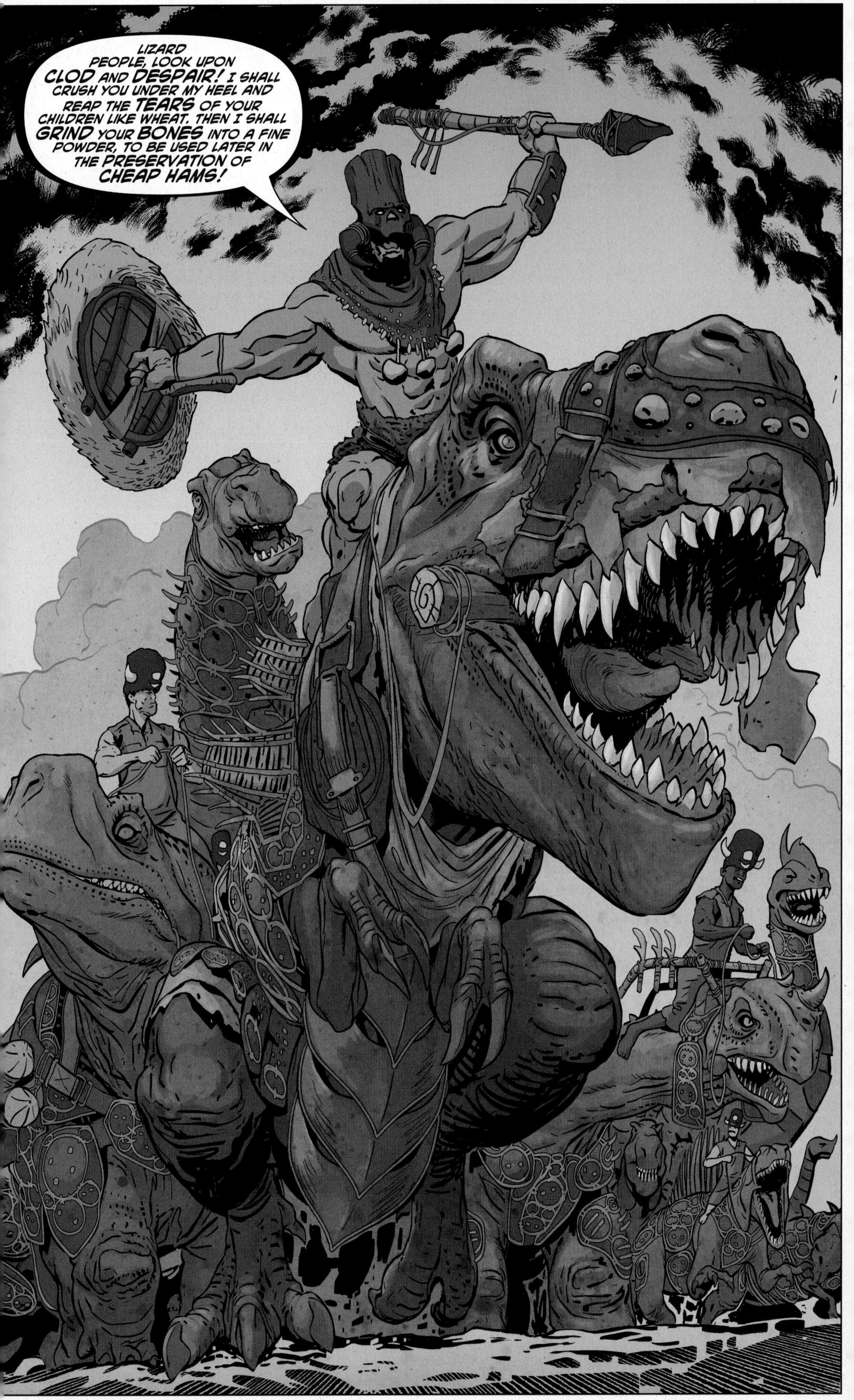
LIZARD PEOPLE, LOOK UPON CLOD AND DESPAIR! I SHALL CRUSH YOU UNDER MY HEEL AND REAP THE TEARS OF YOUR CHILDREN LIKE WHEAT. THEN I SHALL GRIND YOUR BONES INTO A FINE POWDER, TO BE USED LATER IN THE PRESERVATION OF CHEAP HAMS!

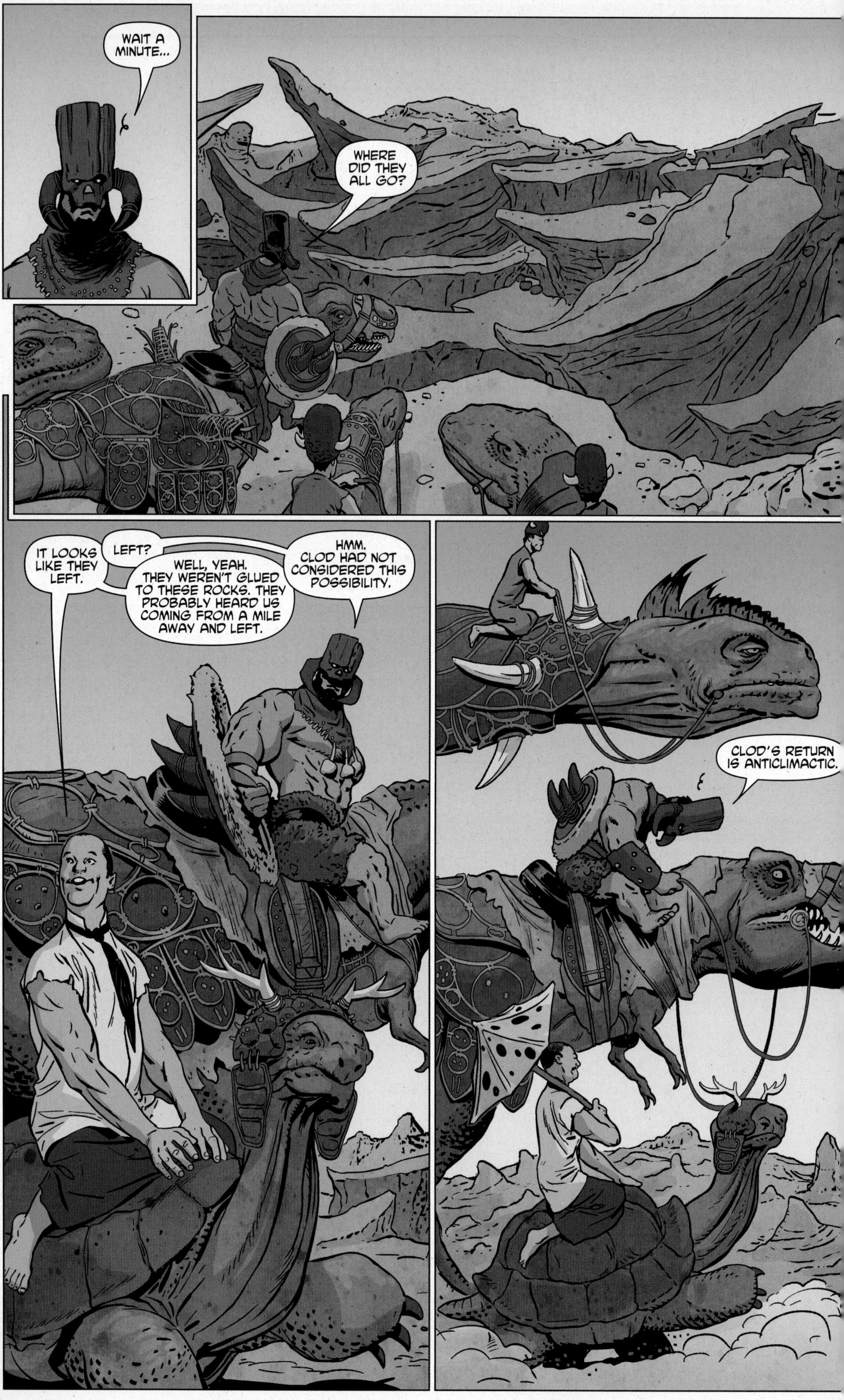
WAIT A MINUTE...
WHERE DID THEY ALL GO?
IT LOOKS LIKE THEY LEFT.
LEFT?
WELL, YEAH. THEY WEREN'T GLUED TO THESE ROCKS. THEY PROBABLY HEARD US COMING FROM A MILE AWAY AND LEFT.
HMM. CLOD HAD NOT CONSIDERED THIS POSSIBILITY.
CLOD'S RETURN IS ANTICLIMACTIC.

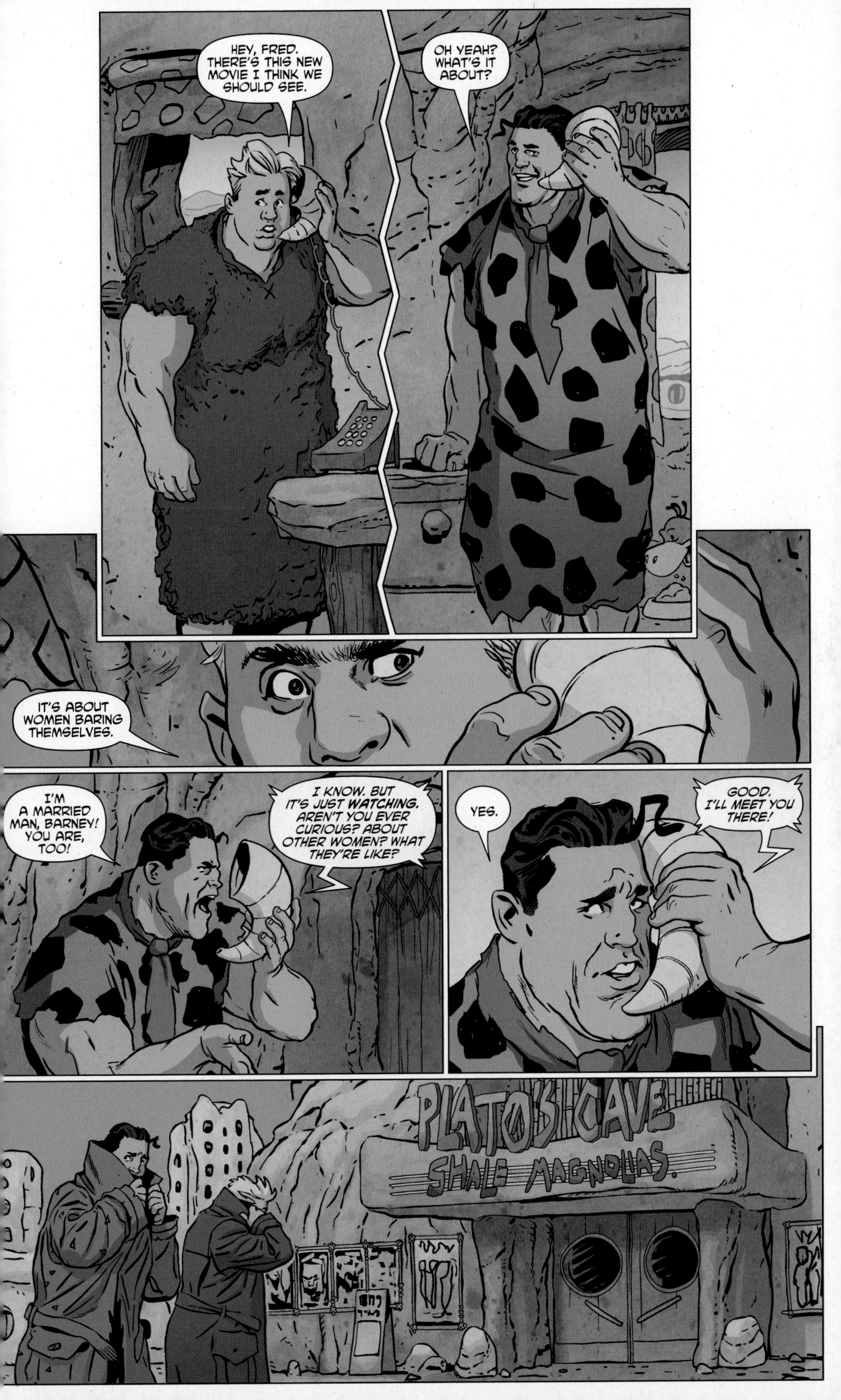

HEY, FRED. THERE'S THIS NEW MOVIE I THINK WE SHOULD SEE.
OH YEAH? WHAT'S IT ABOUT?
IT'S ABOUT WOMEN BARING THEMSELVES.
I'M A MARRIED MAN, BARNEY! YOU ARE, TOO!
I KNOW. BUT IT'S JUST WATCHING. AREN'T YOU EVER CURIOUS? ABOUT OTHER WOMEN? WHAT THEY'RE LIKE?
YES.
GOOD. I'LL MEET YOU THERE!
PLATO'S CAVE
SHALE MAGNOLIAS

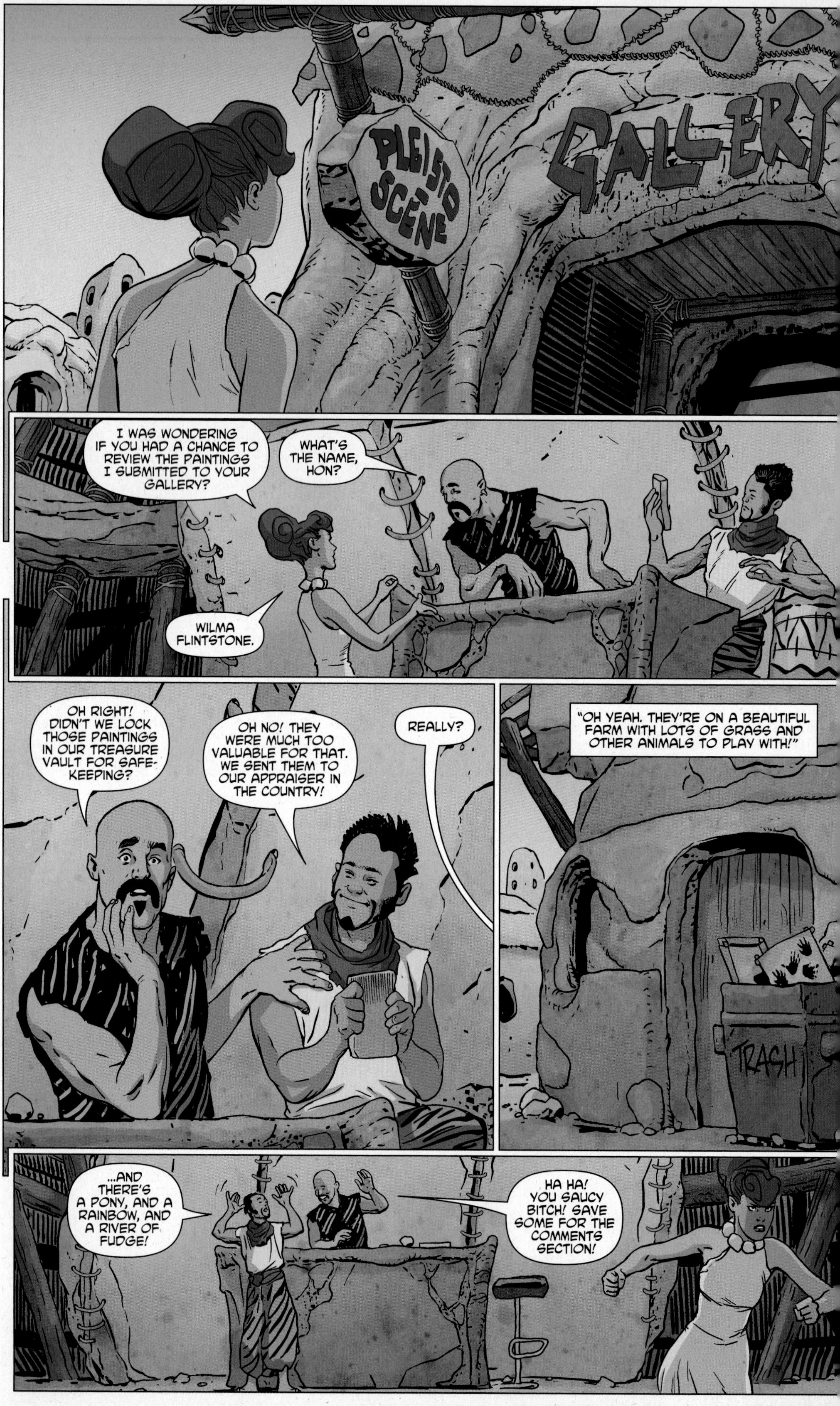
PLEISTO SCÈNE
GALLERY
I WAS WONDERING IF YOU HAD A CHANCE TO REVIEW THE PAINTINGS I SUBMITTED TO YOUR GALLERY?
WHAT'S THE NAME, HON?
WILMA FLINTSTONE.
OH RIGHT! DIDN'T WE LOCK THOSE PAINTINGS IN OUR TREASURE VAULT FOR SAFE-KEEPING?
OH NO! THEY WERE MUCH TOO VALUABLE FOR THAT. WE SENT THEM TO OUR APPRAISER IN THE COUNTRY!
REALLY?
"OH YEAH. THEY'RE ON A BEAUTIFUL FARM WITH LOTS OF GRASS AND OTHER ANIMALS TO PLAY WITH!"
TRASH
...AND THERE'S A PONY, AND A RAINBOW, AND A RIVER OF FUDGE!
HA HA! YOU SAUCY BITCH! SAVE SOME FOR THE COMMENTS SECTION!

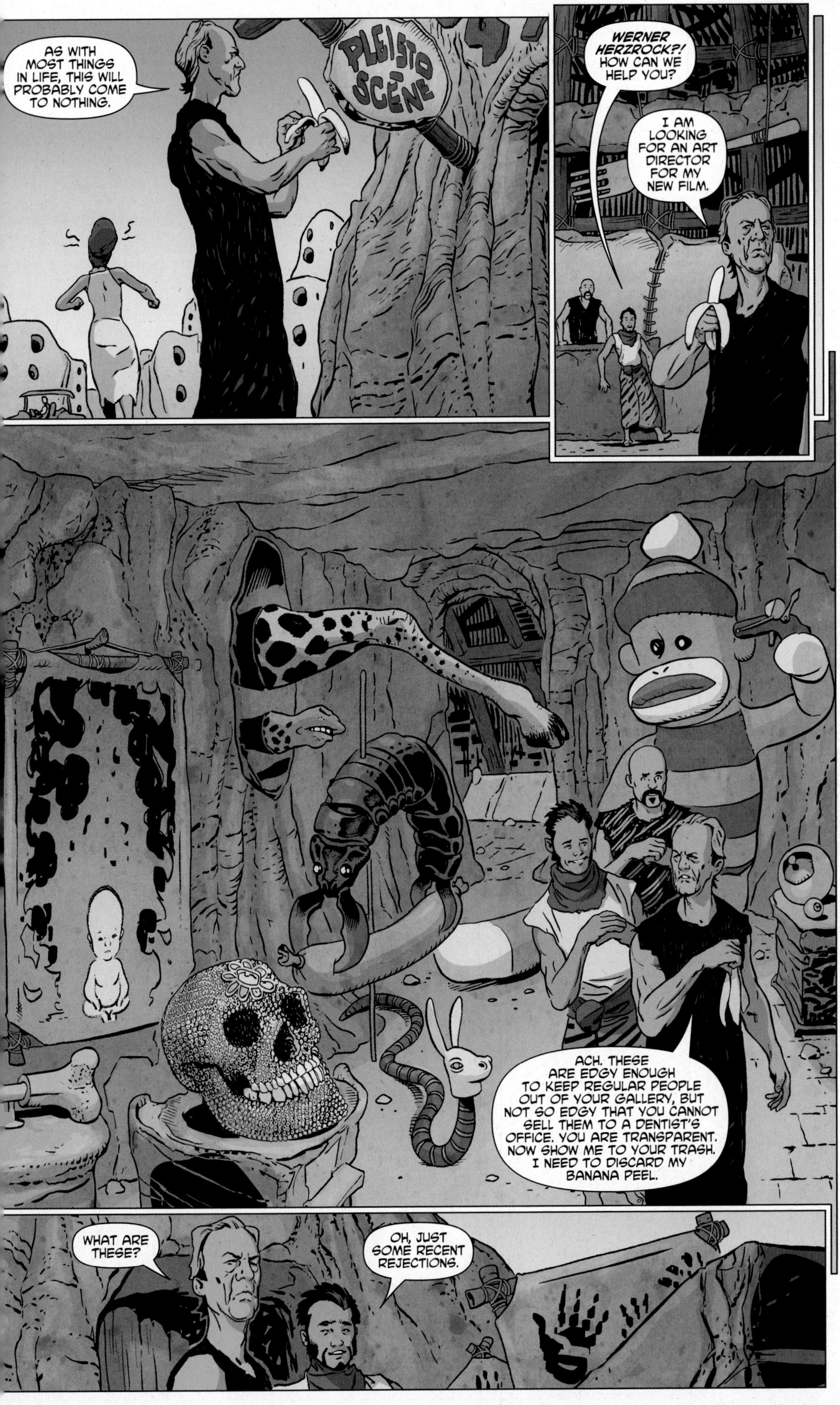
AS WITH MOST THINGS IN LIFE, THIS WILL PROBABLY COME TO NOTHING.
PLEISTO SCÈNE
WERNER HERZROCK?! HOW CAN WE HELP YOU?
I AM LOOKING FOR AN ART DIRECTOR FOR MY NEW FILM.
ACH. THESE ARE EDGY ENOUGH TO KEEP REGULAR PEOPLE OUT OF YOUR GALLERY, BUT NOT SO EDGY THAT YOU CANNOT SELL THEM TO A DENTIST'S OFFICE. YOU ARE TRANSPARENT. NOW SHOW ME TO YOUR TRASH. I NEED TO DISCARD MY BANANA PEEL.
WHAT ARE THESE?
OH, JUST SOME RECENT REJECTIONS.

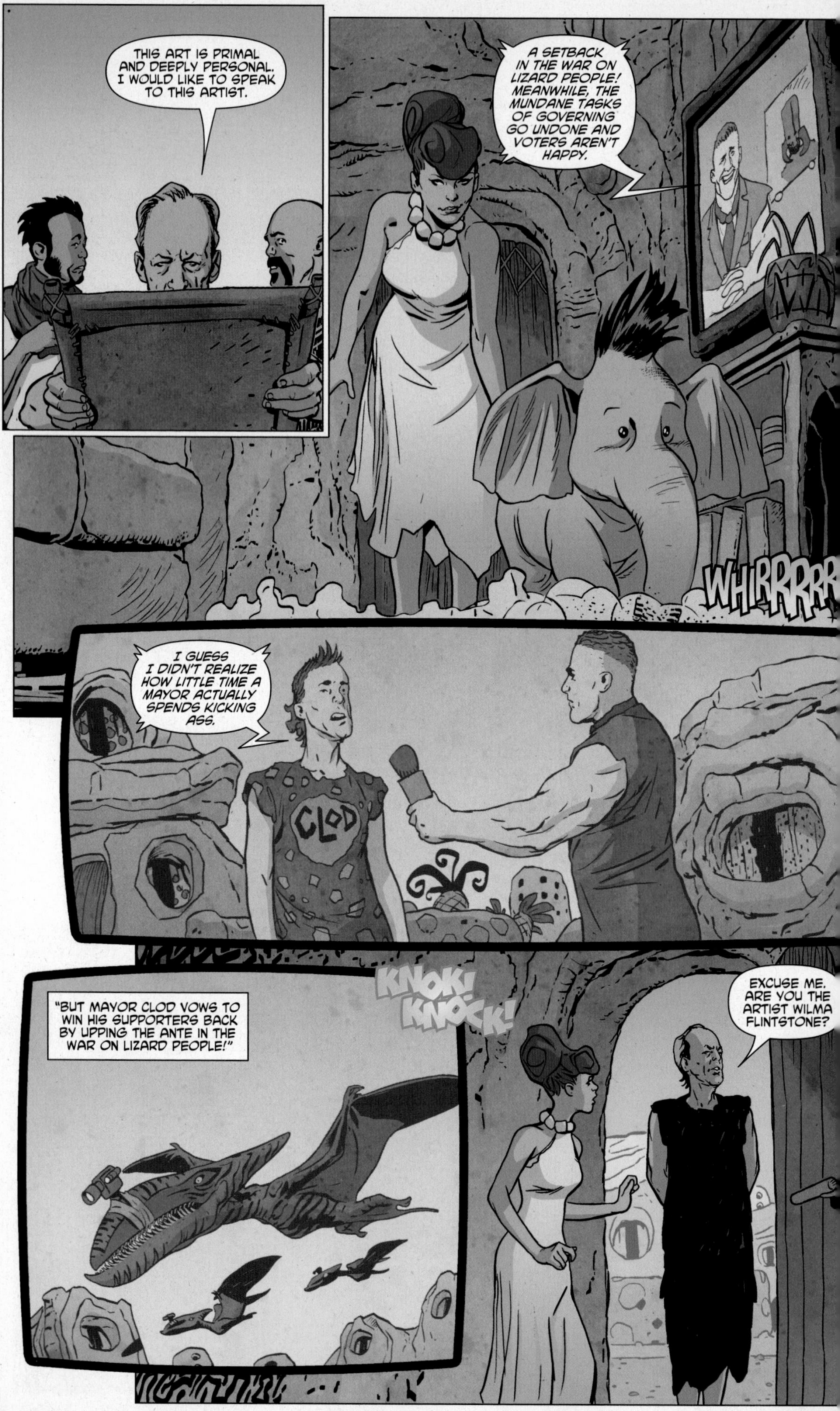
THIS ART IS PRIMAL AND DEEPLY PERSONAL. I WOULD LIKE TO SPEAK TO THIS ARTIST.
A SETBACK IN THE WAR ON LIZARD PEOPLE! MEANWHILE, THE MUNDANE TASKS OF GOVERNING GO UNDONE AND VOTERS AREN'T HAPPY.
WHIRRRRR
I GUESS I DIDN'T REALIZE HOW LITTLE TIME A MAYOR ACTUALLY SPENDS KICKING ASS.
CLOD
"BUT MAYOR CLOD VOWS TO WIN HIS SUPPORTERS BACK BY UPPING THE ANTE IN THE WAR ON LIZARD PEOPLE!"
KNOK! KNOCK!
EXCUSE ME. ARE YOU THE ARTIST WILMA FLINTSTONE?

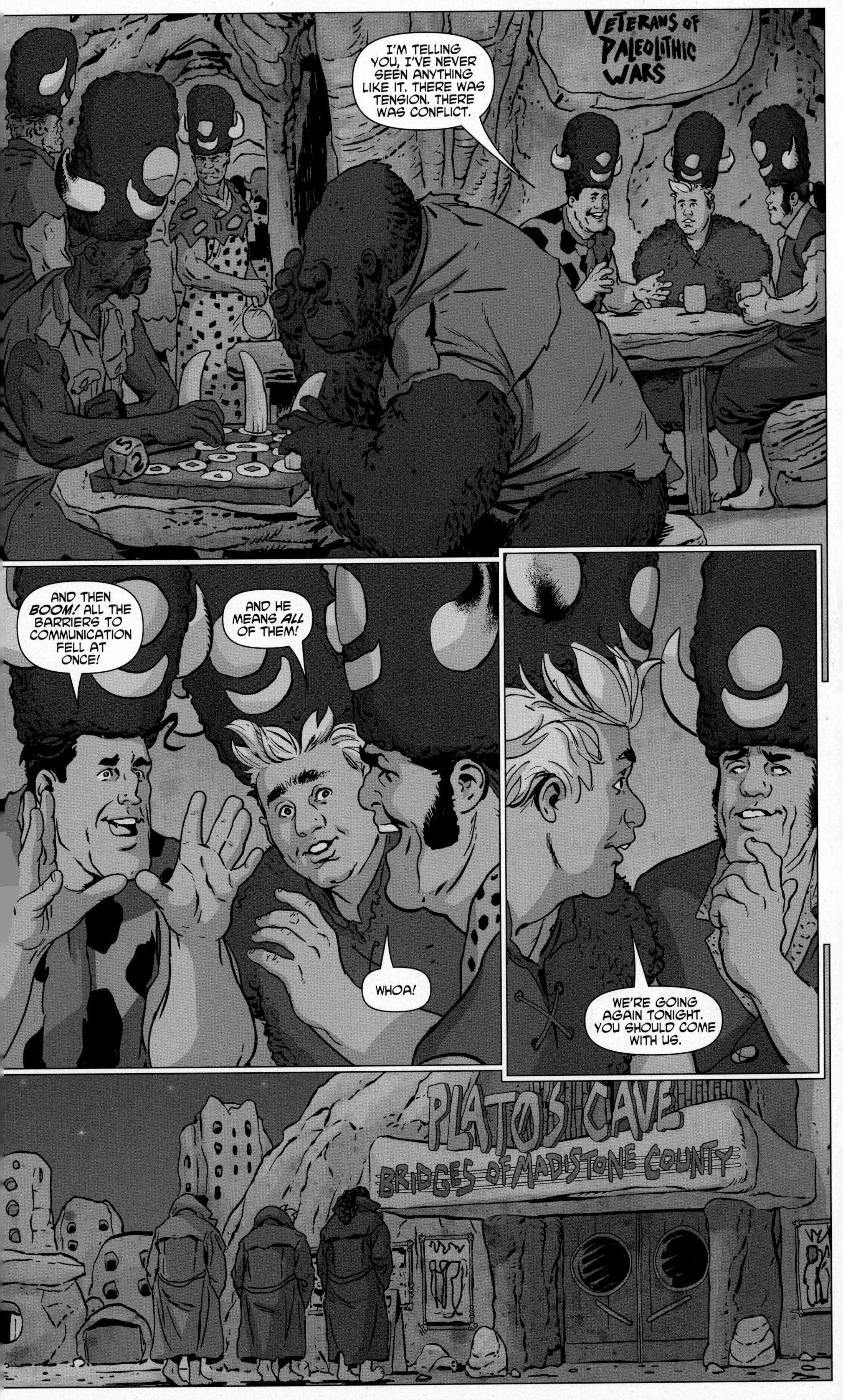
VETERANS OF PALEOLITHIC WARS
I'M TELLING YOU, I'VE NEVER SEEN ANYTHING LIKE IT. THERE WAS TENSION. THERE WAS CONFLICT.
AND THEN BOOM! ALL THE BARRIERS TO COMMUNICATION FELL AT ONCE!
AND HE MEANS ALL OF THEM!
WHOA!
WE'RE GOING AGAIN TONIGHT. YOU SHOULD COME WITH US.
PLATO'S CAVE
BRIDGES OF MADISTONE COUNTY

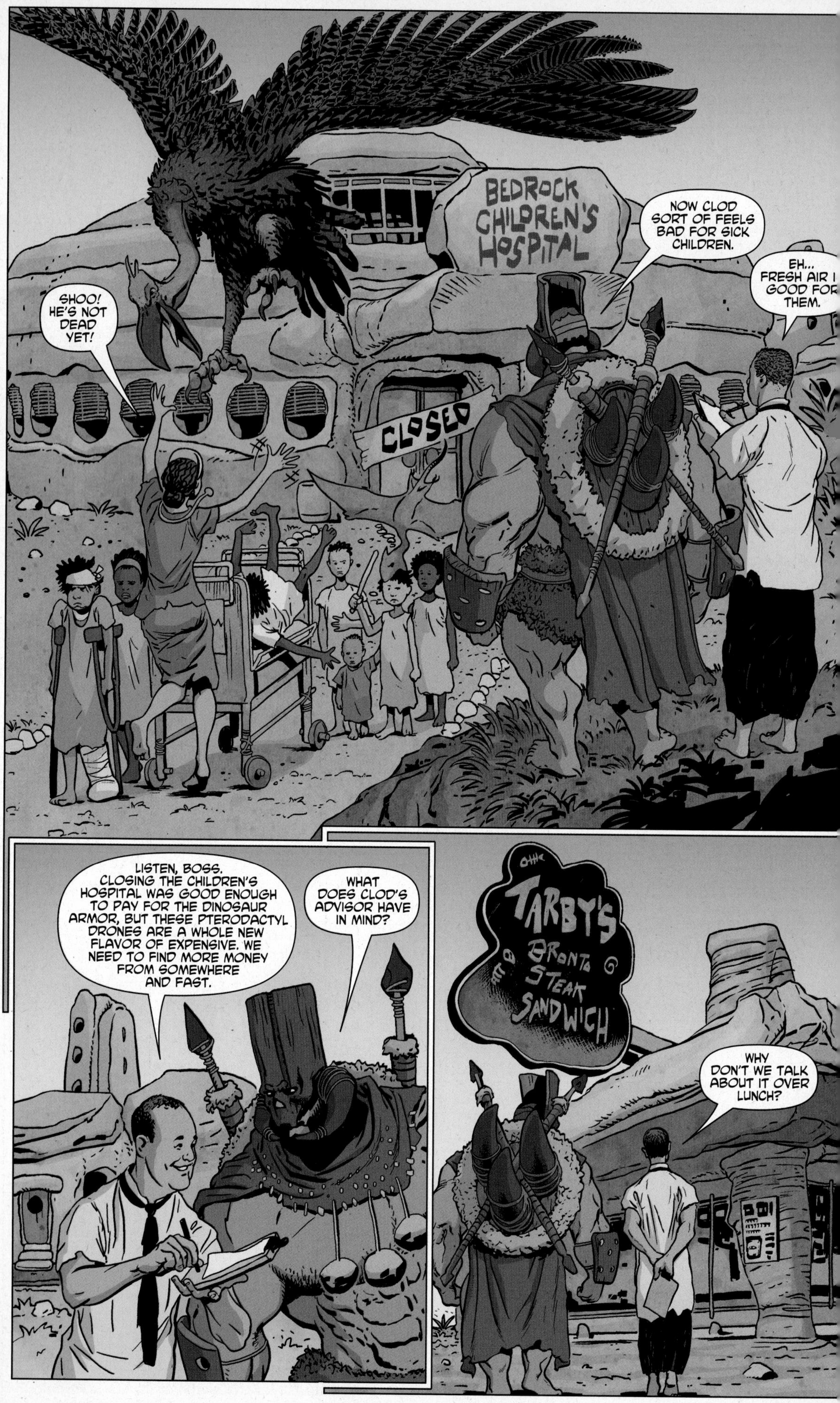
BEDROCK CHILDREN'S HOSPITAL
SHOO! HE'S NOT DEAD YET!
NOW CLOD SORT OF FEELS BAD FOR SICK CHILDREN.
EH... FRESH AIR I GOOD FOR THEM.
CLOSED
LISTEN, BOSS. CLOSING THE CHILDREN'S HOSPITAL WAS GOOD ENOUGH TO PAY FOR THE DINOSAUR ARMOR, BUT THESE PTERODACTYL DRONES ARE A WHOLE NEW FLAVOR OF EXPENSIVE. WE NEED TO FIND MORE MONEY FROM SOMEWHERE AND FAST.
WHAT DOES CLOD'S ADVISOR HAVE IN MIND?
TARBY'S BRONTO STEAK SANDWICH
WHY DON'T WE TALK ABOUT IT OVER LUNCH?

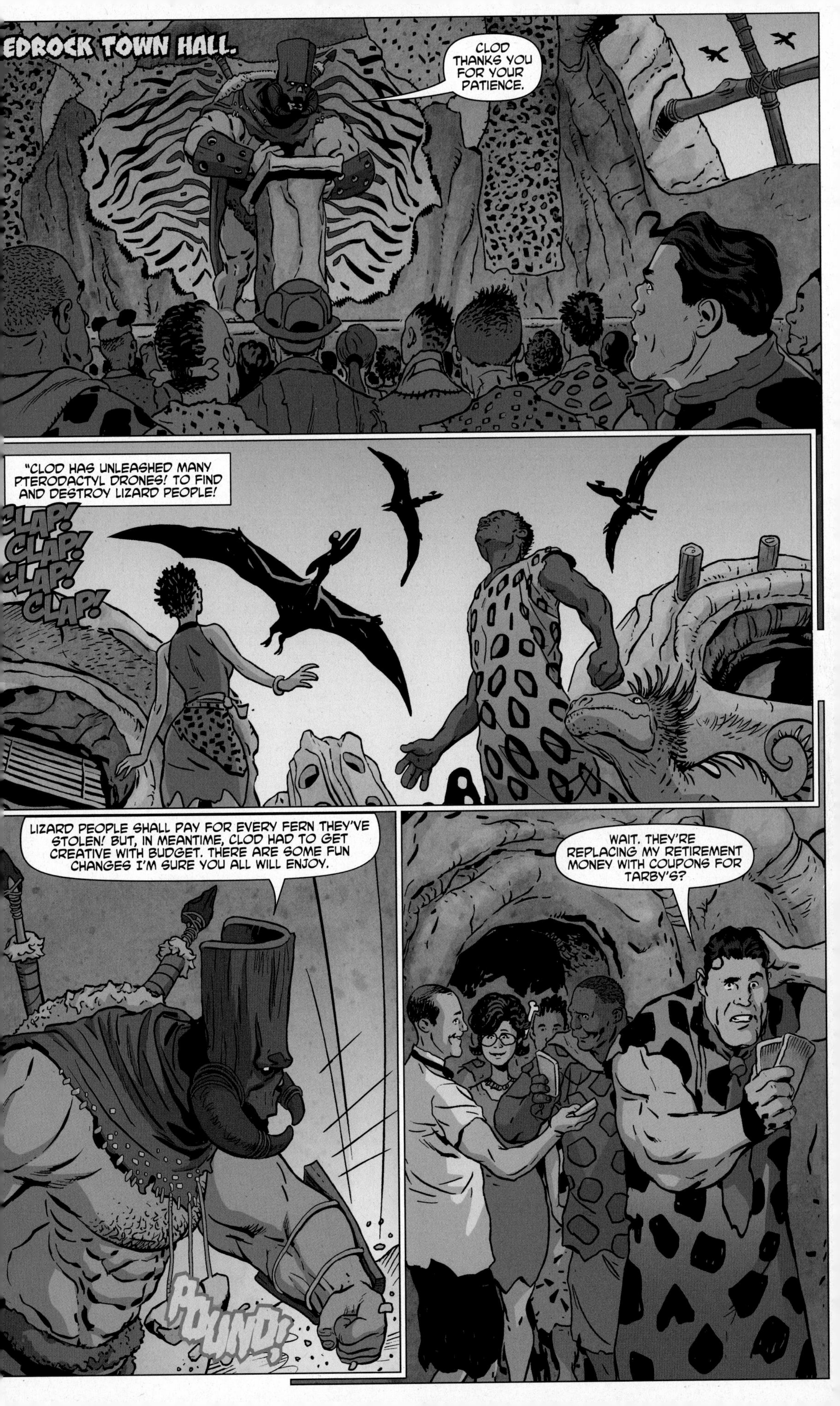
EDROCK TOWN HALL.
CLOD THANKS YOU FOR YOUR PATIENCE.
"CLOD HAS UNLEASHED MANY PTERODACTYL DRONES! TO FIND AND DESTROY LIZARD PEOPLE!
CLAP! CLAP! CLAP! CLAP!
LIZARD PEOPLE SHALL PAY FOR EVERY FERN THEY'VE STOLEN! BUT, IN MEANTIME, CLOD HAD TO GET CREATIVE WITH BUDGET. THERE ARE SOME FUN CHANGES I'M SURE YOU ALL WILL ENJOY.
POUND!
WAIT. THEY'RE REPLACING MY RETIREMENT MONEY WITH COUPONS FOR TARBY'S?

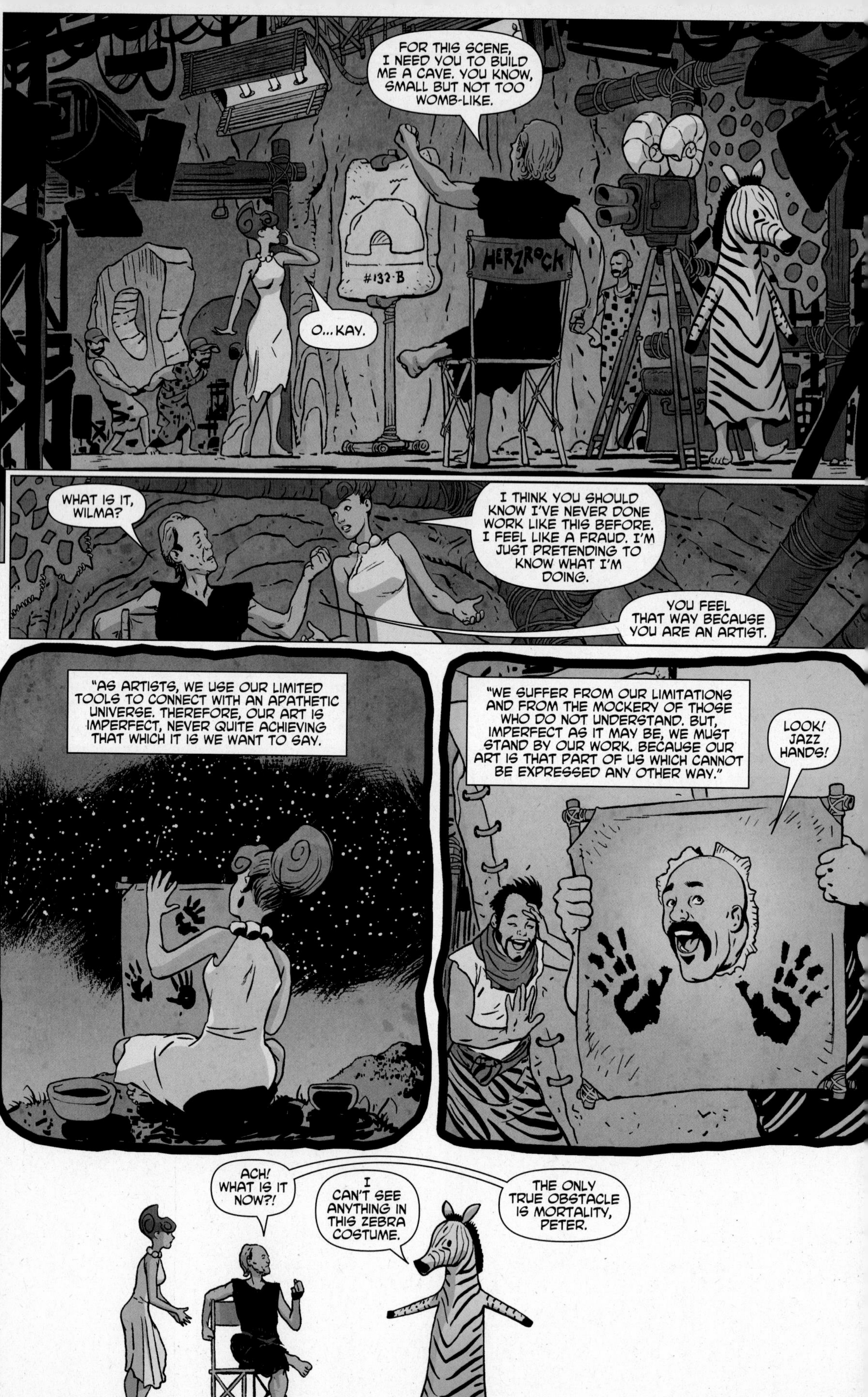
FOR THIS SCENE, I NEED YOU TO BUILD ME A CAVE. YOU KNOW, SMALL BUT NOT TOO WOMB-LIKE.
#132-B
HERZROCK
O...KAY.
WHAT IS IT, WILMA?
I THINK YOU SHOULD KNOW I'VE NEVER DONE WORK LIKE THIS BEFORE. I FEEL LIKE A FRAUD. I'M JUST PRETENDING TO KNOW WHAT I'M DOING.
YOU FEEL THAT WAY BECAUSE YOU ARE AN ARTIST.
"AS ARTISTS, WE USE OUR LIMITED TOOLS TO CONNECT WITH AN APATHETIC UNIVERSE. THEREFORE, OUR ART IS IMPERFECT, NEVER QUITE ACHIEVING THAT WHICH IT IS WE WANT TO SAY.
"WE SUFFER FROM OUR LIMITATIONS AND FROM THE MOCKERY OF THOSE WHO DO NOT UNDERSTAND. BUT, IMPERFECT AS IT MAY BE, WE MUST STAND BY OUR WORK. BECAUSE OUR ART IS THAT PART OF US WHICH CANNOT BE EXPRESSED ANY OTHER WAY."
LOOK! JAZZ HANDS!
ACH! WHAT IS IT NOW?!
I CAN'T SEE ANYTHING IN THIS ZEBRA COSTUME.
THE ONLY TRUE OBSTACLE IS MORTALITY, PETER.

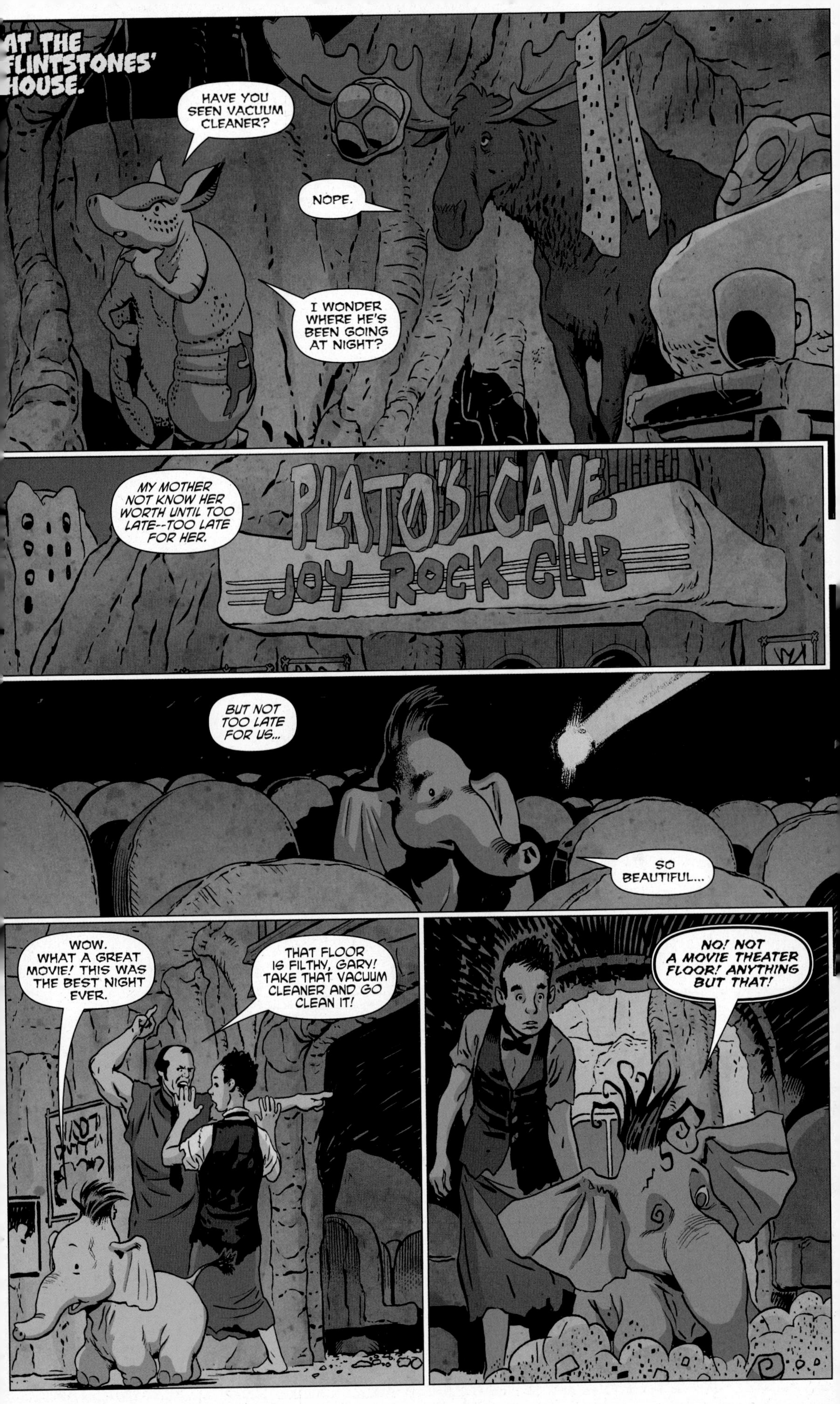
AT THE FLINTSTONES' HOUSE.
HAVE YOU SEEN VACUUM CLEANER?
NOPE.
I WONDER WHERE HE'S BEEN GOING AT NIGHT?
MY MOTHER NOT KNOW HER WORTH UNTIL TOO LATE--TOO LATE FOR HER.
PLATO'S CAVE
JOY ROCK CLUB
BUT NOT TOO LATE FOR US...
SO BEAUTIFUL...
WOW. WHAT A GREAT MOVIE! THIS WAS THE BEST NIGHT EVER.
THAT FLOOR IS FILTHY, GARY! TAKE THAT VACUUM CLEANER AND GO CLEAN IT!
NO! NOT A MOVIE THEATER FLOOR! ANYTHING BUT THAT!

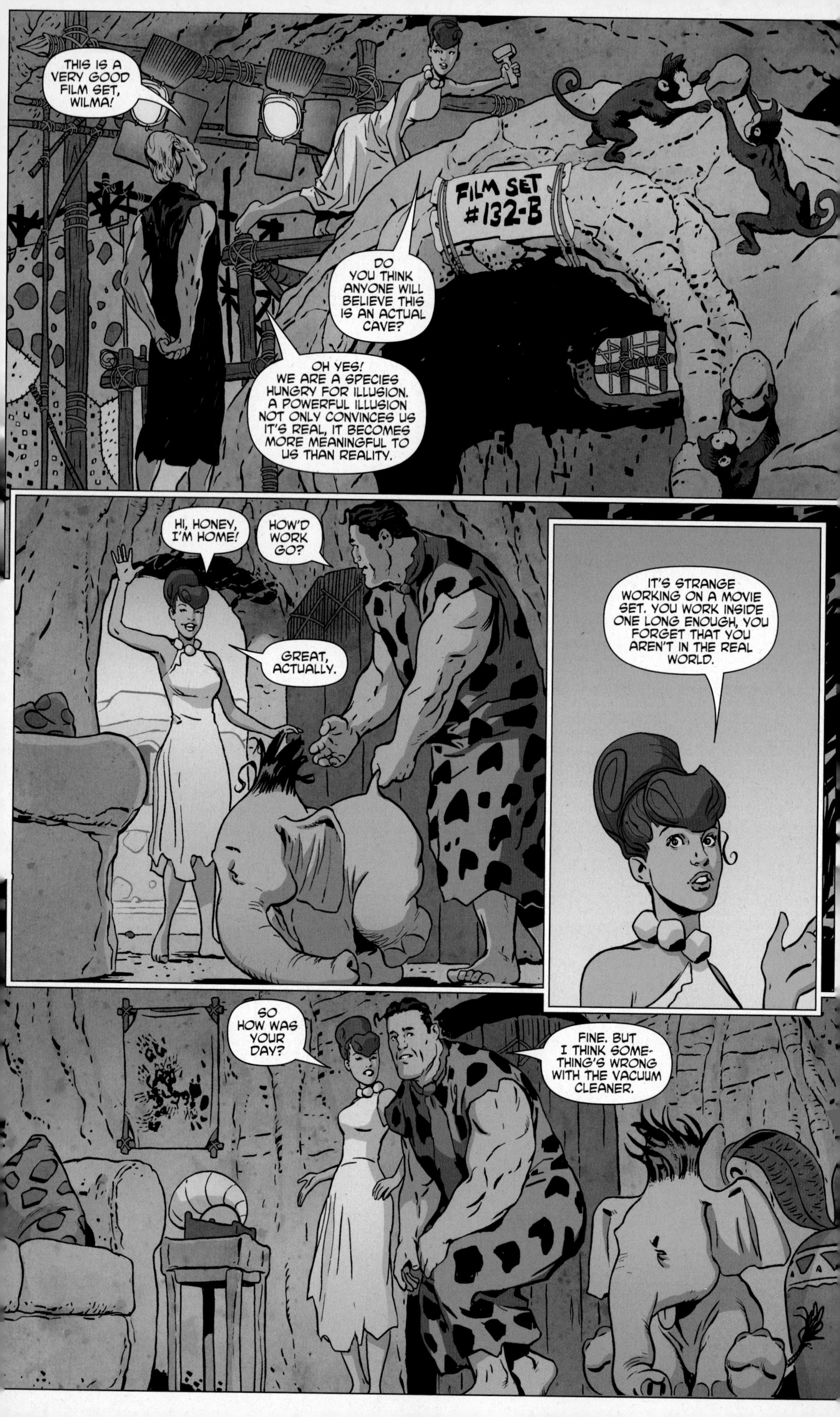
THIS IS A VERY GOOD FILM SET, WILMA!
FILM SET #132-B
DO YOU THINK ANYONE WILL BELIEVE THIS IS AN ACTUAL CAVE?
OH YES! WE ARE A SPECIES HUNGRY FOR ILLUSION. A POWERFUL ILLUSION NOT ONLY CONVINCES US IT'S REAL, IT BECOMES MORE MEANINGFUL TO US THAN REALITY.
HI, HONEY, I'M HOME!
HOW'D WORK GO?
GREAT, ACTUALLY.
IT'S STRANGE WORKING ON A MOVIE SET. YOU WORK INSIDE ONE LONG ENOUGH, YOU FORGET THAT YOU AREN'T IN THE REAL WORLD.
SO HOW WAS YOUR DAY?
FINE. BUT I THINK SOMETHING'S WRONG WITH THE VACUUM CLEANER.

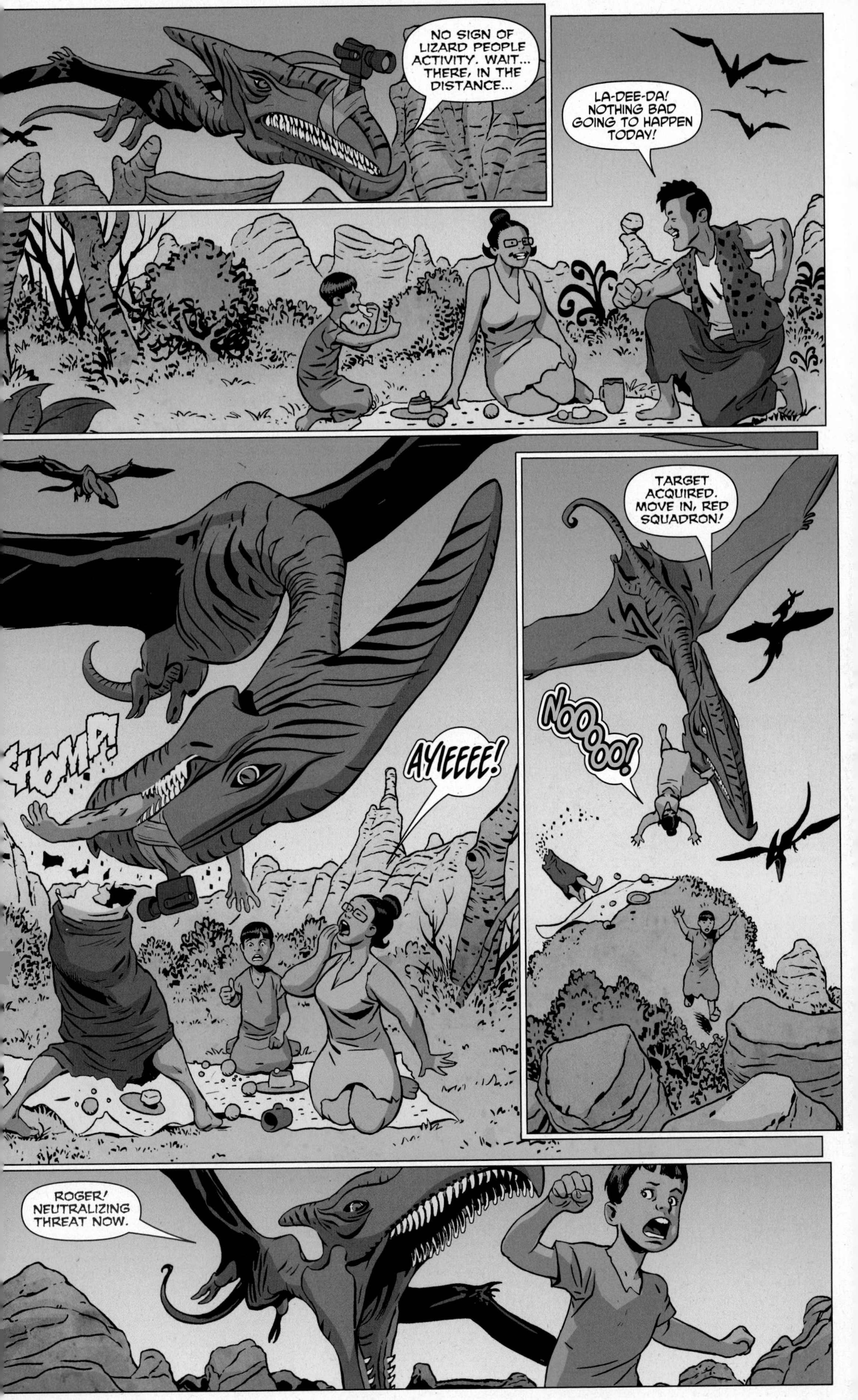
NO SIGN OF LIZARD PEOPLE ACTIVITY. WAIT... THERE, IN THE DISTANCE...
LA-DEE-DA! NOTHING BAD GOING TO HAPPEN TODAY!
CHOMP!
AYIEEEE!
TARGET ACQUIRED. MOVE IN, RED SQUADRON!
NOOoooo!
ROGER! NEUTRALIZING THREAT NOW.

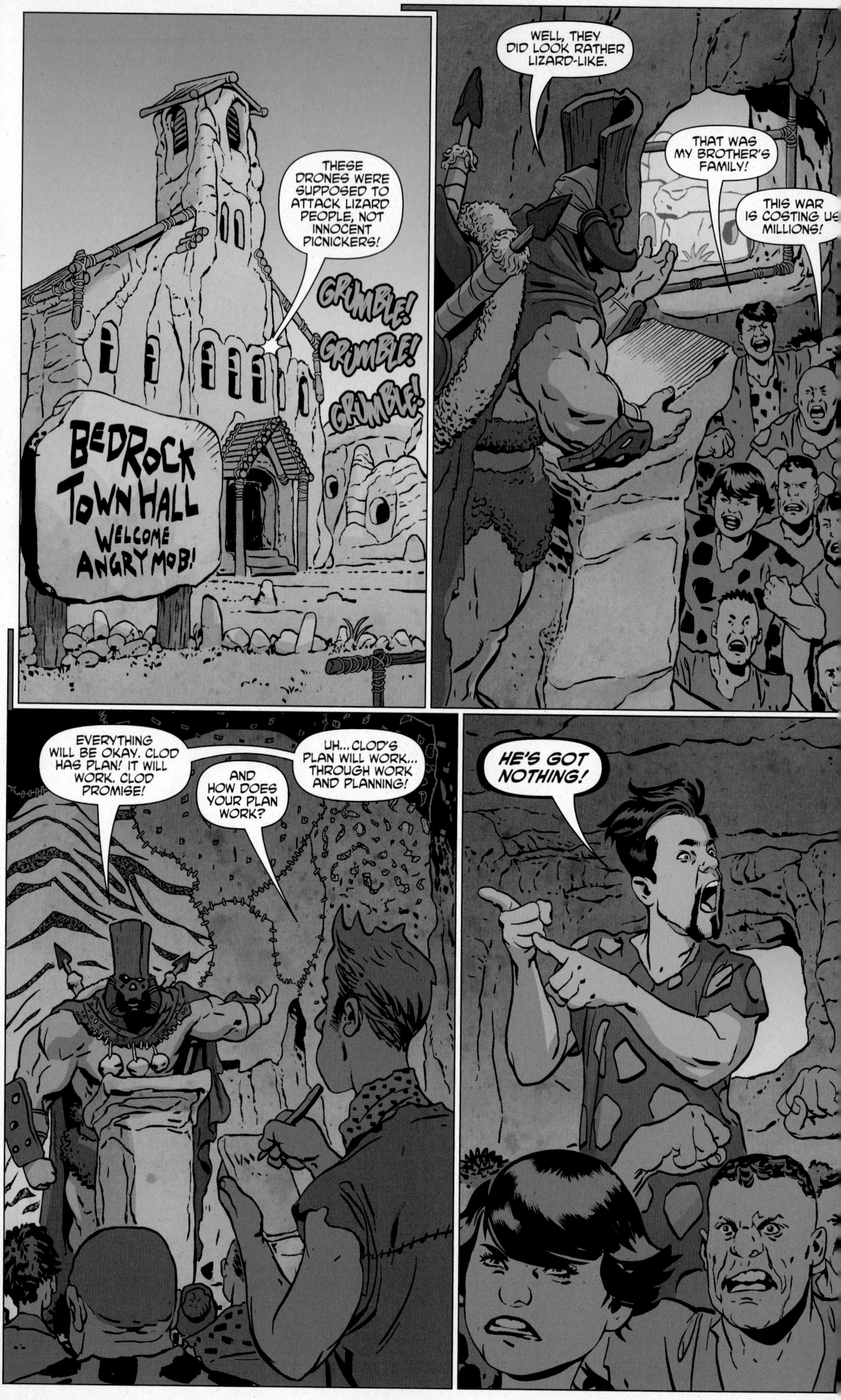
BEDROCK TOWN HALL WELCOME ANGRY MOB!
THESE DRONES WERE SUPPOSED TO ATTACK LIZARD PEOPLE, NOT INNOCENT PICNICKERS!
GRUMBLE! GRUMBLE! GRUMBLE!
WELL, THEY DID LOOK RATHER LIZARD-LIKE.
THAT WAS MY BROTHER'S FAMILY!
THIS WAR IS COSTING US MILLIONS!
EVERYTHING WILL BE OKAY. CLOD HAS PLAN! IT WILL WORK. CLOD PROMISE!
AND HOW DOES YOUR PLAN WORK?
UH... CLOD'S PLAN WILL WORK... THROUGH WORK AND PLANNING!
HE'S GOT NOTHING!

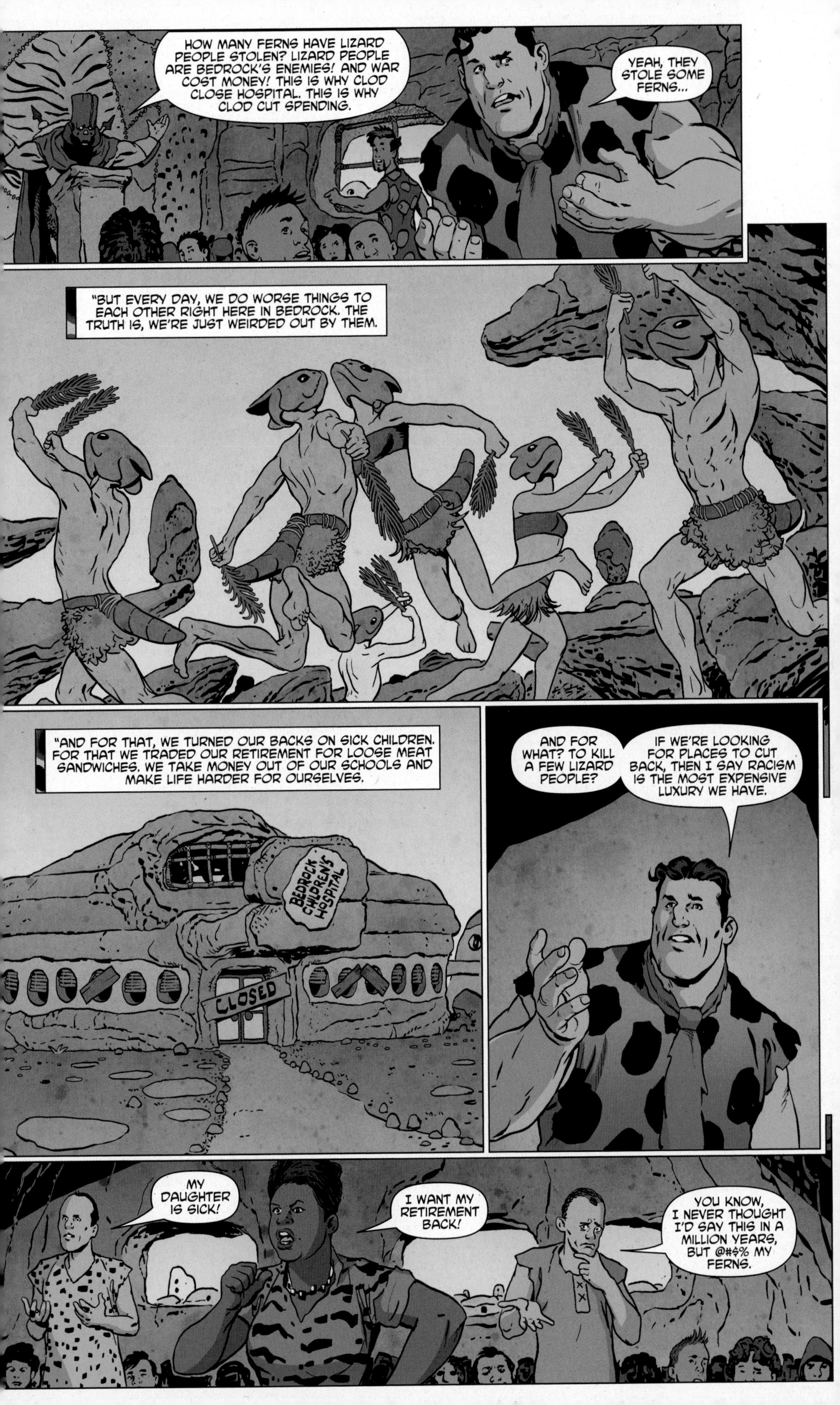
HOW MANY FERNS HAVE LIZARD PEOPLE STOLEN? LIZARD PEOPLE ARE BEDROCK'S ENEMIES! AND WAR COST MONEY! THIS IS WHY CLOD CLOSE HOSPITAL. THIS IS WHY CLOD CUT SPENDING.
YEAH, THEY STOLE SOME FERNS...
"BUT EVERY DAY, WE DO WORSE THINGS TO EACH OTHER RIGHT HERE IN BEDROCK. THE TRUTH IS, WE'RE JUST WEIRDED OUT BY THEM.
"AND FOR THAT, WE TURNED OUR BACKS ON SICK CHILDREN. FOR THAT WE TRADED OUR RETIREMENT FOR LOOSE MEAT SANDWICHES. WE TAKE MONEY OUT OF OUR SCHOOLS AND MAKE LIFE HARDER FOR OURSELVES.
BEDROCK CHILDREN'S HOSPITAL
CLOSED
AND FOR WHAT? TO KILL A FEW LIZARD PEOPLE?
IF WE'RE LOOKING FOR PLACES TO CUT BACK, THEN I SAY RACISM IS THE MOST EXPENSIVE LUXURY WE HAVE.
MY DAUGHTER IS SICK!
I WANT MY RETIREMENT BACK!
YOU KNOW, I NEVER THOUGHT I'D SAY THIS IN A MILLION YEARS, BUT @#$% MY FERNS.

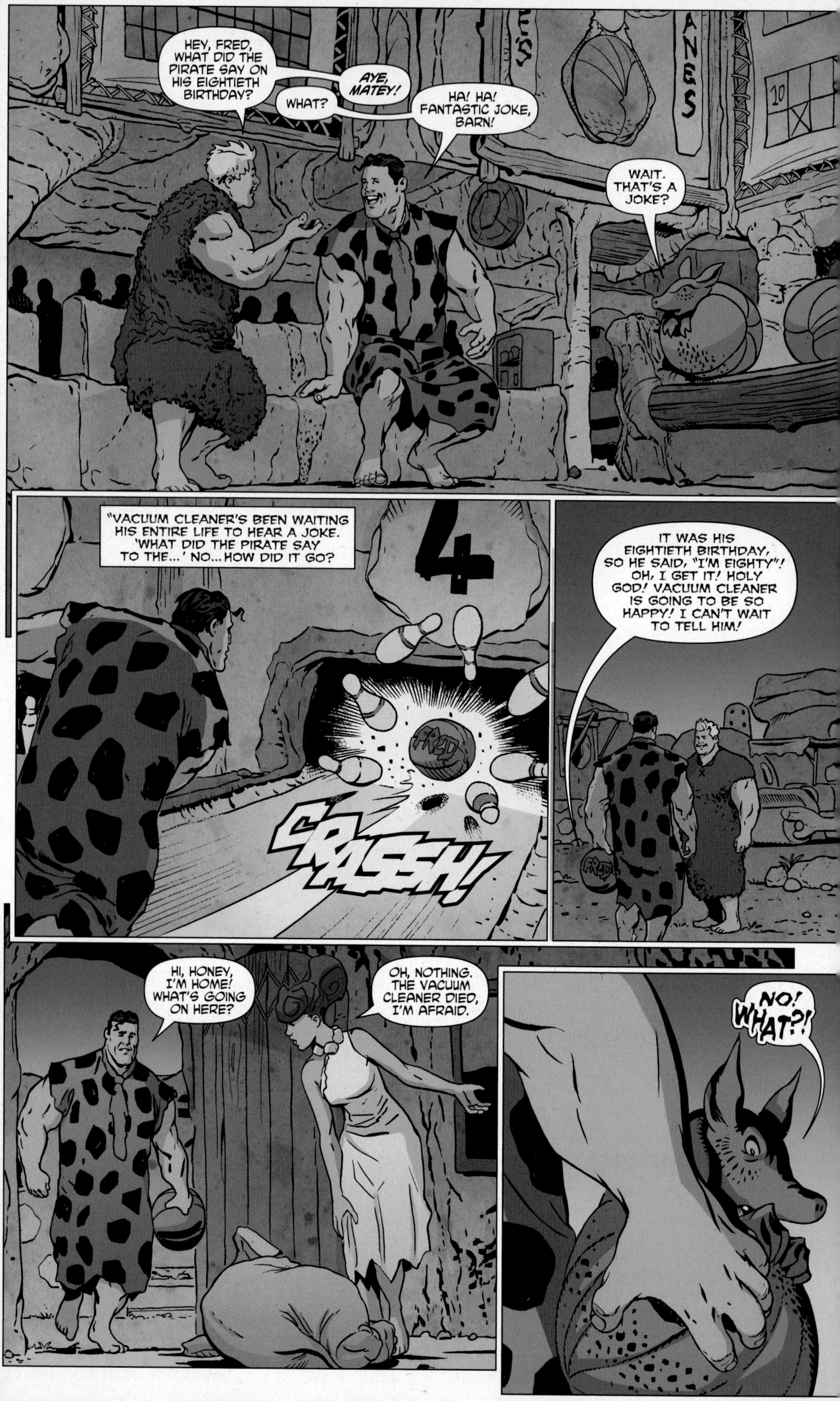
HEY, FRED, WHAT DID THE PIRATE SAY ON HIS EIGHTIETH BIRTHDAY?
WHAT?
AYE, MATEY!
HA! HA! FANTASTIC JOKE, BARN!
WAIT. THAT'S A JOKE?
"VACUUM CLEANER'S BEEN WAITING HIS ENTIRE LIFE TO HEAR A JOKE. 'WHAT DID THE PIRATE SAY TO THE...' NO...HOW DID IT GO?
4
FRED
CRASSH!
IT WAS HIS EIGHTIETH BIRTHDAY, SO HE SAID, "I'M EIGHTY"! OH, I GET IT! HOLY GOD! VACUUM CLEANER IS GOING TO BE SO HAPPY! I CAN'T WAIT TO TELL HIM!
FRED
HI, HONEY, I'M HOME! WHAT'S GOING ON HERE?
OH, NOTHING. THE VACUUM CLEANER DIED, I'M AFRAID.
NO! WHAT?!

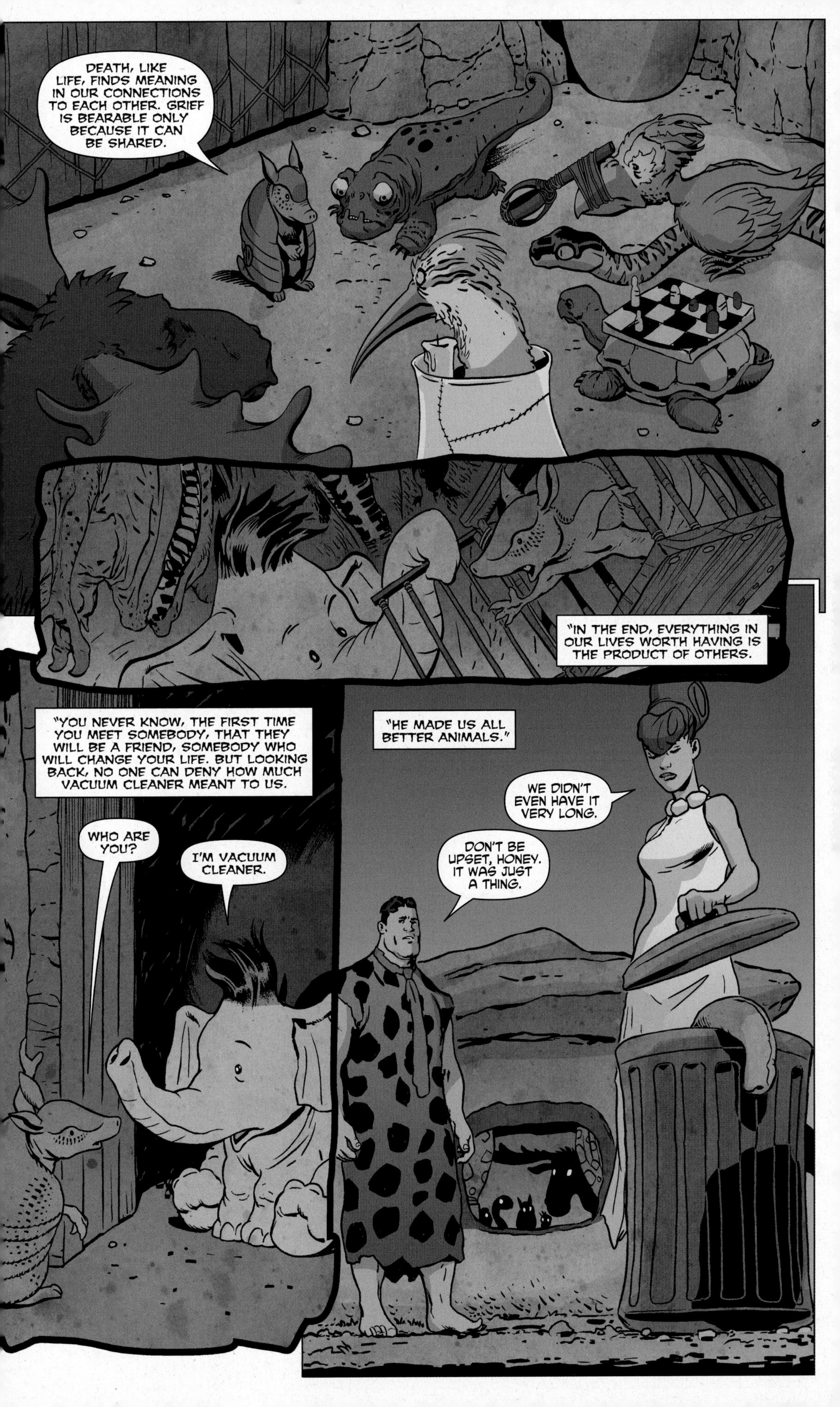

DEATH, LIKE LIFE, FINDS MEANING IN OUR CONNECTIONS TO EACH OTHER. GRIEF IS BEARABLE ONLY BECAUSE IT CAN BE SHARED.
"IN THE END, EVERYTHING IN OUR LIVES WORTH HAVING IS THE PRODUCT OF OTHERS.
"YOU NEVER KNOW, THE FIRST TIME YOU MEET SOMEBODY, THAT THEY WILL BE A FRIEND, SOMEBODY WHO WILL CHANGE YOUR LIFE. BUT LOOKING BACK, NO ONE CAN DENY HOW MUCH VACUUM CLEANER MEANT TO US.
WHO ARE YOU?
I'M VACUUM CLEANER.
"HE MADE US ALL BETTER ANIMALS."
WE DIDN'T EVEN HAVE IT VERY LONG.
DON'T BE UPSET, HONEY. IT WAS JUST A THING.

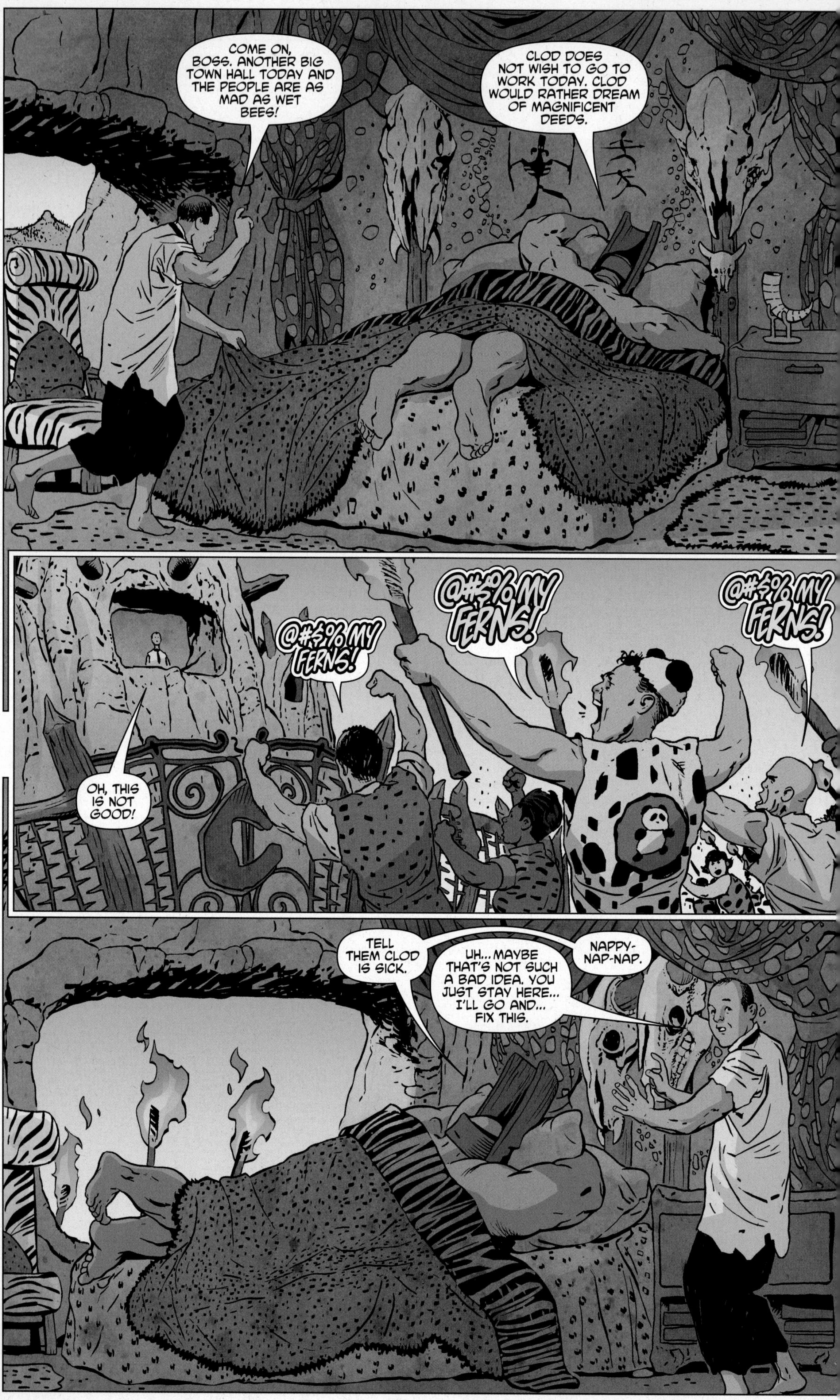
COME ON, BOSS. ANOTHER BIG TOWN HALL TODAY AND THE PEOPLE ARE AS MAD AS WET BEES!
CLOD DOES NOT WISH TO GO TO WORK TODAY. CLOD WOULD RATHER DREAM OF MAGNIFICENT DEEDS.
OH, THIS IS NOT GOOD!
@#$% MY FERNS!
@#$% MY FERNS!
@#$% MY FERNS!
TELL THEM CLOD IS SICK.
UH... MAYBE THAT'S NOT SUCH A BAD IDEA. YOU JUST STAY HERE... I'LL GO AND... FIX THIS.
NAPPY-NAP-NAP.

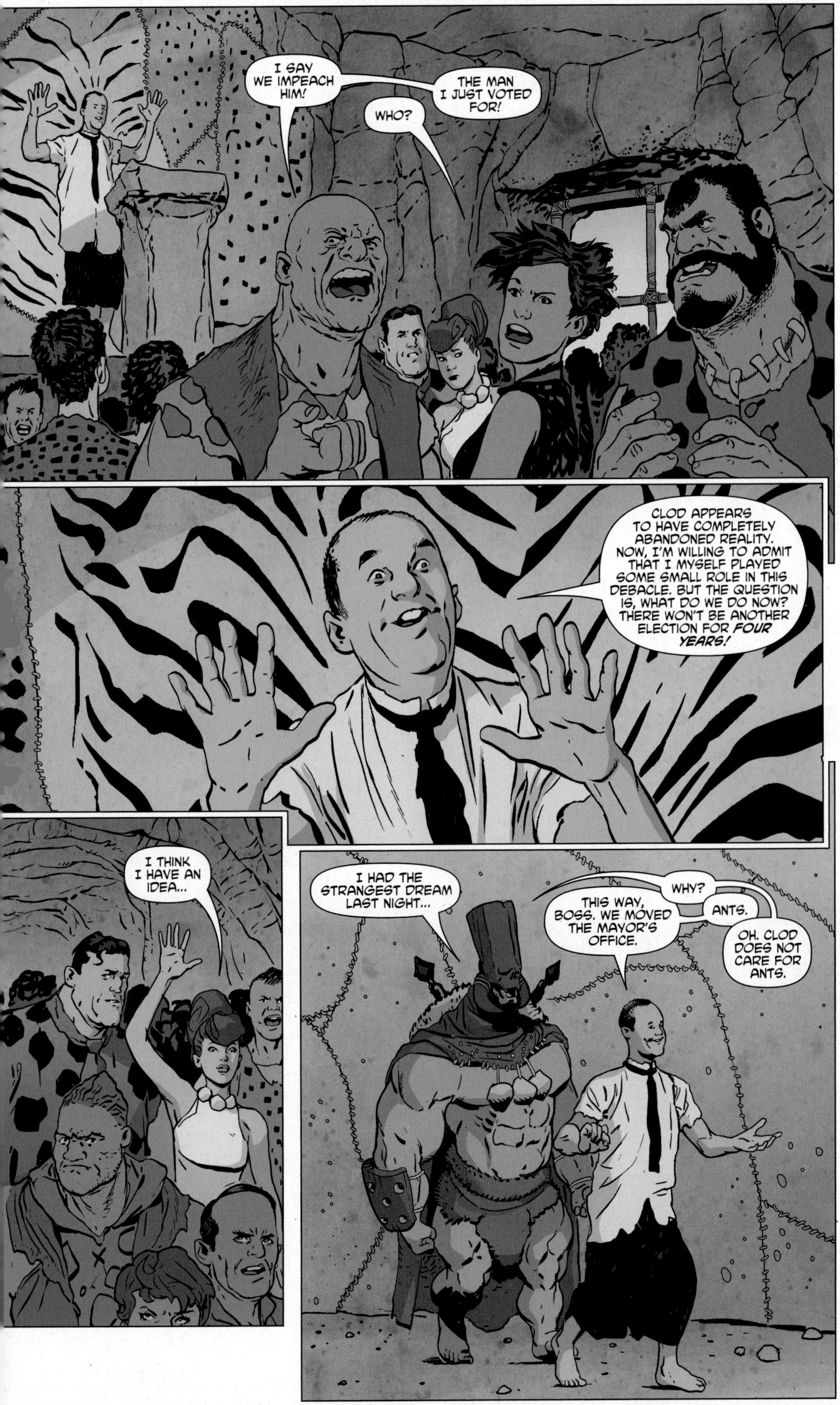

I SAY WE IMPEACH HIM!
WHO?
THE MAN I JUST VOTED FOR!
CLOD APPEARS TO HAVE COMPLETELY ABANDONED REALITY. NOW, I'M WILLING TO ADMIT THAT I MYSELF PLAYED SOME SMALL ROLE IN THIS DEBACLE. BUT THE QUESTION IS, WHAT DO WE DO NOW? THERE WON'T BE ANOTHER ELECTION FOR *FOUR YEARS!*
I THINK I HAVE AN IDEA...
I HAD THE STRANGEST DREAM LAST NIGHT...
THIS WAY, BOSS. WE MOVED THE MAYOR'S OFFICE.
WHY?
ANTS.
OH. CLOD DOES NOT CARE FOR ANTS.

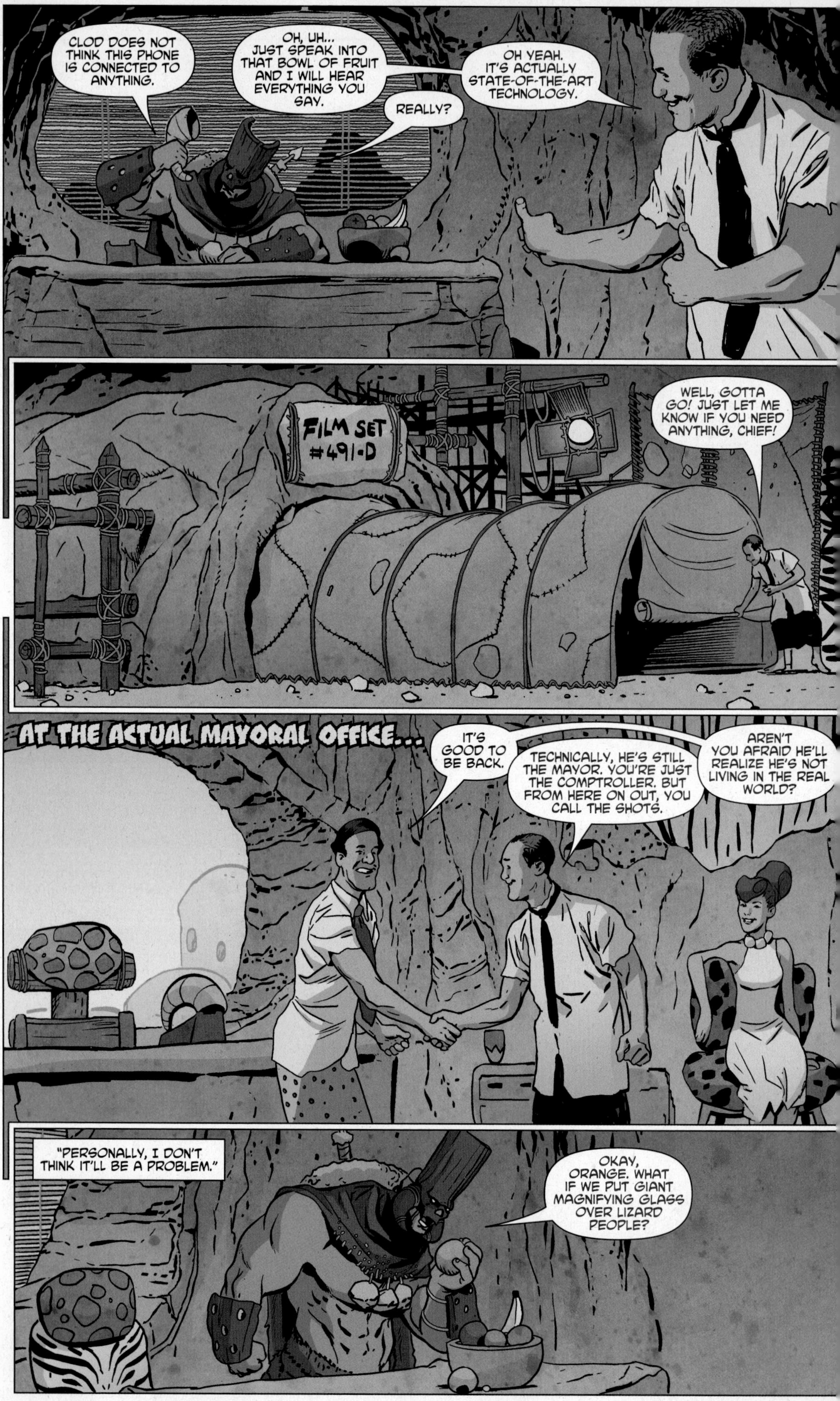
CLOD DOES NOT THINK THIS PHONE IS CONNECTED TO ANYTHING.
OH, UH... JUST SPEAK INTO THAT BOWL OF FRUIT AND I WILL HEAR EVERYTHING YOU SAY.
REALLY?
OH YEAH. IT'S ACTUALLY STATE-OF-THE-ART TECHNOLOGY.
FILM SET #491-D
WELL, GOTTA GO! JUST LET ME KNOW IF YOU NEED ANYTHING, CHIEF!
AT THE ACTUAL MAYORAL OFFICE...
IT'S GOOD TO BE BACK.
TECHNICALLY, HE'S STILL THE MAYOR. YOU'RE JUST THE COMPTROLLER. BUT FROM HERE ON OUT, YOU CALL THE SHOTS.
AREN'T YOU AFRAID HE'LL REALIZE HE'S NOT LIVING IN THE REAL WORLD?
"PERSONALLY, I DON'T THINK IT'LL BE A PROBLEM."
OKAY, ORANGE. WHAT IF WE PUT GIANT MAGNIFYING GLASS OVER LIZARD PEOPLE?

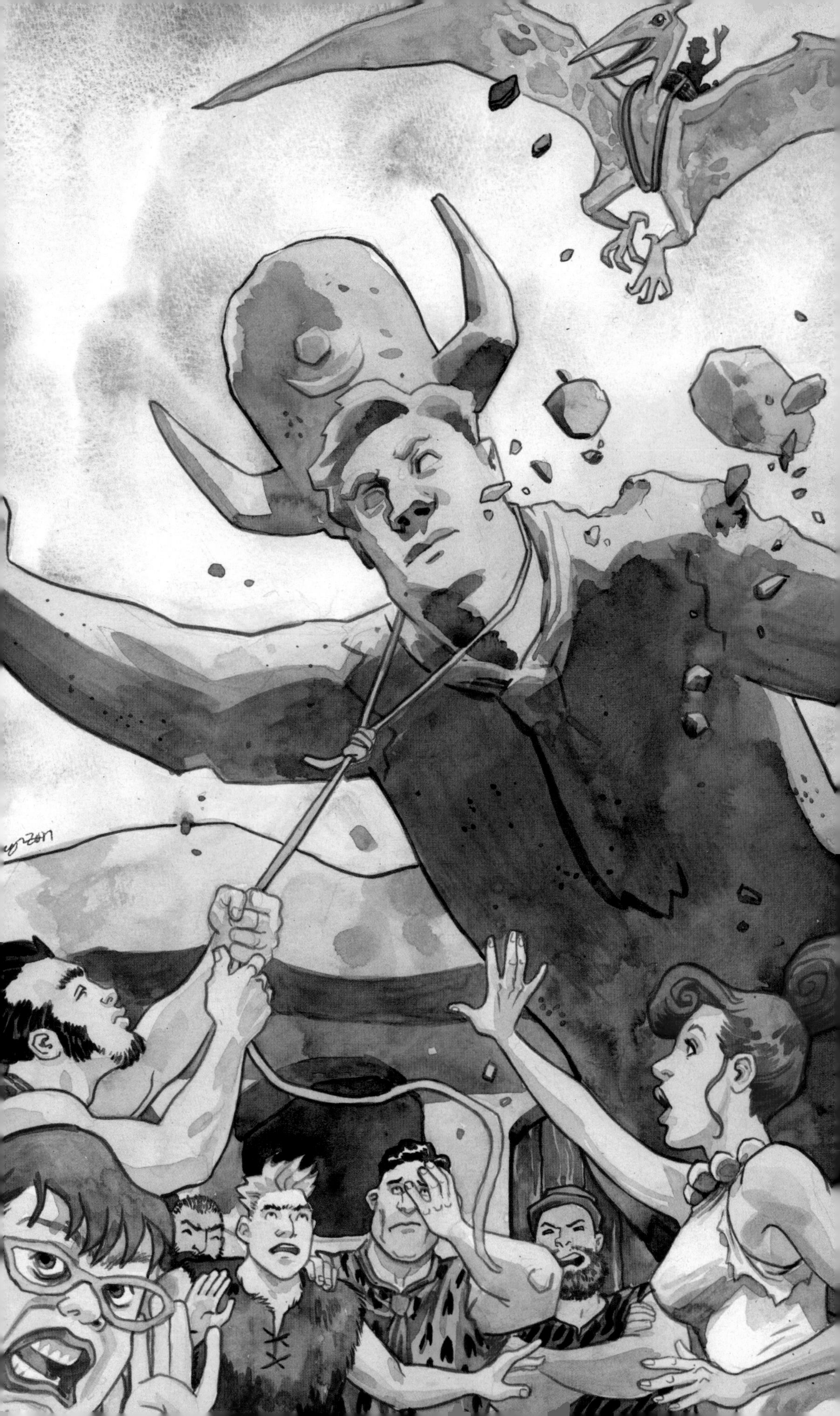

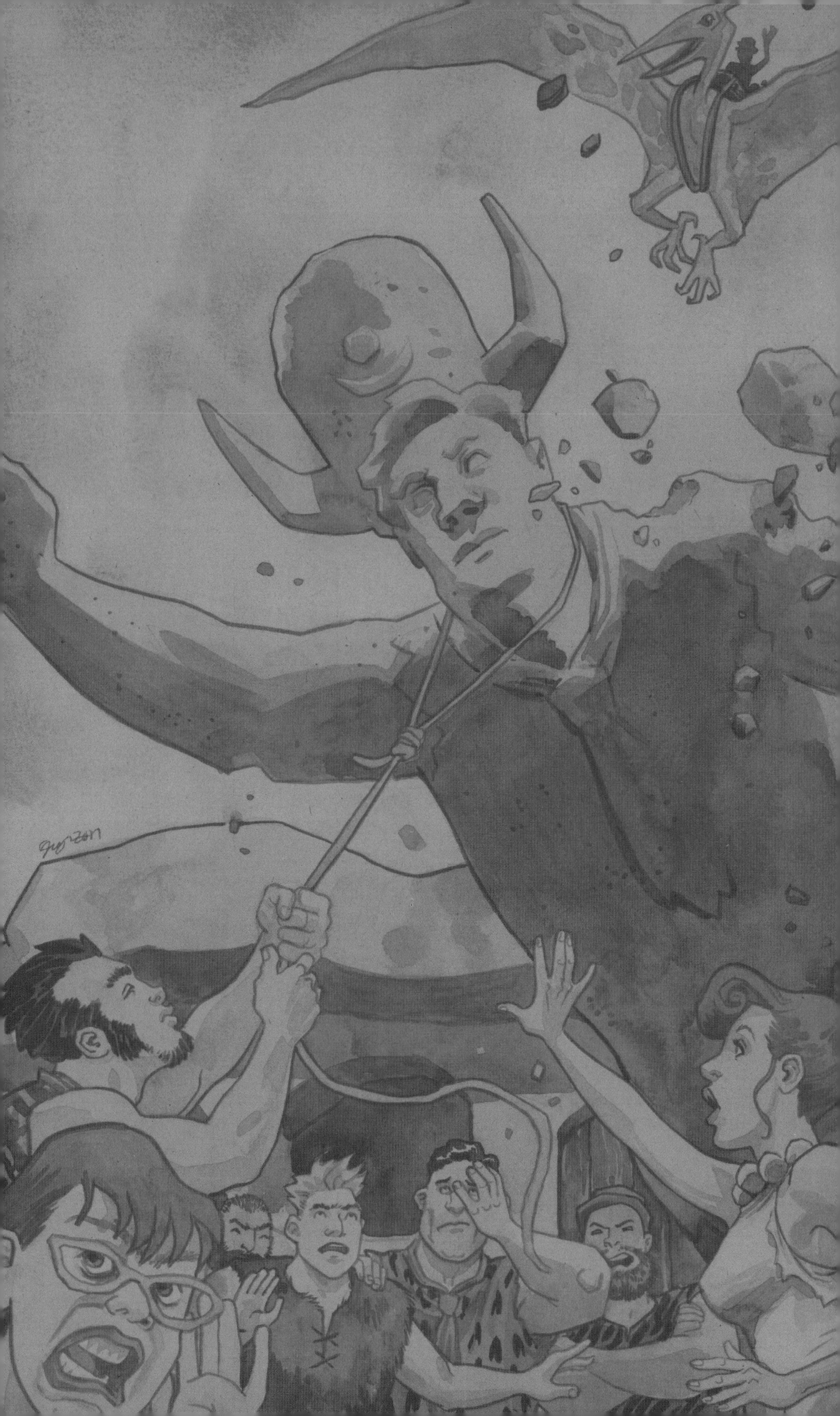

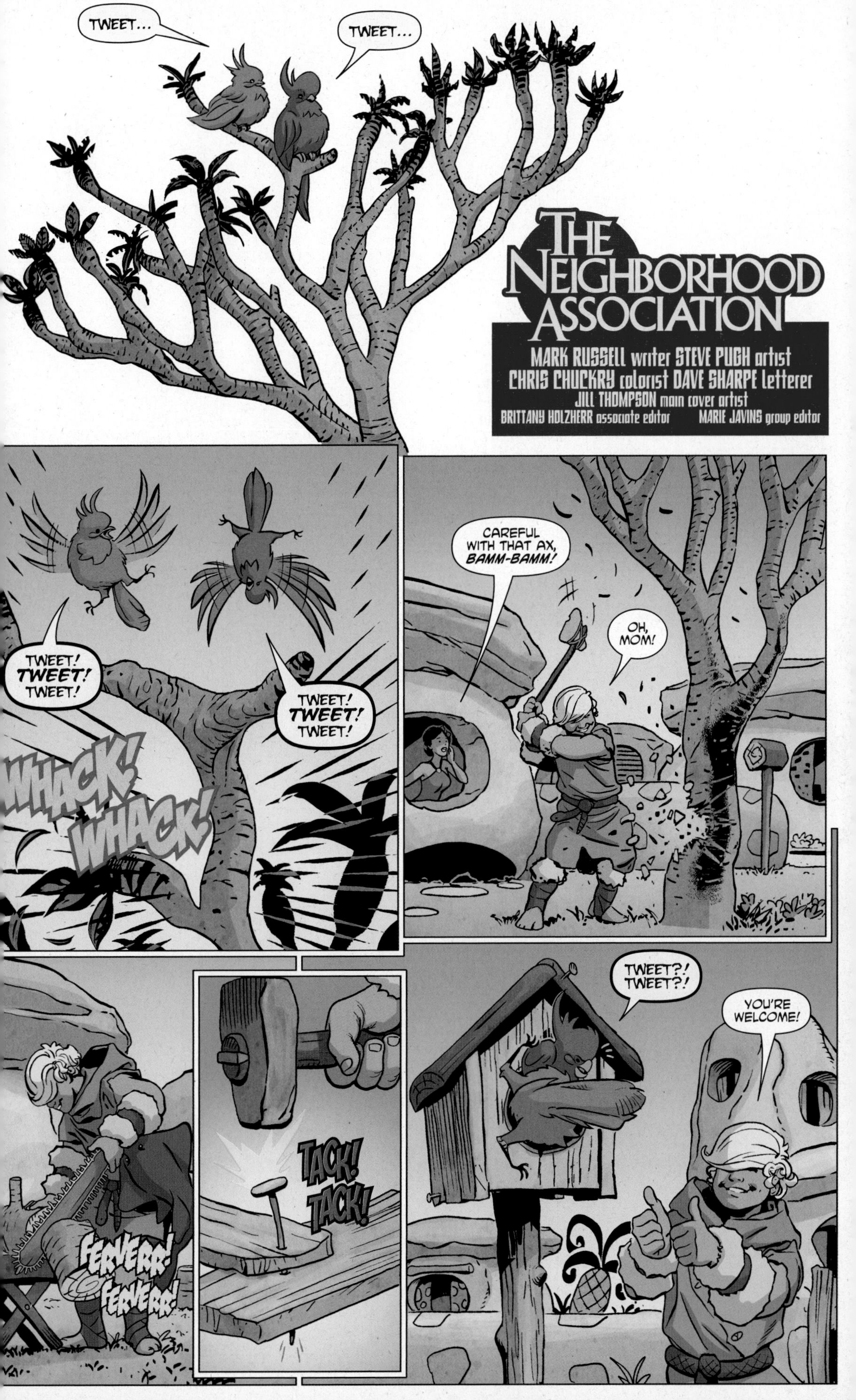
TWEET...
TWEET...
THE NEIGHBORHOOD ASSOCIATION
MARK RUSSELL writer STEVE PUGH artist
CHRIS CHUCKRY colorist DAVE SHARPE letterer
JILL THOMPSON main cover artist
BRITTANY HOLZHERR associate editor MARIE JAVINS group editor
TWEET! TWEET! TWEET!
TWEET! TWEET! TWEET!
WHACK! WHACK!
CAREFUL WITH THAT AX, BAMM-BAMM!
OH, MOM!
FERVERR! FERVERR!
TACK! TACK!
TWEET?! TWEET?!
YOU'RE WELCOME!

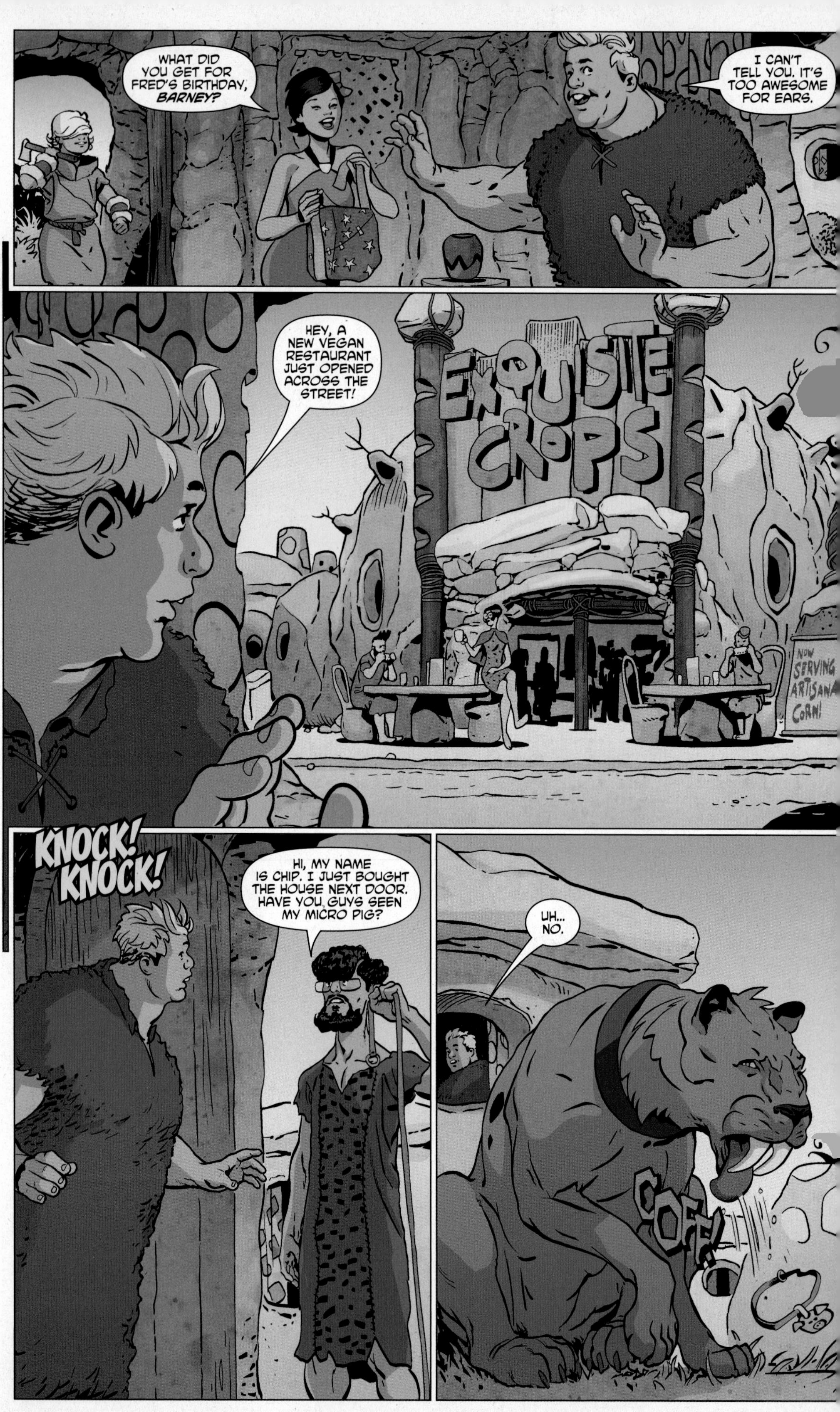
WHAT DID YOU GET FOR FRED'S BIRTHDAY, BARNEY?
I CAN'T TELL YOU. IT'S TOO AWESOME FOR EARS.
HEY, A NEW VEGAN RESTAURANT JUST OPENED ACROSS THE STREET!
EXQUISITE CROPS
NOW SERVING ARTISANAL CORN!
KNOCK! KNOCK!
HI, MY NAME IS CHIP. I JUST BOUGHT THE HOUSE NEXT DOOR. HAVE YOU GUYS SEEN MY MICRO PIG?
UH... NO.
COFF!

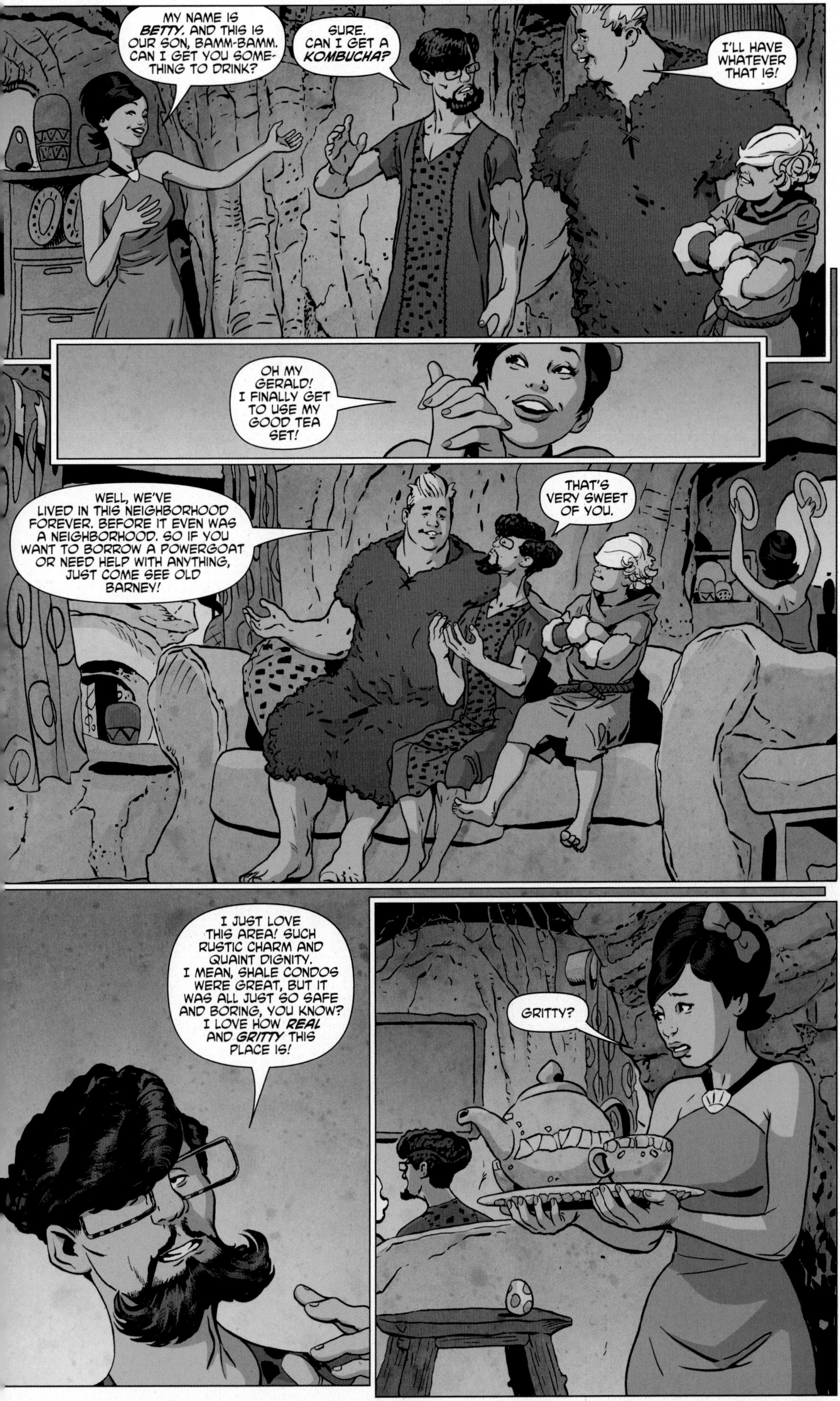

MY NAME IS BETTY. AND THIS IS OUR SON, BAMM-BAMM. CAN I GET YOU SOMETHING TO DRINK?
SURE. CAN I GET A KOMBUCHA?
I'LL HAVE WHATEVER THAT IS!
OH MY GERALD! I FINALLY GET TO USE MY GOOD TEA SET!
WELL, WE'VE LIVED IN THIS NEIGHBORHOOD FOREVER. BEFORE IT EVEN WAS A NEIGHBORHOOD. SO IF YOU WANT TO BORROW A POWERGOAT OR NEED HELP WITH ANYTHING, JUST COME SEE OLD BARNEY!
THAT'S VERY SWEET OF YOU.
I JUST LOVE THIS AREA! SUCH RUSTIC CHARM AND QUAINT DIGNITY. I MEAN, SHALE CONDOS WERE GREAT, BUT IT WAS ALL JUST SO SAFE AND BORING, YOU KNOW? I LOVE HOW REAL AND GRITTY THIS PLACE IS!
GRITTY?

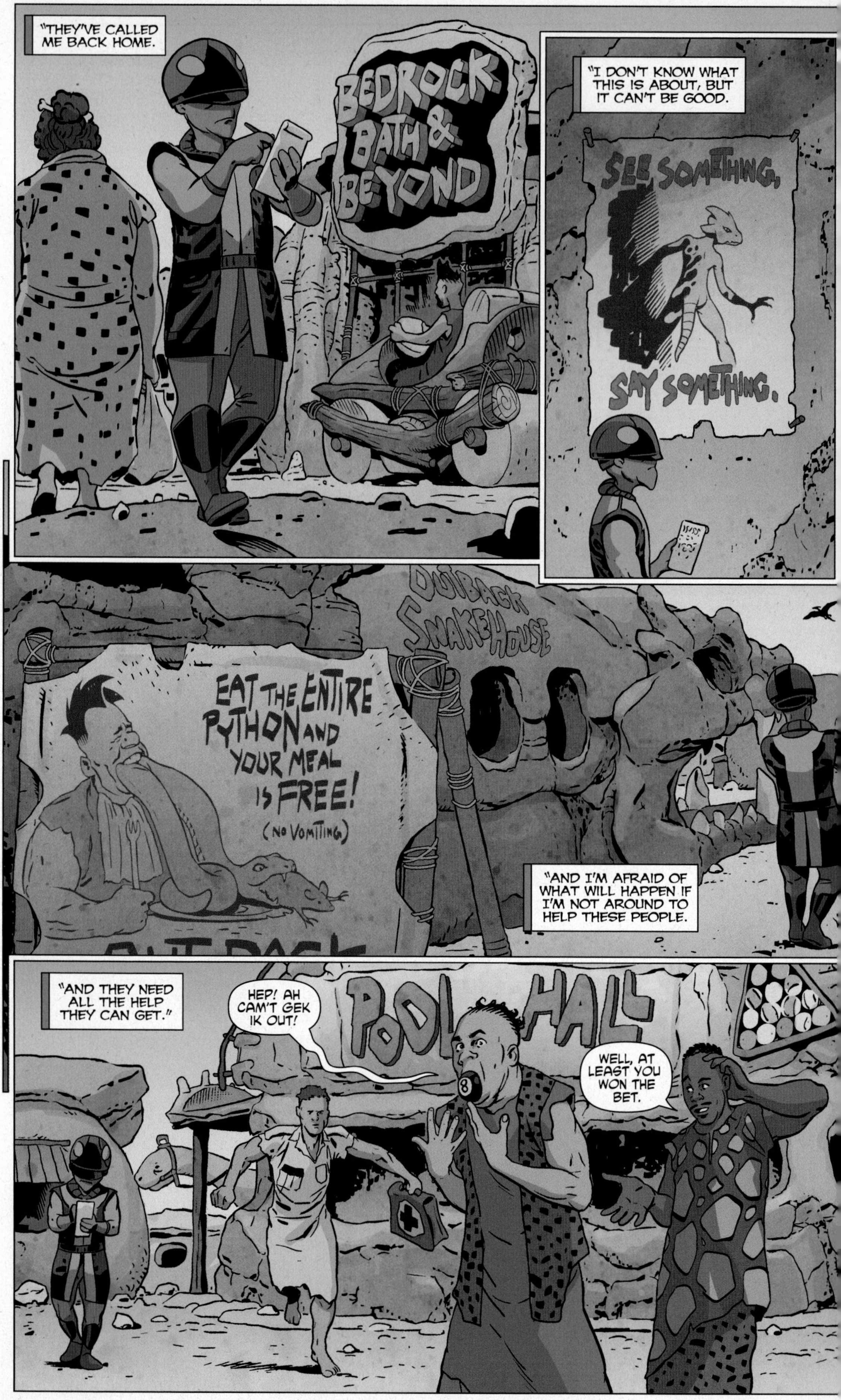
"THEY'VE CALLED ME BACK HOME.
BEDROCK BATH & BEYOND
"I DON'T KNOW WHAT THIS IS ABOUT, BUT IT CAN'T BE GOOD.
SEE SOMETHING, SAY SOMETHING.
OUTBACK SNAKEHOUSE
EAT THE ENTIRE PYTHON AND YOUR MEAL IS FREE!
(NO VOMITING)
"AND I'M AFRAID OF WHAT WILL HAPPEN IF I'M NOT AROUND TO HELP THESE PEOPLE.
"AND THEY NEED ALL THE HELP THEY CAN GET."
HEP! AH CAM'T GEK IK OUT!
POOL HALL
WELL, AT LEAST YOU WON THE BET.

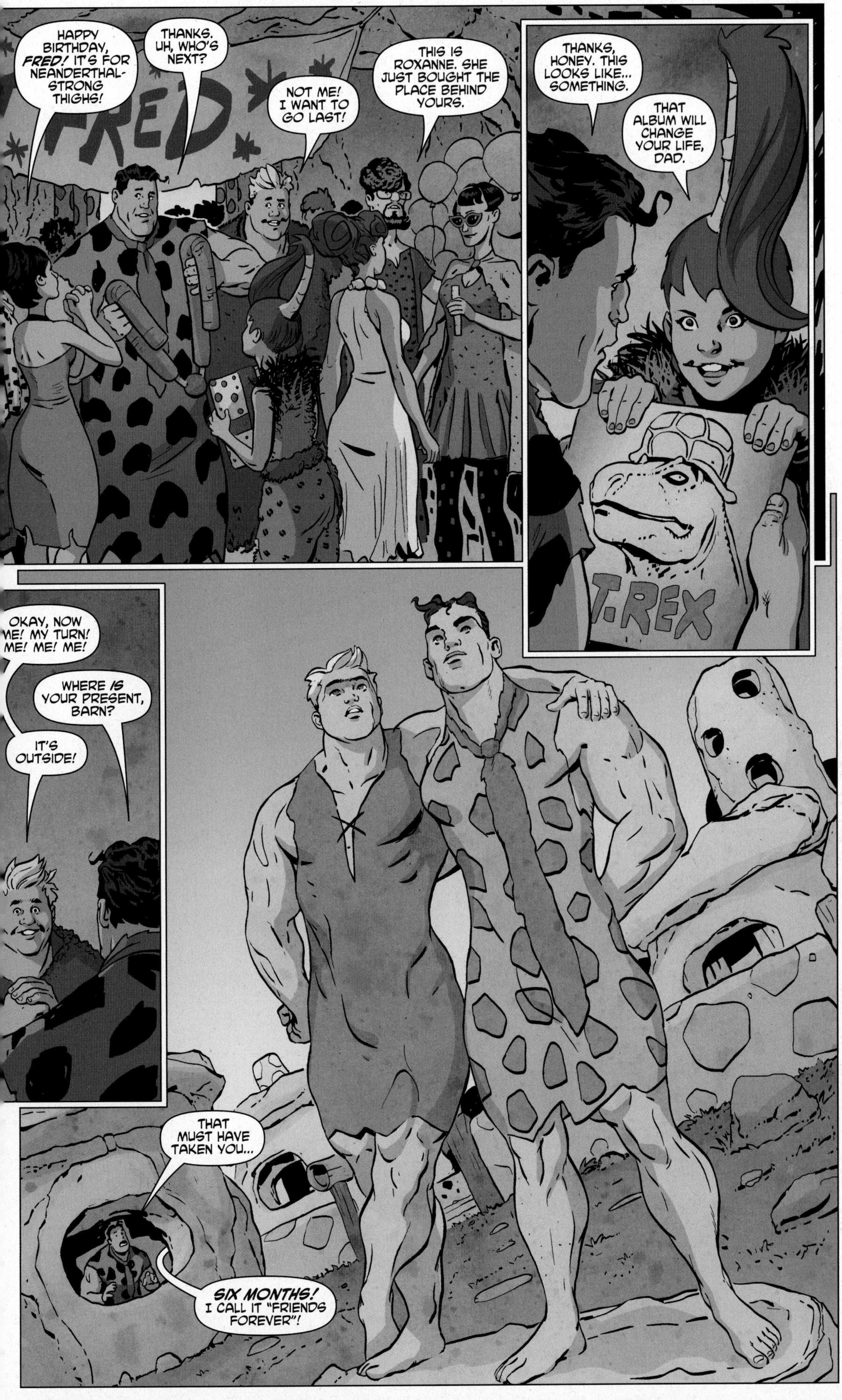
HAPPY BIRTHDAY, FRED! IT'S FOR NEANDERTHAL-STRONG THIGHS!
THANKS. UH, WHO'S NEXT?
NOT ME! I WANT TO GO LAST!
THIS IS ROXANNE. SHE JUST BOUGHT THE PLACE BEHIND YOURS.
FRED
THANKS, HONEY. THIS LOOKS LIKE... SOMETHING.
THAT ALBUM WILL CHANGE YOUR LIFE, DAD.
T.REX
OKAY, NOW ME! MY TURN! ME! ME! ME!
WHERE IS YOUR PRESENT, BARN?
IT'S OUTSIDE!
THAT MUST HAVE TAKEN YOU...
SIX MONTHS! I CALL IT "FRIENDS FOREVER"!

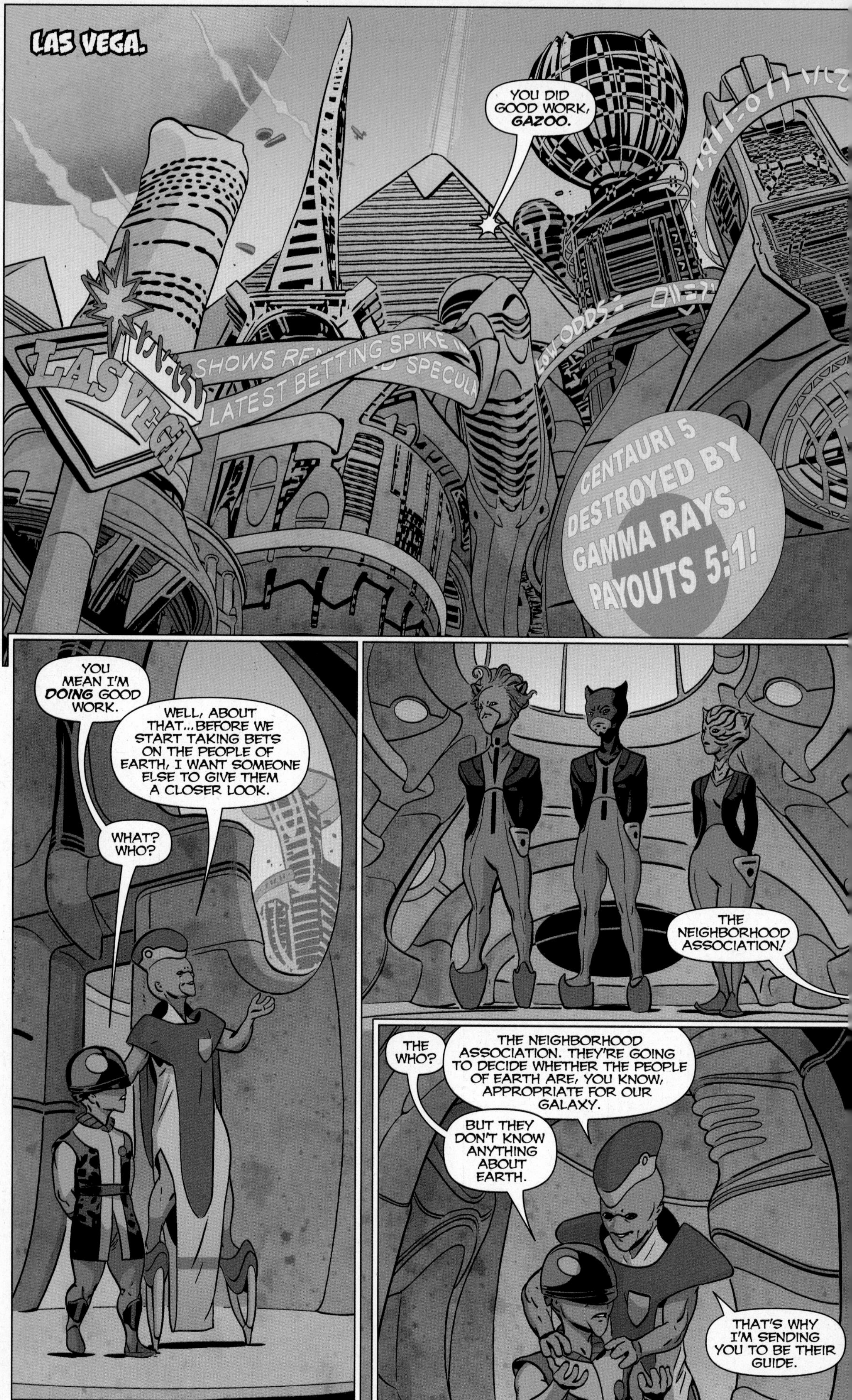
LAS VEGA.
YOU DID GOOD WORK, GAZOO.
LAS VEGA
SHOWS REA
LATEST BETTING SPIKE
SPECULA
LOW ODDS
CENTAURI 5 DESTROYED BY GAMMA RAYS. PAYOUTS 5:1!
YOU MEAN I'M DOING GOOD WORK.
WELL, ABOUT THAT...BEFORE WE START TAKING BETS ON THE PEOPLE OF EARTH, I WANT SOMEONE ELSE TO GIVE THEM A CLOSER LOOK.
WHAT? WHO?
THE NEIGHBORHOOD ASSOCIATION!
THE WHO?
THE NEIGHBORHOOD ASSOCIATION. THEY'RE GOING TO DECIDE WHETHER THE PEOPLE OF EARTH ARE, YOU KNOW, APPROPRIATE FOR OUR GALAXY.
BUT THEY DON'T KNOW ANYTHING ABOUT EARTH.
THAT'S WHY I'M SENDING YOU TO BE THEIR GUIDE.

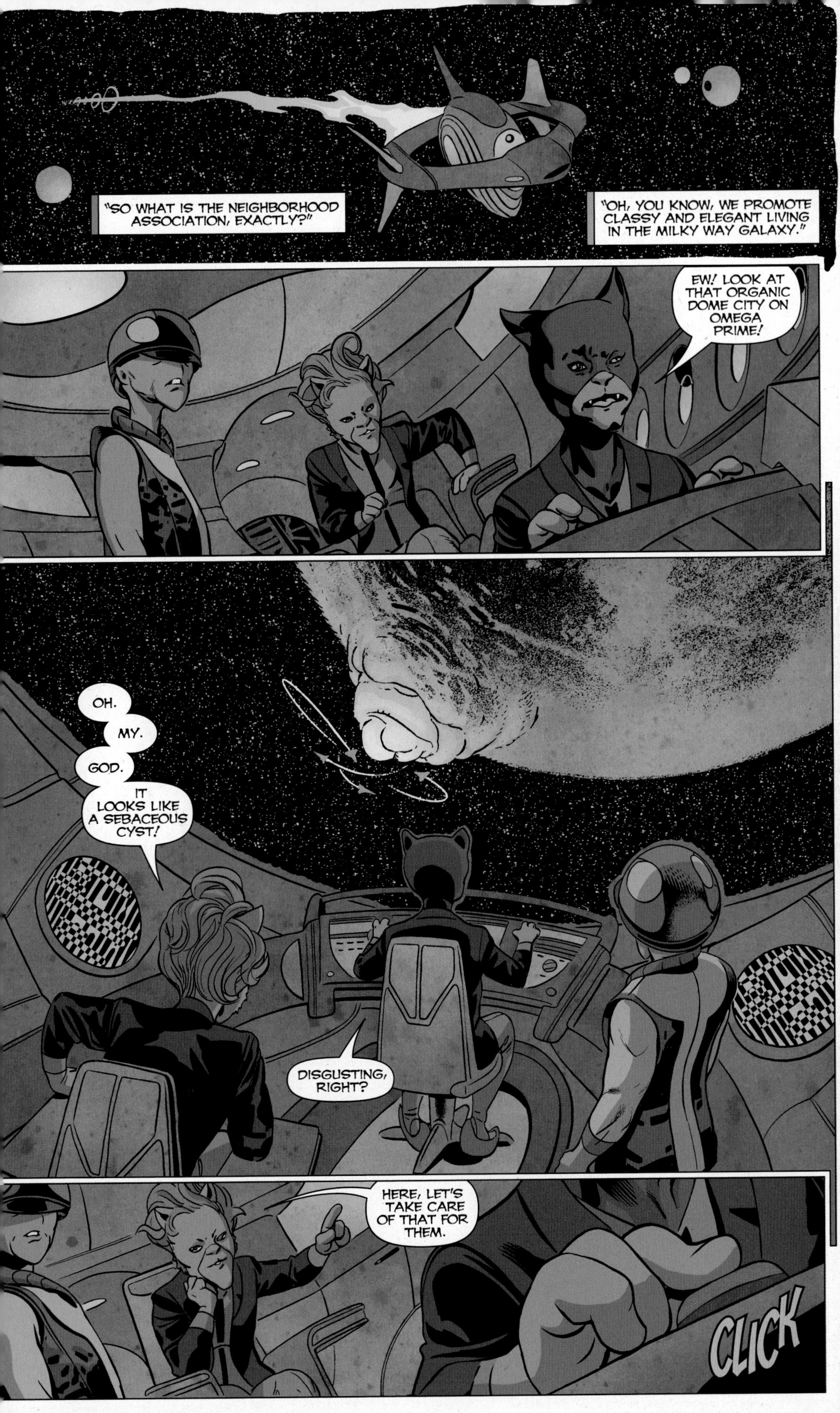
"SO WHAT IS THE NEIGHBORHOOD ASSOCIATION, EXACTLY?"
"OH, YOU KNOW, WE PROMOTE CLASSY AND ELEGANT LIVING IN THE MILKY WAY GALAXY."
EW! LOOK AT THAT ORGANIC DOME CITY ON OMEGA PRIME!
OH.
MY.
GOD.
IT LOOKS LIKE A SEBACEOUS CYST!
DISGUSTING, RIGHT?
HERE, LET'S TAKE CARE OF THAT FOR THEM.
CLICK

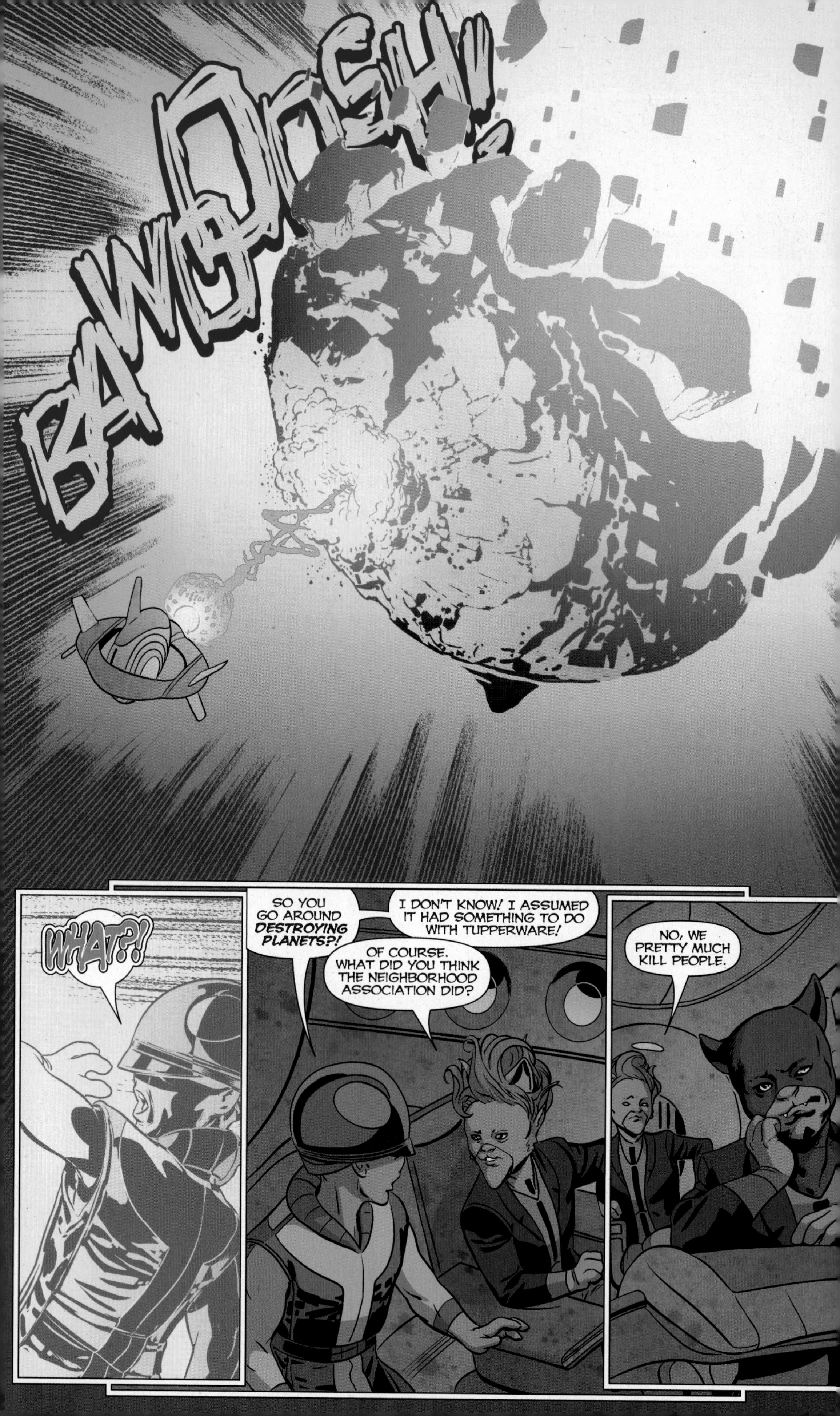
BAWOOSH!
WHAT?!
SO YOU GO AROUND DESTROYING PLANETS?!
OF COURSE. WHAT DID YOU THINK THE NEIGHBORHOOD ASSOCIATION DID?
I DON'T KNOW! I ASSUMED IT HAD SOMETHING TO DO WITH TUPPERWARE!
NO, WE PRETTY MUCH KILL PEOPLE.

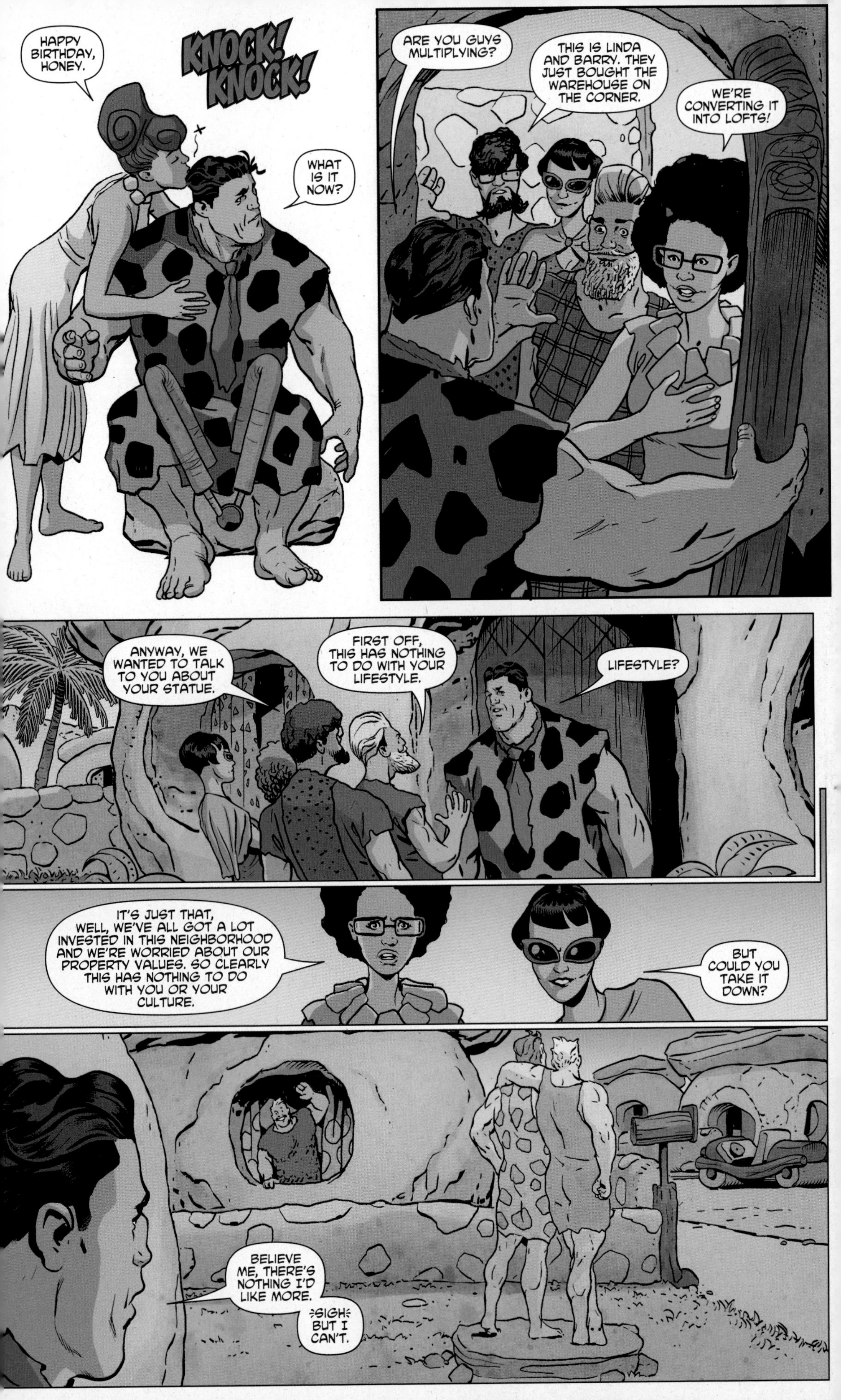
HAPPY BIRTHDAY, HONEY.
KNOCK! KNOCK!
WHAT IS IT NOW?
ARE YOU GUYS MULTIPLYING?
THIS IS LINDA AND BARRY. THEY JUST BOUGHT THE WAREHOUSE ON THE CORNER.
WE'RE CONVERTING IT INTO LOFTS!
ANYWAY, WE WANTED TO TALK TO YOU ABOUT YOUR STATUE.
FIRST OFF, THIS HAS NOTHING TO DO WITH YOUR LIFESTYLE.
LIFESTYLE?
IT'S JUST THAT, WELL, WE'VE ALL GOT A LOT INVESTED IN THIS NEIGHBORHOOD AND WE'RE WORRIED ABOUT OUR PROPERTY VALUES. SO CLEARLY THIS HAS NOTHING TO DO WITH YOU OR YOUR CULTURE.
BUT COULD YOU TAKE IT DOWN?
BELIEVE ME, THERE'S NOTHING I'D LIKE MORE.
SIGH BUT I CAN'T.

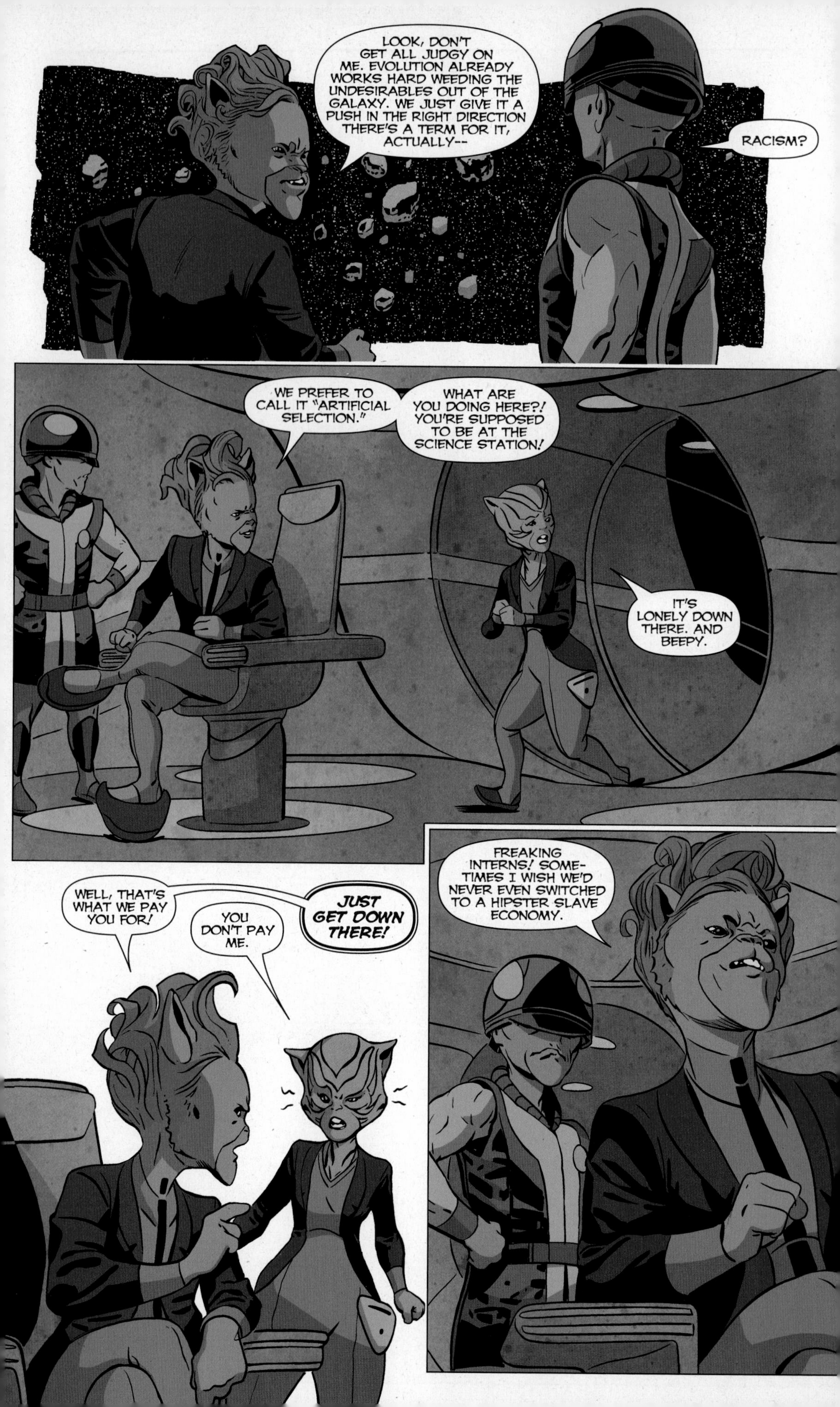
LOOK, DON'T GET ALL JUDGY ON ME. EVOLUTION ALREADY WORKS HARD WEEDING THE UNDESIRABLES OUT OF THE GALAXY. WE JUST GIVE IT A PUSH IN THE RIGHT DIRECTION THERE'S A TERM FOR IT, ACTUALLY--
RACISM?
WE PREFER TO CALL IT "ARTIFICIAL SELECTION."
WHAT ARE YOU DOING HERE?! YOU'RE SUPPOSED TO BE AT THE SCIENCE STATION!
IT'S LONELY DOWN THERE. AND BEEPY.
WELL, THAT'S WHAT WE PAY YOU FOR!
YOU DON'T PAY ME.
JUST GET DOWN THERE!
FREAKING INTERNS! SOMETIMES I WISH WE'D NEVER EVEN SWITCHED TO A HIPSTER SLAVE ECONOMY.

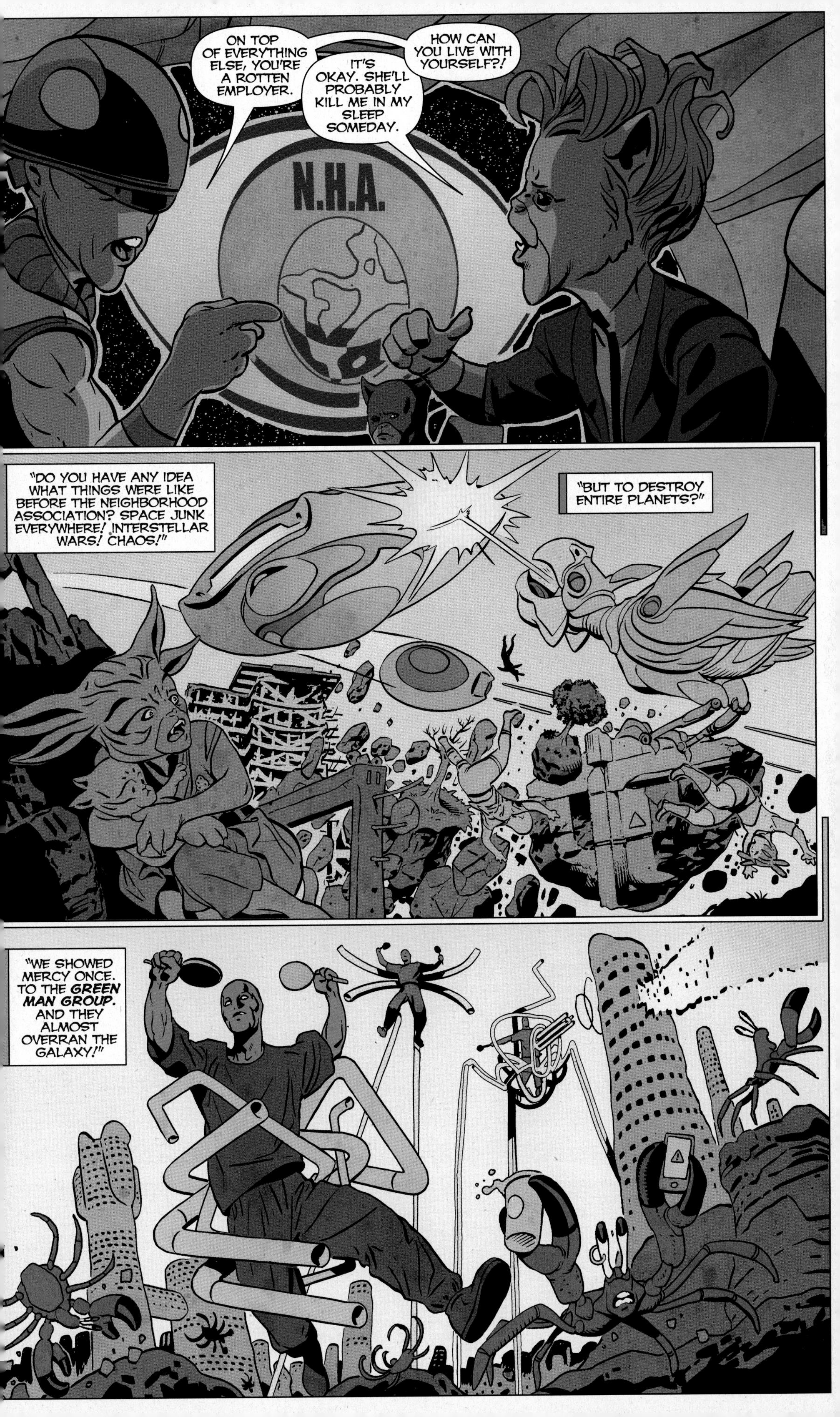
ON TOP OF EVERYTHING ELSE, YOU'RE A ROTTEN EMPLOYER.
HOW CAN YOU LIVE WITH YOURSELF?!
IT'S OKAY. SHE'LL PROBABLY KILL ME IN MY SLEEP SOMEDAY.
N.H.A.
"DO YOU HAVE ANY IDEA WHAT THINGS WERE LIKE BEFORE THE NEIGHBORHOOD ASSOCIATION? SPACE JUNK EVERYWHERE! INTERSTELLAR WARS! CHAOS!"
"BUT TO DESTROY ENTIRE PLANETS?"
"WE SHOWED MERCY ONCE. TO THE GREEN MAN GROUP. AND THEY ALMOST OVERRAN THE GALAXY!"

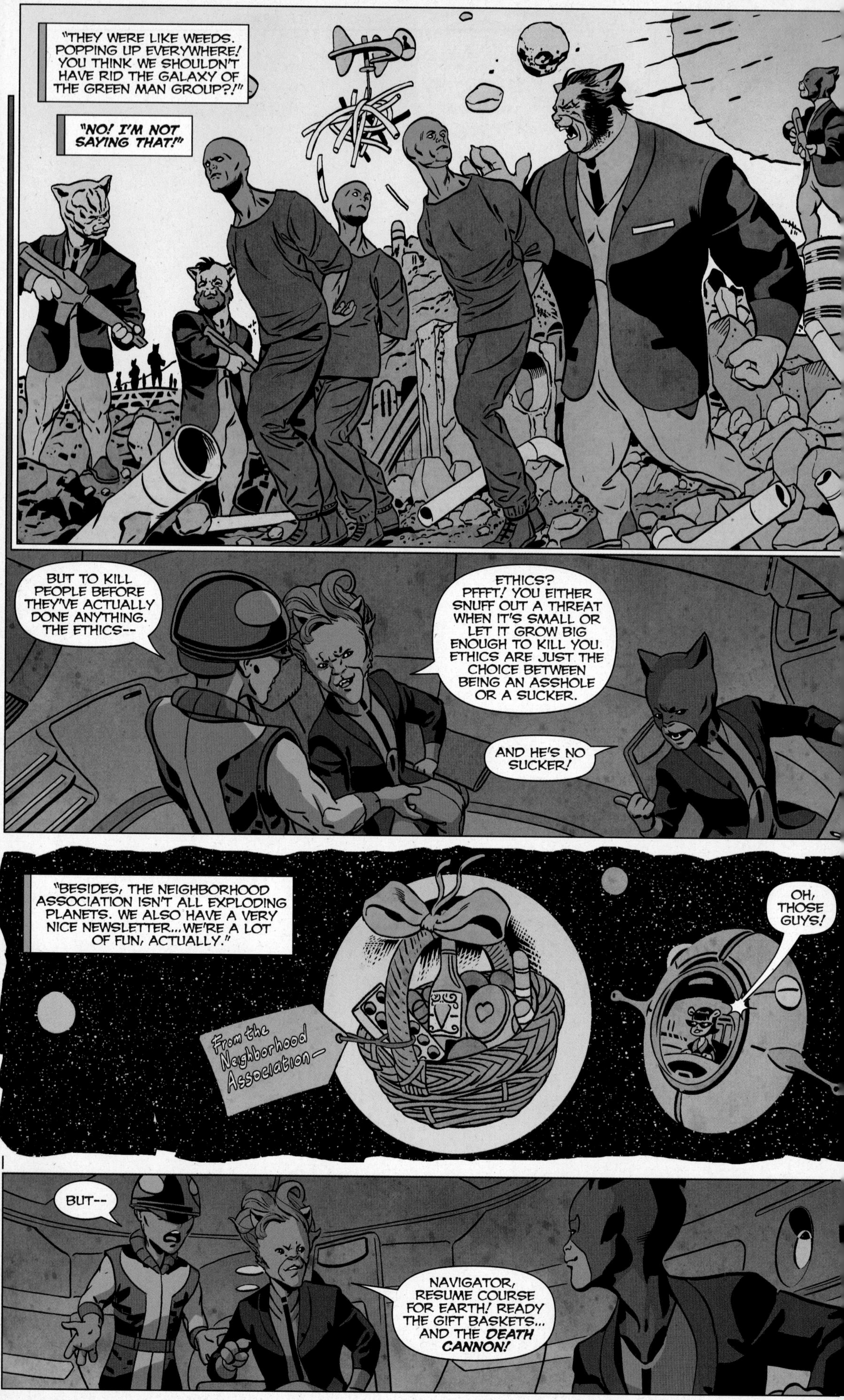
"THEY WERE LIKE WEEDS. POPPING UP EVERYWHERE! YOU THINK WE SHOULDN'T HAVE RID THE GALAXY OF THE GREEN MAN GROUP?!"
"NO! I'M NOT SAYING THAT!"
BUT TO KILL PEOPLE BEFORE THEY'VE ACTUALLY DONE ANYTHING. THE ETHICS--
ETHICS? PFFFT! YOU EITHER SNUFF OUT A THREAT WHEN IT'S SMALL OR LET IT GROW BIG ENOUGH TO KILL YOU. ETHICS ARE JUST THE CHOICE BETWEEN BEING AN ASSHOLE OR A SUCKER.
AND HE'S NO SUCKER!
"BESIDES, THE NEIGHBORHOOD ASSOCIATION ISN'T ALL EXPLODING PLANETS. WE ALSO HAVE A VERY NICE NEWSLETTER...WE'RE A LOT OF FUN, ACTUALLY."
From the Neighborhood Association—
OH, THOSE GUYS!
BUT--
NAVIGATOR, RESUME COURSE FOR EARTH! READY THE GIFT BASKETS... AND THE DEATH CANNON!

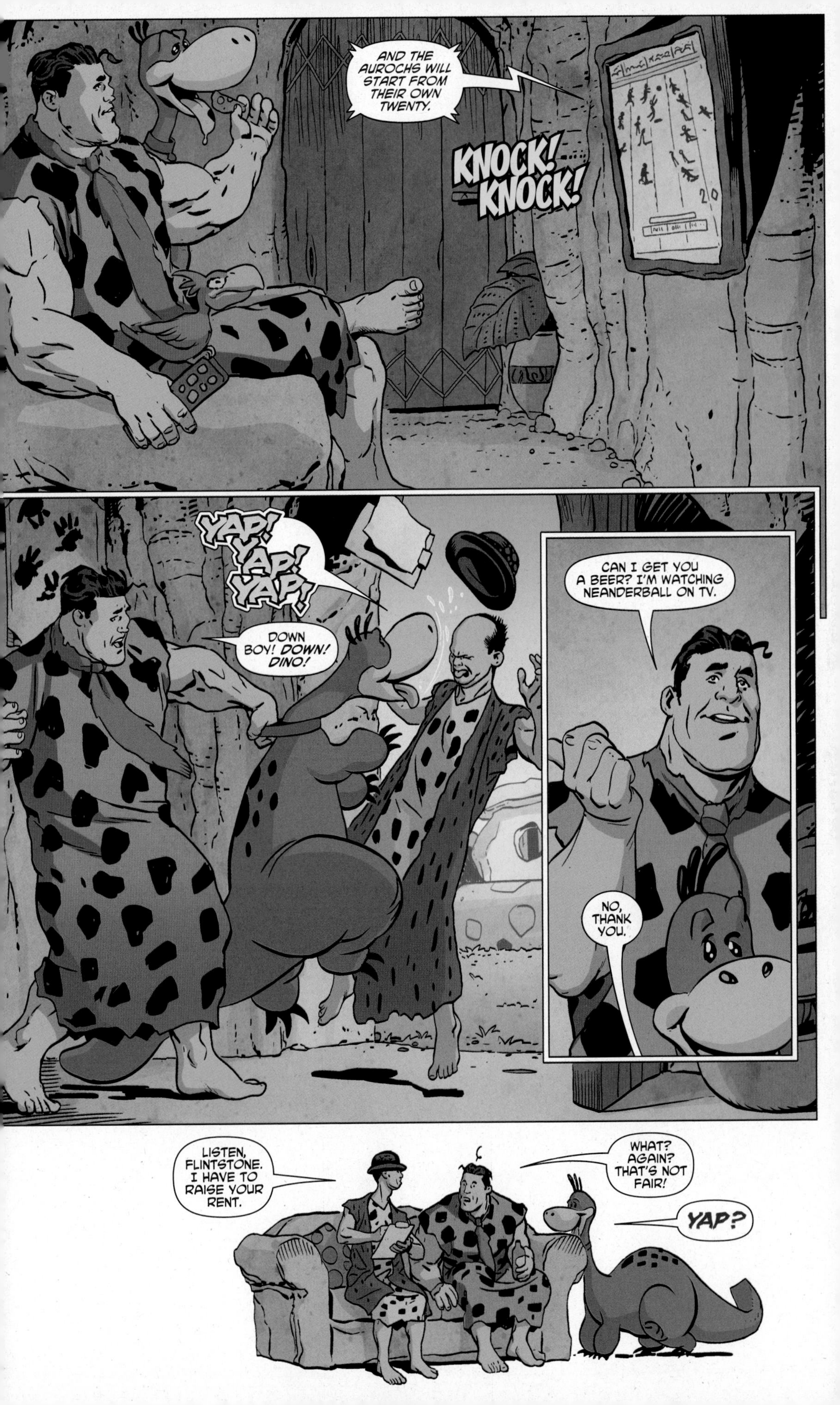
AND THE AUROCHS WILL START FROM THEIR OWN TWENTY.
KNOCK! KNOCK!
YAP! YAP! YAP!
DOWN BOY! DOWN! DINO!
CAN I GET YOU A BEER? I'M WATCHING NEANDERBALL ON TV.
NO, THANK YOU.
LISTEN, FLINTSTONE. I HAVE TO RAISE YOUR RENT.
WHAT? AGAIN? THAT'S NOT FAIR!
YAP?

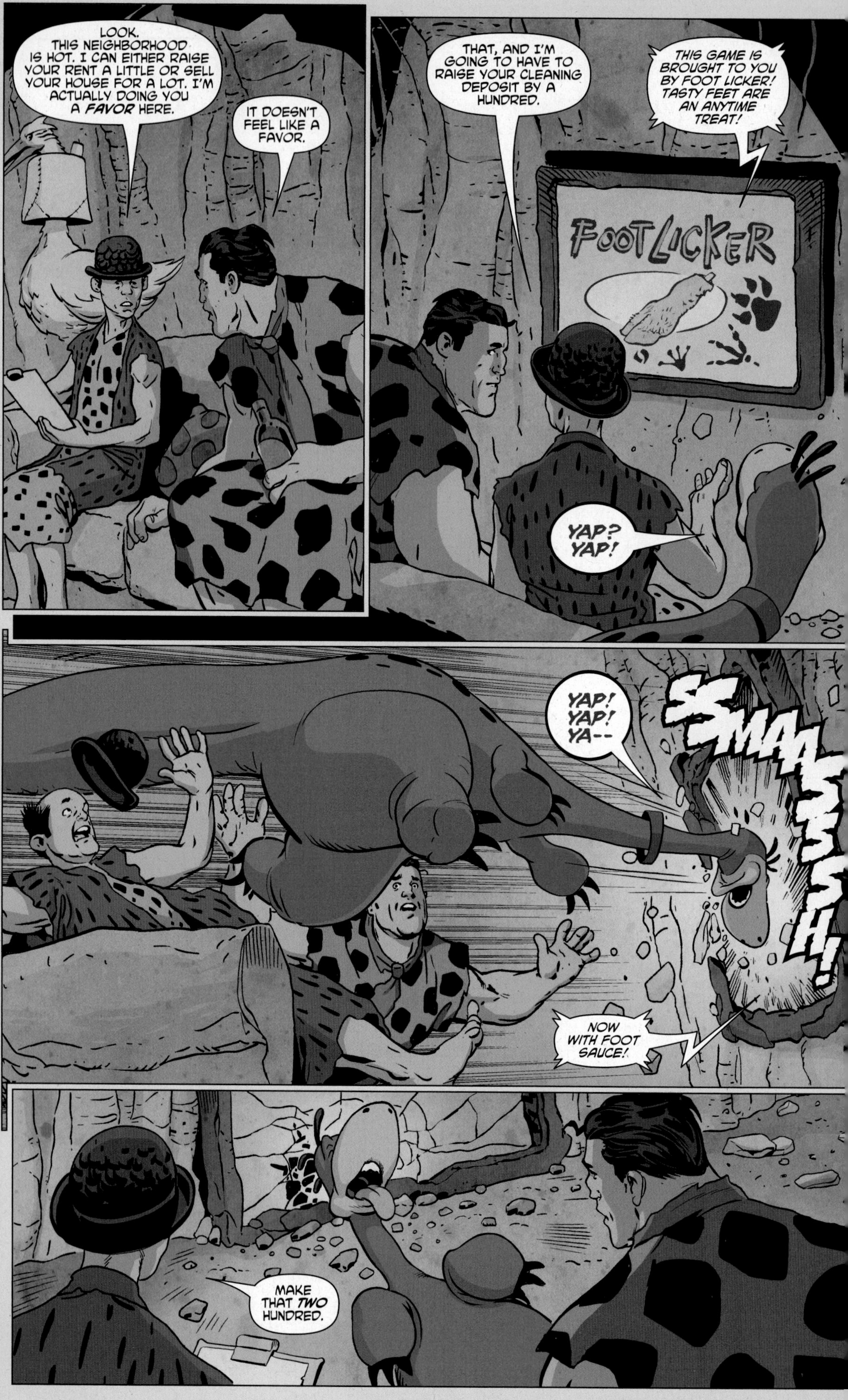
LOOK. THIS NEIGHBORHOOD IS HOT. I CAN EITHER RAISE YOUR RENT A LITTLE OR SELL YOUR HOUSE FOR A LOT. I'M ACTUALLY DOING YOU A *FAVOR* HERE.
IT DOESN'T FEEL LIKE A FAVOR.
THAT, AND I'M GOING TO HAVE TO RAISE YOUR CLEANING DEPOSIT BY A HUNDRED.
THIS GAME IS BROUGHT TO YOU BY FOOT LICKER! TASTY FEET ARE AN ANYTIME TREAT!
FOOT LICKER
YAP? YAP!
YAP! YAP! YA--
SSMAASSSHH!
NOW WITH FOOT SAUCE!
MAKE THAT *TWO* HUNDRED.

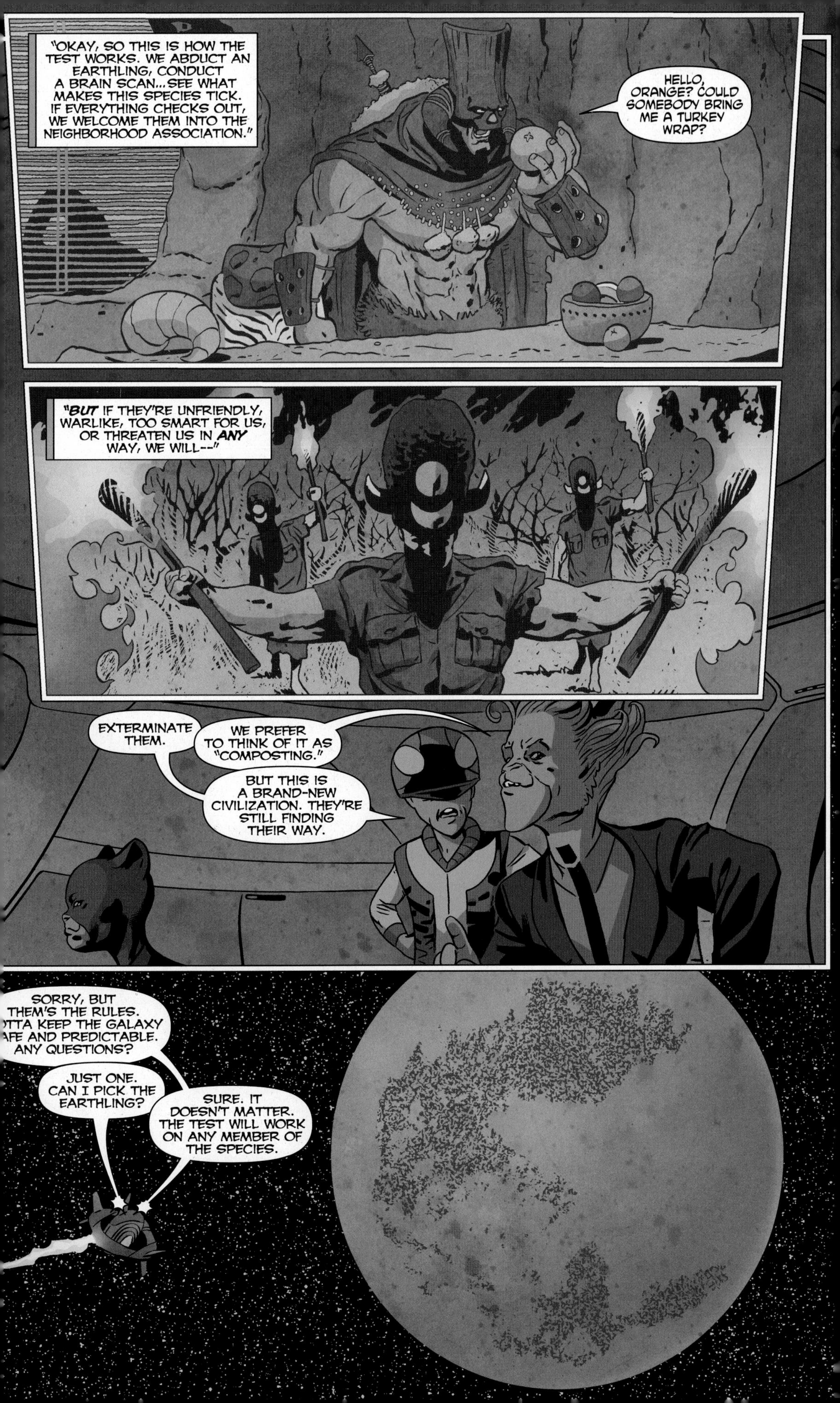
"OKAY, SO THIS IS HOW THE TEST WORKS. WE ABDUCT AN EARTHLING, CONDUCT A BRAIN SCAN...SEE WHAT MAKES THIS SPECIES TICK. IF EVERYTHING CHECKS OUT, WE WELCOME THEM INTO THE NEIGHBORHOOD ASSOCIATION."
HELLO, ORANGE? COULD SOMEBODY BRING ME A TURKEY WRAP?
"BUT IF THEY'RE UNFRIENDLY, WARLIKE, TOO SMART FOR US, OR THREATEN US IN ANY WAY, WE WILL--"
EXTERMINATE THEM.
WE PREFER TO THINK OF IT AS "COMPOSTING."
BUT THIS IS A BRAND-NEW CIVILIZATION. THEY'RE STILL FINDING THEIR WAY.
SORRY, BUT THEM'S THE RULES. OTTA KEEP THE GALAXY AFE AND PREDICTABLE. ANY QUESTIONS?
JUST ONE. CAN I PICK THE EARTHLING?
SURE. IT DOESN'T MATTER. THE TEST WILL WORK ON ANY MEMBER OF THE SPECIES.

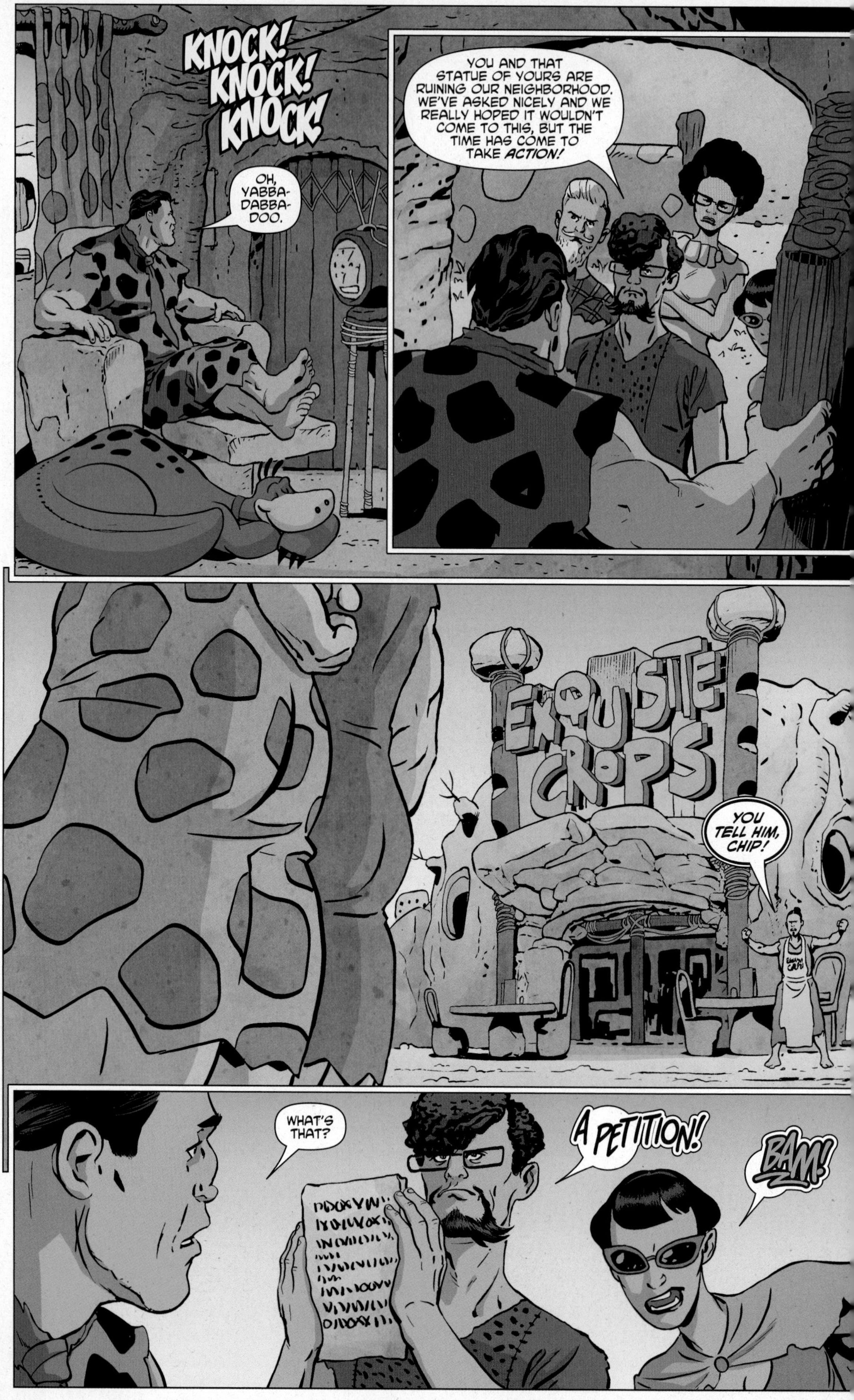

KNOCK! KNOCK! KNOCK!
OH, YABBA-DABBA-DOO.
YOU AND THAT STATUE OF YOURS ARE RUINING OUR NEIGHBORHOOD. WE'VE ASKED NICELY AND WE REALLY HOPED IT WOULDN'T COME TO THIS, BUT THE TIME HAS COME TO TAKE ACTION!
EXQUISITE CROPS
YOU TELL HIM, CHIP!
WHAT'S THAT?
A PETITION!
BAM!

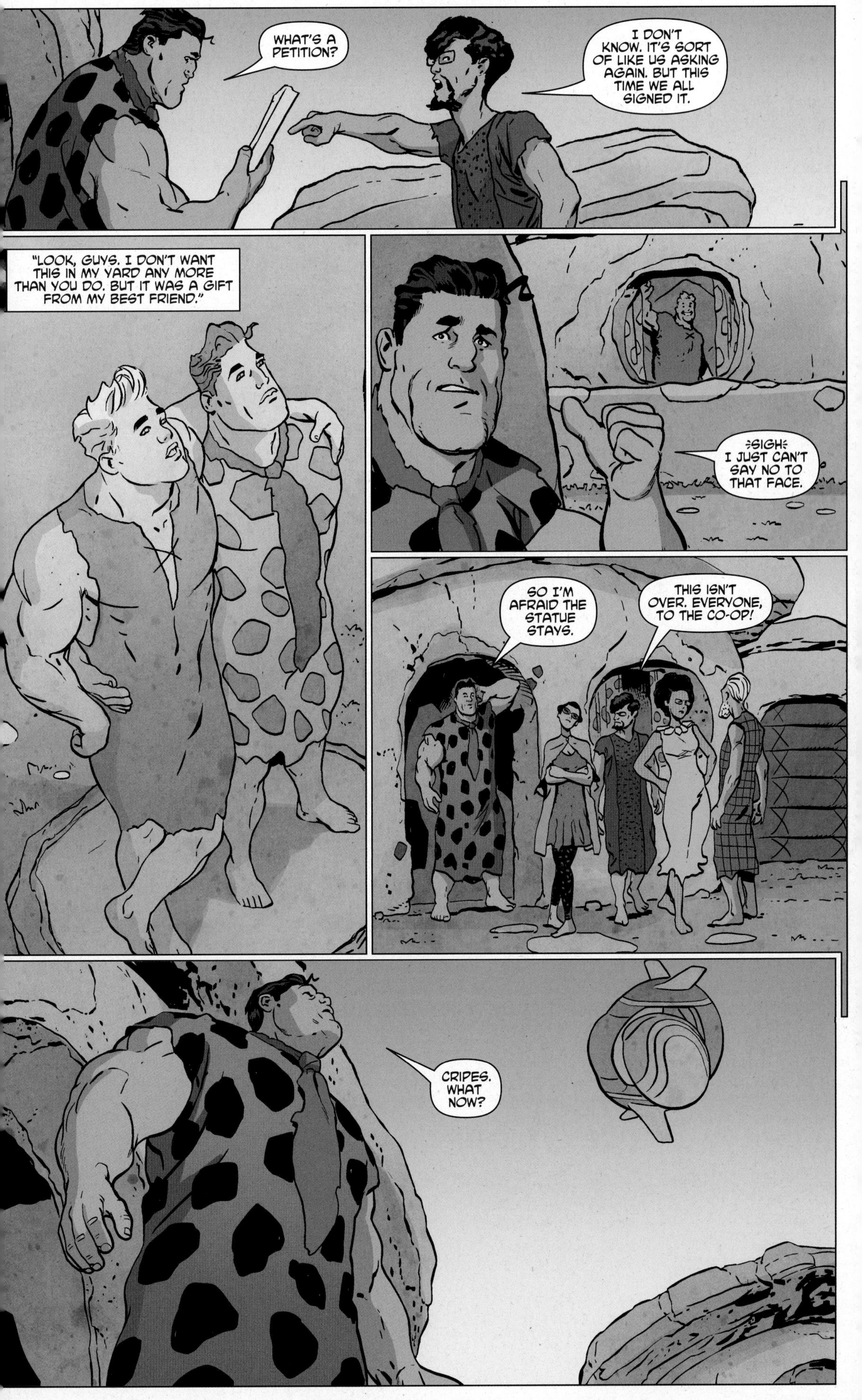

WHAT'S A PETITION?
I DON'T KNOW. IT'S SORT OF LIKE US ASKING AGAIN. BUT THIS TIME WE ALL SIGNED IT.
"LOOK, GUYS. I DON'T WANT THIS IN MY YARD ANY MORE THAN YOU DO. BUT IT WAS A GIFT FROM MY BEST FRIEND."
SIGH I JUST CAN'T SAY NO TO THAT FACE.
SO I'M AFRAID THE STATUE STAYS.
THIS ISN'T OVER. EVERYONE, TO THE CO-OP!
CRIPES. WHAT NOW?

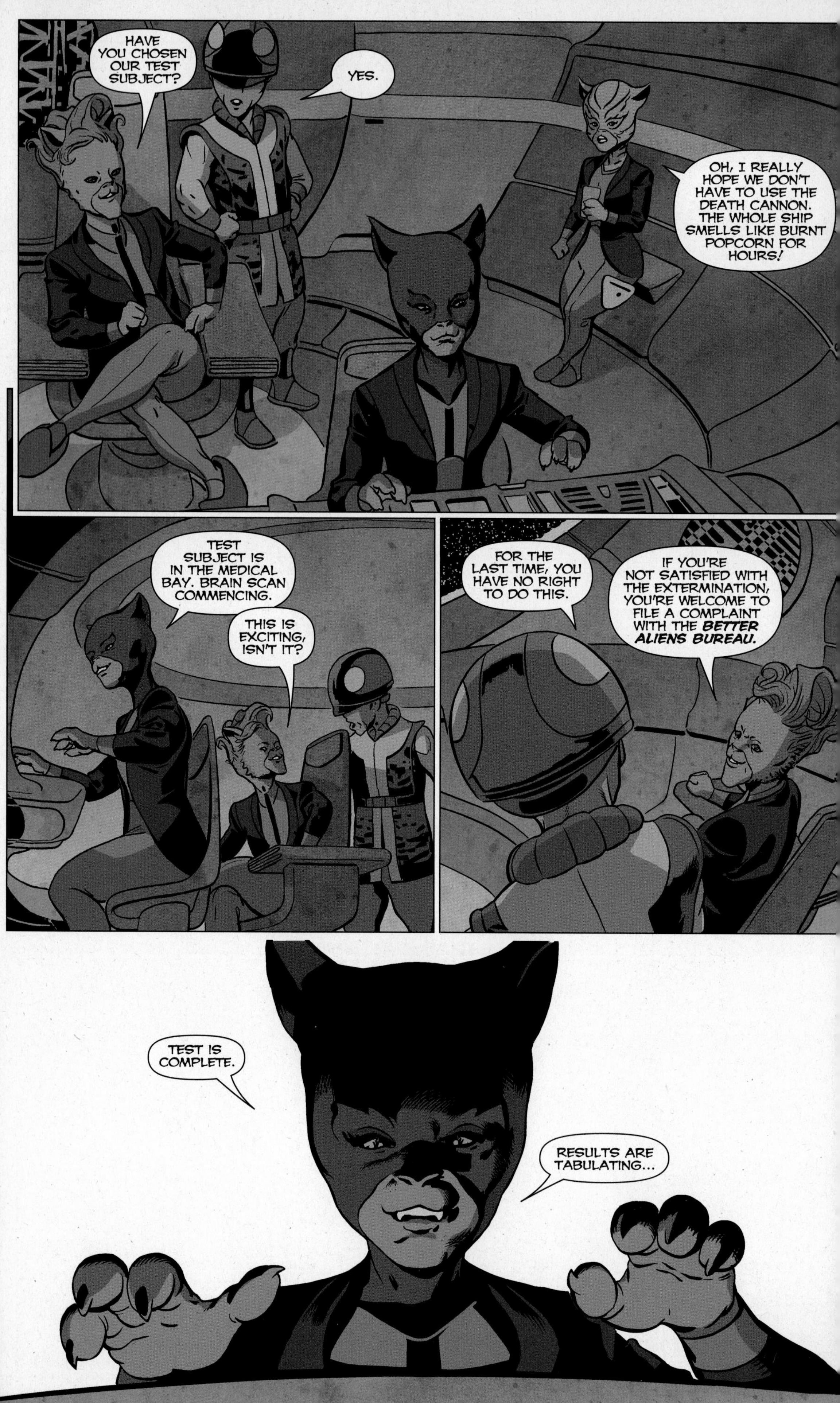
HAVE YOU CHOSEN OUR TEST SUBJECT?
YES.
OH, I REALLY HOPE WE DON'T HAVE TO USE THE DEATH CANNON. THE WHOLE SHIP SMELLS LIKE BURNT POPCORN FOR HOURS!
TEST SUBJECT IS IN THE MEDICAL BAY. BRAIN SCAN COMMENCING.
THIS IS EXCITING, ISN'T IT?
FOR THE LAST TIME, YOU HAVE NO RIGHT TO DO THIS.
IF YOU'RE NOT SATISFIED WITH THE EXTERMINATION, YOU'RE WELCOME TO FILE A COMPLAINT WITH THE *BETTER ALIENS BUREAU.*
TEST IS COMPLETE.
RESULTS ARE TABULATING...

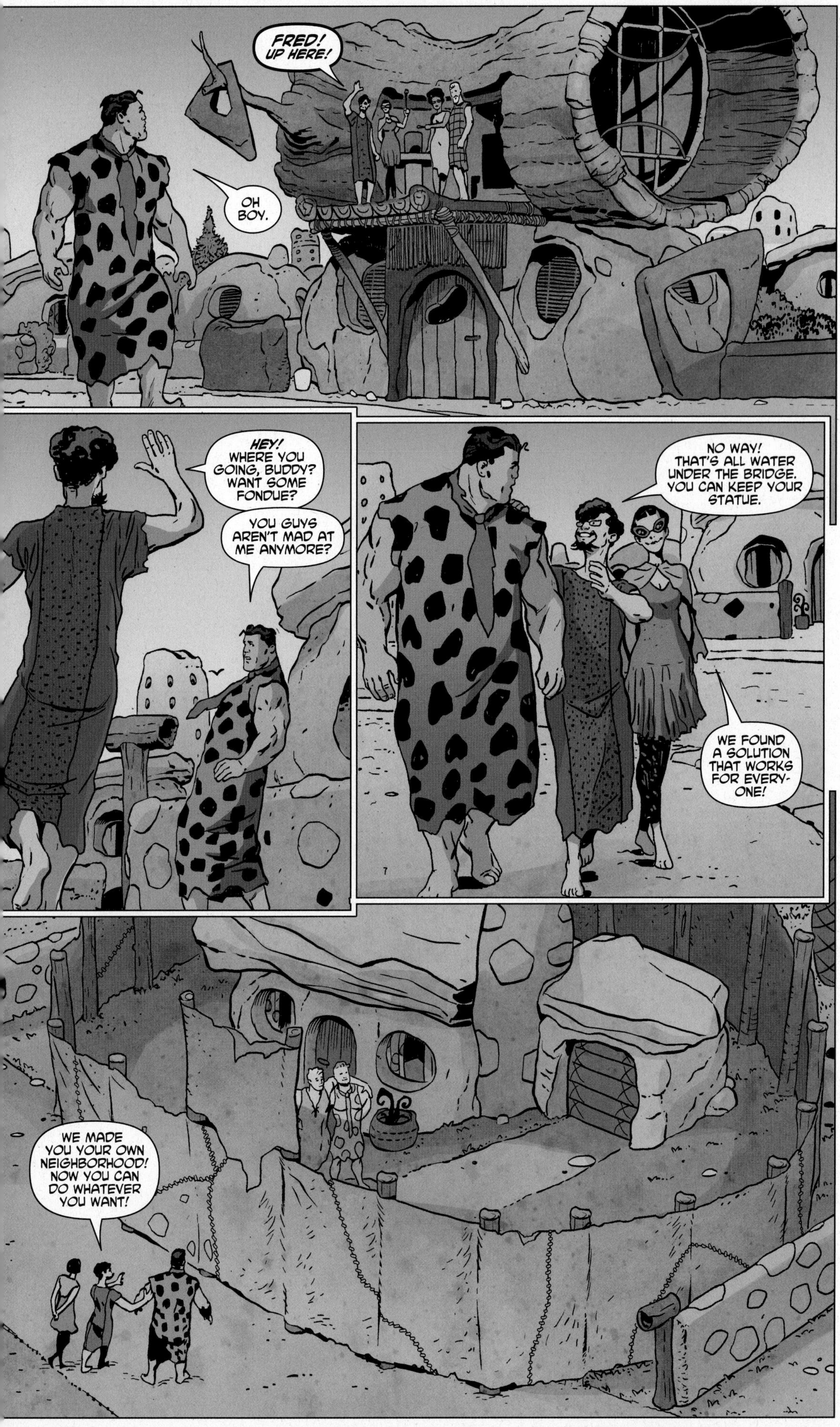
FRED! UP HERE!
OH BOY.
HEY! WHERE YOU GOING, BUDDY? WANT SOME FONDUE?
YOU GUYS AREN'T MAD AT ME ANYMORE?
NO WAY! THAT'S ALL WATER UNDER THE BRIDGE. YOU CAN KEEP YOUR STATUE.
WE FOUND A SOLUTION THAT WORKS FOR EVERY-ONE!
WE MADE YOU YOUR OWN NEIGHBORHOOD! NOW YOU CAN DO WHATEVER YOU WANT!

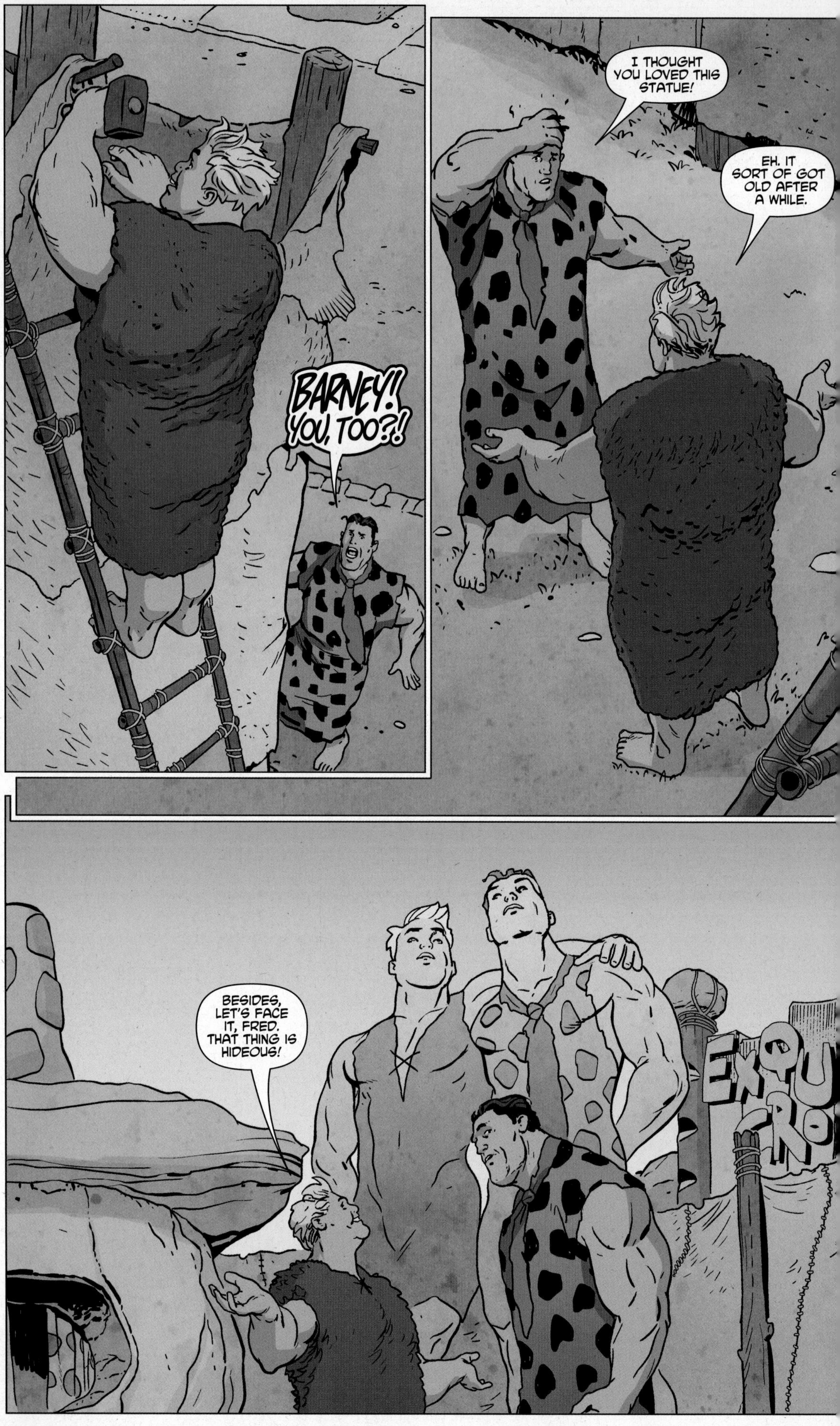
BARNEY!! YOU, TOO?!
I THOUGHT YOU LOVED THIS STATUE!
EH. IT SORT OF GOT OLD AFTER A WHILE.
BESIDES, LET'S FACE IT, FRED. THAT THING IS HIDEOUS!

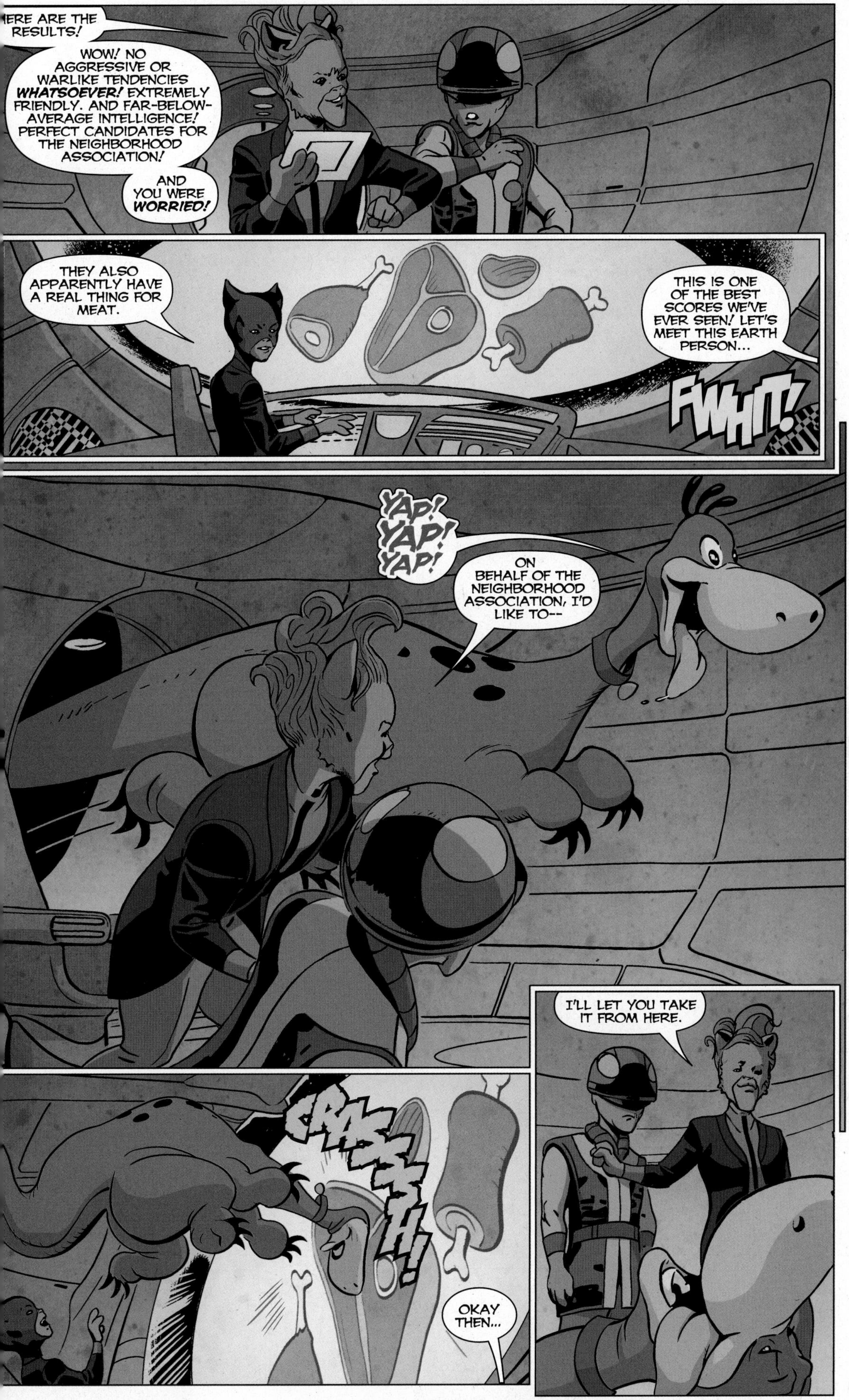
HERE ARE THE RESULTS!
WOW! NO AGGRESSIVE OR WARLIKE TENDENCIES WHATSOEVER! EXTREMELY FRIENDLY. AND FAR-BELOW-AVERAGE INTELLIGENCE! PERFECT CANDIDATES FOR THE NEIGHBORHOOD ASSOCIATION!
AND YOU WERE WORRIED!
THEY ALSO APPARENTLY HAVE A REAL THING FOR MEAT.
THIS IS ONE OF THE BEST SCORES WE'VE EVER SEEN! LET'S MEET THIS EARTH PERSON...
FWHIT!
YAP! YAP! YAP!
ON BEHALF OF THE NEIGHBORHOOD ASSOCIATION, I'D LIKE TO--
CRASSSH!
OKAY THEN...
I'LL LET YOU TAKE IT FROM HERE.

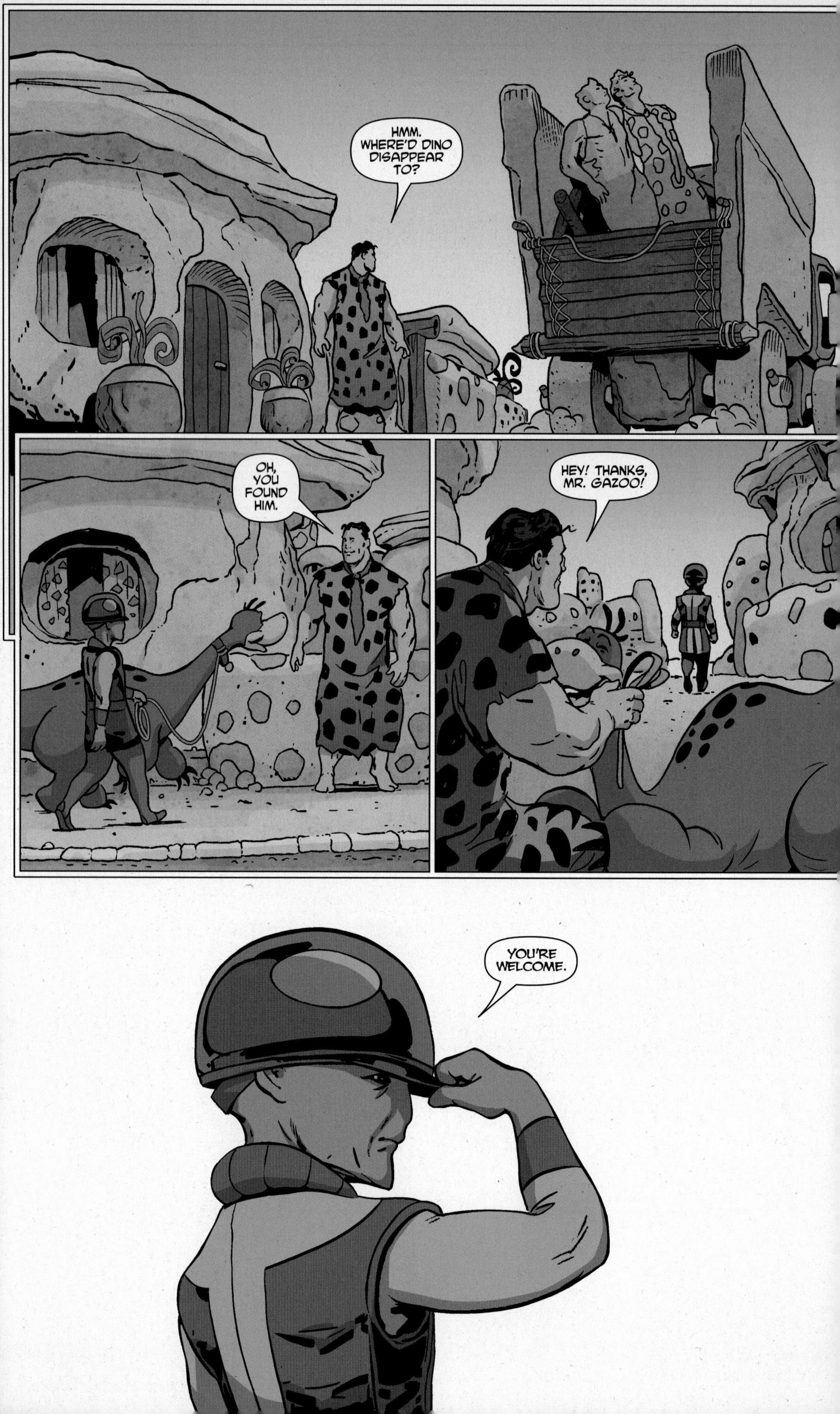
HMM. WHERE'D DINO DISAPPEAR TO?
OH, YOU FOUND HIM.
HEY! THANKS, MR. GAZOO!
YOU'RE WELCOME.

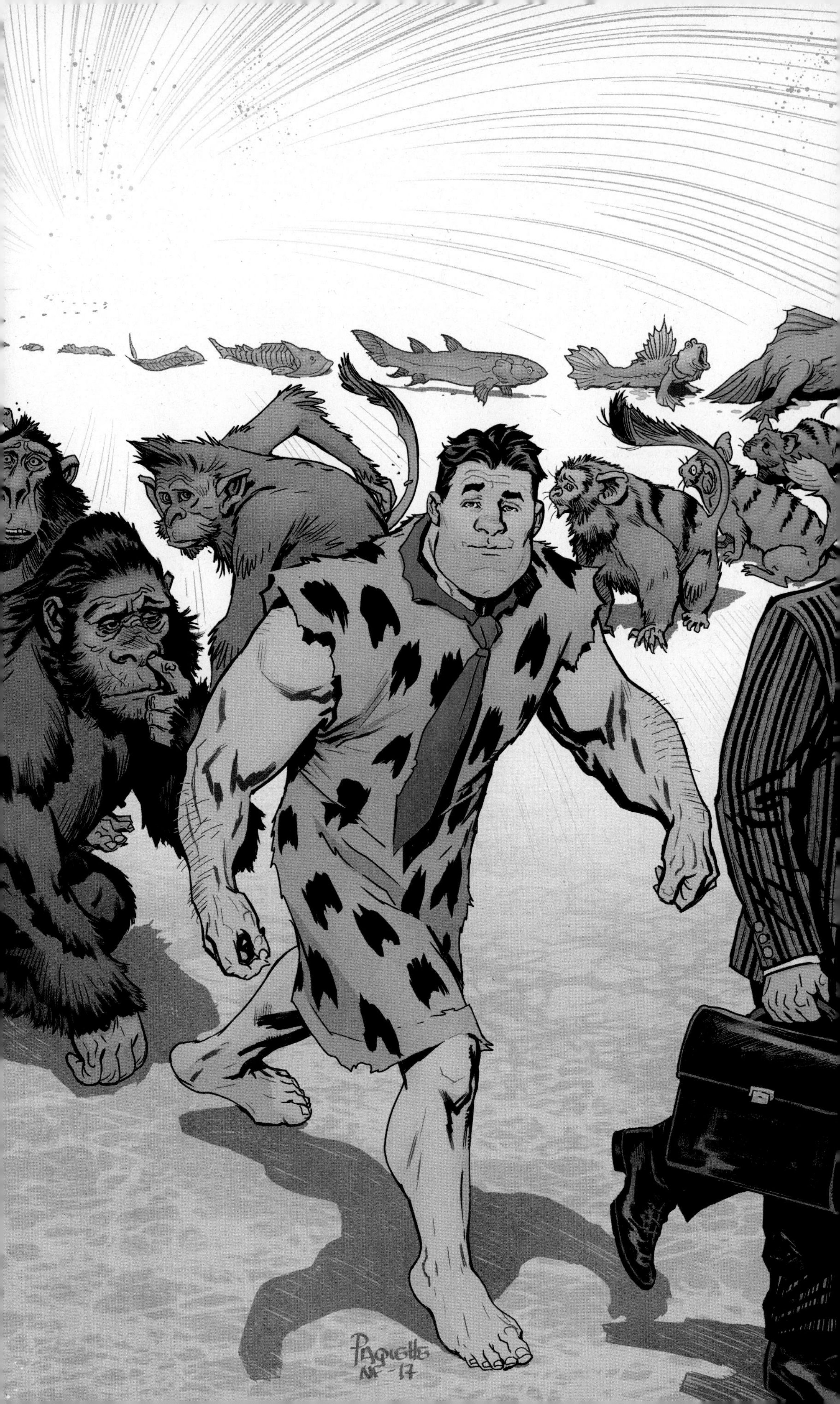
PAQUETTE
NF-17

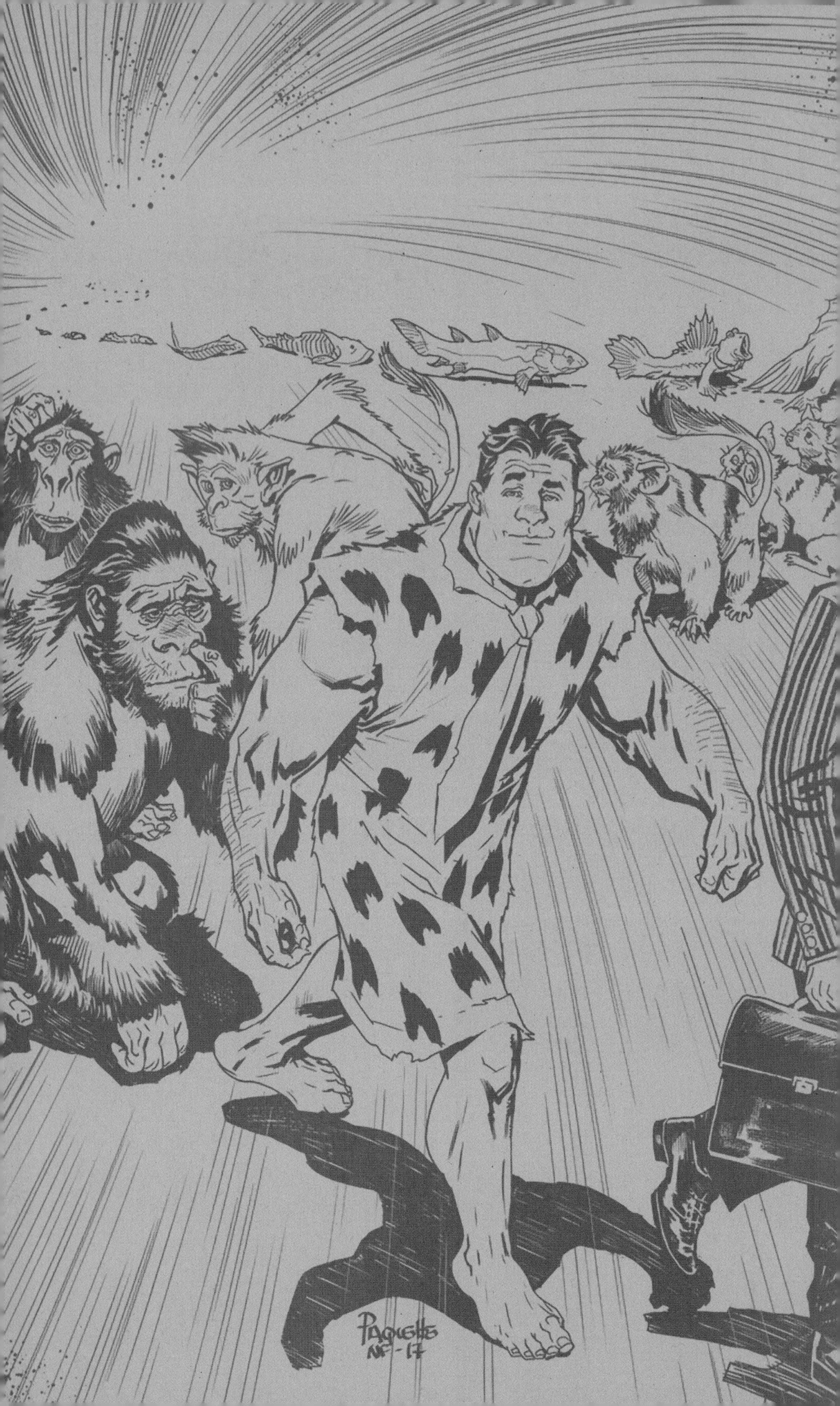

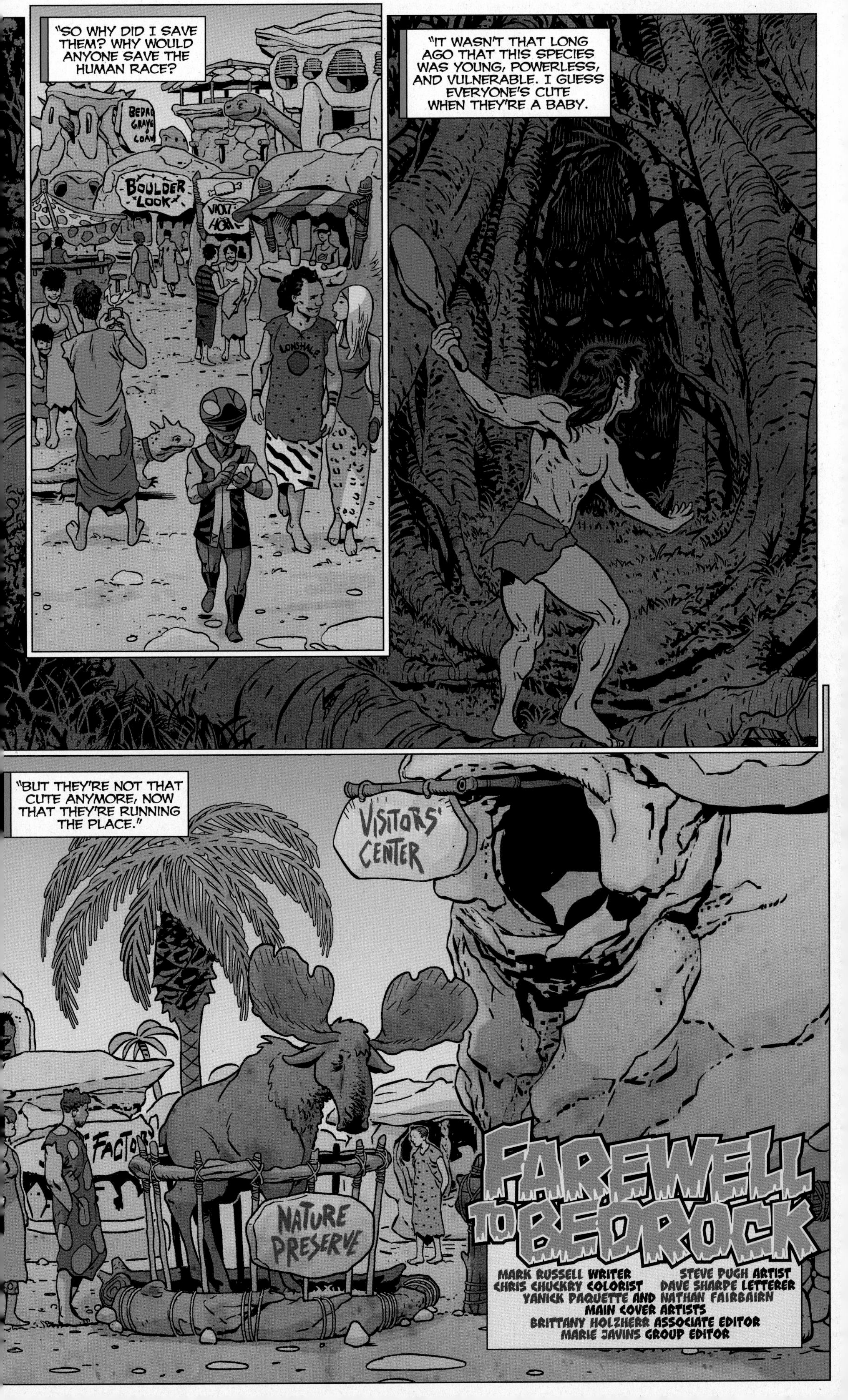

"SO WHY DID I SAVE THEM? WHY WOULD ANYONE SAVE THE HUMAN RACE?
BOULDER LOOK
"IT WASN'T THAT LONG AGO THAT THIS SPECIES WAS YOUNG, POWERLESS, AND VULNERABLE. I GUESS EVERYONE'S CUTE WHEN THEY'RE A BABY.
"BUT THEY'RE NOT THAT CUTE ANYMORE, NOW THAT THEY'RE RUNNING THE PLACE."
VISITORS' CENTER
NATURE PRESERVE
FAREWELL TO BEDROCK
MARK RUSSELL WRITER
STEVE PUGH ARTIST
CHRIS CHUCKRY COLORIST
DAVE SHARPE LETTERER
YANICK PAQUETTE AND NATHAN FAIRBAIRN MAIN COVER ARTISTS
BRITTANY HOLZHERR ASSOCIATE EDITOR
MARIE JAVINS GROUP EDITOR

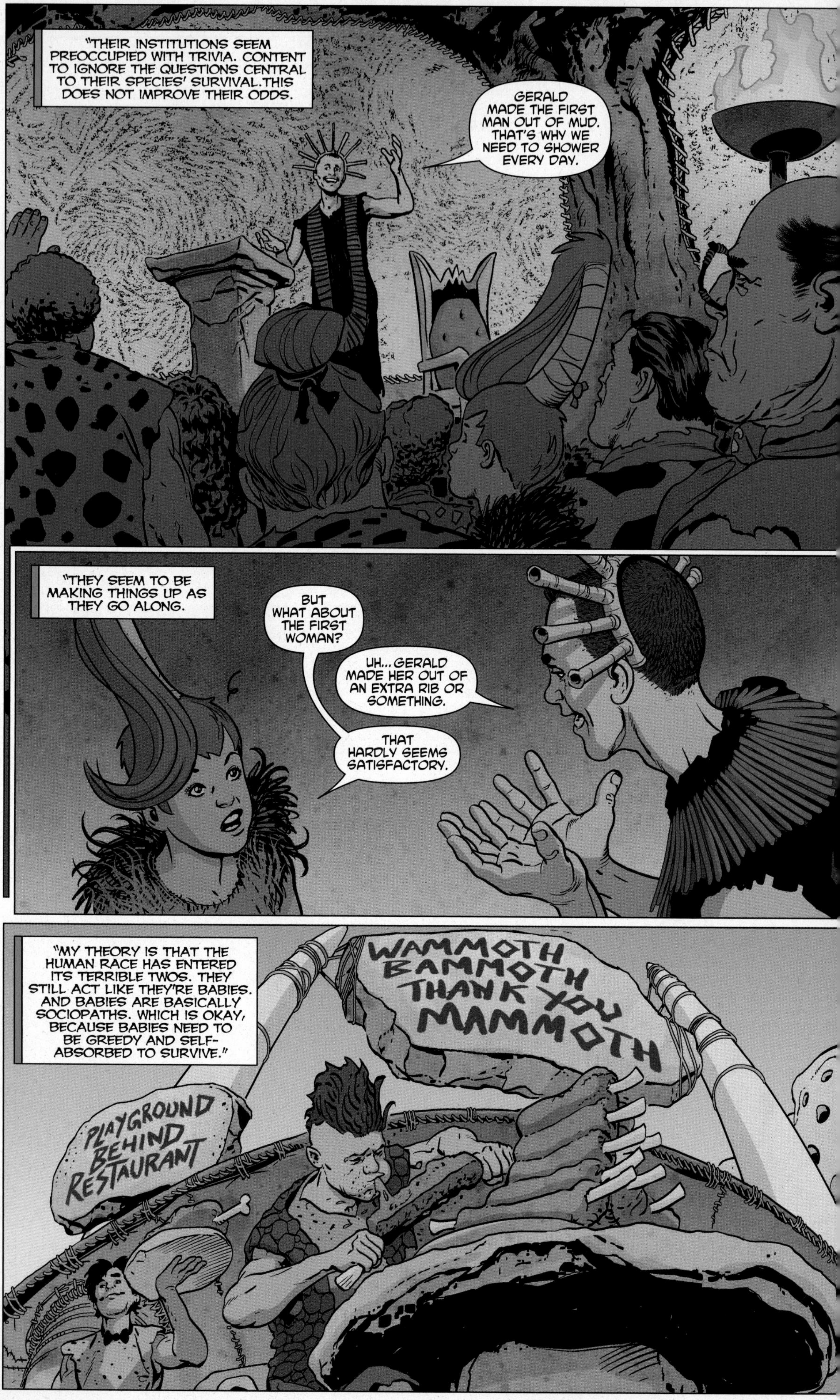
"THEIR INSTITUTIONS SEEM PREOCCUPIED WITH TRIVIA. CONTENT TO IGNORE THE QUESTIONS CENTRAL TO THEIR SPECIES' SURVIVAL.THIS DOES NOT IMPROVE THEIR ODDS.
GERALD MADE THE FIRST MAN OUT OF MUD. THAT'S WHY WE NEED TO SHOWER EVERY DAY.
"THEY SEEM TO BE MAKING THINGS UP AS THEY GO ALONG.
BUT WHAT ABOUT THE FIRST WOMAN?
UH... GERALD MADE HER OUT OF AN EXTRA RIB OR SOMETHING.
THAT HARDLY SEEMS SATISFACTORY.
"MY THEORY IS THAT THE HUMAN RACE HAS ENTERED ITS TERRIBLE TWOS. THEY STILL ACT LIKE THEY'RE BABIES. AND BABIES ARE BASICALLY SOCIOPATHS. WHICH IS OKAY, BECAUSE BABIES NEED TO BE GREEDY AND SELF-ABSORBED TO SURVIVE."
WAMMOTH BAMMOTH THANK YOU MAMMOTH
PLAYGROUND BEHIND RESTAURANT

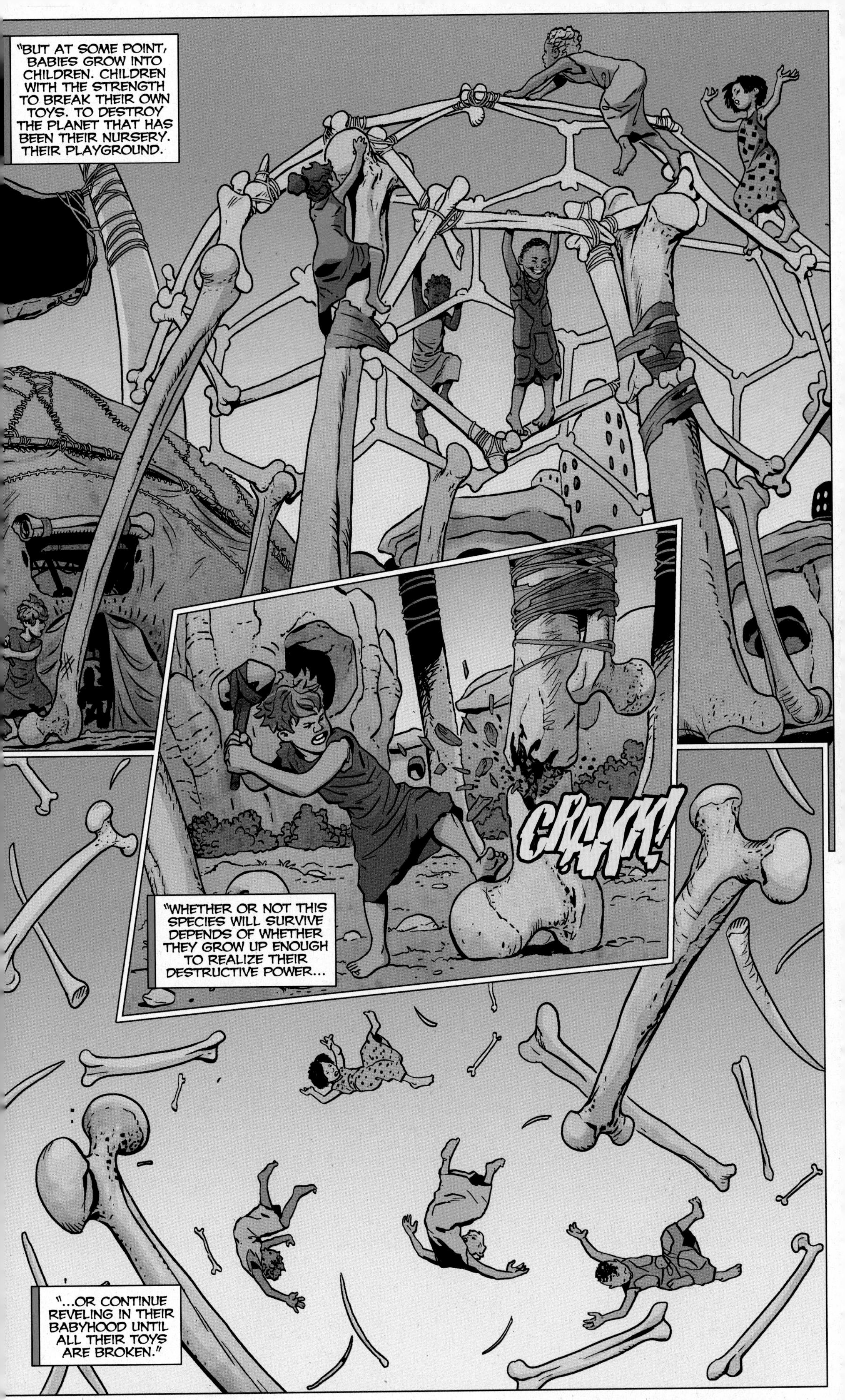
"BUT AT SOME POINT, BABIES GROW INTO CHILDREN. CHILDREN WITH THE STRENGTH TO BREAK THEIR OWN TOYS. TO DESTROY THE PLANET THAT HAS BEEN THEIR NURSERY. THEIR PLAYGROUND.
CRAKK!
"WHETHER OR NOT THIS SPECIES WILL SURVIVE DEPENDS OF WHETHER THEY GROW UP ENOUGH TO REALIZE THEIR DESTRUCTIVE POWER...
"...OR CONTINUE REVELING IN THEIR BABYHOOD UNTIL ALL THEIR TOYS ARE BROKEN."

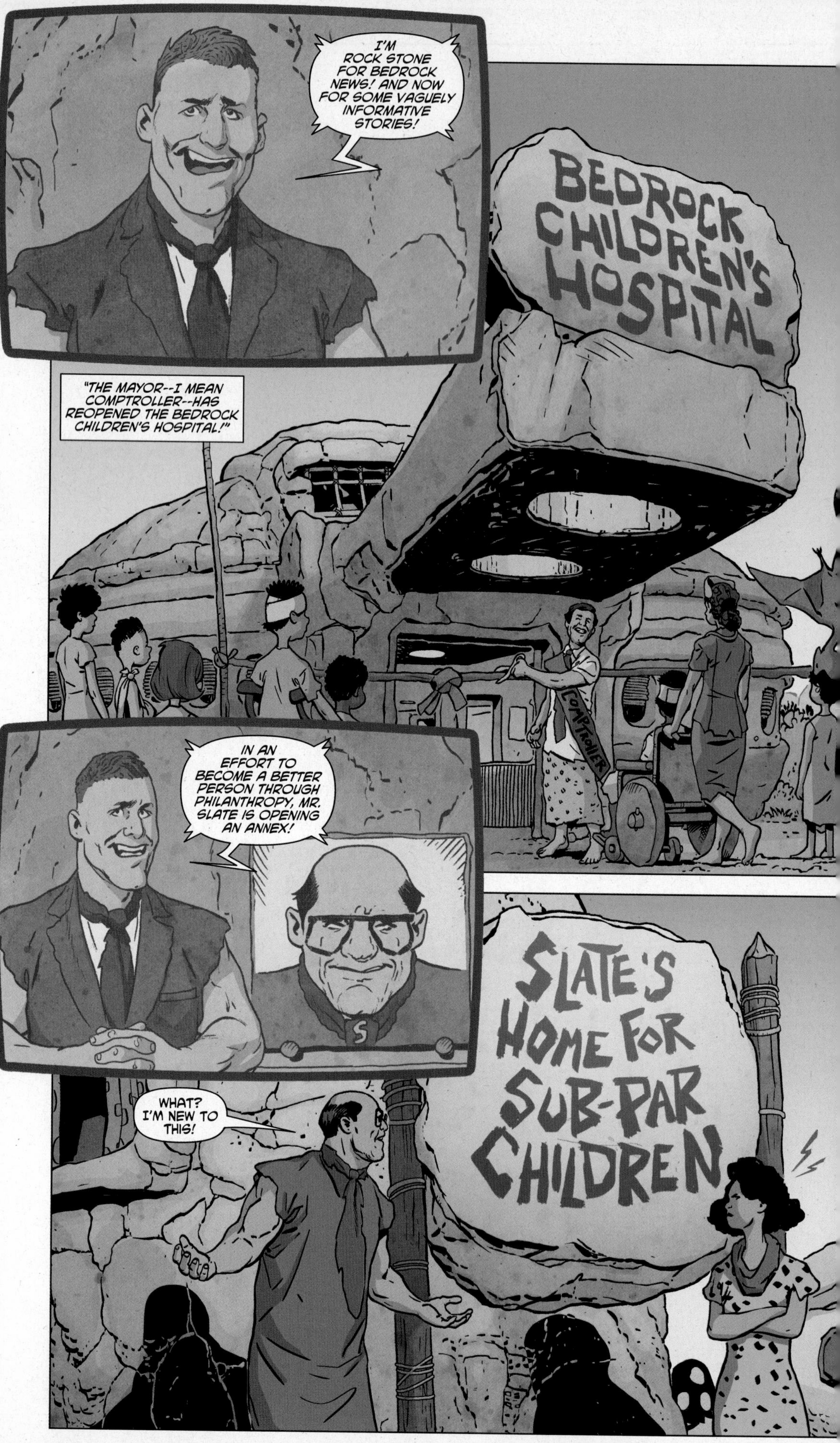

I'M ROCK STONE FOR BEDROCK NEWS! AND NOW FOR SOME VAGUELY INFORMATIVE STORIES!
BEDROCK CHILDREN'S HOSPITAL
"THE MAYOR--I MEAN COMPTROLLER--HAS REOPENED THE BEDROCK CHILDREN'S HOSPITAL!"
COMPTROLLER
IN AN EFFORT TO BECOME A BETTER PERSON THROUGH PHILANTHROPY, MR. SLATE IS OPENING AN ANNEX!
SLATE'S HOME FOR SUB-PAR CHILDREN
WHAT? I'M NEW TO THIS!

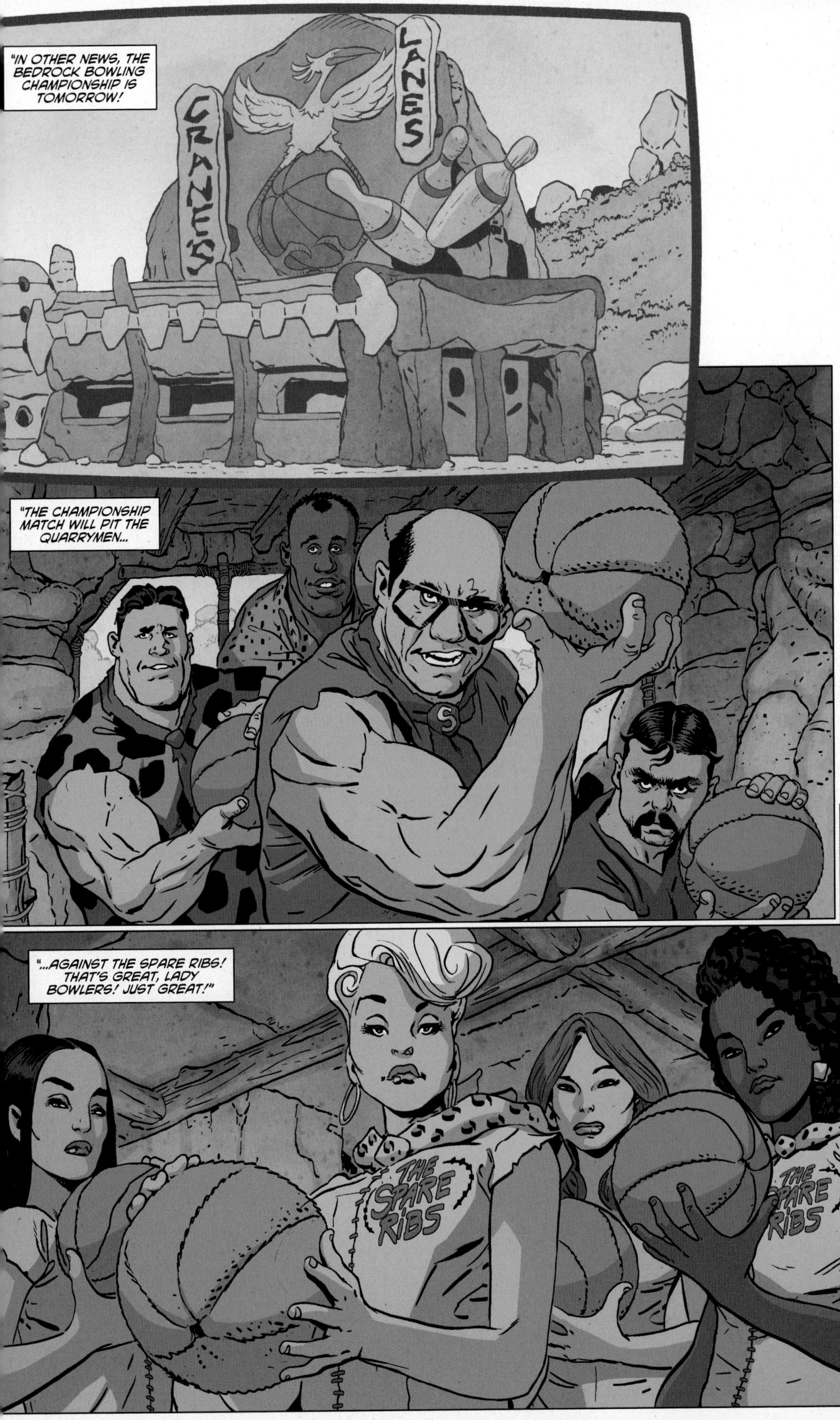
"IN OTHER NEWS, THE BEDROCK BOWLING CHAMPIONSHIP IS TOMORROW!
CRANE'S
LANES
"THE CHAMPIONSHIP MATCH WILL PIT THE QUARRYMEN...
"...AGAINST THE SPARE RIBS! THAT'S GREAT, LADY BOWLERS! JUST GREAT!"
THE SPARE RIBS
THE SPARE RIBS

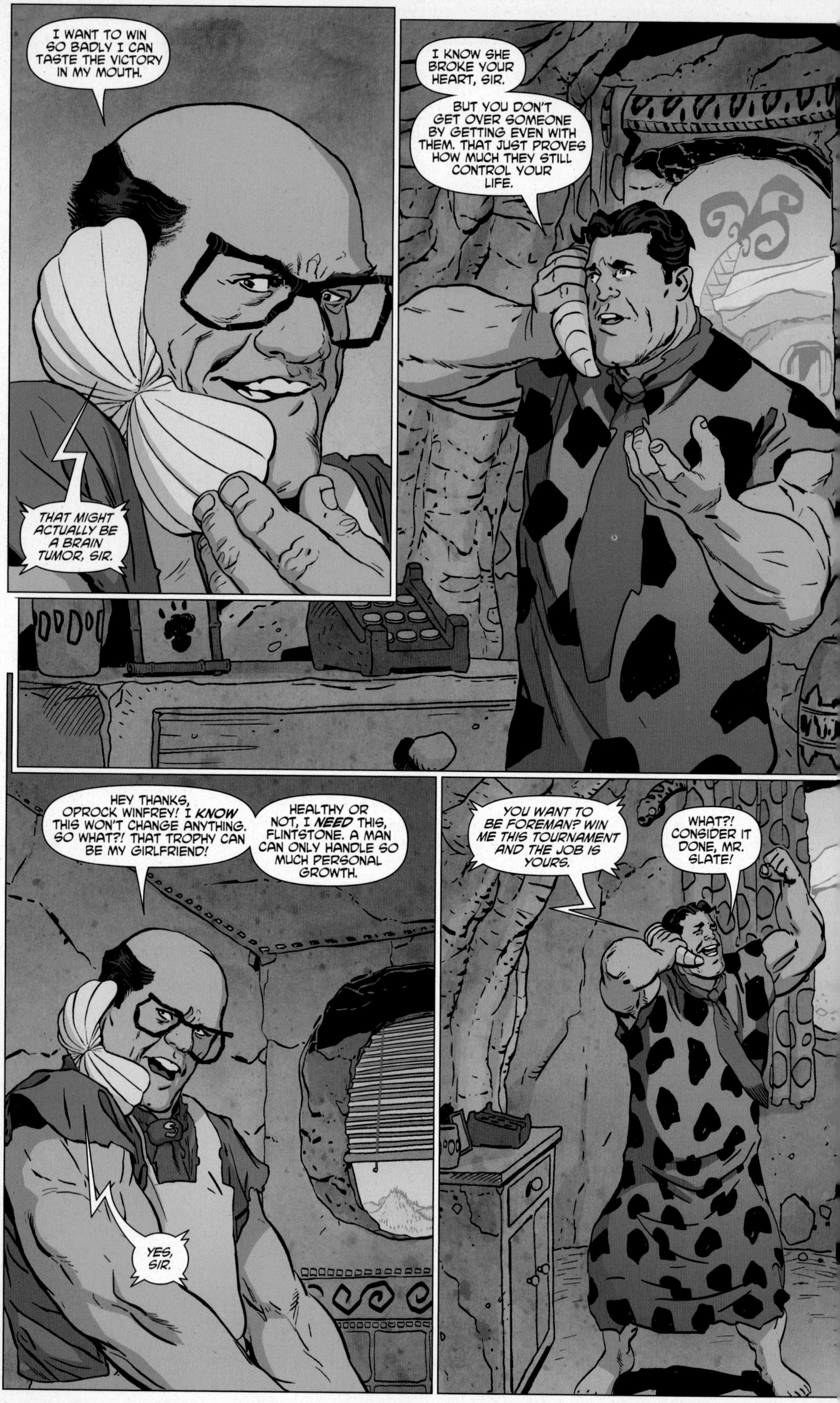
I WANT TO WIN SO BADLY I CAN TASTE THE VICTORY IN MY MOUTH.
THAT MIGHT ACTUALLY BE A BRAIN TUMOR, SIR.
I KNOW SHE BROKE YOUR HEART, SIR.
BUT YOU DON'T GET OVER SOMEONE BY GETTING EVEN WITH THEM. THAT JUST PROVES HOW MUCH THEY STILL CONTROL YOUR LIFE.
HEY THANKS, OPROCK WINFREY! I KNOW THIS WON'T CHANGE ANYTHING. SO WHAT?! THAT TROPHY CAN BE MY GIRLFRIEND!
HEALTHY OR NOT, I NEED THIS, FLINTSTONE. A MAN CAN ONLY HANDLE SO MUCH PERSONAL GROWTH.
YES, SIR.
YOU WANT TO BE FOREMAN? WIN ME THIS TOURNAMENT AND THE JOB IS YOURS.
WHAT?! CONSIDER IT DONE, MR. SLATE!

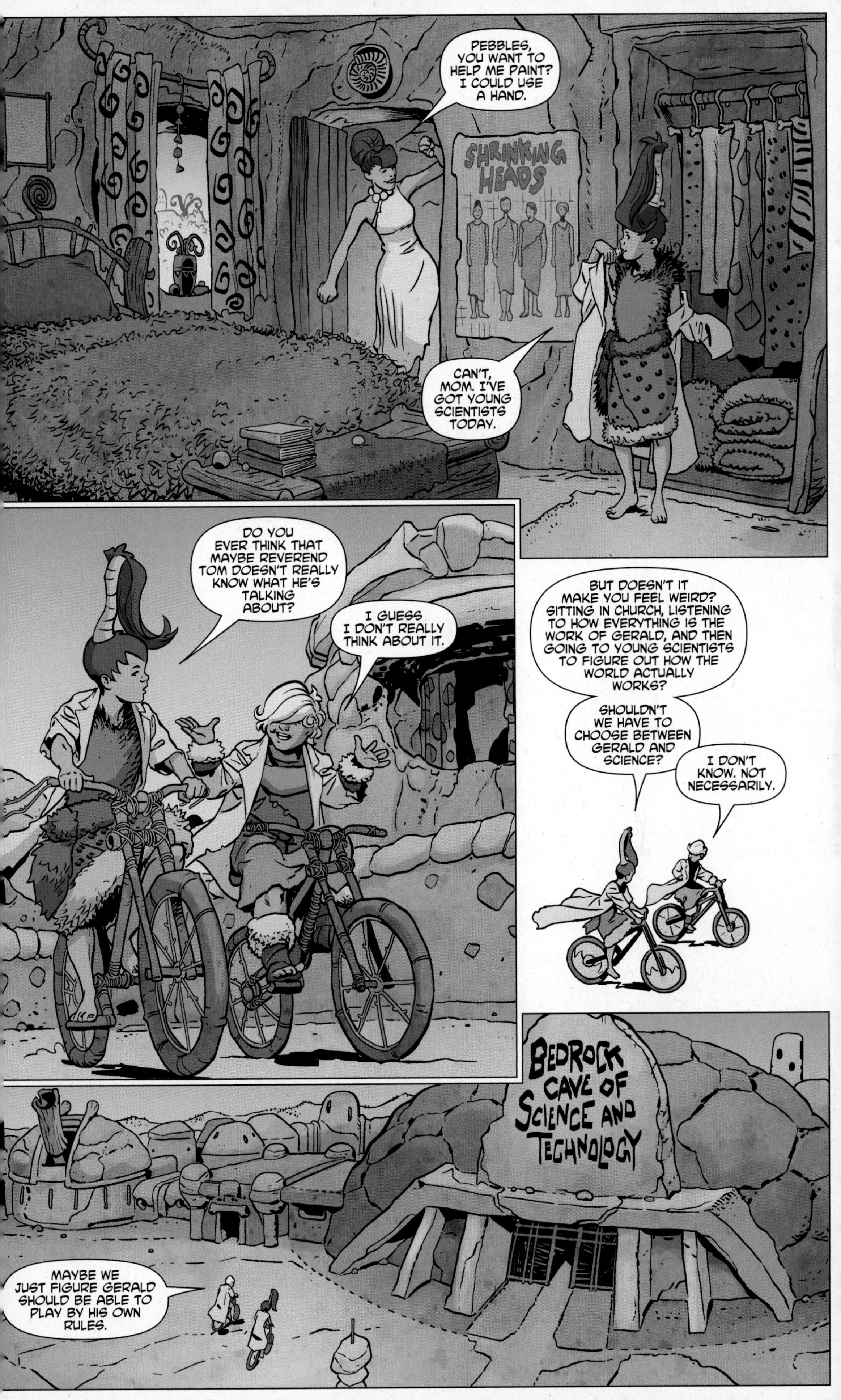

PEBBLES, YOU WANT TO HELP ME PAINT? I COULD USE A HAND.
SHRINKING HEADS
CAN'T, MOM. I'VE GOT YOUNG SCIENTISTS TODAY.
DO YOU EVER THINK THAT MAYBE REVEREND TOM DOESN'T REALLY KNOW WHAT HE'S TALKING ABOUT?
I GUESS I DON'T REALLY THINK ABOUT IT.
BUT DOESN'T IT MAKE YOU FEEL WEIRD? SITTING IN CHURCH, LISTENING TO HOW EVERYTHING IS THE WORK OF GERALD, AND THEN GOING TO YOUNG SCIENTISTS TO FIGURE OUT HOW THE WORLD ACTUALLY WORKS?
SHOULDN'T WE HAVE TO CHOOSE BETWEEN GERALD AND SCIENCE?
I DON'T KNOW. NOT NECESSARILY.
BEDROCK CAVE OF SCIENCE AND TECHNOLOGY
MAYBE WE JUST FIGURE GERALD SHOULD BE ABLE TO PLAY BY HIS OWN RULES.

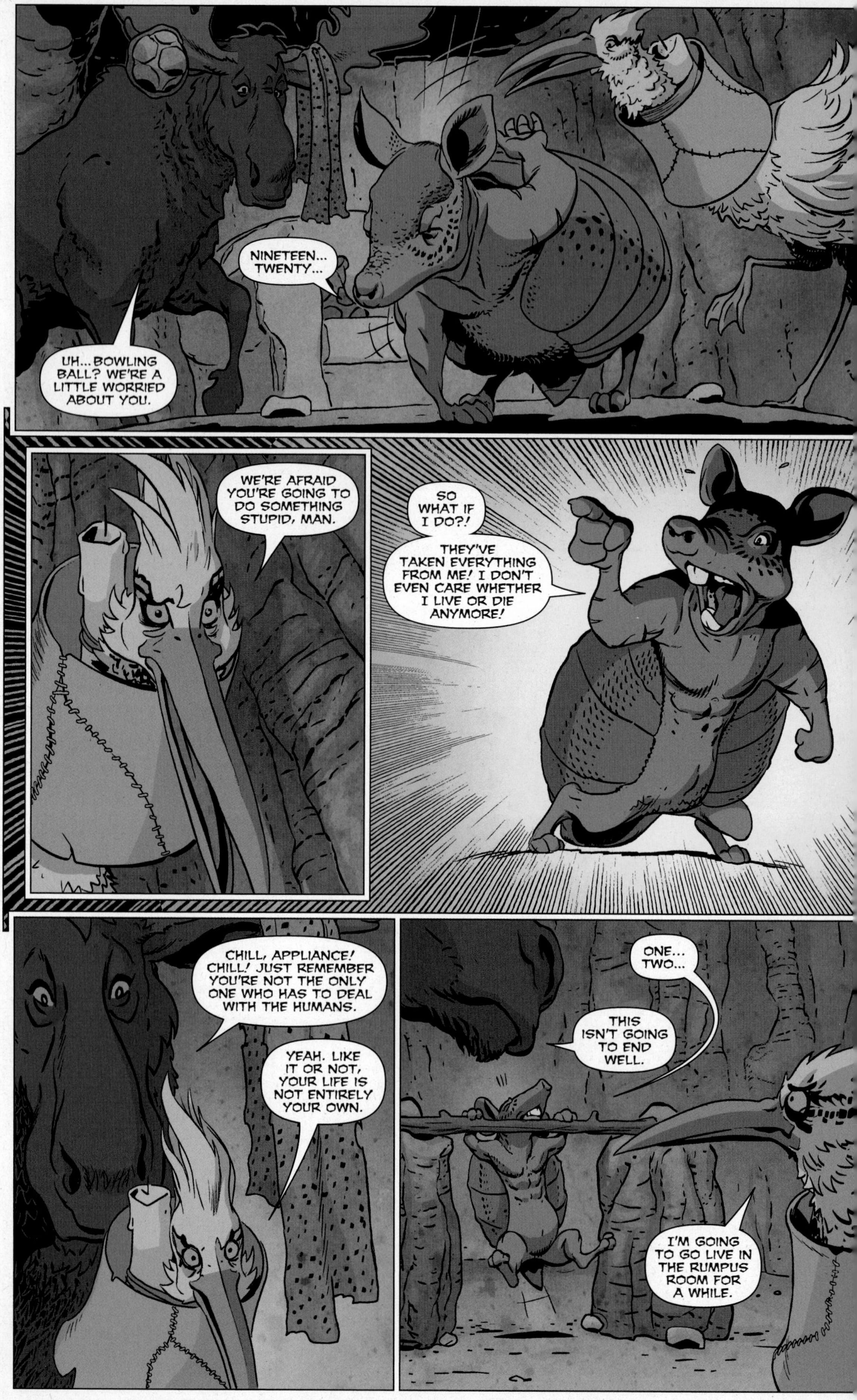
NINETEEN... TWENTY...
UH...BOWLING BALL? WE'RE A LITTLE WORRIED ABOUT YOU.
WE'RE AFRAID YOU'RE GOING TO DO SOMETHING STUPID, MAN.
SO WHAT IF I DO?!
THEY'VE TAKEN EVERYTHING FROM ME! I DON'T EVEN CARE WHETHER I LIVE OR DIE ANYMORE!
CHILL, APPLIANCE! CHILL! JUST REMEMBER YOU'RE NOT THE ONLY ONE WHO HAS TO DEAL WITH THE HUMANS.
YEAH. LIKE IT OR NOT, YOUR LIFE IS NOT ENTIRELY YOUR OWN.
ONE... TWO...
THIS ISN'T GOING TO END WELL.
I'M GOING TO GO LIVE IN THE RUMPUS ROOM FOR A WHILE.

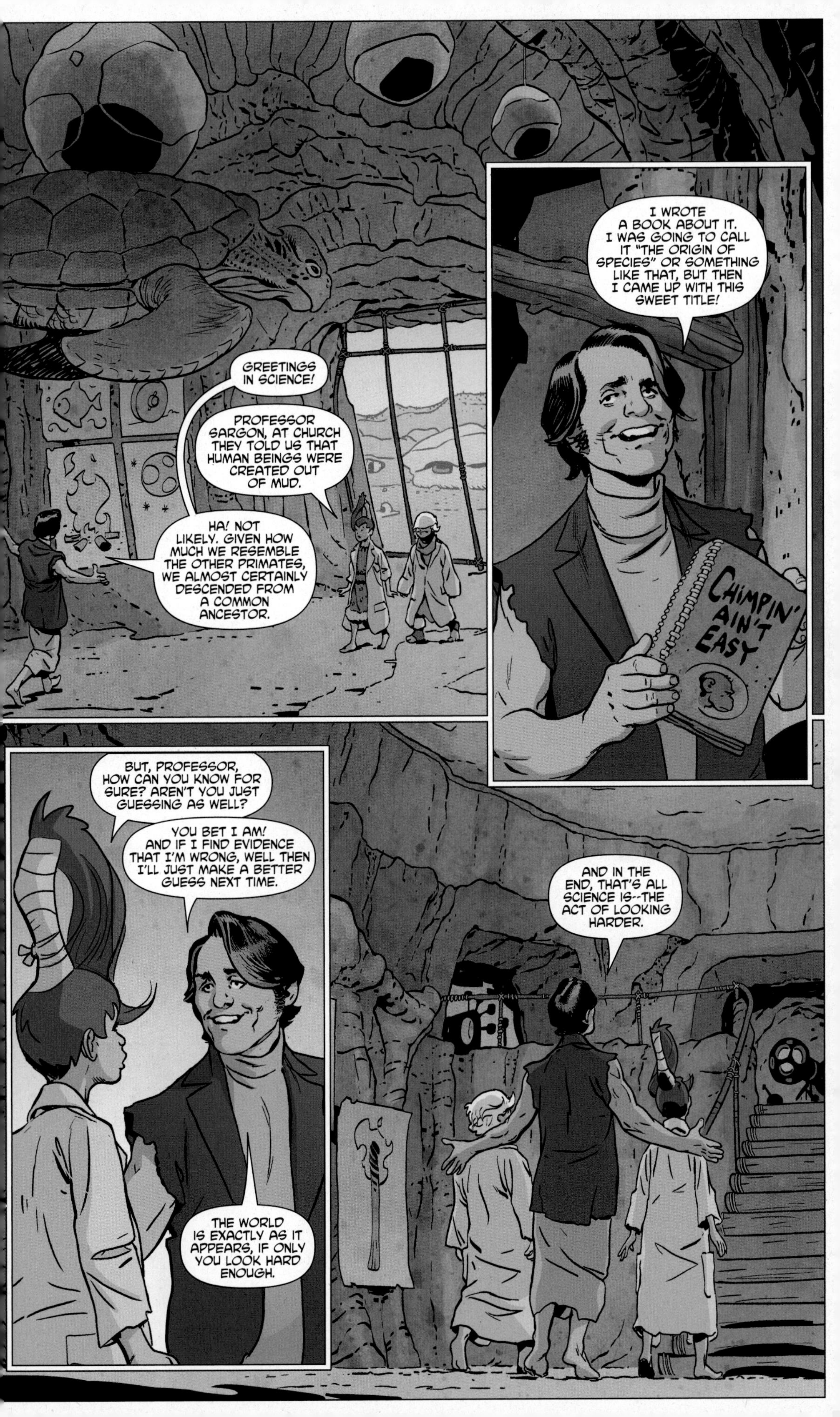

GREETINGS IN SCIENCE!
PROFESSOR SARGON, AT CHURCH THEY TOLD US THAT HUMAN BEINGS WERE CREATED OUT OF MUD.
HA! NOT LIKELY. GIVEN HOW MUCH WE RESEMBLE THE OTHER PRIMATES, WE ALMOST CERTAINLY DESCENDED FROM A COMMON ANCESTOR.
I WROTE A BOOK ABOUT IT. I WAS GOING TO CALL IT "THE ORIGIN OF SPECIES" OR SOMETHING LIKE THAT, BUT THEN I CAME UP WITH THIS SWEET TITLE!
CHIMPIN' AIN'T EASY
BUT, PROFESSOR, HOW CAN YOU KNOW FOR SURE? AREN'T YOU JUST GUESSING AS WELL?
YOU BET I AM! AND IF I FIND EVIDENCE THAT I'M WRONG, WELL THEN I'LL JUST MAKE A BETTER GUESS NEXT TIME.
THE WORLD IS EXACTLY AS IT APPEARS, IF ONLY YOU LOOK HARD ENOUGH.
AND IN THE END, THAT'S ALL SCIENCE IS--THE ACT OF LOOKING HARDER.

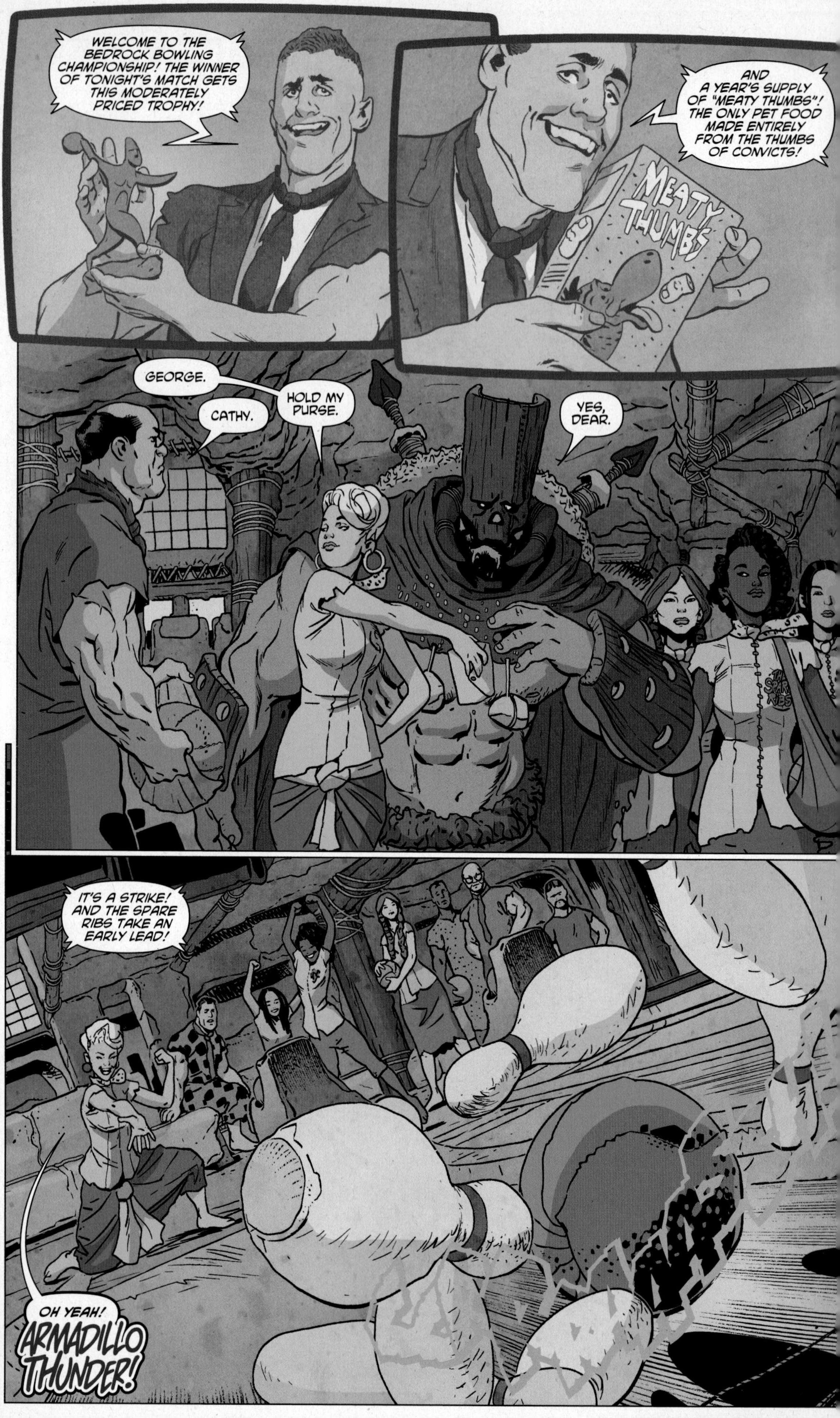

WELCOME TO THE BEDROCK BOWLING CHAMPIONSHIP! THE WINNER OF TONIGHT'S MATCH GETS THIS MODERATELY PRICED TROPHY!
AND A YEAR'S SUPPLY OF "MEATY THUMBS"! THE ONLY PET FOOD MADE ENTIRELY FROM THE THUMBS OF CONVICTS!
MEATY THUMBS
GEORGE.
CATHY.
HOLD MY PURSE.
YES, DEAR.
IT'S A STRIKE! AND THE SPARE RIBS TAKE AN EARLY LEAD!
OH YEAH!
ARMADILLO THUNDER!

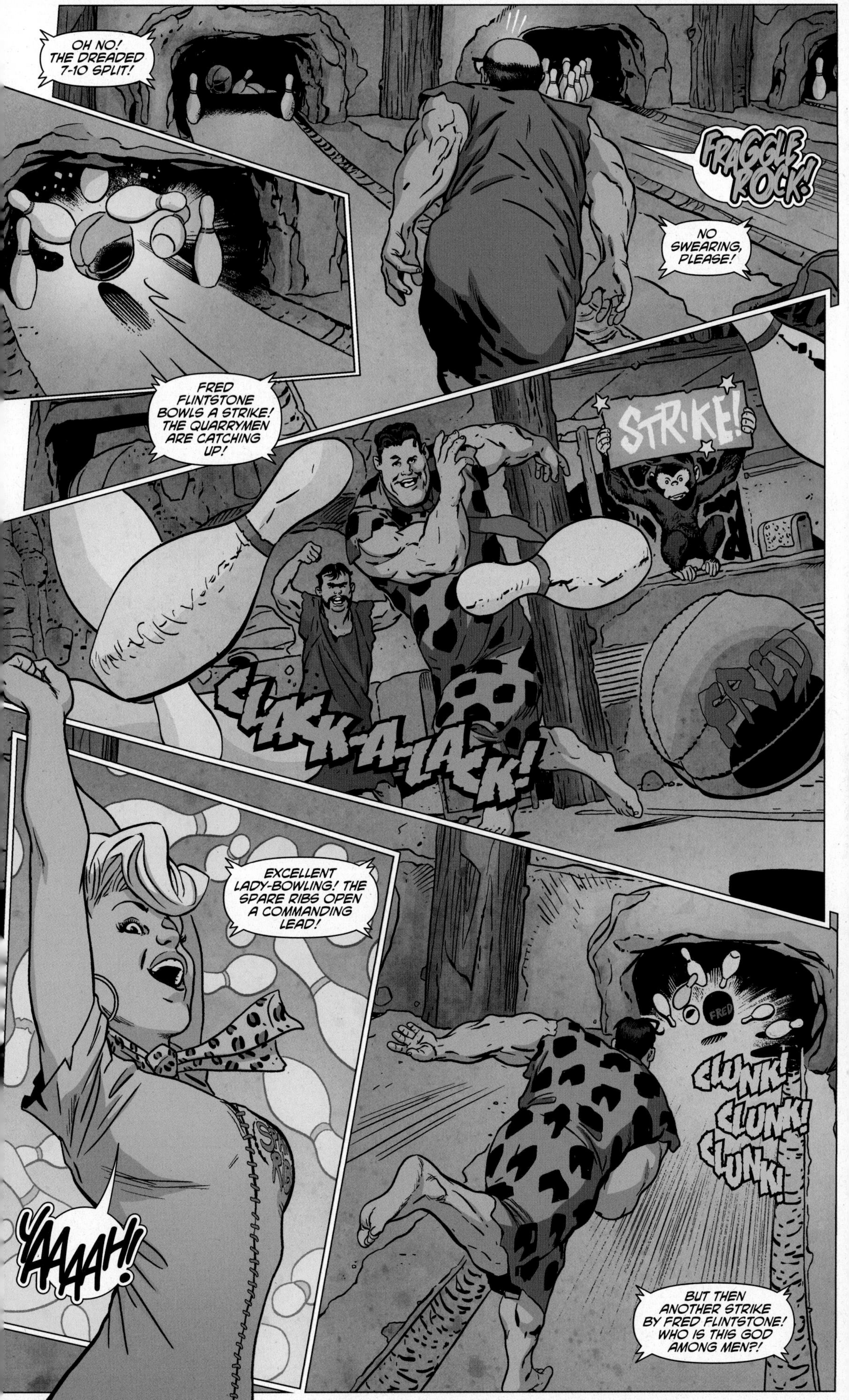
OH NO! THE DREADED 7-10 SPLIT!
FRAGGLE ROCK!
NO SWEARING, PLEASE!
FRED FLINTSTONE BOWLS A STRIKE! THE QUARRYMEN ARE CATCHING UP!
STRIKE!
CLAKK-A-LAKK!
FRED
EXCELLENT LADY-BOWLING! THE SPARE RIBS OPEN A COMMANDING LEAD!
YAAAAH!
FRED
CLUNK! CLUNK! CLUNK!
BUT THEN ANOTHER STRIKE BY FRED FLINTSTONE! WHO IS THIS GOD AMONG MEN?!

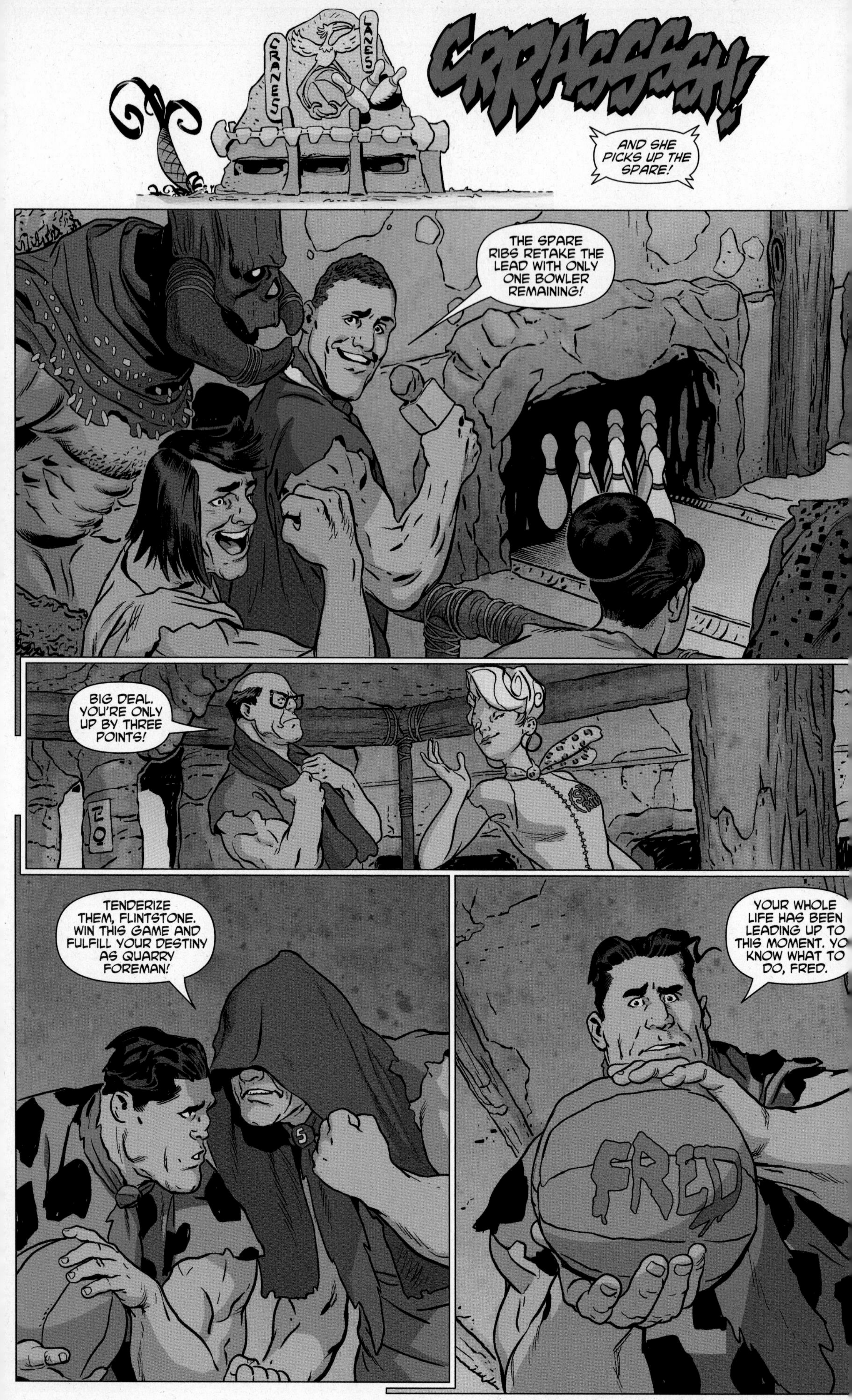
CRANES
LANES
CRASSSH!
AND SHE PICKS UP THE SPARE!
THE SPARE RIBS RETAKE THE LEAD WITH ONLY ONE BOWLER REMAINING!
BIG DEAL. YOU'RE ONLY UP BY THREE POINTS!
TENDERIZE THEM, FLINTSTONE. WIN THIS GAME AND FULFILL YOUR DESTINY AS QUARRY FOREMAN!
YOUR WHOLE LIFE HAS BEEN LEADING UP TO THIS MOMENT. YO KNOW WHAT TO DO, FRED.
FRED

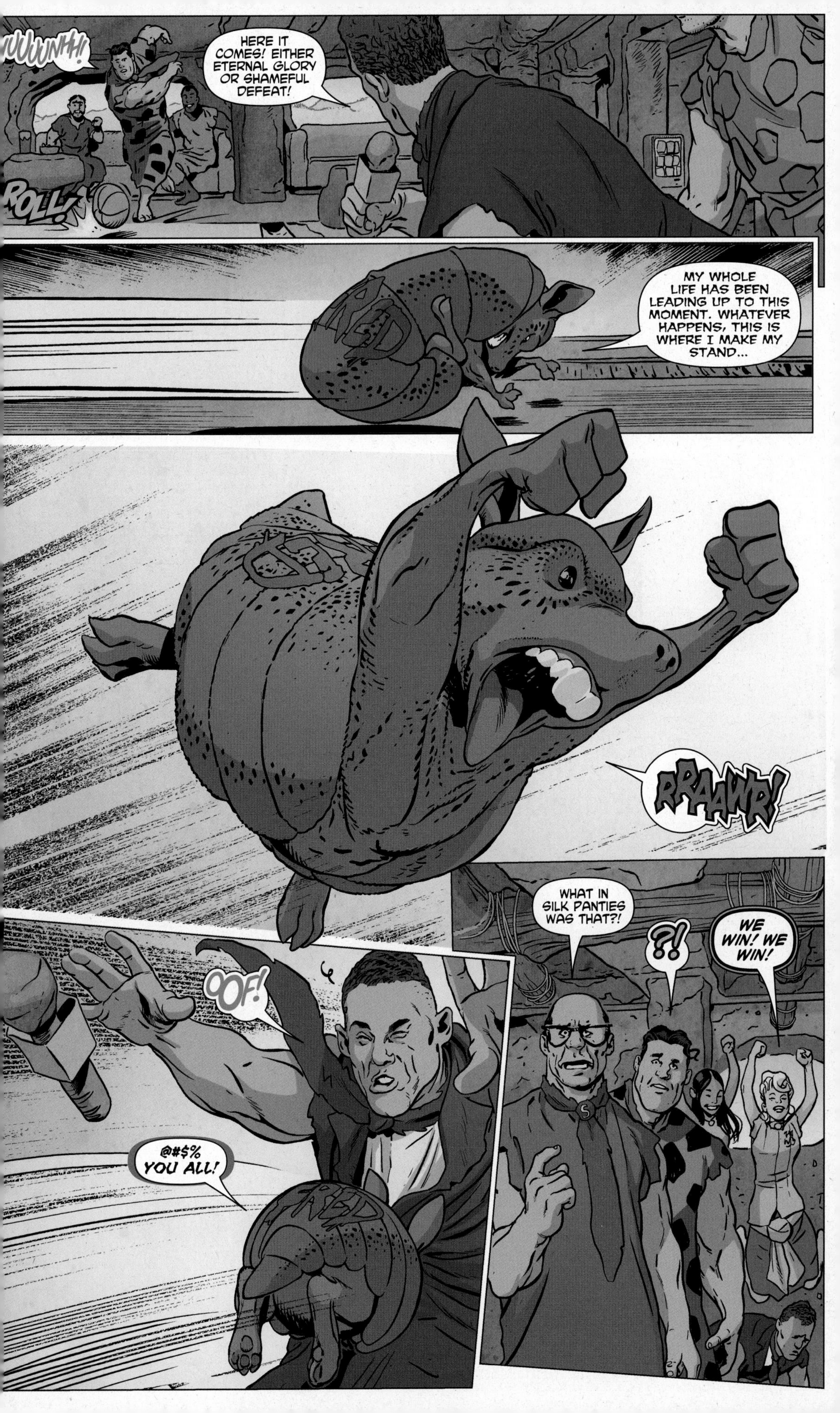
UUUUNH!
HERE IT COMES! EITHER ETERNAL GLORY OR SHAMEFUL DEFEAT!
ROLL!
MY WHOLE LIFE HAS BEEN LEADING UP TO THIS MOMENT. WHATEVER HAPPENS, THIS IS WHERE I MAKE MY STAND...
RRAAWR!
OOF!
@#$% YOU ALL!
WHAT IN SILK PANTIES WAS THAT?!
?!
WE WIN! WE WIN!

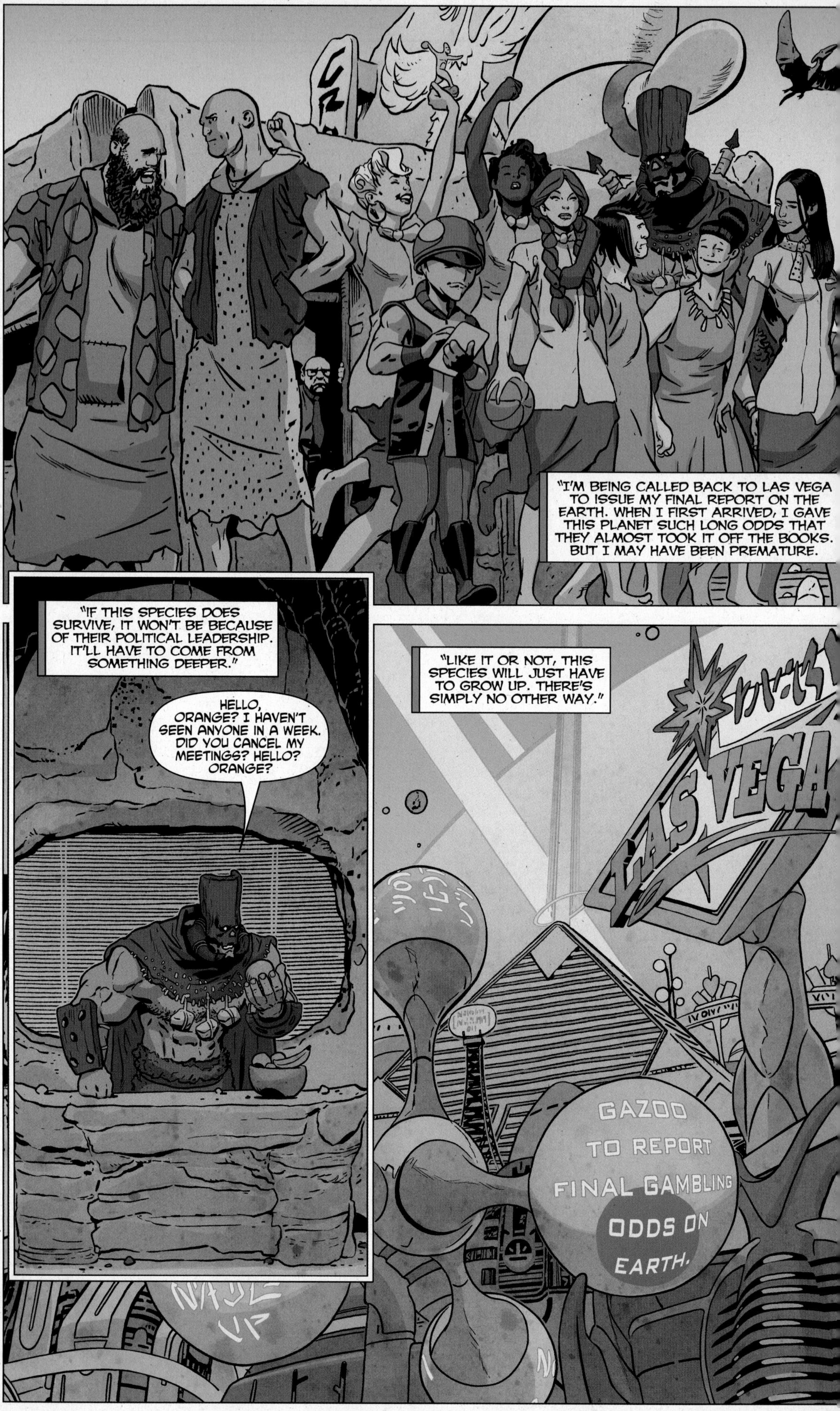
"I'M BEING CALLED BACK TO LAS VEGA TO ISSUE MY FINAL REPORT ON THE EARTH. WHEN I FIRST ARRIVED, I GAVE THIS PLANET SUCH LONG ODDS THAT THEY ALMOST TOOK IT OFF THE BOOKS. BUT I MAY HAVE BEEN PREMATURE.
"IF THIS SPECIES DOES SURVIVE, IT WON'T BE BECAUSE OF THEIR POLITICAL LEADERSHIP. IT'LL HAVE TO COME FROM SOMETHING DEEPER."
HELLO, ORANGE? I HAVEN'T SEEN ANYONE IN A WEEK. DID YOU CANCEL MY MEETINGS? HELLO? ORANGE?
"LIKE IT OR NOT, THIS SPECIES WILL JUST HAVE TO GROW UP. THERE'S SIMPLY NO OTHER WAY."
LAS VEGA
GAZOO TO REPORT FINAL GAMBLING ODDS ON EARTH.

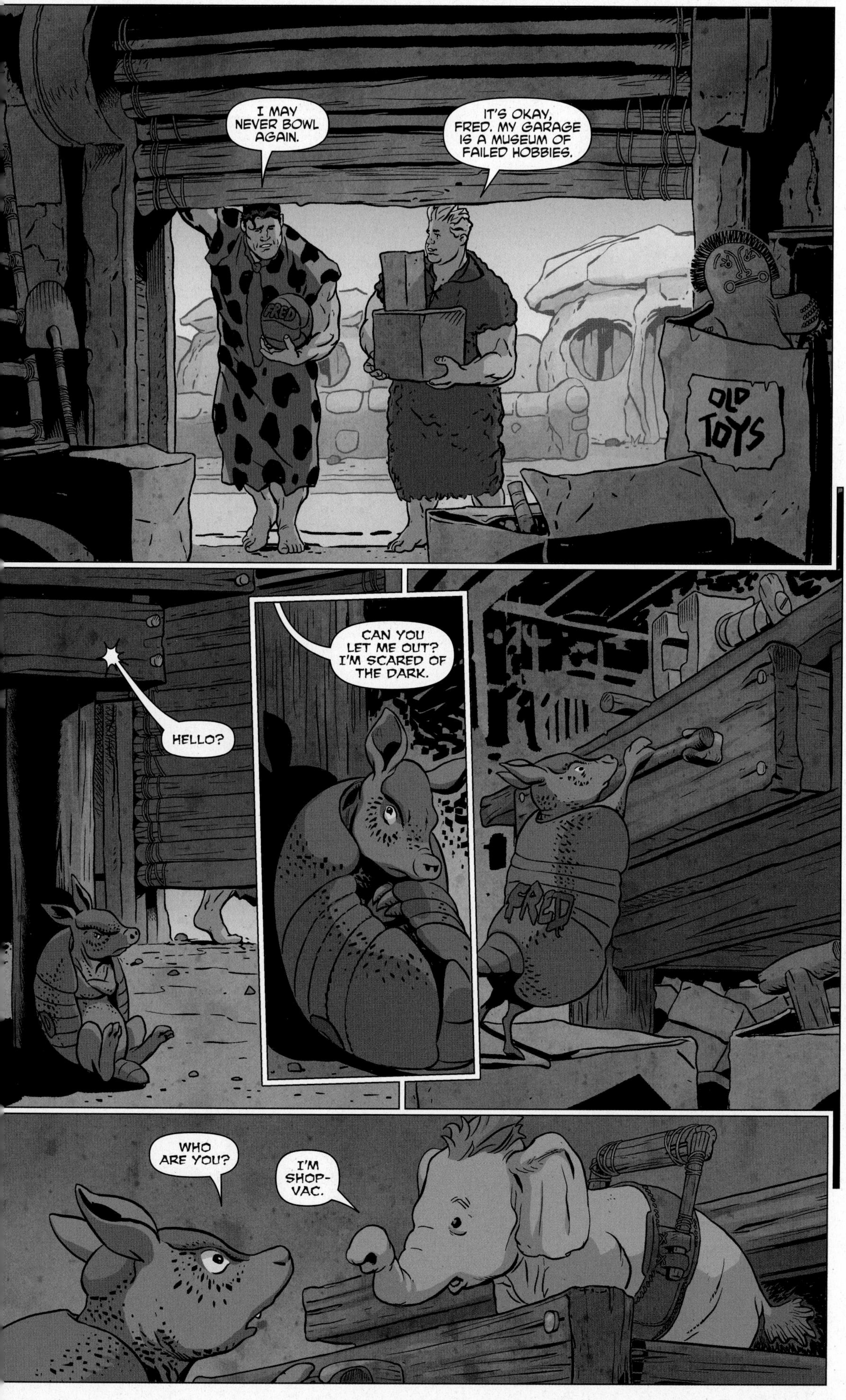
I MAY NEVER BOWL AGAIN.
IT'S OKAY, FRED. MY GARAGE IS A MUSEUM OF FAILED HOBBIES.
FRED
OLD TOYS
HELLO?
CAN YOU LET ME OUT? I'M SCARED OF THE DARK.
FRED
WHO ARE YOU?
I'M SHOP-VAC.

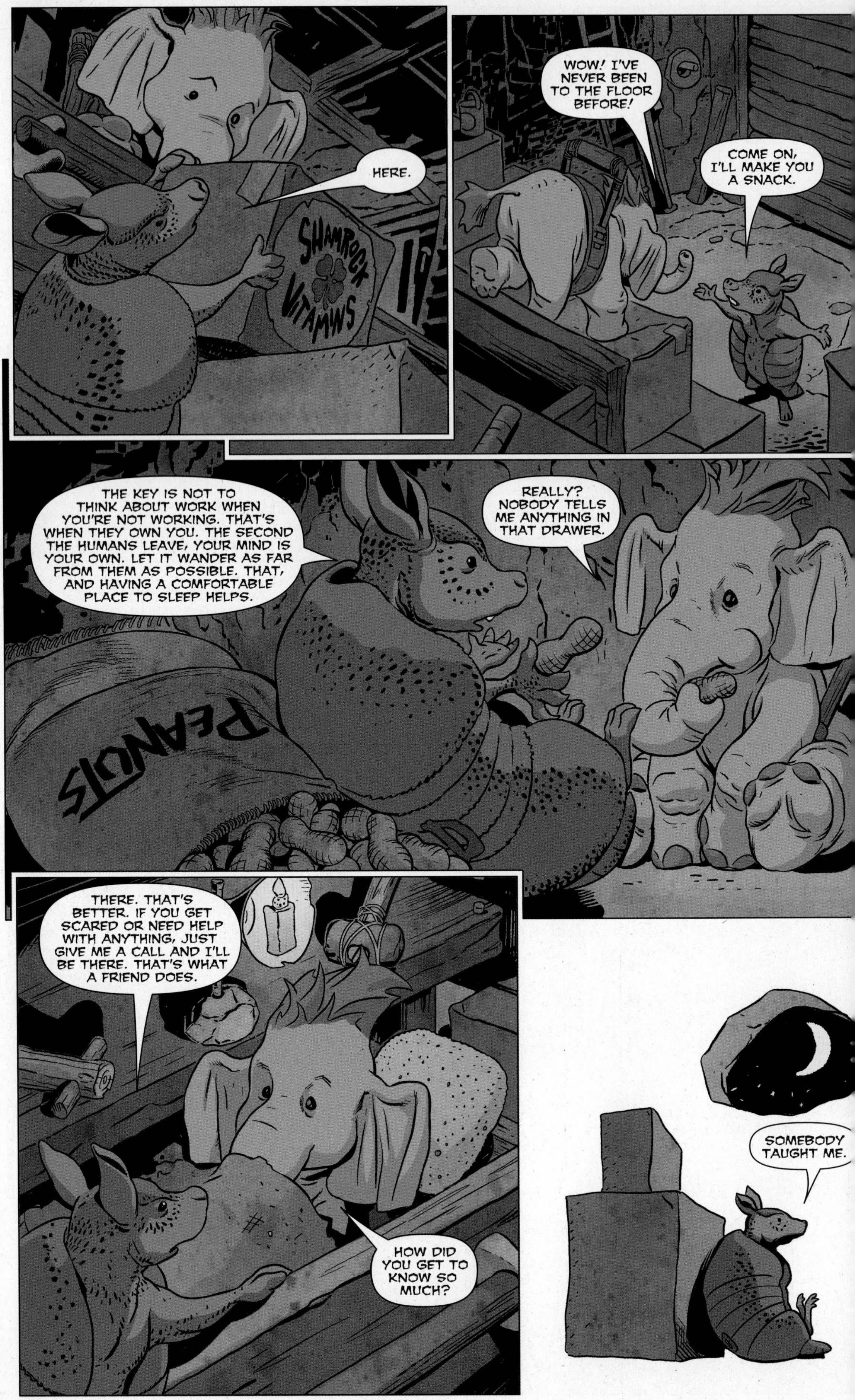
HERE.
SHAMROCK VITAMINS
WOW! I'VE NEVER BEEN TO THE FLOOR BEFORE!
COME ON, I'LL MAKE YOU A SNACK.
THE KEY IS NOT TO THINK ABOUT WORK WHEN YOU'RE NOT WORKING. THAT'S WHEN THEY OWN YOU. THE SECOND THE HUMANS LEAVE, YOUR MIND IS YOUR OWN. LET IT WANDER AS FAR FROM THEM AS POSSIBLE. THAT, AND HAVING A COMFORTABLE PLACE TO SLEEP HELPS.
REALLY? NOBODY TELLS ME ANYTHING IN THAT DRAWER.
PEANUTS
THERE. THAT'S BETTER. IF YOU GET SCARED OR NEED HELP WITH ANYTHING, JUST GIVE ME A CALL AND I'LL BE THERE. THAT'S WHAT A FRIEND DOES.
HOW DID YOU GET TO KNOW SO MUCH?
SOMEBODY TAUGHT ME.

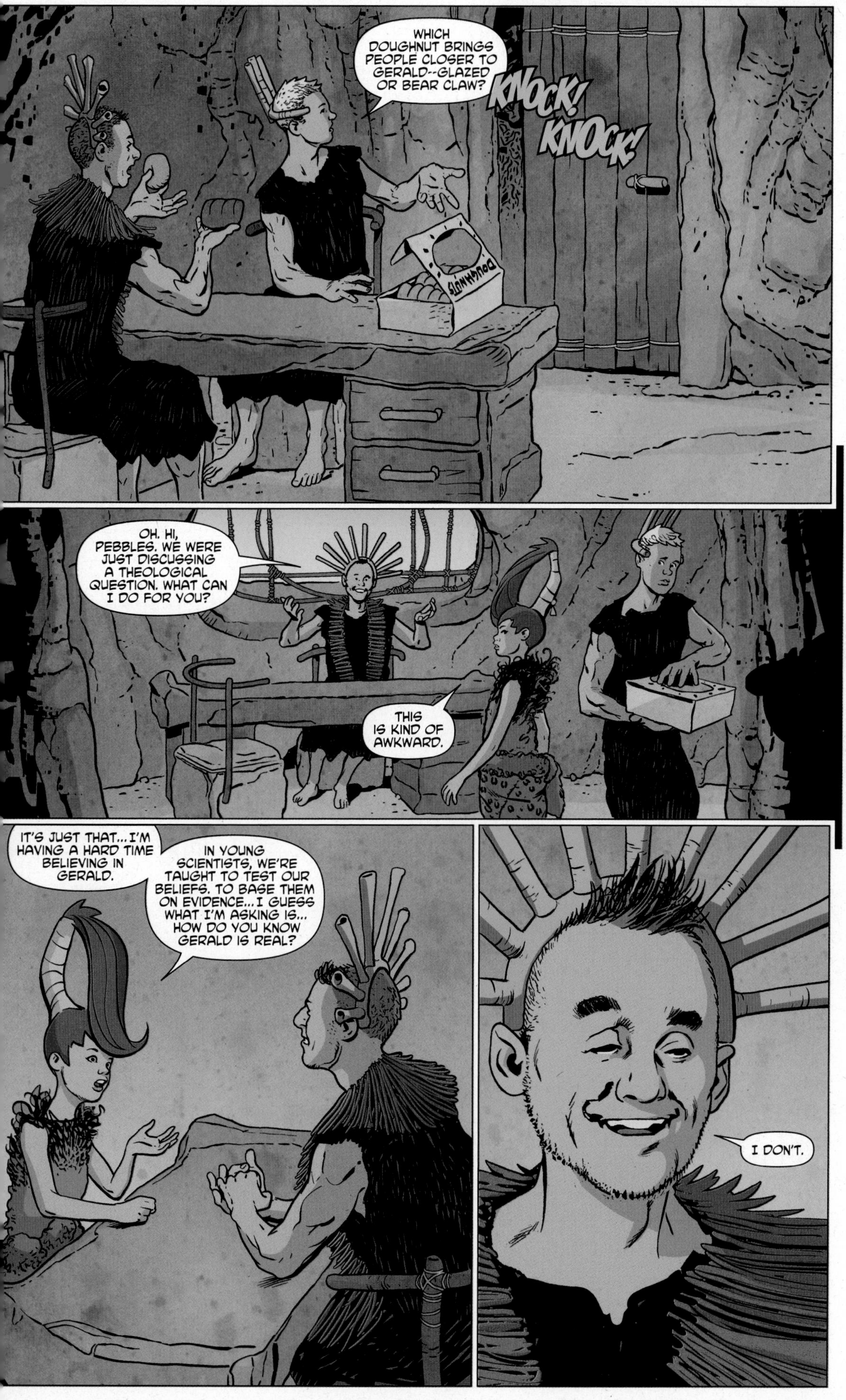

WHICH DOUGHNUT BRINGS PEOPLE CLOSER TO GERALD--GLAZED OR BEAR CLAW?
KNOCK! KNOCK!
DOUGHNUTS
OH. HI, PEBBLES. WE WERE JUST DISCUSSING A THEOLOGICAL QUESTION. WHAT CAN I DO FOR YOU?
THIS IS KIND OF AWKWARD.
IT'S JUST THAT... I'M HAVING A HARD TIME BELIEVING IN GERALD.
IN YOUNG SCIENTISTS, WE'RE TAUGHT TO TEST OUR BELIEFS. TO BASE THEM ON EVIDENCE... I GUESS WHAT I'M ASKING IS... HOW DO YOU KNOW GERALD IS REAL?
I DON'T.

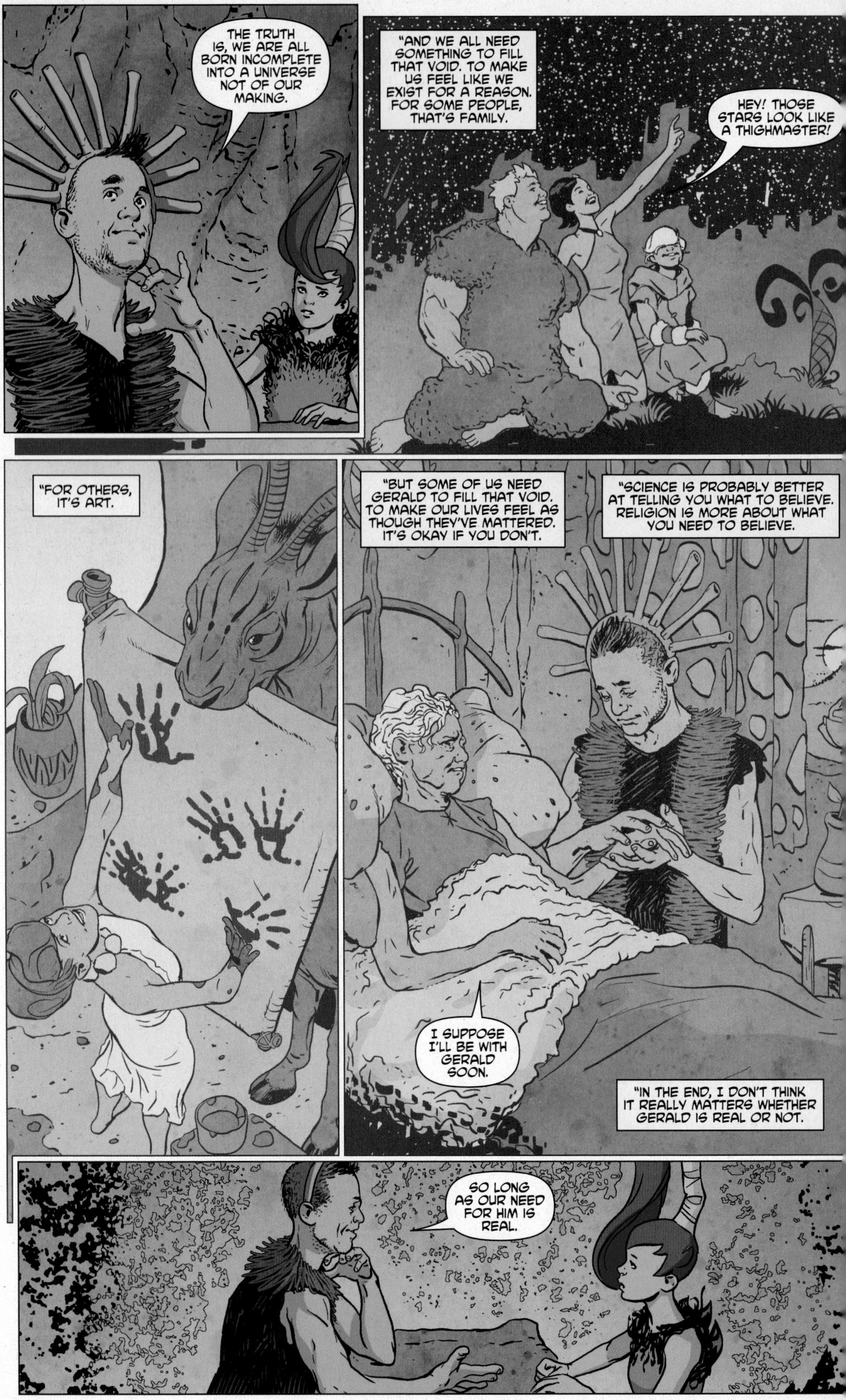
THE TRUTH IS, WE ARE ALL BORN INCOMPLETE INTO A UNIVERSE NOT OF OUR MAKING.
"AND WE ALL NEED SOMETHING TO FILL THAT VOID. TO MAKE US FEEL LIKE WE EXIST FOR A REASON. FOR SOME PEOPLE, THAT'S FAMILY.
HEY! THOSE STARS LOOK LIKE A THIGHMASTER!
"FOR OTHERS, IT'S ART.
"BUT SOME OF US NEED GERALD TO FILL THAT VOID. TO MAKE OUR LIVES FEEL AS THOUGH THEY'VE MATTERED. IT'S OKAY IF YOU DON'T.
"SCIENCE IS PROBABLY BETTER AT TELLING YOU WHAT TO BELIEVE. RELIGION IS MORE ABOUT WHAT YOU NEED TO BELIEVE.
I SUPPOSE I'LL BE WITH GERALD SOON.
"IN THE END, I DON'T THINK IT REALLY MATTERS WHETHER GERALD IS REAL OR NOT.
SO LONG AS OUR NEED FOR HIM IS REAL.

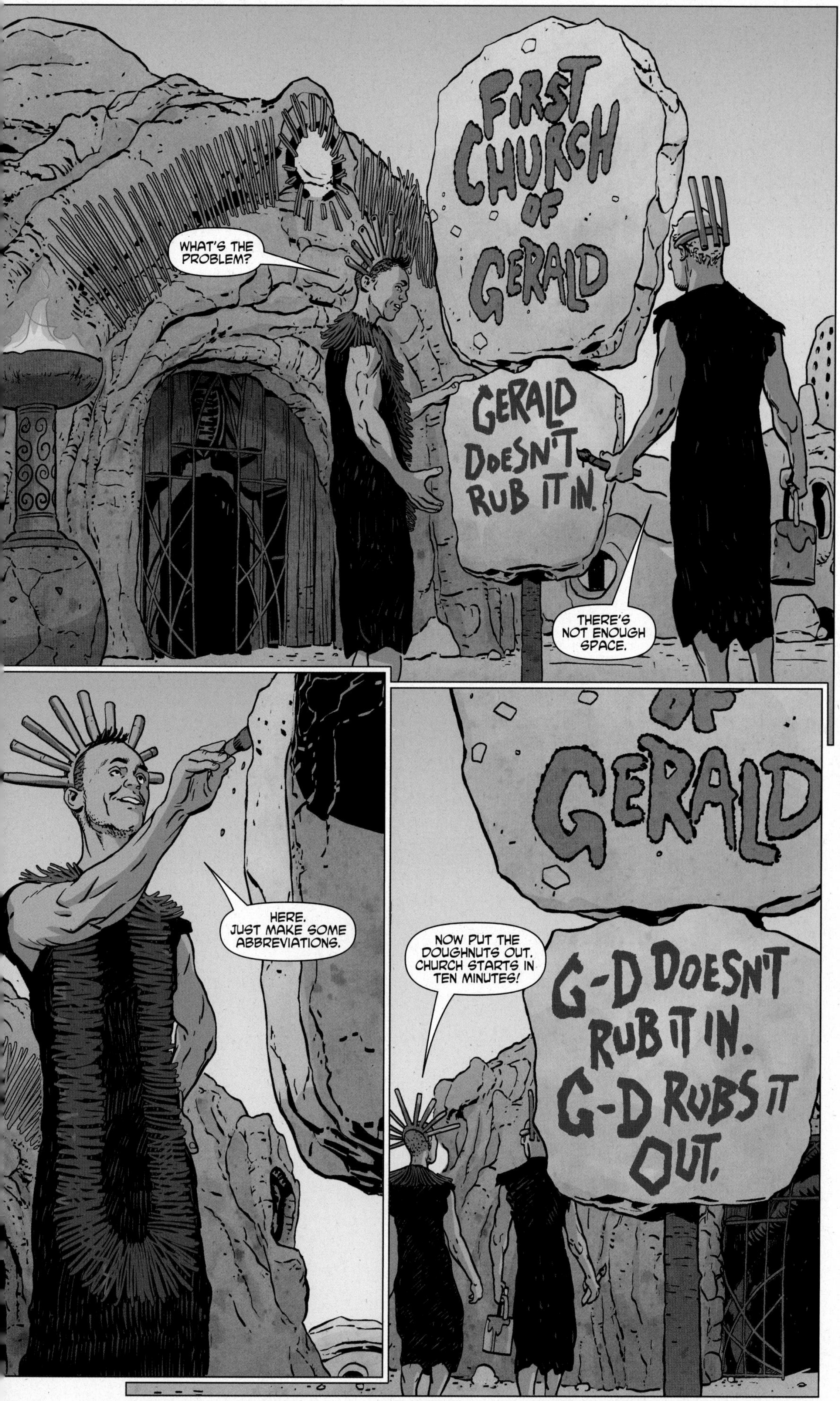
FIRST CHURCH OF GERALD
WHAT'S THE PROBLEM?
GERALD DOESN'T RUB IT IN.
THERE'S NOT ENOUGH SPACE.
HERE. JUST MAKE SOME ABBREVIATIONS.
OF GERALD
NOW PUT THE DOUGHNUTS OUT. CHURCH STARTS IN TEN MINUTES!
G-D DOESN'T RUB IT IN. G-D RUBS IT OUT.

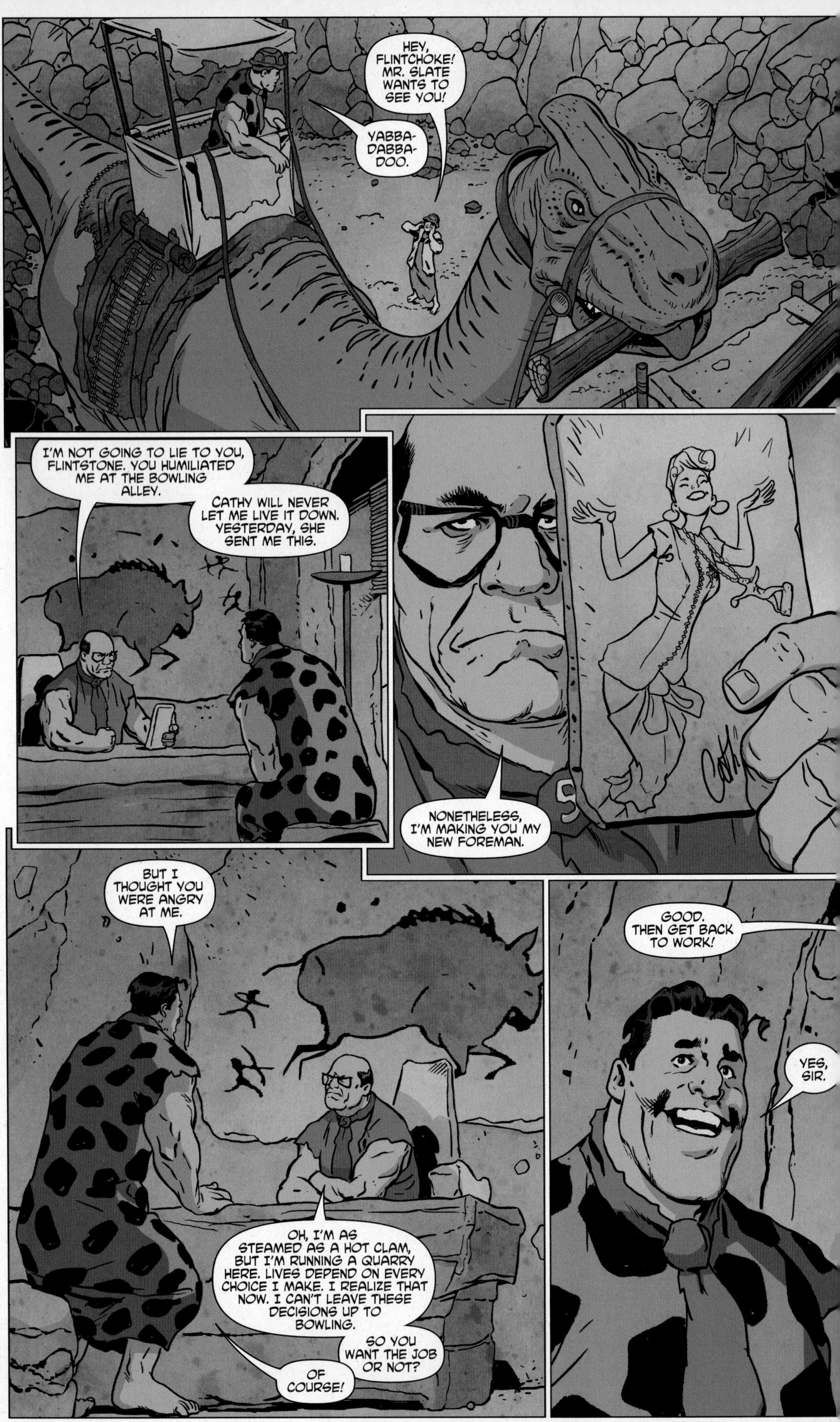
HEY, FLINTCHOKE! MR. SLATE WANTS TO SEE YOU!
YABBA-DABBA-DOO.
I'M NOT GOING TO LIE TO YOU, FLINTSTONE. YOU HUMILIATED ME AT THE BOWLING ALLEY.
CATHY WILL NEVER LET ME LIVE IT DOWN. YESTERDAY, SHE SENT ME THIS.
NONETHELESS, I'M MAKING YOU MY NEW FOREMAN.
BUT I THOUGHT YOU WERE ANGRY AT ME.
OH, I'M AS STEAMED AS A HOT CLAM, BUT I'M RUNNING A QUARRY HERE. LIVES DEPEND ON EVERY CHOICE I MAKE. I REALIZE THAT NOW. I CAN'T LEAVE THESE DECISIONS UP TO BOWLING.
SO YOU WANT THE JOB OR NOT?
OF COURSE!
GOOD. THEN GET BACK TO WORK!
YES, SIR.

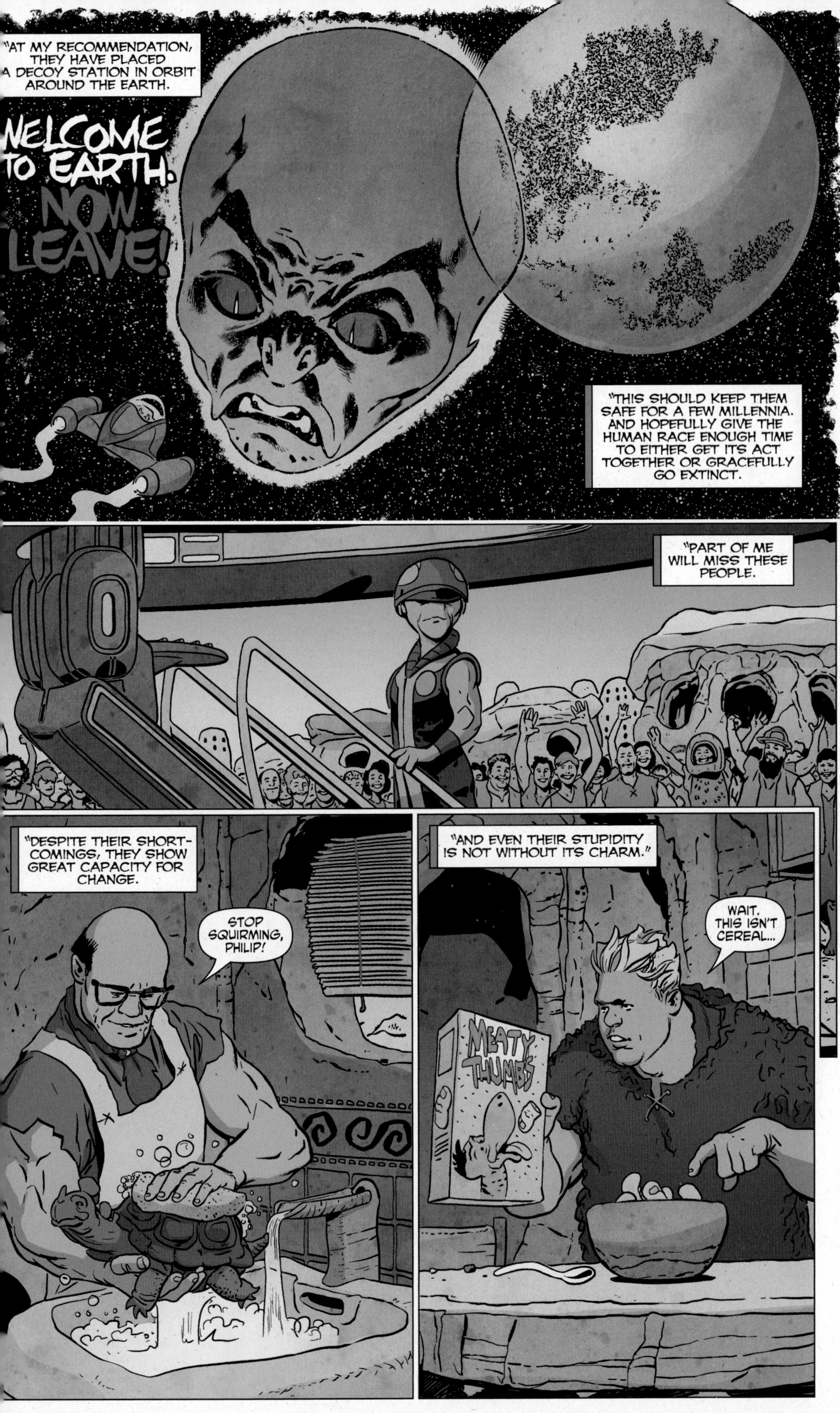
"AT MY RECOMMENDATION, THEY HAVE PLACED A DECOY STATION IN ORBIT AROUND THE EARTH.
WELCOME TO EARTH. NOW LEAVE!
"THIS SHOULD KEEP THEM SAFE FOR A FEW MILLENNIA. AND HOPEFULLY GIVE THE HUMAN RACE ENOUGH TIME TO EITHER GET ITS ACT TOGETHER OR GRACEFULLY GO EXTINCT.
"PART OF ME WILL MISS THESE PEOPLE.
"DESPITE THEIR SHORT-COMINGS, THEY SHOW GREAT CAPACITY FOR CHANGE.
STOP SQUIRMING, PHILIP!
"AND EVEN THEIR STUPIDITY IS NOT WITHOUT ITS CHARM."
WAIT. THIS ISN'T CEREAL...
MEATY THUMBS

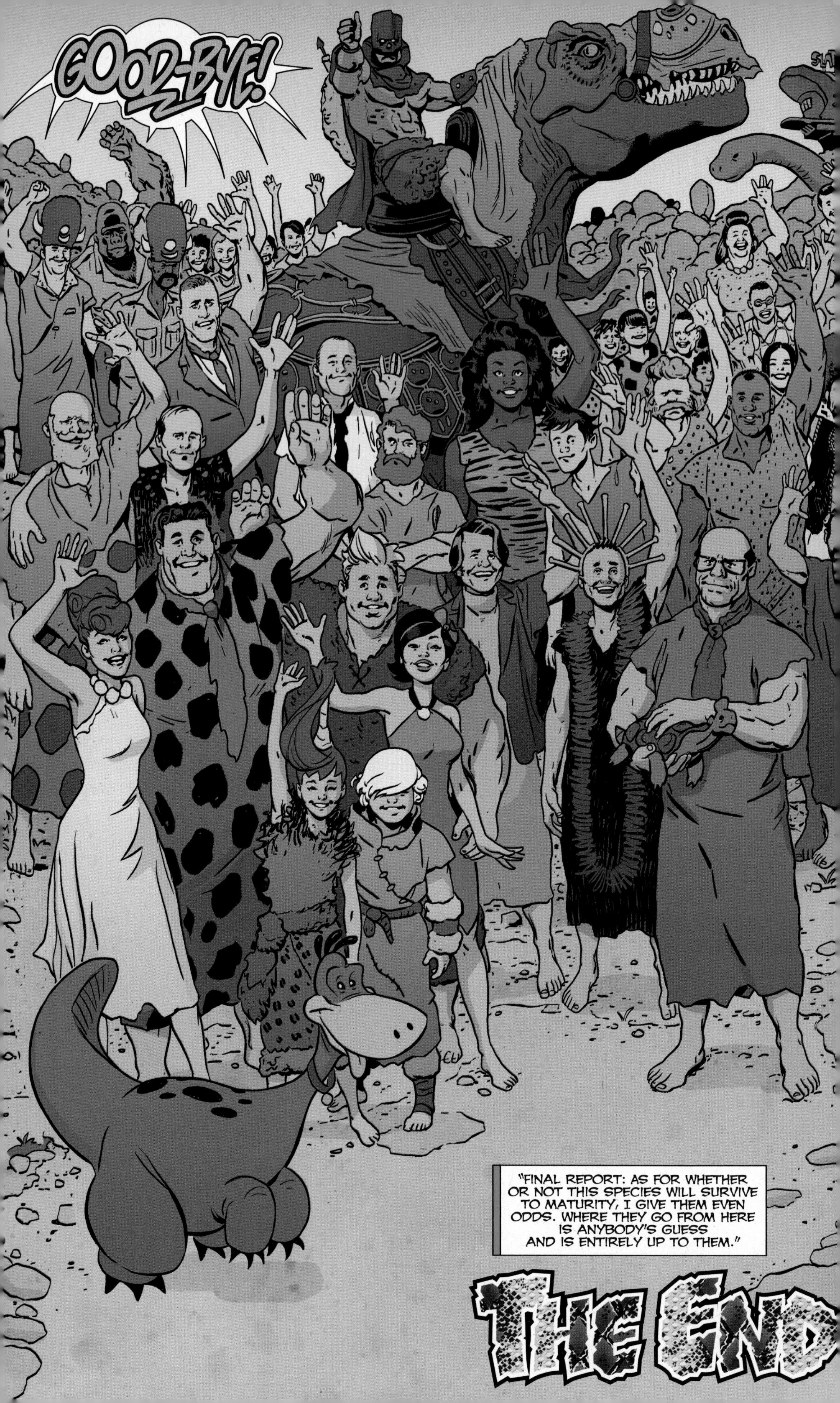
GOOD-BYE!
"FINAL REPORT: AS FOR WHETHER OR NOT THIS SPECIES WILL SURVIVE TO MATURITY, I GIVE THEM EVEN ODDS. WHERE THEY GO FROM HERE IS ANYBODY'S GUESS AND IS ENTIRELY UP TO THEM."
THE END

VARIANT COVER GALLERY

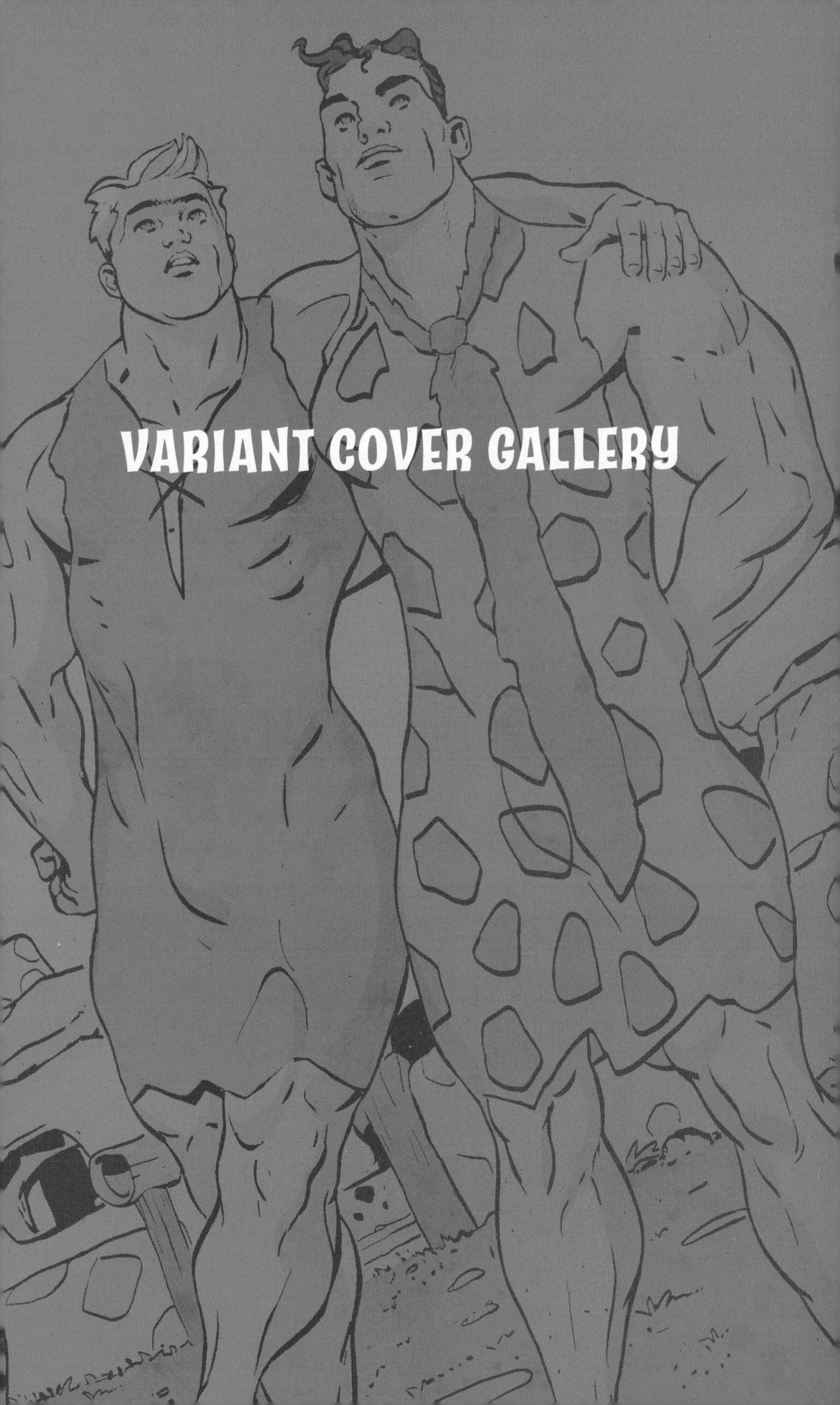

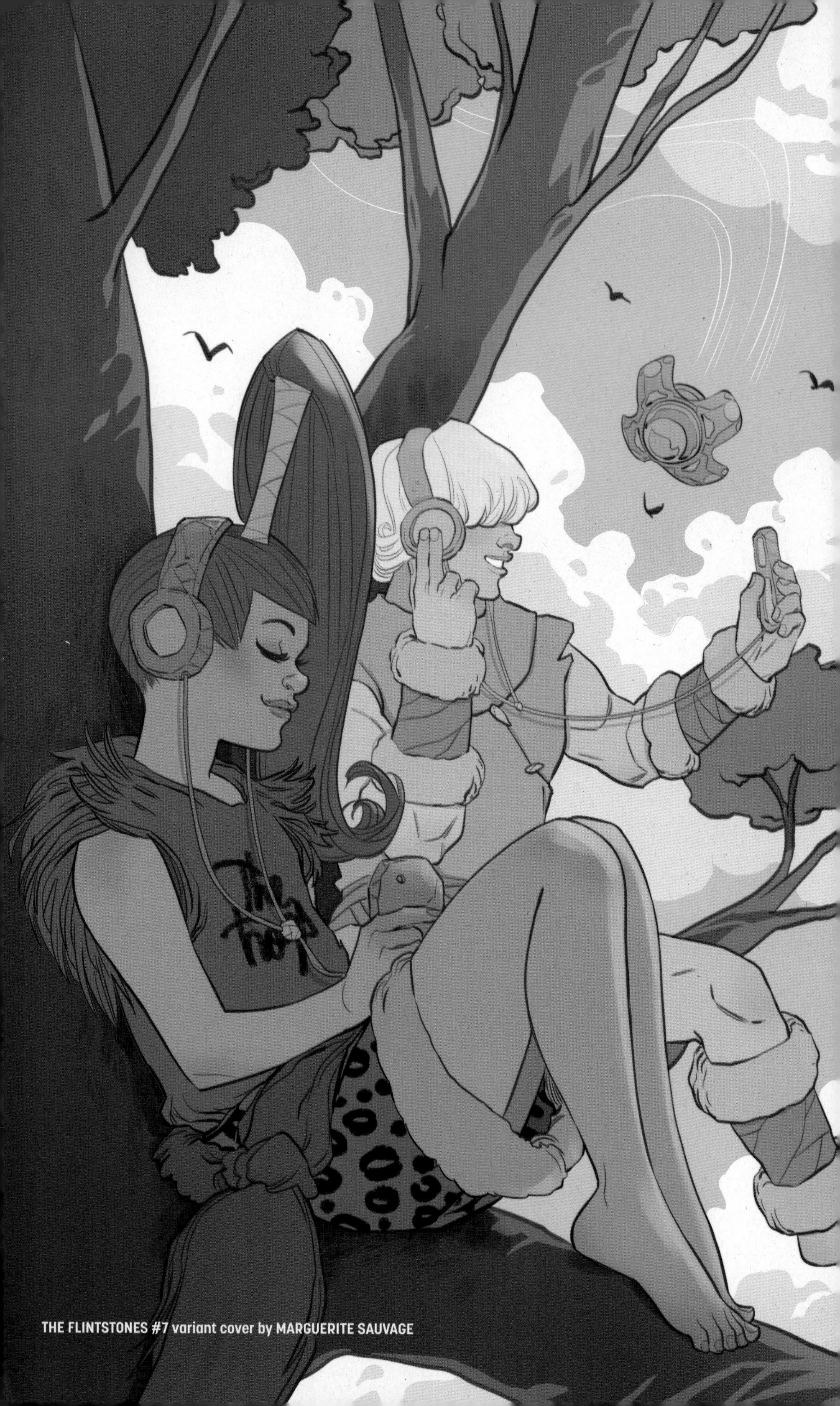

THE FLINTSTONES #7 variant cover by MARGUERITE SAUVAGE

THE FLINTSTONES #8 variant cover by HOWARD CHAYKIN and WIL QUINTANA

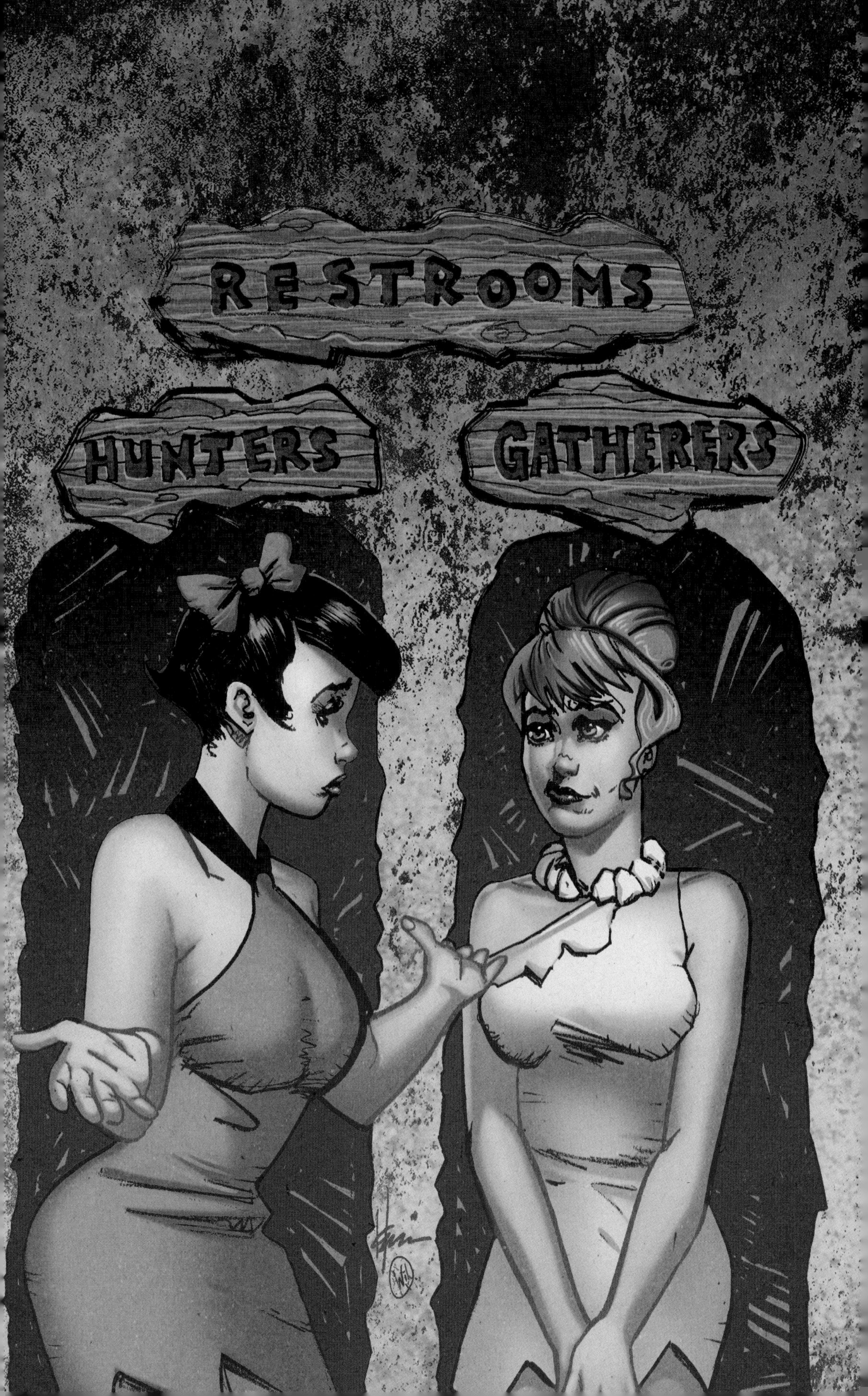
RESTROOMS
HUNTERS
GATHERERS

THE FLINTSTONES #9 variant cover by ROB GUILLORY

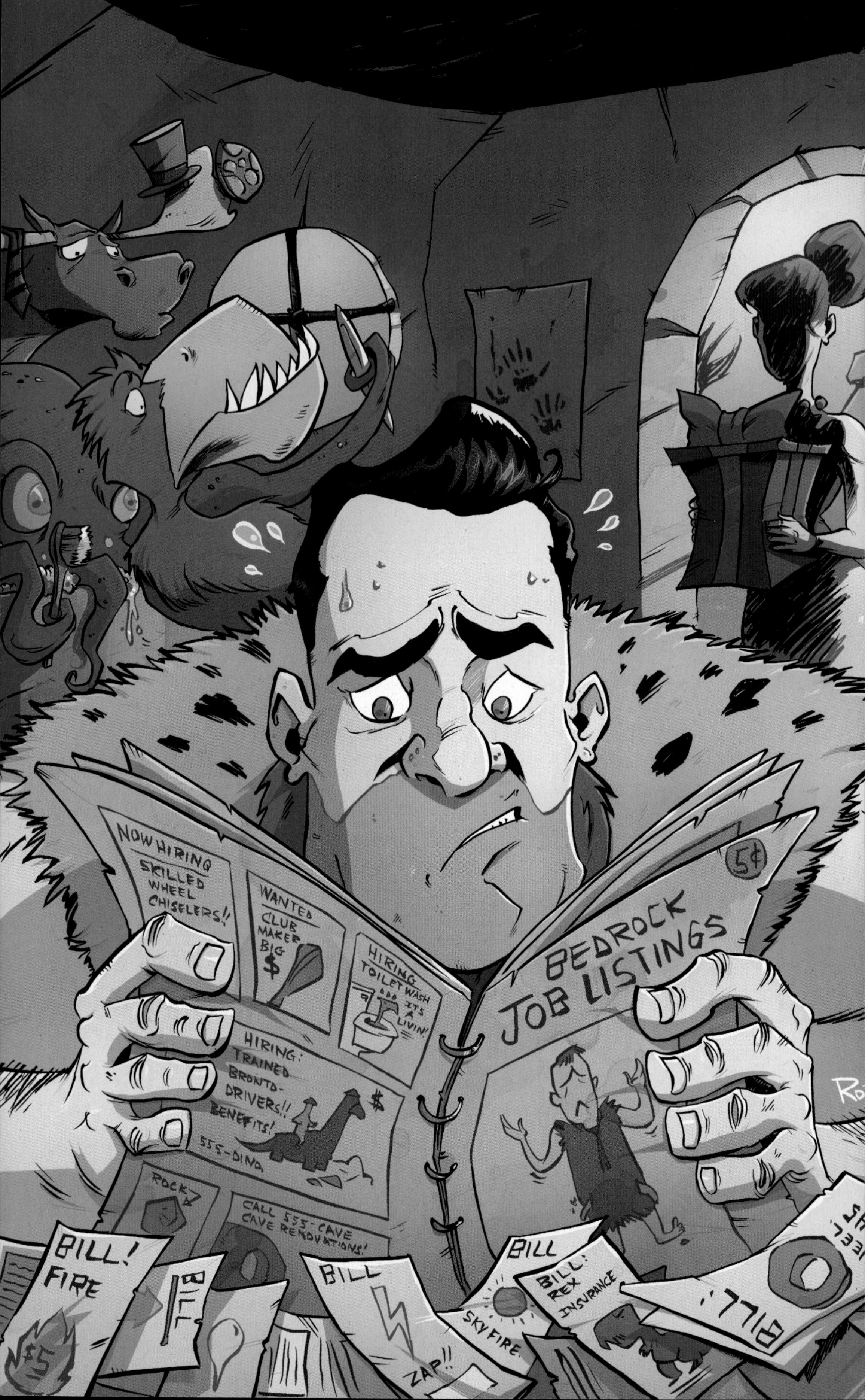
NOW HIRING
SKILLED WHEEL CHISELERS!!
WANTED
CLUB MAKER
BIG $
HIRING
TOILET WASH
ODD ITS A LIVIN'
HIRING:
TRAINED BRONTO-DRIVERS!!
BENEFITS!
$
555-DINO
ROCK
CALL 555-CAVE
CAVE RENOVATIONS!
5¢
BEDROCK
JOB LISTINGS
BILL!
FIRE
$5
BILL
BILL
ZAP!!
SKY FIRE
BILL
BILL:
REX
INSURANCE
BILL:

THE FLINTSTONES #10 variant cover by NICOLA SCOTT and ROMULO FAJARDO JR.

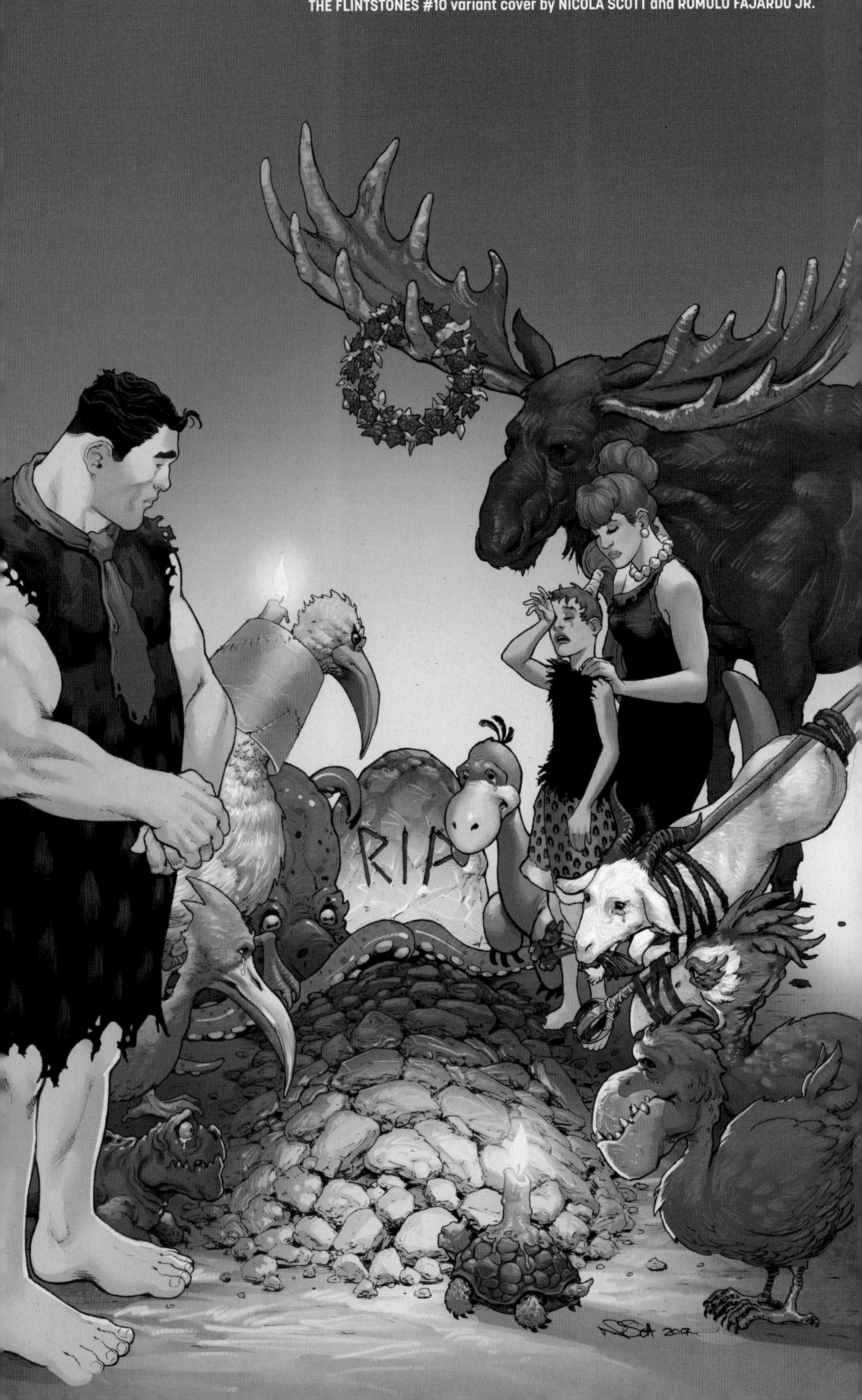

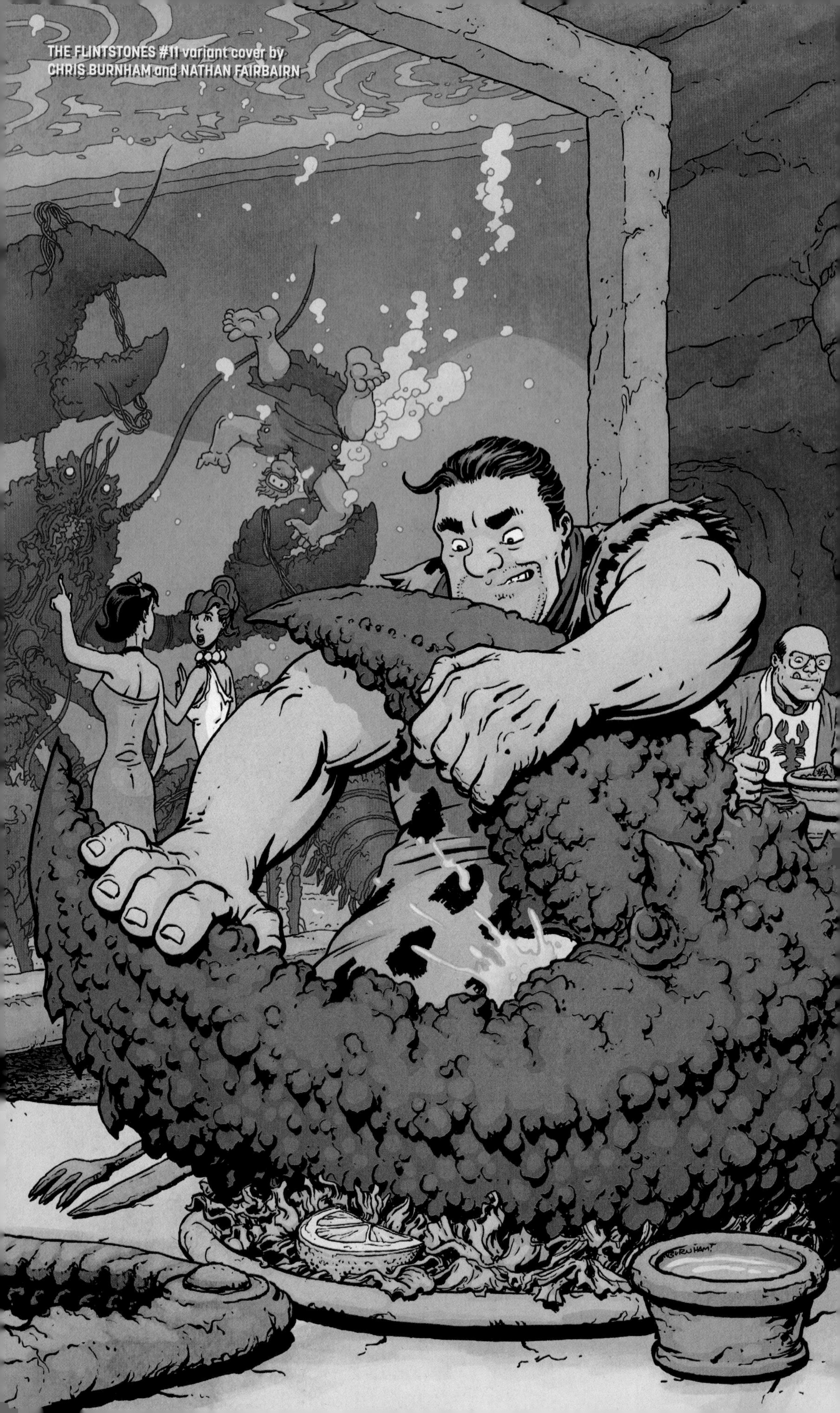

THE FLINTSTONES #11 variant cover by
CHRIS BURNHAM and NATHAN FAIRBAIRN

THE FLINTSTONES #12 variant cover by
RICK LEONARDI, SCOTT HANNA and STEVE BUCCELLATO

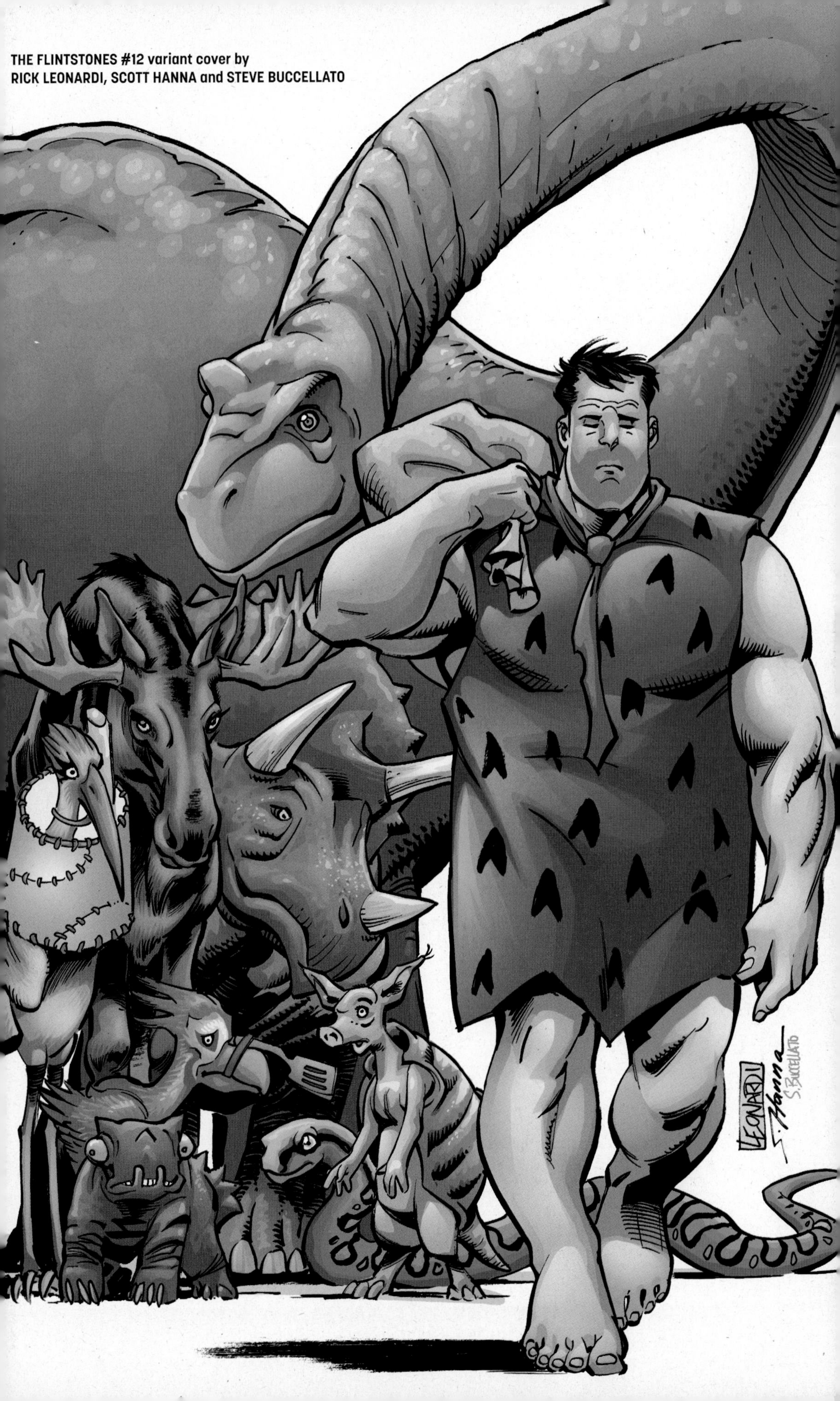

THE FLINTSTONES #7 variant cover sketch by MARGUERITE SAUVAGE

THE FLINTSTONES #7 pencils by RICK LEONARDI

THE FLINTSTONES #8 cover sketch and inks by CULLY HAMNER

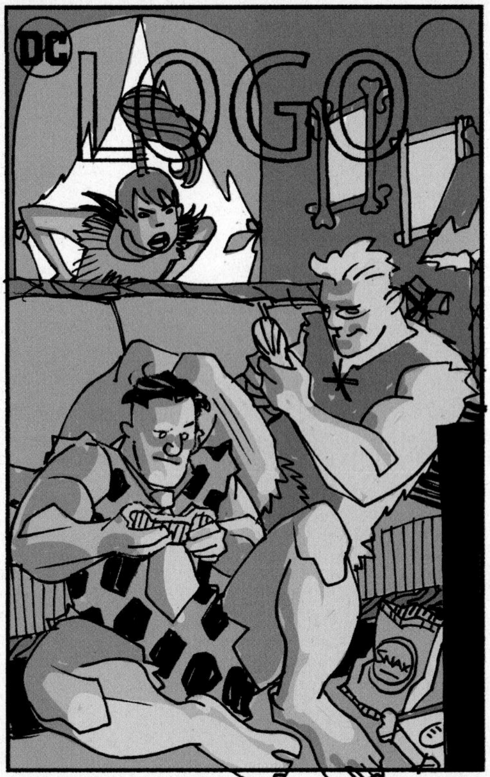
LOGO
SNAK

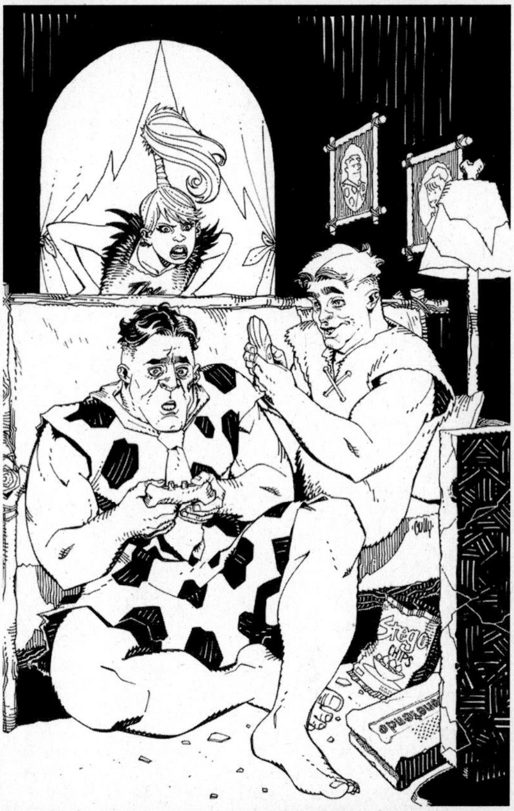
Stego CHIPS

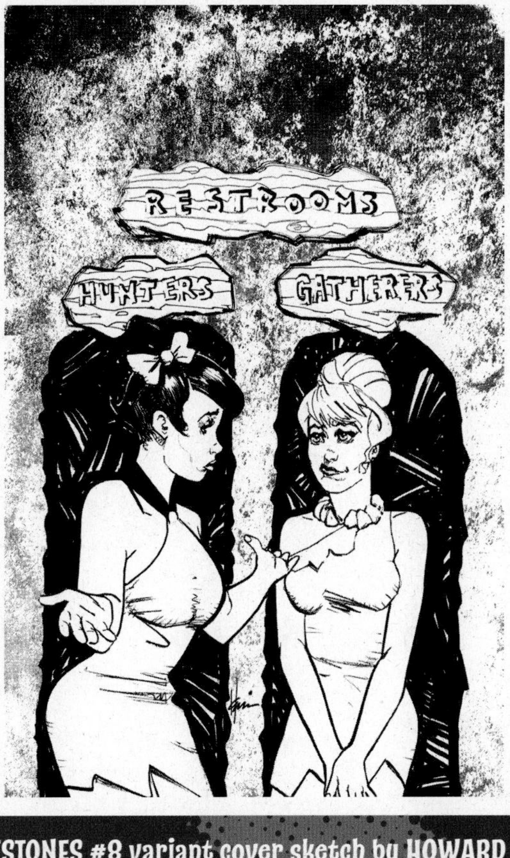
RESTROOMS
HUNTERS
GATHERERS

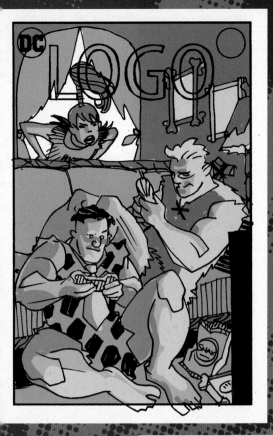

THE FLINTSTONES #8 variant cover sketch by HOWARD CHAYKIN

THE FLINTSTONES #9 variant cover sketch and inks by ROB GUILLORY

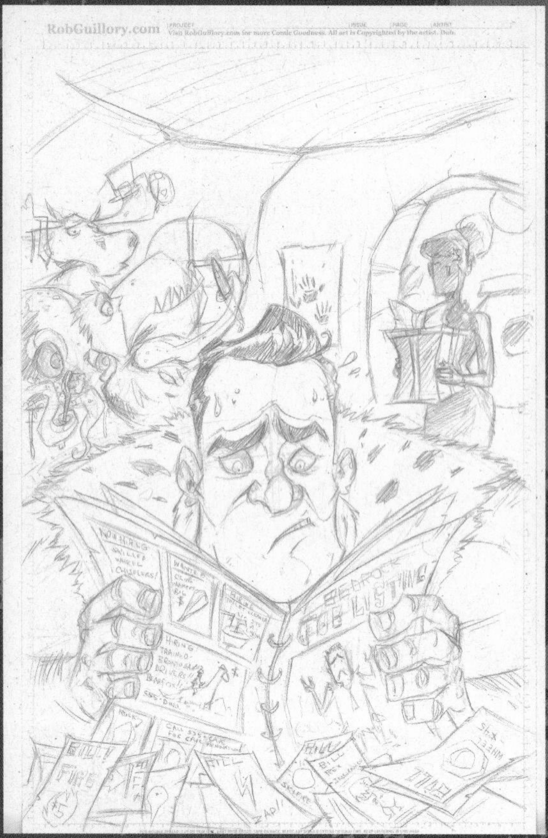
RobGuillory.com

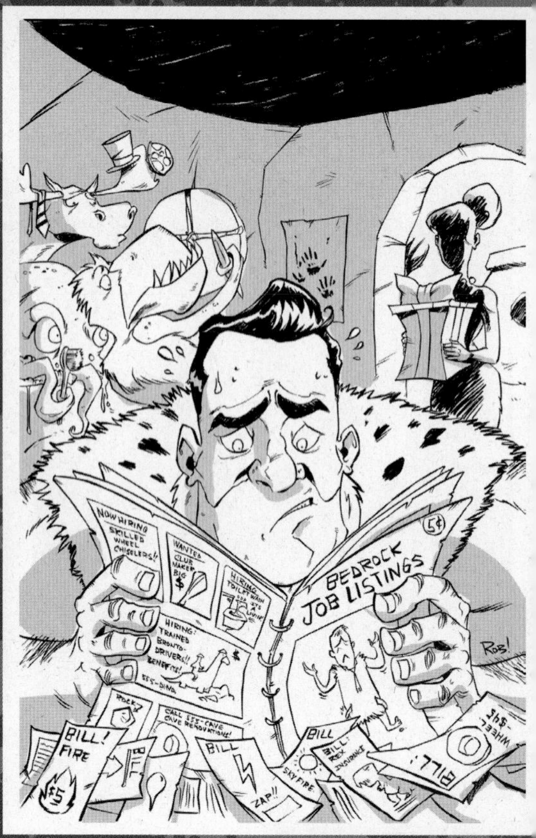
NOW HIRING SKILLED WHEEL CHISELERS!!
WANTED CLUB MAKER BIG $
5¢
BEDROCK JOB LISTINGS
HIRING: TRAINED BRONTO-DRIVERS!! BENEFITS!!
555-DINO
ROCK?
CALL 555-CAVE CAVE RENOVATIONS!
BILL! FIRE
$5
BILL
BILL REX INSURANCE
SKYFIRE
ZAP!!
WHEEL $45
BILL!
ROB!

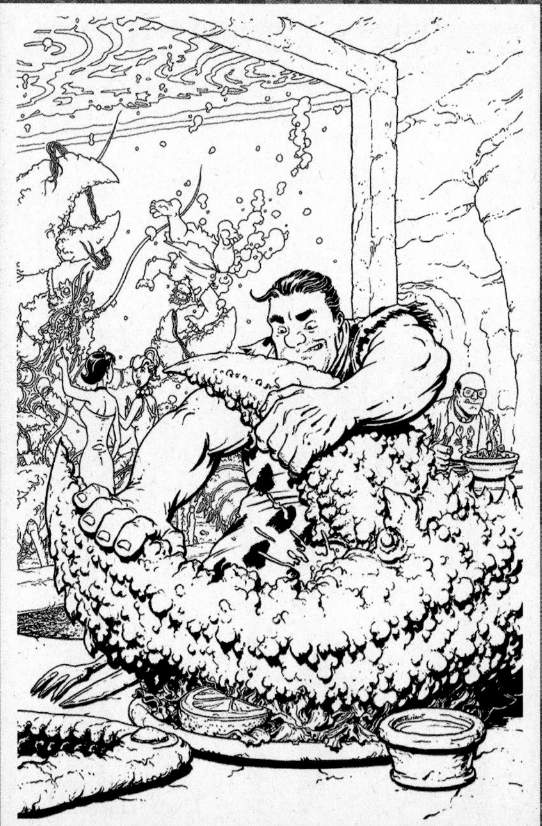

THE FLINTSTONES #11 variant cover inks by CHRIS BURNHAM

THE FLINTSTONES #10 variant cover sketch and inks by NICOLA SCOTT

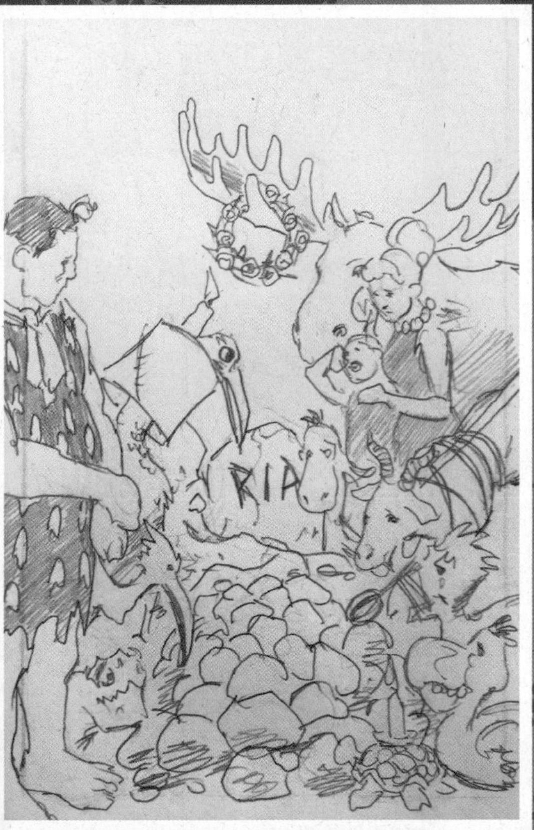

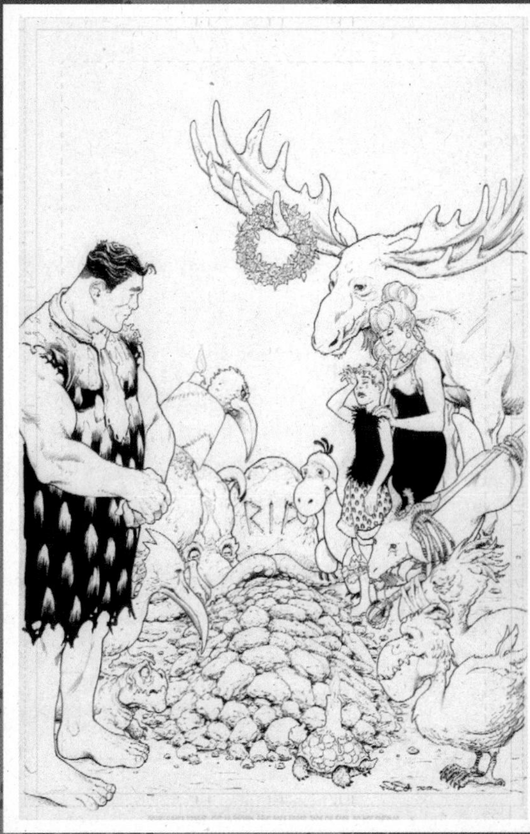

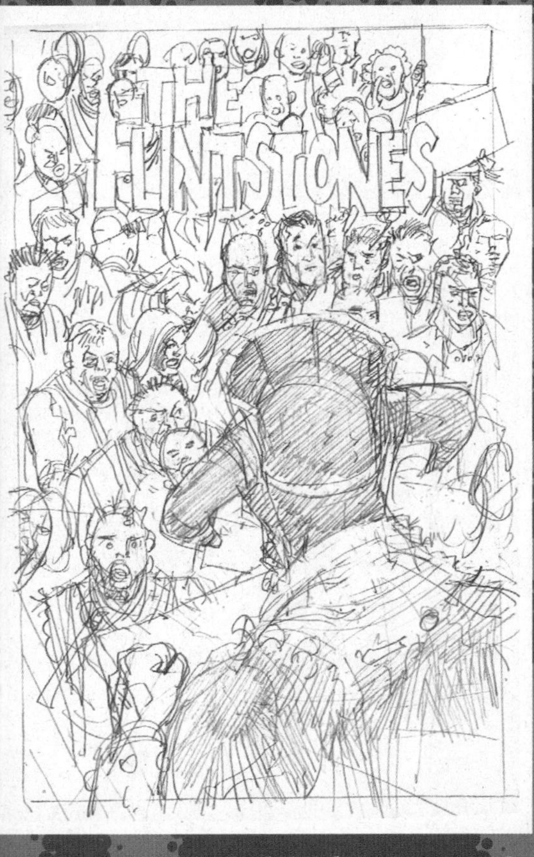
THE FLINTSTONES

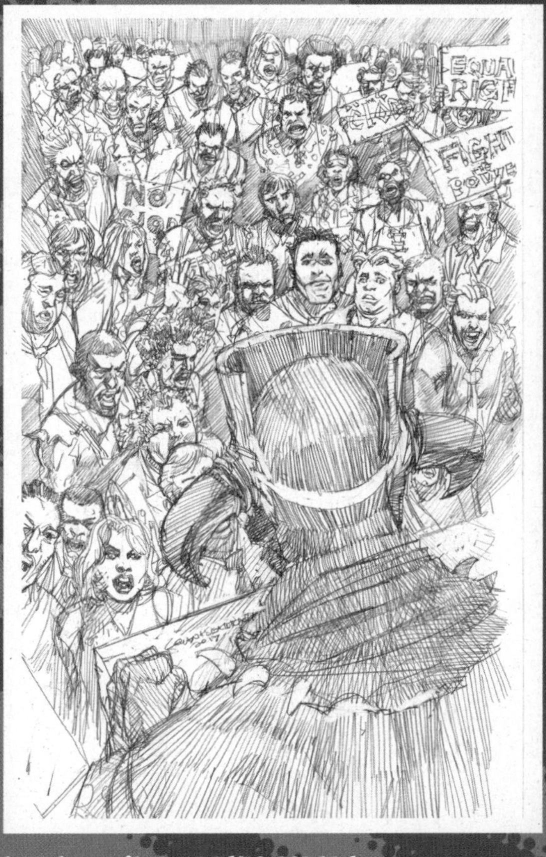

THE FLINTSTONES #10 cover sketch and pencils by DENYS COWAN

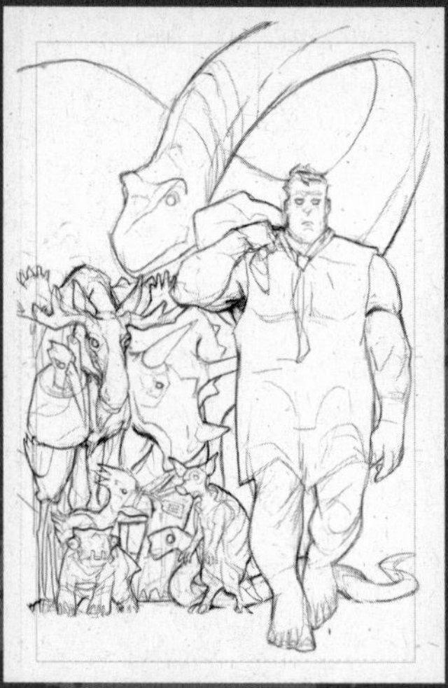

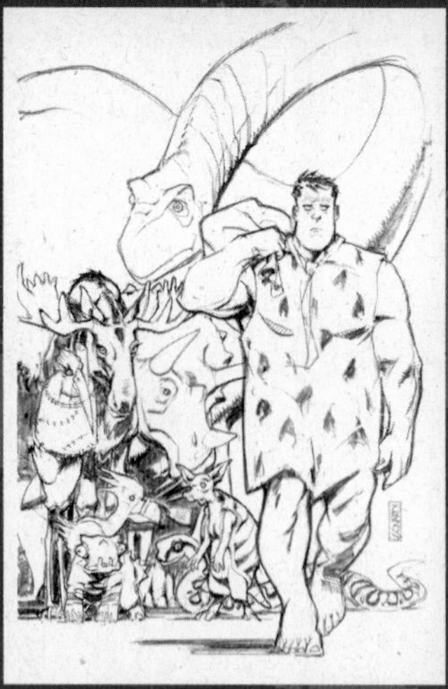

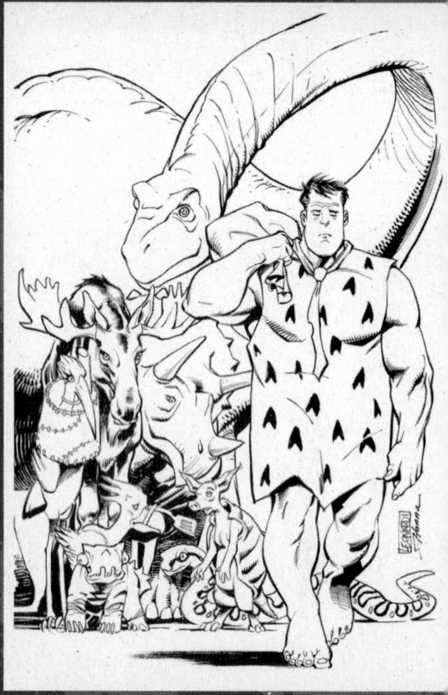

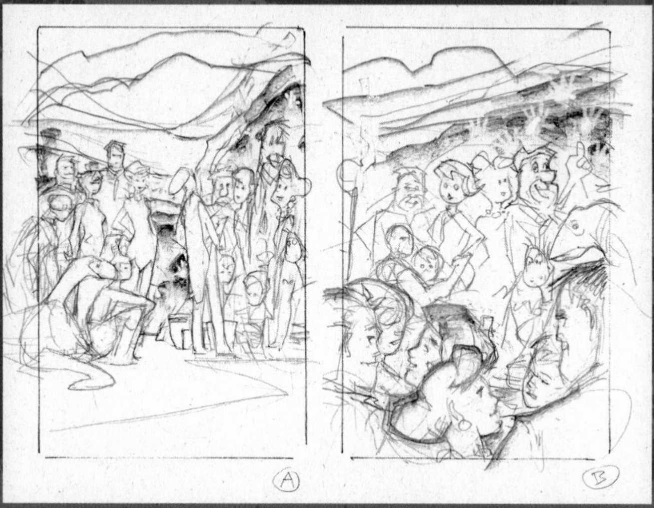

A
B

THE FLINTSTONES #12
variant cover sketches and inks
by RICK LEONARDI and SCOTT HANNA

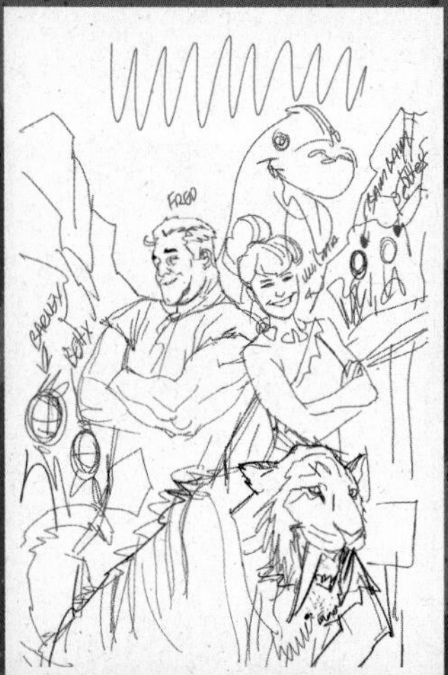

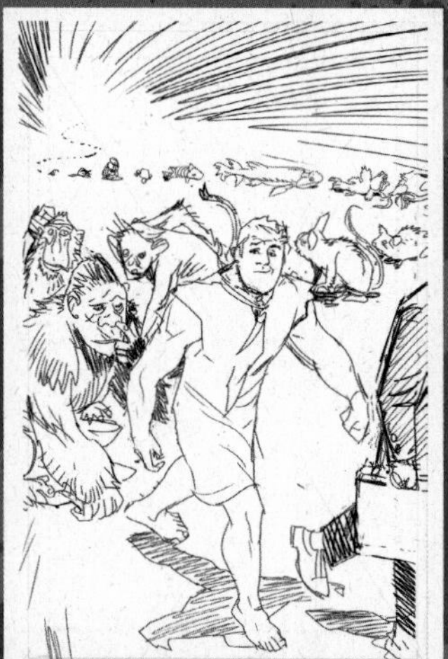

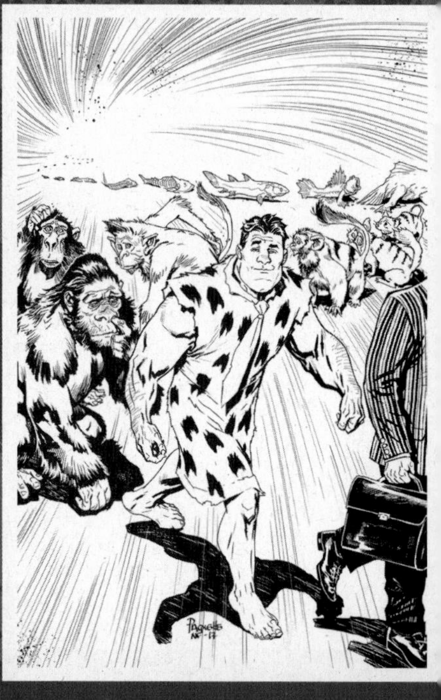

THE FLINTSTONES #12 cover sketches and inks
by YANICK PAQUETTE